LIVING ENVIRONMENTS FOR DEVELOPMENTALLY RETARDED PERSONS

LIVING ENVIRONMENTS FOR DEVELOPMENTALLY RETARDED PERSONS

Edited by

H. Carl Haywood, Ph.D.

and

J. R. Newbrough, Ph.D.

George Peabody College
Vanderbilt University

University Park Press
Baltimore

UNIVERSITY PARK PRESS
International Publishers in Science, Medicine, and Education
300 North Charles Street
Baltimore, Maryland 21201

Copyright © 1981 by University Park Press

Typeset by Maryland Composition Company
Manufactured in the United States of America by
The Maple Press Company

Library of Congress Cataloging in Publication Data
Main entry under title:

Living environments for developmentally retarded
persons.

Bibliography: p.
Includes indexes.
1. Mentally handicapped—Care and treatment—
Addresses, essays, lectures. 2. Developmentally
disabled—Care and treatment—Addresses, essays,
lectures. 3. Group homes for handicapped—
Addresses, essays, lectures. 4. Environmental
psychology—Addresses, essays, lectures.
I. Haywood, H. Carl, 1931–   II. Newbrough,
J. R. [DNLM: 1. Mental retardation—Rehabilitation. 2. Social environment. WM 308 L785]

HV3004.L58   362.3'83   81-863
ISBN 0-8391-1663-2   AACR2

Contents

I   SOCIAL-ECOLOGICAL CONCEPTS AND DEVELOPMENTALLY RETARDED PERSONS

II   THE COMMUNITY ORIENTATION

List of Contributors

John R. Aiello, Ph.D.
Associate Professor of Psychology
Department of Psychology
Douglass College
Rutgers—The State University
New Brunswick, New Jersey 08903

David A. Balla, Ph.D.
Associate Professor of Psychology
Child Study Center
Department of Psychology
Box 11A Yale Station
Yale University
New Haven, Connecticut 06520

Michael J. Begab, Ph.D.
Vice President
University Park Press
300 North Charles Street
Baltimore, Maryland 21201

Gershon Berkson, Ph.D.
Research Scientist IV
Illinois Institute for the Study of
  Developmental Disabilities
Behavioral Sciences Building, Box
  4348
University of Illinois at Chicago
  Circle
Chicago, Illinois 60680

Douglas Biklen, Ph.D.
Associate Professor of Special
  Education and Planning
Director, Center on Human Policy
Syracuse University
Syracuse, New York 13210

Burton Blatt, Ed.D.
Professor of Special Education
Dean, School of Education
Syracuse University
Huntington Hall
150 Marshall Street
Syracuse, New York 13210

Robert Bogdan, Ed.D.
Professor of Education and
  Sociology
School of Education
Syracuse University
Huntington Hall
150 Marshall Street
Syracuse, New York 13210

Cary Cherniss, Ph.D.
Research Scientist
Illinois Institute for Developmental
  Disabilities
1640 West Roosevelt Road
Chicago, Illinois 60608

Daniel W. Close, Ph.D.
Research Associate
Rehabilitation Research and
  Training Center in Mental
  Retardation
College of Education,
Clinical Services Building
University of Oregon
Eugene, Oregon 97403

Jeffrey L. Crawford, Ph.D.
Director, Clinical Systems
  Development
Information Sciences Division
Rockland Research Institute
Orangeburg, New York 10962

Robert B. Edgerton, Ph.D.
Professor
Departments of Anthropology
  and Psychiatry
Socio-Behavioral Research Group
Neuropsychiatric Institute
The Center for the Health Sciences
UCLA, 760 Westwood Plaza
Los Angeles, California 90024

H. Carl Haywood, Ph.D.
Professor of Psychology and of
  Neurology
Director, John F. Kennedy Center
  for Research on Education and
  Human Development
Box 40, Peabody College
Vanderbilt University
Nashville, Tennessee 37203

Matthew P. Janicki, Ph.D.
Director, Bureau of Program
  Research and Planning
State of New York, Office of
  Mental Retardation and
  Developmental Disabilities
44 Holland Avenue
Albany, New York 12229

Keith T. Kernan, Ph.D.
Associate Research Anthropologist
Department of Psychiatry
Socio-Behavioral Research Group
Neuropsychiatric Institute
The Center for the Health Sciences
UCLA, 760 Westwood Plaza
Los Angeles, California 90024

Chris Kiernan, Ph.D.
Deputy Director
Thomas Coram Research Unit
Institute of Education
University of London
41 Brunswick Square
London WC1N 1AZ
England

Michael S. Klein, Psychology
  Fellow
Department of Psychology
University of Vermont
Burlington, Vermont 05401

Lewis L. Langness, Ph.D.
Professor
Departments of Psychiatry and
  Anthropology
Socio-Behavioral Research Group
Neuropsychiatric Institute
The Center for the Health Sciences
UCLA, 760 Westwood Plaza
Los Angeles, California 90024

Rudolf H. Moos, Ph.D.
Professor, Department of Psychiatry
  and Behavioral Sciences
Director, Social Ecology Laboratory
Stanford University and Veterans
  Administration Medical Center
Palo Alto, California 94305

J. R. Newbrough, Ph.D.
Professor of Psychology and
  Education
Coordinator, Center for Community
  Studies
John F. Kennedy Center for
  Research on Education and
  Human Development
Box 319, Peabody College
Vanderbilt University
Nashville, Tennessee 37203

Gail O'Connor, Ph.D.
Research Investigator
Office of Research
Planning and Research Division
Department of Social and Health
  Services
Olympia, Washington 98504

Susan L. Peterson
Graduate Teaching Fellow
Rehabilitation Research and
  Training Center in Mental
  Retardation
College of Education
Clinical Services Building
University of Oregon
Eugene, Oregon 97403

Stephen A. Richardson, Ph.D.
Professor of Pediatrics and
  Community Health
Department of Pediatrics
Albert Einstein College of Medicine
  of Yeshiva University
1300 Morris Park Avenue
Bronx, New York 10461

Daniel Romer, Ph.D.
Consultant, Illinois Institute for the
  Study of Developmental
  Disabilities
Apartment 2203, 1750 North Clark
Chicago, Illinois 60614

Phil Schoggen, Ph.D.
Professor and Chairperson
Department of Human Development
  and Family Studies
New York State College of Human
  Ecology
Martha Van Rensselaer Hall
Cornell University
Ithaca, New York 14850

Lona Davis Spencer, Ph.D.
Owen Graduate School of
  Management
Vanderbilt University
Alexander Hall
2505 West End Avenue
Nashville, Tennessee 37203

Paul E. Stucky, B.A.
Research Assistant
Department of Psychology and
  Human Development
Box 319, Peabody College
Vanderbilt University
Nashville, Tennessee 37203

Steven J. Taylor, Ph.D.
Assistant Professor of Special
  Education
Senior Staff Associate
Center on Human Policy
Syracuse University
Syracuse, New York 13210

Donna E. Thompson, Ph.D.
Faculty of Arts and Science
Department of Psychology
Psychology Building
New York University
6 Washington Place, Room 550
New York, New York 10003

Jim Turner, Ph.D.
Assistant Professor of Psychiatry
Socio-Behavioral Research Group
Neuropsychiatric Institute
The Center for the Health Sciences
UCLA, 760 Westwood Plaza
Los Angeles, California 90024

Abraham H. Wandersman, Ph.D.
Associate Professor of Psychology
Department of Psychology
University of South Carolina
Columbia, South Carolina 29208

Foreword

Historically, the term "mental retardation" has carried a strong connotation of concern with purely intrapersonal, psychological, or neurological processes. The problem seemed to be located primarily, if not entirely within the deviant individual. Thus, efforts toward amelioration were focused on trying to "fix" what was "wrong" with the retarded person.

Over the past decade, we have seen the emergence of new concerns for the environment and especially for improved understanding of environment-behavior relations. The new field, known as environmental psychology, has placed heavy emphasis on how aspects of the physical and man-made environments are related to human behavior. Here, the concern is with environmental determinants of behavior.

Given these very disparate, if not fundamentally opposed emphases on the person in mental retardation and on the environment in environmental psychology, some readers may be surprised to find in this volume a collection of theoretical and empirical papers by scholars and researchers in the field of mental retardation that sound very much as if they had been written by some of the newer writers in the field of environmental psychology, who go beyond concern for the physical environment to include social-ecological factors in relation to behavior. One chapter, for example, stresses the importance of the immediate context of behavior by pointing out that behavior that is adaptive in one setting may be entirely maladaptive in another—a statement that applies to mentally retarded as well as to nonretarded persons. Another paper asserts that in order to understand the behavior of mentally retarded persons, it is important to examine living environments not only for their provision for security, health, and physical care, but also for the development of cognitive skills and opportunities for satisfying social relationships. This is not the first book to be concerned with environment-behavior relations in mentally retarded persons. Previous works in this tradition include: Farber's (1968) *Mental Retardation: Its Social Context and Consequences*; Baumeister and Butterfield's (1970) *Residential Facilities for the Mentally Retarded*; Haywood's (1970) *Social-Cultural Aspects of Mental Retardation*; and Begab and Richardson's (1975) *The Mentally Retarded and Society: A Social Science Perspective*.

The main message common to the papers in this volume is that we need more and better research to improve our understanding of how living environments can enhance the quality of life for mentally retarded persons. That such a call should come from scientists in mental retardation research seems entirely appropriate. Recall that the pioneer studies by Skeels, Dye, and Skodak in the 1930s and the follow-ups to those studies showed the importance of stimulating environments for the intellectual development of young developmentally delayed children. Thus, long before the emergence of the environmental psychology specialty, scientists in mental retardation research were concerned with environment-behavior relations. The studies described in the present volume document the still seriously underdeveloped state of our knowledge in this complex field of study.

This volume appears at a particularly appropriate time because of the vigor of the present debate among concerned workers in mental retardation over the trend toward deinstitutionalization. There is still controversy over the environmental circumstances under which the goals of normalization can best be achieved. These papers include important contributions toward the ultimate resolution of this debate.

Phil Schoggen

Preface

Contemporary concern for the care, treatment, education, and habilitation of mentally retarded and other handicapped persons is both unusually great (in an historical sense) and extraordinarily complex, encompassing several interacting dimensions. The major questions generated by this concern are at least five:

Who? This is the assessment/diagnostic question, reflecting the realistic observation that a maximal level of services will not be provided to every individual who seeks them, so some decisions must be made about those who are most in need of habilitative services.

When? This is the question regarding optimal timing of services. Current emphasis is placed heavily on early diagnosis and on early treatment of a variety of developmental disorders, including mental retardation. There is simultaneously less tolerance now than in the past for institutionalization of children. Thus, the "when" question interacts with other questions.

Why? This is the goals question, reflecting growing recognition that the goals of habilitative services need to be specified clearly for each individual, and that the nature of the services needs to follow from the goals.

What? This is the programs question, perhaps the most difficult of all to resolve, reflecting some recognition that we are still far from having reliable knowledge regarding which forms of care, treatment, education, and habilitation are likely to be most efficacious.

Where? This is a new question, not seriously considered in explicit form prior to the last 15 or 20 years, but it reflects a growing awareness of the importance of settings and of their influence on behavior and development.

The "where" question constitutes the primary emphasis of this book. Even though we are concerned in this volume primarily with the nature of different settings and their potential influence on the behavior and development of mentally retarded persons, every author represented here shows an acute awareness of the most complex interactions among the five dimensions of concern listed above. No single author in this volume has maintained the universal superiority of one group of settings over another group of settings. The authors have chosen instead to discuss settings characteristics in terms of the developmental needs and the personal assets of retarded persons, the needs of those who work with them, the nature of individual programs, the stages of development, and the goals of programs.

The authors represented in this volume share a social-ecological orientation, recognizing that the behavior and development of retarded persons is a function not only of individual differences in the nature of such persons, but also, to a very large extent, of the physical and social characteristics of their environments as well. Those who hold this view are heavily indebted to the scientific tradition of behavioral ecology or environmental psychology, in which there is explicit recognition of the differential influence of settings on behavior and development. Similarly, scientists who subscribe to the social-ecological point of view are indebted to the transactional tradition in the social and behavioral sciences with its emphasis upon the dynamic nature of person-person and person-environment interactions and the consequent necessity of simultaneously studying each of the components in a series of social transactions as well as the transactional process itself. In other words, there is explicit recognition of the reciprocal nature of person-setting influence. Complicating that reciprocal person-setting relationship is the extremely broad range of individual differences that one encounters among human beings in general and among developmentally retarded persons in particular. Such individual differences in strengths, weaknesses, abilities, ages, degrees of handicap, preferences, and hundreds of other dimensions dictate an extremely complex range of settings and settings characteristics in order to provide for optimal matching of persons and settings. In addition, settings must be conceptualized to include both physical and social aspects, making the settings side of the person-setting equation almost as complex as the persons side. In the context of living environments for developmentally retarded persons, the relevant social aspect of settings includes caregivers and other staff members, peers, friends, family, and neighborhood residents. Still another complicating observation is the logical idea that person-setting matches are not permanent but are instead dynamic. Therefore, a truly development-enhancing setting will become obsolete as its development-enhancing momentum declines, and the person component in that match will need to move to the next, more demanding, more enhancing, and less restricting setting. Thus, scientists who work under a social-ecological orientation recognize that person-setting matches are less permanent than are either persons or settings, and they look forward to the possibility of arranging such matches hierarchically in order to reflect and to contribute to an optimal developmental sequence.

The foregoing broad characteristics of a social-ecological orientation are derived from a relatively new set of sociopolitical issues and questions that have arisen gradually over the last 20 years. These include 1) some direct outgrowths of the worldwide human rights movement; 2) a relatively new approach to habilitative treatment, referred to as normalization; 3) a widespread movement to depopulate large residential institutions, especially those with an essentially custodial orientation; and 4) the judicial concept of the least restrictive environment.

Specific outgrowths of the worldwide human rights movement that have had substantial effects on services to handicapped persons include the concepts of right to treatment, right to education, and the somewhat less explicit idea of a right to participation in community affairs. Professional interest has been focused on the concomitant questions of whether it is possible to secure and exercise such rights in some residential settings, particularly institutional settings in which large numbers of persons of similar disability have been aggregated and have been the objects of impersonal care, political economy, and professional neglect, perhaps as often as or more often than they have received caring, adequate, well-planned, and development-enhancing treatment.

A simultaneous development has been the idea (referred to as the principle of normalization) that arranging the circumstances of life for mentally retarded persons to be as much like those of nonretarded persons as possible constitutes an efficacious approach to the care and treatment of retarded persons. In other words, normalization has been introduced as a potential method for enhancing the development of a variety of handicapped persons, including those who are mentally retarded. The more sensible ones of those who have written extensively on that idea do not maintain that retarded persons should be treated the same as nonretarded persons, but they do maintain that arranging the circumstances of their lives (housing, work, social interactions, expectations) more nearly like those of nonretarded persons would pay off in behavior and development that is less deviant. Although these ideas have not been empirically tested, they have guided the construction of a large number of service programs and have stimulated widespread interest in reducing the range of differences between settings for retarded and nonretarded persons.

The deinstitutionalization movement has exceedingly complex roots, probably beginning with fairly frequent observations that residents of large public institutions not only did not get better, but frequently actually got worse over time. Thus, there was great disappointment with the apparent outcome of this form of treatment. At the same time, research on the development of intelligence, although not yet conclusive, has seemed to accumulate steadily toward the generalization that intellectual development is to some degree a function of variations in environmental circumstances and in experience, and that such circumstances and experiences may bring about shifts in intelligence, both upward and downward. Continued residence in large institutions for mentally retarded persons has been associated so often with declining intelligence rather than with intellectual growth that alternatives have been sought, sometimes with the belief that almost any alternative would represent an improvement. Unfortunately, the effects of many of the alternative environments have not been systematically investigated, using developmental criteria. Thus, although there is a generalized feeling that large public institutions for mentally retarded persons are not doing the job that they were intended to do, there is much less agreement on the nature of the most desirable alternatives.

A major force in the provision of services to mentally retarded and other handicapped persons in the last 20 years has been litigation and judicial action. An influential concept that was a direct product of judicial action is the idea of the least restrictive environment. In a now famous case heard in Federal District Court in the State of Alabama, Judge Frank Johnson ruled, as part of a broad decision on proper care and treatment of mentally retarded and mentally ill persons, that each such individual should reside and function in the least restrictive environment that is compatible with that individual's welfare and development. In other words, the court held that maximum liberty is a legitimate and specifiable goal of residential and treatment services for retarded persons, but also explicitly recognized the importance of individual differences in requirements. Another important aspect of the least restrictive environment concept is the obvious necessity to determine, on an individual basis, the developmental needs of retarded persons in order to match those needs with environments that not only will be responsive to the needs, but that will also have the least restricting effect on each individual's liberty.

Taken together, these four sociopolitical ideas have lent great urgency to the emphasis upon settings and upon person-setting interactions. In addition, they have given rise to some scientific and professional problems that follow directly from the sociopolitical issues. One such problem is how best to reconcile the extremely broad range of individual differences found in mentally retarded persons with the tendency of the law to deal in very broad generalizations. Although it might be true in the legal sense that the majority, or even the vast majority, of mentally retarded persons should not reside in institutions for the mentally retarded because such placements would not be responsive to their developmental needs, it might also be true that there are some individuals who would be served best in such settings. Much time, money, and scientific effort will be required to work out those relationships. A related scientific and professional issue is the need for developmental and personal criteria in the evaluation of settings and of person-setting matches. We need to design research on the efficacy of different residential settings in such a way that the settings will be evaluated against criteria that reflect the development and personal adjustment of the residents. Although that might seem to be an obvious point, some evaluation research on settings for retarded persons has already appeared in which the criteria are neither personal nor developmental, but are designed to reflect the goodness of fit between the settings and the philosophical principles that determine where retarded persons should live and work. A highly related need is for new research models that will enhance the search for person-environment matching formulae. Such models, and their accompanying statistical procedures, will need to take into account a wide variety of person and settings variables. Statistical models that might prove to be useful in this regard include those associated with transactional research, such as cross-lag correlation, time series analysis, canonical correlation, path analysis, and similar models that have multiple regression at their roots.

The overriding need is for scientists and professionals in this field to learn to ask their questions before answering them. The current state of the art in determining the most appropriate settings for retarded persons sometimes seems hysterical and dogmatic rather than objective or scientific. Many professionals in the field of mental retardation services have reached conclusions about where retarded persons ought to live and work, and then have begun to gather data to support those conclusions. At the very least, we can learn to ask the questions first. In many respects, the papers in this volume have been designed to do exactly that.

This volume has been stimulated by and is based upon a small professional conference on alternative living environments for mentally retarded persons sponsored jointly by the John F. Kennedy Center for Research on Education and Human Development of George Peabody College for Teachers (now of Vanderbilt University) and the Tennessee Department of Mental Health and Mental Retardation, held in June 1977. The book does not contain all of the papers presented at that conference, nor can it possibly reflect the richness of discussion and idea exchange that took place among the participants. Discussions at the conference gave rise to new work, which in turn gave rise to new papers, some of which are presented in this volume. The composition of the conference was both deliberate and unusual. The sponsors made a determined effort to assemble in one place a group of participants who would represent primary professional concerns in social-ecological theory and research, day-to-day delivery of services to mentally retarded persons, and the public policy domain. The primary goal of the conference was to stimulate thought (and even controversy) by assessing the present state of knowledge with respect to mentally retarded persons and their possible range of living environments, to call attention to the areas of most glaring ignorance, to raise some caution flags in the rapid evolution of service delivery models, and to point some directions for systematic research and program evaluation. The participants clearly recognized the embryonic stage of development of this field of inquiry, and therefore did not propose to provide definitive answers. Even casual readers will observe that that expectation was realized!

The selection of chapters for this volume represents rather closely the diversity of professional concerns of the conference participants: from theory to empirical research to personal experience; from defense of institutional models (with necessary improvement) to exclusive enthusiasm for community alternatives; from concerns motivated entirely by conceptual curiosity to concerns that are the product of administrative responsibility for programs and services that we do not yet know how to provide.

The volume is organized in four sections, each section and its component chapters approaching the problem of living environments for developmentally retarded persons from a unique direction, but unified overall by a social-ecological orientation. Phil Schoggen's foreword sets forth a task, not only for this volume but for this field of investigation for some time to come: it challenges social and behavioral scientists to build on the base of environmental psychology and to pay more attention to the differences in behavior that are products of the interaction of persons and settings. Section I, containing the chapters of Balla and Klein, Richardson, and Stucky and Newbrough, is concerned primarily with social-ecological concepts and their relevance to applied research with mentally retarded persons. In that section the stage is set by Balla and Klein's effort toward classification, the classical starting point for scientific enterprises. Richardson makes the social-ecological perspective relevant to the quest for appropriate settings for the development and functioning of retarded persons, building on data supplied largely through the methods of sociology. Stucky and Newbrough present the rather novel idea that, within the social-ecological perspective, enhancing the mental health of mentally retarded persons is both a primary goal and a reasonable expectation, provided one views individual retarded persons in the context of their physical and social environments and sees each of the interacting components of their environments as a potential contributor to mental health.

With the stage set conceptually, Section II, reflecting the major direction of service change in this field over the last ten years, is concerned with several aspects of community placement of mentally retarded persons. First, Janicki presents a *tour d'horizon* of research on community placement. Cherniss considers group home placement of retarded persons in the context of organizational design, and in the process suggests some principles that can serve to guide the development of community alternatives to institutionalization. A closely related, but slightly broader context of community adaptation of mildly retarded adults is reflected in the chapter by Kernan, Turner, Langness, and Edgerton, who serve to reinforce the social science perspective of the book. Not content to focus entirely upon residential settings, these authors consider the possibilities of work and other personally significant activity and extend the boundaries of the social environment of retarded persons into work places and generalized community settings. Such broadening of the horizons of retarded persons is continued in the chapter by Close, O'Connor, and Peterson, whose work is concerned with the use of habilitation services by the residents of community residential facilities, such as group homes. Taking a social-psychological point of view, Crawford, Thompson, and Aiello consider the community placement of retarded persons from clinical and environmental standpoints.

Section III serves to sharpen the most prominent contemporary issues in residential placement. Begab points out not only the problems with residential institutions, but also some values that are often overlooked. His essential point of view, that many of the problems with the institutional model are not inherent in the model but are products of inadequate implementation, is in sharp contrast to the points of view expressed in the chapter by Bogdan, Biklen, Blatt, and Taylor, who are convinced that too little good inheres in the institutional model for that model to be continued. In that same section, the chapter by Kiernan constitutes a status report on residential programs in England and Wales. Such a report is especially relevant to this field of inquiry, because it was a handful of British social and behavioral scientists (Jack Tizard, Ann and Alan Clarke, Neil O'Connor, and a very few others) who started much of the present concern for the effects of different living environments on the development of mentally retarded persons and whose experimental service programs in the United Kingdom set new patterns for residential services that are just now being replicated widely in other parts of the world.

Section IV is oriented toward practical problems at the level of

individual mentally retarded persons and the clinicians and administrators who are charged with their care, treatment, education, and
habilitation. The necessity to evaluate sheltered environments for retarded people constitutes the primary concern of the chapter by Wandersman and Moos, and Haywood discusses the characteristics and
particular problems of mentally retarded persons in atypical settings
(prisons, juvenile correctional facilities, and psychiatric hospitals). The
applied implication of both chapters is that retarded persons behave
differently in different settings, and that therefore it must be possible
to engineer settings in such a way as to elicit satisfying and development-enhancing behavior. The final two papers are both unusual and
very personal. Spencer actually posed as a retarded resident of a residential institution and lived for a short time among the regular residents. Her paper is a reaction to that experience nine years later,
revealing that the personal impact of that experience has not diminished
significantly over time. In an almost equally personal way, Berkson
and Romer relate their experiences in studying retarded residents of
group homes in a large city, as well as their firsthand knowledge of
problems encountered by administrators of small residential programs.
Their paper constitutes an effort to bring together what is known about
the requirements of residential programs for retarded persons and to
interpret those requirements in the light of practical problems that
service providers encounter regularly. In addition to their intrinsic
importance, these papers constitute an attempt to overcome the communication barriers between scientists and practitioners. Whether they
have succeeded in doing so is less important than the fact that they
have begun to do so.

The editors are indebted to the authors of these papers and to the
other participants in the living environments conference for their cooperation, hard work, and stimulating thought, and to the hundreds of
mentally retarded persons who have been the subjects of systematic
study, much of which is reflected in these papers. We are especially
grateful to Dona Tapp, the technical editor who spent many hours
imposing order and editorial consistency, checking references, and
making sense out of ambiguous sentences. We acknowledge, with additional thanks, the organizational, artistic, and clerical assistance of
Betty Ladd, Deborah Keim, Norma Morris, Jennifer McDowell, Sue
Byrns, Jon Loranger, Betty James, and Lyn Devine.

In the hope that research on living environments for developmentally retarded persons will continue, and that knowledge so generated will ultimately improve the level of services to retarded persons
and the quality of life for them, we have assigned whatever royalties

may accrue from the sale of this volume to Vanderbilt University, for the exclusive use of the John F. Kennedy Center for Research on Education and Human Development.

H.C.H.

LIVING ENVIRONMENTS FOR DEVELOPMENTALLY RETARDED PERSONS

SOCIAL-ECOLOGICAL CONCEPTS AND DEVELOPMENTALLY RETARDED PERSONS

Living Environments for Developmentally Retarded Persons
Edited by H. Carl Haywood and J. R. Newbrough
Copyright 1981   University Park Press   Baltimore

Labels for and Taxonomies of Environments for Retarded Persons

David A. Balla, Ph.D.
Child Study Center
Department of Psychology
Box 11A Yale Station
Yale University
New Haven, Connecticut 06520

Michael S. Klein
Department of Psychology
University of Vermont
Burlington, Vermont 05401

The purposes of this chapter are: 1) to suggest that, to date, our efforts to classify caregiving environments for retarded persons have important similarities to historical efforts to classify individuals; 2) to propose a possible way of classifying environments that might circumvent the difficulties encountered in the classification of persons, especially those considered atypical.

In our view, there have been three phases in the development of classification schemes for atypical persons. First, there have been informal taxonomies for atypical behavior that involve concepts such as craziness, stupidity, or blindness. These informal classifications of atypicality have considerable generality across cultures (Murphy, 1976). Second, at least in our culture, there has been an effort to formalize these classifications, from the time of Kraepelin to the pres-

Preparation of this report was supported by Research Grant IID-03008 from the National Institute of Child Health and Human Development, U.S. Public Health Service.

ent day. These efforts at more efficient classification of individuals are still in active progress, as shown by the recent revision of the terminology and classification manual of the American Association on Mental Deficiency (Grossman, 1973), the imminent appearance of the third edition of the *Diagnostic and Statistical Manual* of the American Psychiatric Association, the efforts of the World Health Organization in the classification of disorders of children, and the proposed classification scheme of The Group for the Advancement of Psychiatry. Finally, there have been reactions to the classification of individuals in such diverse fields as criminology (Becker, 1963), mental illness (Scheff, 1966), mental retardation (Farber, 1968; Mercer, 1973), and blindness (Scott, 1969). These reactions are most clearly seen in the context of the development of labeling theory concerning deviant individuals, in radical labeling positions, such as those of Scheff (1966) and Goffman (1963), and in more moderate positions, such as those of Mercer (1973) and Scott (1969). Current thought concerning the classification of children has been summarized recently by Hobbs and his collaborators (1975).

A recurring criticism of both informal and formal taxonomies of individuals is that the labels acquire a great deal of excess meaning. Even an informal term, such as "blind," seems to have overtones of social incompetency and dependency. Similarly, when an individual is classified as mentally retarded, the classification is interpreted by many to mean that the person is totally incapable of learning and profiting from experience, rather than that the person has an IQ less than 70, some decrement in adaptive behavior, and that these difficulties arose at some point in the developmental period.

We may well be recreating the history of classification of individuals in our classification of care settings for retarded persons. For example, in the area of mental retardation, we are now essentially at the stage of having only an informal taxonomy of environments, but this informal taxonomy has already acquired a great deal of excess meaning. An example of our current taxonomy should serve to illustrate this point. Many observers agree that an institution is an inadequate caregiving facility; however, it is not clear what an institution is. There seems to be an informal consensus that institution means a large facility, probably with a population of more than 1,000, located far from population centers, with an antihumanistic caregiving philosophy. There also seems to be a consensus that small caregiving facilities located in urban community settings are not institutions. Because of these preoccupations, we think it is fair to say that almost any clinicians in the field of mental retardation, given a choice between placing a retarded person in a large institution or in a small community-based facility, would automatically place the person in the community facility, even if they knew nothing of the social-psychological realities of the two settings. The work of Butler (Butler and Bjaanes, 1977; 1978) and Edgerton (Edgerton, 1975; Edgerton, Eyman, and Silverstein, 1975) has suggested that such a decision might be mistaken. The most reasonable conclusion from these investigators' data is that small community-based facilities may often be just as demeaning and nonnormalized as are the large facilities they were meant to replace. This example suggests that our informal taxonomies of environments differ in a crucial respect from our taxonomies of individuals. The informal taxonomies of individuals and the formal efforts that have arisen from them have been concerned with classifying deviant individuals, while informal taxonomies of environments seem to polarize the designations "good" and "bad." The characteristic that the taxonomies have in common is their excess meaning.

More recently, formal attempts at the classification of environments have been undertaken. Fredricksen (1972) has suggested that the first task for environmental taxonomists is to develop a set of attributes or dimensions by which environments can be classified. The work of Barker and his colleagues (Barker and Gump, 1964) on undermanning in behavior settings is one such taxonomy. Moos and his colleagues (1974) have devoted a great deal of effort to developing a taxonomy that incorporates a wide range of environments, from total institution to family settings. This work is especially interesting because the authors have argued convincingly that a wide variety of environments, including psychiatric wards, correctional facilities, military basic training companies, university dormitories, junior and senior high school classrooms, work environments, and even families (Moos, 1974), can be classified empirically along a limited number of dimensions. These dimensions are: relationship (or the amount of involvement, support, and expressiveness within the setting), personal development or goal orientation, and system maintenance and change. These dimensions have been found to be generally stable across settings. Therefore, there is some reason to believe that it might be possible to have a very general taxonomy of environments.

CAREGIVING ENVIRONMENTS

Although environmental psychologists have begun to develop taxonomies of environments, difficulties arise immediately when we begin to apply this work to the area of mental retardation. The most important problem is that most of the work to date has been concerned with environments for people who are at least potentially capable of totally independent functioning. Thus, relatively little attention has been given to the caregiving aspects of environments, aspects that are of crucial concern to retarded persons. When we shift our attention to caregiving environments, we have to consider one environment that has only recently begun to receive the attention of taxonomists—the family. We find it difficult to incorporate the dimensions discussed by Barker (Barker and Gump, 1964), and by Moos in most of his work (Moos, 1974), into an intuitive framework of at least the caregiving dimensions of family environments.

Some efforts in the area of mental retardation, especially the work of Farber (1964, 1975), might be viewed as a sophisticated taxonomy of the family environment of retarded persons. In Farber's view, the adaptation of the family to the presence of a retarded member goes through a systematic series of phases. These phases are: 1) the labeling phase, 2) the normalization phase, 3) the mobilization phase, 4) the revisionist phase, 5) the polarization phase, and 6) the elimination phase. The environments of retarded individuals might be demonstrably different depending on the particular phases of adaptation their families are in at a given time. The social deprivation scale of Zigler, Butterfield, and Goff (1966) can be seen as another taxonomy of families. These authors have suggested that the pre-institutional environments of retarded individuals can be classified along four dimensions. These dimensions are: 1) Familial Harmony, which is the degree of parental rejection or neglect of the child; 2) Parental Attitude, which is the desire of the parents to institutionalize the child; 3) Familial Richness, which is the intellectual and economic level of the parents; and 4) Continuity of Residence, which is the number of sets of parent figures experienced by the child.

In the area of mental retardation, Butler and Bjaanes (1977) have proposed a classification for a limited range of caregiving settings for retarded persons. These investigators have proposed that community care facilities can be classified into at least three types: therapeutic, custodial, and maintenance. This work represents the only attempt that we know of to develop a formal taxonomy of environments for retarded persons.

Because the major taxonomies of environments developed to date are not directly applicable to the goal of categorizing care settings for retarded persons, we are proposing here a framework for the possible development of such a taxonomy. Several aims have guided this effort. First, we are convinced that any unidimensional taxonomy will be less than adequate. The experiences of such investigators and groups as the Group for the Advancement of Psychiatry, Rutter and his colleagues (Rutter et al., 1969), and Hobbs (1975) in the classification of individuals have strongly suggested the advantages of a multidimensional taxonomy. In addition, when environments are classified on more than one dimension, consumers of services for retarded persons can multiply their options in choosing environments best suited to their goals. For example, a setting that provides excellent humanistic care for a severely retarded child may still have no program directed toward education or cognitive development. An environmental taxonomy would separate these dimensions in such a way that, if a consumer were more interested in a setting that provided humane care and less interested in one that provided cognitive development, it would be possible for him to make an informed choice.

Our second goal is to develop a classification scheme that has as little excess meaning as possible. A major difficulty with informal taxonomies of individuals is the inevitable excess meaning they carry. It seems to us that the general understanding of the term "group home," e.g., care in the community, normalization, and the enhancement of contact with others in the community, has become the antithesis of institution. It is our conviction that it is possible to develop a taxonomy with enough precision that the assignment of excess meaning to the categories would be difficult and unnecessary.

Our final goal, which might not yet be possible, is to make the dimensions of the taxonomy applicable to environments ranging from the family setting to school environments to total large central institutions. It may be, as Goffman (1961) has suggested, that the characteristics of total institutions are unique, making comparisons with a family irrelevant.

DIMENSIONS OF A POSSIBLE TAXONOMY

Balla (1976) has suggested four dimensions along which institutions might be compared. The first of these is quality of life, an important issue in the taxonomy of care settings for retarded individuals. At some level this dimension certainly could incorporate environments from the family to the total institution. For example, is nutrition for retarded persons adequate? From our reading of numerous case records of retarded individuals, it is not certain that every retarded person has enough to eat. Also, what is the quality of the transactions between clients and important persons in their lives (Balla, 1966; Edgerton, 1975; Strain and Shores, 1977)? Are the transactions supportive of growth and development, or are they punitive, neutral, or nonexistent? There have been attempts to assess some aspects of this dimension. King, Raynes, and Tizard (1971) have developed a scale that quantifies child management practices. Both Gunzberg (1973) and Wolfensberger (1972) have suggested measures to assess the extent to which a setting enhances the quality of life. It should be noted that, in many ways, we are suggesting nothing more than a systematized case history. However, much is lost between the level of the practitioner and the level of our ideologies concerning optimal care settings. We often erroneously assume that, if an environment has been labeled "family," it is the least restrictive or most normalized setting possible. In addition, case histories of environments other than families are seldom taken.

Gottlieb (1977) has presented some evidence that the quality of life in school for mainstreamed children may not be as good as that for children in segregated special education classrooms. Given the widespread acceptance of, and enthusiasm for, mainstreamed classrooms, this is an instance in which our labels for environments may be carrying such excess meaning as to hinder our understanding of the actual experiences of children receiving special education.

At the level of institutional environments, there is evidence that the quality of life in small community-based facilities is better than that in large central institutions (Balla, 1976; King et al., 1971; McCormick, Balla, and Zigler, 1975). However, Butler and Bjaanes (1977; 1978) and Edgerton and his colleagues (Edgerton, 1975; Edgerton et al., 1975) have presented evidence indicating that, although large may be bad, that does not mean that small is good. These authors have demonstrated convincingly that life in group homes may be just as demeaning and restrictive as life in many large central institutions.

The second dimension of environments, concerning the behavioral growth and development of clients in institutions, has probably been as responsible as any other for the adverse view of institutions prevalent in the area of mental retardation today. It has been reported that groups of institutionalized retarded individuals are less intelligent or less developmentally advanced than are supposedly comparable groups of home-reared individuals (Carr, 1970; Centerwall and Centerwall, 1960; Lyle, 1959, 1960a, 1960b; Shipe and Shotwell, 1965; Stedman et al., 1962). Superiority in home-reared individuals has been found in such diverse areas of behavior as discrimination learning (Kaufman, 1963), level of abstraction on a vocabulary test (Badt, 1958), the ability to conceptualize an emotional continuum (Iscoe and McCann, 1965), and the ability to form a learning set (Harter, 1967). Demonstrations of beneficial effects of institutions have usually been overlooked. Yando and Zigler (1971), however, found institutionalized retarded persons to be more autonomous in their problem solving than noninstitutionalized retarded persons. Mueller and Weaver (1964) found a consistent language advantage in favor of a group of institutionalized retarded children as compared to a matched sample of home-reared day school children. Unfortunately, in the majority of these studies even the most basic characterization of family and institutional environments is missing, making it impossible to reconcile inconsistent findings. Furthermore, we do not know whether the institutionalized children in the above studies differed in some crucial respects from the noninstitutionalized children before their admission, a factor that introduces the possibility of biased selection. Thus, even in this body of literature we are not on very firm ground in asserting that family environments are superior to institutional environments on the dimension of promoting behavioral growth.

When we change from the question of the relative advantages of family and institutional environments in promoting behavioral growth to the question of inter-institutional comparisons, we find practically no evidence that our informal taxonomies of types of institutions are in any way reliable. In one study, Balla, Butterfield, and Zigler (1974) evaluated residents in four institutions ranging in size from approximately 400 to approximately 2,000 residents. There was also considerable variation in cost, number of aides per resident, and employee turnover rate. Residents were examined within 6 months of their admission date, and again after 2.5 years of institutional experience. Measures of mental age (MA), IQ, responsiveness to social reinforcement, verbal dependency, extent of imitation of adults, and behavioral variability were obtained. Contrary to our most pessimistic views concerning the effects of institutions, considerable evidence of psychological growth on the part of the residents was found. Over the course of 2.5 years, in all of the institutions the residents became less verbally dependent, less imitative, and more variable in their behavior. IQ level did not change, and MA level increased. Residents in the largest of the institutions were more responsive to social reinforcement than were residents in the other three institutions. With this exception, institution size was not related to the behavior or development of the residents. It seems most reasonable to conclude that institution size was not an important determinant of behavioral development in the 400 to 2,000 population range.

Using a cross-sectional rather than longitudinal design, Balla, Kossan, and Zigler (1976) conducted another study of the behavior of residents in five regional centers and two central institutions in Connecticut. The regional centers ranged in size from 12 to 290 persons, while the average size of the large central institutions was 1,633 persons, with a range from 1,453 to 1,813 persons. Measures of responsiveness to social reinforcement, wariness of adults, and imitation of adults were obtained. With one exception, no behavioral differences were found between persons residing in the two central institutions and persons residing in the five regional centers. There were also no behavioral differences between persons residing in the largest regional center with a population of 290 and persons in the smallest regional center with a population of 12. Given the widespread assumption that small institutions are invariably superior to larger institutions, we were surprised to find so few significant differences in behavioral functioning between residents in institutions so different in size.

Our informal taxonomies of environments, judged by the extent to which they promote growth and development of retarded persons, have only the status of labels at this time. These labels have taken on great excess meaning. Many people assume that there is a great deal of firm evidence that family environments promote greater psychological growth than do all types of institutional environments, and that there is firm knowledge that small community-based institutions are more effective than large central institutions, but available evidence does not support these assumptions.

Another way of classifying environments for retarded persons would be to compare them in terms of the extent to which they promote the independence of the participants. At this stage of our knowledge, perhaps the best measure of the effects of institutional settings would be discharge rates for groups of clients at comparable developmental levels. To accomplish such a comparison, we would have to develop a way of scaling numerous living arrangements along some dimension, such as degree of restrictiveness. If a person were discharged from a central institution to a prison, his environment would most probably be more restrictive, even though he was on the roster of discharged clients. It might be somewhat difficult to use this dimension for individuals who live with their families, but it certainly seems possible that the fate of home-related versus institutionalized children is greatly influenced by the degree of autonomy their environments permit or require of them.

The final dimension along which we classify environments is the extent to which they facilitate involvement in the community. A major criticism of traditional institutional settings has been that they are so far removed geographically from population centers that any kind of involvement of the residents in noninstitutional community life is impossible, and involvement of the noninstitutional community with retarded persons is also extraordinarily difficult (Sarason, Zitnay, and Grossman, 1971). This dimension of environments is perhaps the closest to some key concepts in the care of retarded persons at this time, e.g., "normalization" and the "least restrictive environment." We believe that the greater the extent of a person's contact with his natural community, the more normalized is his environment and the less restrictive is his setting. We think environments ranging from families to central institutions could be classified along this dimension. One primitive way of doing this would be on a physical or geographic basis: how far is the home or institution from stores, churches, community centers, schools, playgrounds, or bus stops? Is the home or institution accessible by public transportation? Once such a geographic assessment is made, we could observe the number of contacts with the community by residents in different types of environments. We suspect that a retarded person who lives in a family, in a very small institutional setting, or by himself, will not automatically have greater involvement with his community than will a person who lives in a more traditional residential setting. Such a speculation has been supported by the work of Butler and his colleagues (Butler and Bjaanes, 1977; 1978).

SUMMARY

Our thinking concerning environments for mentally retarded persons is at the stage of informal taxonomies. Many of these classifications carry a great deal of excess meaning, whether the terms be large institution, developmental center, or mainstreamed classroom. The small amount of research that has been done to date in actually comparing different environments for retarded persons has failed to support current popular and professional beliefs. There have been a few attempts at classification in the field of environmental psychology, but, as we see it, these taxonomies are not directly applicable to the area of mental retardation. We suggest that investigators in the area of environments for retarded persons begin more formal taxonomies. If this effort were successful, it might be possible to revise the mistaken belief of a great number of professionals, as well as of the public, that the classification of individuals does far more harm than good.

ACKNOWLEDGMENTS

Michael Begab assisted in the clarification of several of the ideas presented in this paper. The authors are grateful to Barbara Kaufman, Marilyn Carroll, and Edward Zigler for their critical comments on a previous draft of this manuscript. Margaret Houghton and Peppie Weiss were of great assistance in the preparation of this paper.

REFERENCES

Badt, M. I. 1958. Level of abstraction in vocabulary definitions of mentally retarded school children. Am. J. Ment. Defic. 63:241–246.
Balla, D. 1966. The verbal action of the environment on institutionalized and

noninstitutionalized retardates and normal children of two social classes. Unpublished doctoral dissertation, Yale University.

Balla, D. A. 1976. Relationship of institution size to quality of care: A review of the literature. Am. J. Ment. Defic. 81:117–124.

Balla, D., Butterfield, E. C., and Zigler, E. 1974. Effects of institutionalization on retarded children: A longitudinal cross-institutional investigation. Am. J. Ment. Defic. 78:530–549.

Balla, D., Kossan, N., and Zigler, E. 1976. Effects of preinstitutional history and institutionalization on the behavior of the retarded. Unpublished manuscript, Yale University.

Barker, R., and Gump, P. 1964. Big School, Small School. Stanford University Press, Stanford.

Becker, H. S. 1963. Outsiders. Free Press, New York.

Butler, E. W., and Bjaanes, A. T. 1977. A typology of community care facilities and differential normalization outcomes. In: P. Mittler (ed.), Research to Practice in Mental Retardation, Vol. 1. Care and Intervention, pp. 337–347. University Park Press, Baltimore.

Butler, E. W., and Bjaanes, A. 1978. Activities and the use of time by retarded persons in community care facilities. In: G. P. Sackett (ed.), Observing Behavior, Vol. 1. Theory and Applications in Mental Retardation, pp. 379–400. University Park Press, Baltimore.

Carr, J. 1970. Mental and motor development in young mongol children. J. Ment. Defic. Res. 14:205–220.

Centerwall, S. A., and Centerwall, W. R. 1960. A study of children with mongolism reared in home compared to those reared away from home. Pediatrics 25:678–685.

Edgerton, R. B. 1975. Issues relating to the quality of life among mentally retarded persons. In: M. J. Begab and S. A. Richardson (eds.), The Mentally Retarded and Society: A Social Science Perspective, pp. 127–140. University Park Press, Baltimore.

Edgerton, R. B., Eyman, R. K., and Silverstein, A. B. 1975. Mental retardation system. In: N. Hobbs (ed.), Issues in the Classification of Children, Vol. 2, pp. 62–87. Jossey-Bass, Inc., Pubs., San Francisco.

Farber, B. 1964. Family: Organization and Interaction. Chandler Publishing Company, San Francisco.

Farber, B. 1968. Mental retardation: Its Social Context and Social Consequences. Houghton Mifflin Company, Boston.

Farber, B. 1975. Family adaptations to severely mentally retarded children. In: M. J. Begab and S. A. Richardson (eds.), The Mentally Retarded and Society: A Social Science Perspective, pp. 247–266. University Park Press, Baltimore.

Fredericksen, N. 1972. Toward a taxonomy of situations. Am. Psychol. 27:114–123.

Goffman, E. 1961. Asylums: Essays on the Social Situation of Mental Patients and Other Inmates. Doubleday and Company, Inc., New York.

Goffman, E. 1963. Stigma: Notes on the Management of Spoiled Identity. Prentice-Hall, Inc., Englewood Cliffs, N.J.

Gottlieb, J. 1977. Attitudes toward mainstreaming retarded children and some possible effects on educational practices. In: P. Mittler (ed.), Research to Practice in Mental Retardation, Vol 1. Care and Intervention, pp. 35–44. University Park Press, Baltimore.

Grossman, H. (ed.), 1973. Manual on Terminology and Classification in Mental Retardation, 1973 Revision. American Association on Mental Deficiency, Washington.

Gunzberg, H. C. 1973. The physical environment of the mentally handicapped, VIII—"39 steps" leading towards normalized living practices in living units for the mentally handicapped. Br. J. Ment. Subnormal. 37:91–99.

Harter, S. 1967. Mental age, IQ, and motivational factors in the discrimination learning set performance of normal and retarded children. J. Exp. Child Psychol. 5:123–141.

Hobbs, N. 1975. The Futures of Children. Jossey-Bass, Inc., Pubs., San Francisco.

Iscoe, I., and McCann, B. 1965. The perception of an emotional continuum by older and younger mental retardates. J. Pers. Soc. Psychol. 1:383–385.

Kaufman, M. 1963. The formation of a learning set in institutionalized and non-institutionalized mental defectives. Am. J. Ment. Defic. 67:601–605.

King, R. D., Raynes, N. V., and Tizard, J. 1971. Patterns of Residential Care: Sociological Studies in Institutions for Handicapped Children. Routledge and Kegan Paul, London.

Lyle, J. G. 1959. The effect of an institution environment on the verbal development of imbecile children: I. Verbal intelligence. J. Ment. Defic. Res. 3:122–128.

Lyle, J. G. 1960a. The effect of an institution environment upon the verbal development of imbecile children: II. Speech and language. J. Ment. Defic. Res. 4:1–13.

Lyle, J. G. 1960b. The effect of an institution environment upon the verbal development of imbecile children: III. The Brooklands residential family unit. J. Ment. Defic. Res. 4:14–23.

McCormick, M., Balla, D., and Zigler, E. 1975. Resident-care practices in institutions for retarded persons: A cross-institutional, cross-cultural study. Am. J. Ment. Defic. 80:1–17.

Mercer, J. R. 1973. Labelling the Mentally Retarded. University of California Press, Berkeley.

Moos, R. 1974. Evaluating Treatment Environments: A Social Ecological Approach. John Wiley and Sons, Inc., New York.

Mueller, M. W., and Weaver, S. J. 1964. Psycholinguistic abilities of institutionalized and noninstitutionalized trainable mental retardates. Am. J. Ment. Defic. 68:755–783.

Murphy, J. M. 1976. Psychiatric labeling in cross-cultural perspective. Science 191:1019–1028.

Rutter, M., Lebovici, S., Eisenberg, L., Sneznevskij, A., Sadoun, R., Brooke, E., and Lin, T.Y. 1969. A tri-axial classification of mental disorders in childhood: An international study. J. Child Psychol. Psychiatry 10(1):41–61.

Sarason, S., Zitnay, G., and Grossman, F. 1971. The Creation of a Community Setting. Syracuse University Division of Special Education and Rehabilitation and the Center on Human Policy, Syracuse.

Scheff, T. J. 1966. Being Mentally Ill. Aldine Publishing Company, Chicago.

Scott, R. A. 1969. The Making of Blind Men: A Study in Adult Socialization. Russell Sage Foundation, New York.

Shipe, E., and Shotwell, A. M. 1965. Effect of out-of-home care on mongoloid children: A continuation study. Am. J. Ment. Defic. 69:649–652.

Stedman, D. J., Eichorn, D. E., Griffin, J., and Gooch, B. 1962. A comparative study of growth and development trends of institutionalized and noninstitutionalized retarded children: A summary report. Paper presented at the annual meeting of the American Association on Mental Deficiency, New York.

Strain, P. S., and Shores, R. E. 1977. Social reciprocity: A review of research and educational implications. Except. Child. 43:526–530.

Wolfensberger, W. 1972. The Principle of Normalization in Human Services. National Institute on Mental Retardation, Toronto.

Yando, R., and Zigler, E. 1971. Outer-directedness in the problem-solving of institutionalized and noninstitutionalized normal and retarded children. Dev. Psychol. 4:277–288.

Zigler, E., Butterfield, E. C., and Goff, G. 1966. A measure of preinstitutional social deprivation for institutionalized retardates. Am. J. Ment. Defic. 70:873–885.

Living Environments for Developmentally Retarded Persons
Edited by H. Carl Haywood and J. R. Newbrough
Copyright 1981   University Park Press   Baltimore

Living Environments
An Ecological Perspective

Stephen A. Richardson, Ph.D.
Department of Pediatrics
Albert Einstein College of Medicine
* of Yeshiva University*
1300 Morris Park Avenue
Bronx, New York 10461

Living environments for developmentally retarded persons are a particularly appropriate topic to consider from a social-ecological perspective. To understand mental retardation, one must take into account the interaction between individuals and their social and physical environments over their life courses, including both biological and social factors. Ecology—the concept that emphasizes the interaction between individuals and their environments—is a valuable concept that can expand our understanding, because it encompasses a wide range of variables that are relevant to particular issues and problems. The definition of environment is sometimes restricted to the physical component, but it can also include social and biological components. The ecological concern with the individual is physical, social, and biological, and the overall system is viewed over time to include the study of development and change. It is easy to accept intellectually such a broad concept, but it is difficult to apply social ecology to a specific problem. One must find a means for restricting the number of variables to those that can be managed within a research design, choosing the significant variables salient to the problem, and, having identified these variables, defining them operationally so that they may be incorporated into systematic multivariate description and analysis. In this chapter I discuss the factors and classes of factors that need to be taken into account, from an ecological perspective, in considering living environments for mentally retarded persons.

Living environments are those places where people sleep and spend varying proportions of their evenings, weekends, and holidays. For most people, the living environment is "home." Depending on age and role, a person's living environment may be with his or her family of orientation, with the family of a caregiver other than the parents, with the family of procreation, with friends, relatives, or strangers in some housing arrangement, or the person may be living alone. Children rarely have any choice in their living environments; as they grow up, however, their opportunities for choice increase. These living environments form only part of the inhabitant's overall environment at any time. Other distinctive environments, separated by geography and by use, make up the remainder of the total environment for most people, and include schools or other educational institutions, work settings, recreational facilities, public places, shops, and the living environments of other people. There are also specialized environments, such as those occupied by health, social, and religious institutions.

For a minority of people, the living environment is part of a specialized overall environment that is largely a self-contained institution, separated from the everyday life of the rest of society. Such settings include ships at sea, prisons, army barracks, monasteries, and institutions for the care of chronically ill, physically handicapped, mentally ill, or mentally retarded persons. Depending on the type of institution, a person may be in a residence through personal choice or through having been placed without choice by some politically recognized authority. This type of total institution has been defined as "a place of residence and work where a large number of like-situated individuals, cut off from the wider society for an appreciable period of time, together lead an enclosed, formally administered round of life" (Goffman, 1961, p. xiii). Other institutions conform, in part, to the description of total institutions, but differ in that they are less cut off from the wider society and provide varying degrees of interchange between the internal environment of the institution and the external environment of the wider society. Interchanges may be for purposes of work, recreation, social visits, holidays, or for the provision of a variety of services. Most studies focus only on the internal environment of the institution, yet the relationships between the internal and external environments may be important in understanding the lives of the residents.

When considering the living environments of persons who are mentally retarded, a reasonable starting point is to identify a total population of persons in a given community who have been defined as mentally retarded and to see what their living environments are at a particular age. A study in a city in the United Kingdom shows that, of persons born in 1951 and 1952 who were at any time during their school years administratively classified as mentally retarded and placed in special facilities for mentally retarded persons, 10% were in total-care institutions at age 15 and the remainder were living with parents or parent substitutes. At age 22, 13% of the same population were in total-care institutions (Richardson, 1978).

The living environments for the same study population, with the addition of those classified in the same way from the 1953 birth cohort, have been examined in somewhat more detail (Table 1). The percentage of persons in some form of residential institution is 13%, similar to the percentage for the two birth years of 1951 and 1952. When considering how many additional young adults will require some form of institutional residence as they grow older, it is reasonable to expect that those presently living with parents, and attending a day center that combines certain aspects of a sheltered workshop with social training and recreation, will require some form of institutional residence when their parents can no longer look after them because of infirmity or death. This group constitutes an additional 13% of the total cases, which raises to 26% those who will at some time require some form of institutional residence (although mortality may reduce this percentage). These data suggest that approximately 75% of the adults in the study will not need institutional residential placements.

Innes (1975) surveyed mentally retarded persons of all ages in northeast Scotland and found that throughout their adult years an increasing percentage of the population has as its environment a mental subnormality hospital, while a decreasing percentage lives in noninstitutional homes with parents, spouses, relatives, or others. These epidemiological data suggest that a major concern in the study of living environments for mentally retarded persons must be how to make noninstitutional homes more effective. (Because this chapter deals primarily with residential institutions, this form of living environment is not considered here.) The data also suggest that, because of the increased longevity of the more severely retarded persons, many will

Table 1.   Living environments at age 22 for mentally retarded persons[a] who were born 1951–1953

Living environment	Percentage of persons
In the home of parent, guardian, or relative[b]	60
With a friend, a landlord, or alone	7
With a spouse (with or without other adults in the household)	20
In an institutional residence for the care of the mentally retarded	13

[a] Persons who, at any time during the school years, were administratively classified as mentally retarded and received special services ($N = 114$).

[b] Fifteen of these young adults are, at the time of this writing, attending a day center for adults who are retarded (13% of the cases).

outlive their parents; therefore, greater preparation, thought, and planning must be given to the transition from the parental home to some other form of residence.

Current literature on living environments for mentally retarded persons deals predominantly with total or partial institutional residences. The residences have been characterized in a number of ways that suggest the range of variables considered salient by the respective authors, and include small group homes, workshop dormitories, semi-independent satellite community residences, mental deficiency hospitals, central institutions, regional centers, community residences or care facilities, board-and-care facilities, home-care facilities, foster-care homes, group family homes, and village communities.

In Sweden, a fuller description of types of residential facilities has been used. Separate facilities are described for 1) properly trained, mildly and moderately mentally retarded persons who are able to live in their own flats with frequent assistance; 2) mentally retarded persons who need more training and support, reside in groups of three to five individuals, and require daily assistance; and 3) the most severely handicapped and multiply handicapped persons, who require support day and night and live in groups of four to six. It is emphasized that each arrangement must include residents in an organized daily work schedule in order to support integrated living (Binda, 1975).

Descriptions of living environments are often related to the number of residents. The larger environments tend to be total institutions, such as mental deficiency hospitals or "schools," which, in the United States, are generally run by the state. The smaller ones tend to be described as group homes, hostels, board-and-care facilities, and community residences. The larger institutions are developed and administered by persons with medical backgrounds, while the smaller residences reflect a wide variety of backgrounds in their planning and operation, including education, social work, and the behavioral sciences.

There is considerable debate over the relationship between size of residence and various measures of the quality of life of the residents. Some relationships appear to be reasonably established:

1.   Based on the estimates of Kushlick (1975), a total population of 1,000,000 can be expected to have 1,550 mentally retarded persons who will need residential care. A mental retardation institution with 3,000 residents will draw, then, from a total population or catchment area of approximately 2,000,000. The larger the institution for a given density of population, the greater becomes the average physical distance between the residents and the homes and communities from which they came. The greater the physical distance, the more numerous

the problems of parents and friends in coming to visit the residents and of the residents in visiting their families and friends.

2. The larger the institution, the greater is the physical space required. On the basis of cost and availability of sites, this tends to place the institutions in more isolated and less desirable locations. With less socially desirable locations, it becomes more difficult to attract high-quality staff, and staff are likely to stay for shorter periods. Both of these problems affect quality of care.

3. The agencies providing human services to the region around the institution are less able to meet the needs of the institutional residents the larger the institution is. Thus, medical, social, recreational, and transportation services must be developed within the institutions themselves, making them more like total institutions, with decreased contacts between residents and the surrounding areas.

The present policies supporting the trend toward development of small residences located in communities are based on the assumption that these residences 1) provide opportunities for use of already established community facilities and services, 2) maintain the continuity of relationships between a resident and those who were socially significant to him or her before entering the residence, and 3) offer a gradual and humane transition to the residence and to participation in the activities of the community. It is also believed that, because of more central locations, staff turnover will be lower. What has been recognized less frequently is that to create and maintain these desired conditions requires great skill, effort, and continued attention, and that the opportunities provided by small residences will not be beneficial without these things.

IDEOLOGY AND ENVIRONMENTS

The ideology of those responsible for planning and running various forms of living environments deeply influences the structure, organization, choice of staff, and day-to-day running of the organization. This ideology, frame of reference, or mode of thought derives from professional training and the wisdom and values generally held at the time.

Medical ideology has been one of the major contributors to the structure, functioning, customs, and practice of large, established residential institutions for the mentally retarded. Having been trained in hospitals, physicians who have established residential institutions have used the organizational model they know best—the hospital—thus creating a highly centralized, authoritarian form of organization. The doctor/patient relationship influenced their conception of the role relationships between residents and staff: Residents were regarded as patients, to be treated or acted upon, and were expected to obey and to be passive. Medical training develops a physiological, pathological view, and therefore primary attention is given to bodily functions and needs, disease processes, and pathology. The doctor/patient ideology has largely ignored the resident as a social being with individual social, emotional, and educational needs and as someone with family and community ties. The hospital model of organization has also influenced the physical structure and arrangements of the institutions and their degrees of separateness from surrounding external environments. Although this description may be a traditional view of medical ideology rather than a contemporary one, once an institution is firmly established, vested interests develop among the staff members that greatly increase the difficulties in making changes in the institution. It becomes difficult to sort out the different effects of medical ideology and size of institution, because the large institutions have been run primarily by physicians.

The ideology of an asylum as a place of refuge and protection, where the residents live out their lives largely separated from the outside world, influences the organization and running of some residential institutions. Primrose (1977, p. 263) has suggested that an asylum-like setting may be used for long-stay admissions of persons who are severely physically handicapped and who are admitted at an early age, those whose behavior the community cannot tolerate, and those in whom the precipitating factor is psychotic mental illness and who have had lengthy trials of alternative community provisions before exclusion is sought from the normal surroundings by admission to a hospital. Primrose suggests that the advantage of a large institution is "the ability to form peer groups for the patients, groups where they are no longer the least efficient member and where they are not ridiculed because of their inadequacy; . . . removing stress allows patients to be more relaxed and happy." He further suggests that an asylum is appropriate for the patient who has progressive conditions and whose level of functioning is deteriorating (p. 265). It should be noted that the context of Primose's position is a country where, for many mentally retarded persons, there has been long-term residence in large institutions and where the initial reasons for institutionalization in some cases go back many years to early views about mental retardation, treatment, and services. The present functioning of mentally retarded individuals within such institutions reflects their past experiences and treatment.

The ideologies that have been described represent views less generally held today. More current ideologies, such as those related to an educational-developmental view, normalization, and decentralization, are so readily available in the current literature that it would not be useful to repeat them here. However, implementation of these current concepts involves dealing with residents who were institutionalized at a time when the older ideologies were influential. Thus, the earlier views must first be understood if the newer ideologies are to succeed.

An interesting example of the relation between ideology and the institutionalization of the mentally retarded is given by Nemeth (1975). In the Netherlands, placement is determined by two agencies, Social Services and Mental Health Services. The former placed 23% of the low-grade mentally retarded persons in institutional care, whereas the latter placed 54% there. Nemeth comments that

> A study of the directives of the experts attached to these two organizations reveals a remarkable state of affairs. The social workers are of the opinion that, unless there are indications to the contrary, the mentally retarded person should be kept as long as possible in his home surroundings. The representatives of the Mental Health Authorities, however, take up the opposite standpoint. Their opinion is that, where there are not indications to the contrary, the severer forms of mental retardation always qualify for institutionalization. (Nemeth, 1975, p. 664)

Therefore, when seeking understanding of any particular living environment for mentally retarded individuals, the ideologies and values of those responsible for shaping the environment provide a potentially valuable avenue of exploration, whether it be a large total institution or a family home.

PHYSICAL AND SPATIAL ARRANGEMENTS

The physical arrangements of living environments are often inherited from earlier conceptions and are appropriate to previously conceived, specialized residential structures. Physical structures can shape the behavior of those who live within them, but when changes in thinking or ideology occur, it is often very difficult to change physical structure. Birenbaum and Seiffer (1976) followed adults who were transferred to a community residence with bedrooms shared by only two people after they had slept for years in large wards of mental retardation institutions. The investigators found that, because the residents had had no experience in sharing a room with only one other person, a long period of learning was needed before they could adapt to the new conditions.

It has already been mentioned that the placement of a large residence in an isolated location contributes to its becoming more total in functioning. For community residences, a location near public transportation, educational and vocational facilities, recreational facilities, and shops, as well as the characteristics of the neighbors, can greatly influence the lives of the residents. Planners of residences for mentally retarded individuals are often attracted to suburban or semi-rural locations because of pleasant surroundings and an environment that the planners find congenial. They neglect to consider, however, that the residents will not have their own cars and that public transportation is often poor or nonexistent, leaving the residents dependent on the availability of private cars and on the willingness of others to drive, which severely restricts the residents from leaving the living environment. Freedom of the residents to explore the external environment can also be severely hampered by physical dangers, such as fast-moving traffic. For residents with impairments of physical mobility, physical terrain and man-made structures (e.g., steps) can also impose barriers.

ORGANIZATIONAL AND ADMINISTRATIVE CHARACTERISTICS

Investigators also study a variety of organizational and administrative characteristics of living environments. Zigler and Balla (1977), comparing residential institutions, include in their measures "average number of residents per living unit; cost per resident per day; number of aides per resident; number of professional staff per resident; annual employee turnover rate; volunteer hours per resident per year; and mean institutional I.Q." (p. 6).

King, Raynes, and Tizard (1971) have developed a Child Management Scale to differentiate a range of institutionally oriented practices from inmate- or child-oriented management practices. The scale consists of sets of questions or indicators that describe rigidity of routine, block treatment, depersonalization, and social distance.

The Child Management Scale has been used to identify institutions as being mainly institutionally or child-oriented, in order to examine the organizational characteristics of each type of institution. Damen (1975) used measures of "control structure, coordination, communication, leadership, attitudes concerning the related professional staff and ward staff, and transfers of ward nursing staff" (p. 465) in his study. He found that in the institutionally organized mental retardation facility: 1) there was a more pyramidal stratified control structure, 2) the organizational segments operated more in isolation from each other, 3) professional staff told less to the "front-line" personnel about the situation and the needs of the pupils, 4) there was more of a communication gap between head nurses and "front-line" personnel, 5) nurses talked very infrequently to professional staff, and 6) head nurses and nurses were transferred more frequently (pp. 465–466).

Morris gives an example of how the role of the nurse can influence the environment in a mental subnormality hospital (1969): "Nurses generally suffer from low morale, due to such factors as isolation, lack of involvement in decision making, poor communication, and the doctor's lack of interest in the nurses' work. . . . Thus the traditional emphases on cleanliness, tidiness, orderly behavior, etc. predominate and since little more is expected of nurses, little more is given" (p. 171).

Pratt, Raynes, and Roses (1977) sought to determine which factors in the organization within a large institution for mentally retarded persons were related to differences in the quality of care between the various living units. Direct care workers were questioned about their perceptions of who participated in making administrative decisions. Direct observations were made of supervisors and their subordinates regarding the amount of time spent in various activities related to resident care and administrative activity. The authors found that "the more workers feel themselves involved in decisions affecting their work, the better the quality of care provided for residents on both measures of care, and the higher the staff's morale" (p. 333). The concept of the study is interesting because, although researchers frequently compare residential institutions that are characterized by different descriptive terms, comparisons are made less frequently between institutions having the same descriptive terms. The Pratt et al. (1977) study makes comparisons within the same institution.

A residential institution may be heavily influenced by a parent or controlling authority if the institution is a member of a larger institutional structure, such as a national or state system. The forms of influence include budget and fiscal control, administrative rules, directives and policies, and Civil Service regulations. The overall system of which the institution is a part is also influenced by legislation and political pressures. Cohen (1975) gives an account of such a relationship between state headquarters of the Department of Mental Hygiene in New York and local facilities, but, in general, these influences on the institutions have received little attention.

STAFF-RESIDENT RELATIONSHIPS

Because there is a wide range of variables used to describe organizational and administrative characteristics in living environments, in most cases one is left to infer how they influence the daily behavioral interchanges between staff and residents. There is need for more study of this topic. Goffman (1961) has described how the social conduct of the inmates of psychiatric institutions is shaped in the interest of administrative efficiency. Dentler and Mackler (1961) studied the process by which mentally retarded children were socialized when they entered a residential institution. In the first month, the investigators found 45 mutual friendship choices based on sociometric questions, but only three mutual choices by the second month. This drop was associated with a large number of disciplinary acts by the staff during the first 3 weeks, when the children were being initiated into the institutional behavioral requirements. A sharp dropping-off of disciplinary acts occurred as the children's stay lengthened. The authors concluded: "The ideal end-product, the social outcome we suspect, is a quiet, well-mannered, even subdued young adult. . . . The character of this total institution is incompatible with the goal of maximum fulfillment of individual potentialities" (pp. 251–252). Thormahlen (1965) examined the training given to children by aides in a residential institution and found that such training promoted dependent behavior, rather than self-sufficiency, in the children who were inmates.

In another study of institutions for mentally retarded persons, Morris (1969) devoted a chapter to life and relationships within hospitals. In the summary, she said of the admissions procedure:

> The ritualized exclusion of the relatives symbolizes a denial on the part of the hospital that relatives have feelings and concerns about the patient, and at the same time it establishes the future pattern of relationships between the hospital and the relatives.

> The second factor which we believe emerges from our findings is the ambivalence of all levels of staff in relation to their custodial role. The patients are constantly referred to as "children" by the majority of nursing staff and this is further symbolized by their attitudes to punishments and sanctions. Stopping entertainments or parole, sending patients to bed early, reducing pocket money, these are all methods which would normally be acceptable as a means of social control of children. Yet the great majority of patients in the hospitals studied were adults, and the behavioral norms expected of them were those of adults. (pp. 187–188)

Most studies of living environments are based on information from staff—generally senior staff. It has been assumed too often that, because residents are mentally retarded, they cannot articulate their own concerns and evaluations or provide information that may be relevant to understanding their living environment. The first advocacy for mentally retarded persons developed with the growth of parent organizations. This representation has been broadened and strengthened by professional and volunteer advocates and by recourse to the courts through class actions. Despite the parents' involvement, their views and feelings often are not sought or are ignored in the planning and operation of living environments. In addition, there is the assumption, which is being increasingly questioned, that mentally retarded individuals cannot speak for themselves, and this assumption appears to underlie the tendency for decisions to be made unilaterally by professionals. Parents sometimes contribute to the tendency to ignore retarded children by becoming so accustomed to speaking for their children that they often underestimate their children's ability to speak for themselves.

RESIDENTS OF LIVING
ENVIRONMENTS FOR THE RETARDED

The customary way in which residents of institutions tend to be described is by use of one of three criteria for defining mental retardation: IQ, level of social competence, and diagnosis. Associated handicapping conditions are sometimes also used, as well as demographic variables, such as age, sex, socioeconomic status, and ethnic background. In research, a wide range of psychological variables has been employed, with the particular variable depending on the investigator's interest. For example, Zigler and Balla (1977) examined perseveration, dependency, responsiveness to social reinforcement, and changes in IQ over time. These factors were related to the type of residential facility and to the pre-institutional histories of the residents. In their review of the impact of institutional experience on the behavior and development of retarded persons, Zigler and Balla (1977) concluded by saying: "We are convinced that any comprehensive program of research must take into account not only the behavioral functioning of residents, but the quality of life they experience, the extent to which they maintain contact with the community and whether they are successfully discharged to community placement" (p. 10). It might have been added that the planning and functioning of residences should be carried out with consideration for the previous experiences of the individuals whom the residences are to serve.

Currently, a dominant interest in the field of mental retardation is deinstitutionalization—the resettlement of persons who have lived, often for most of their lives, in large traditional institutions. Many of those who come from long stays in these institutions have, because of their age, length of stay, the location of the institution, and the reason for their initial placement, lost any close ties that they may have had with their families and home communities. Reasons for their initial placement in institutions have varied widely, and many who were placed there were not severely retarded and had no associated functional handicaps. Many have lived in institutions for long periods of time, sometimes from childhood. As a result, their behavior has been adapted to institutional demands and expectations through socialization within the institution. This socialization has also provided few of the experiences necessary to learn the wide array of skills required for effective living in a community—skills needed to hold a job, to have some time sense, to orient oneself and to use public transportation, to obtain needed information, to find and participate in recreational activities, to form relationships with individuals of the opposite sex, to acquire shopping skills, and to share with others. Some of the skills needed in the community, but lacking in those who have lived for long periods in residential institutions, are described by Birenbaum and Seiffer (1976). With this set of needs remaining the focus of attention, it is easy to overlook the fact that this temporary, although major, problem is one that we have inherited because of the pattern of services over the past 50 years.

As stated earlier, a major long-term problem that is currently receiving too little attention is how to meet the needs of mentally retarded persons who have been brought up in their parents' homes and need alternative living arrangements, either because the burden of care becomes too great for the parents, or because there is a breakdown of the family supports through illness, death, or separation. Many of these mentally retarded adults have been living with their parents and attending daily services, such as sheltered workshops or occupation centers. In the previously referred to study, Richardson (1978) found that, at age 22, 20% of the population defined as mentally retarded were living at home with parents and attending an occupation center 5 days a week. Some form of residential care is needed for all these adults when their parents can no longer care for them. However, little systematic planning has been done to provide a humane and orderly transition from the parents' home to a residential facility in the same community, where residents can continue to participate in the external environment they have known while living with their parents. Such a transition can be helped by the support and encouragement of the parents if it is started when the parents are still able-bodied. Without such a transition, it commonly occurs that, at the death or sudden infirmity of the parents, a crisis develops that must be dealt with hastily. Any available residential arrangement is then taken, often far removed from the external environment that the mentally retarded person has known and become accustomed to. Being forced to leave a familiar environment, to live among strangers in an unfamiliar setting, and at the same time to cope with the death of parents who had been the center of their lives is, to say the least, a wrenching and debilitating experience. This situation can be avoided by careful planning of appropriate community residences.

Generally, in the small residences established through deinstitutionalization programs, a high priority is not placed on locating the residence close to the homes of residents' parents, because most residents have lost contact with their families or have retained only loose ties. In addition, those resettled from large institutions often have few or no social ties with the community from which they originally came. By contrast, for mentally retarded persons who come to residences directly from their parents' homes, the location of a residence close to their previous homes is very important for maintaining easy contact between the residents and their families and between residents and other community associates. Close proximity makes visiting between the residential facility and the parents' homes easier, a mutual advantage to the retarded person, his or her family, the staff, and other residents of the residential facility. Moreover, the initial opposition to those community residences designed to serve a limited area of local residents may be considerably less than opposition to residences designed for those coming from long institutional stays.

Unless the differences in the background histories of the persons coming to residential institutions are taken into account, there is danger that the location, staffing, and programs of the residences will develop into patterns that, while suitable for those coming from long-term stays in large institutions, would be inappropriate and possibly harmful to those coming from their parents' homes.

SPECIAL CHARACTERISTICS
OF THE MENTALLY RETARDED

The term "mentally retarded" is applied to people whose intellectual impairments range from mild to severe, and who may or may not have associated functional impairments.

Mentally retarded individuals vary in the extent to which they require modification or supplementation of the experiences usually needed for socialization. The particular age groups and time periods in which they most benefit from certain experiences may differ from those for nonretarded individuals. They also need varying degrees of extra support, care, and supervision. In young adulthood, some are able to manage most of their own affairs, while others require some support, e.g., assistance from parents, spouses, friends and professionals, although not necessarily within the same household. They may need assistance with tasks like reading, writing, filling out forms, and budgeting money, or with solving problems related to associated handicaps. At the other extreme, some of the severely retarded young adults present problems of care so great that, were the young adult to live at home, most families would be unable to cope with the burden of physical care and/or emotional stress, even with the aid of supporting services from the community. These young adults need almost constant supervision and are unable to manage on their own except for short periods of time. They may be able to participate in occupational activities, but only in a sheltered situation.

For some mentally retarded persons, the broadening of their experiences is dependent, in part, on professional management. For those with seizures, control may be possible through carefully monitored medication. When seizures cannot be controlled by medication, supervision and protective equipment may be essential, such as a helmet to guard the head. For those with Down's syndrome, careful attention must be given to respiratory disorders. For those with sensory losses, special training is important. For those with motor problems, provision and training in the use of wheelchairs, prostheses, crutches, and braces may be essential, together with organization of the living environments to eliminate physical obstacles, such as flights of steps. Corrective surgery may be necessary. Depending on the degree of mental retardation and the types of severity of associated impairments, there is need for extra help in obtaining any social or recreational experiences beyond those that most families can supply. Where the family provides the living environment, the need for formal or informal supporting services is greater if the parents themselves have functional impairments and/or if other family members need extra care, support, or supervision.

When persons with a sociopsychological background approach the study of living environments, it is easy to neglect some of the important physical and biological needs of mentally retarded persons, just as it is easy for persons with physiological and medical training to neglect behavioral needs.

MOVING TOWARD AN ECOLOGICAL PERSPECTIVE

This brief and selective view of the classes of variables related to living environments for mentally retarded individuals illustrates the number and range of those variables that have thus far been considered, and gives some indication of the complexity of their interactions.

The variables used for analyses of internal living environments must be considered in relation to external environments and to the values and ideologies of those who influence the living environments. The particular characteristics of living environments need to be related to the residents of those environments, including the interrelationships of those who are responsible and those for whom they are responsible. The transitions to different living environments that mentally retarded persons experience, and, more generally, the history of their experiences, are both critical factors. Finally, the special characteristics of the person who is mentally retarded must be taken into account. Such complexity can easily confound one, yet an ecological view points in this direction.

Influenced by ecological concepts, we have asked how retarded individuals are affected, in the context of their interpersonal relationships and activities, by the environments that they experience. To select from these experiences, we have asked which are the experiences that are important at different ages for the development of language and for the social, cognitive, and physical skills necessary for effective and satisfying participation in the society. The approach is essentially one of socialization, exploring the individual's life history. One man, in his time, plays many parts, and learning these parts is a continuous process that does not stop at the attainment of adulthood. The form and manner of socialization vary, both from one society to another, and within different parts of the same society. Despite this variation, there remain basic experiences that are needed by all. The question is: Which experiences are generally regarded as advantageous and which disadvantageous for social and intellectual development? A large body of research literature exists that deals with this issue, under such rubrics as cultural or human deprivation, maternal deprivation, the culture of poverty, high-risk families, childhood enrichment programs, and the environmental factors contributing to cultural-familial mental retardation.

One of the difficulties in reviewing studies of living environments for retarded persons is that the form of conceptualization changes from studies of large residential institutions to studies of smaller community residences and parental homes. A second difficulty is the absence, in most studies, of a longitudinal view of the persons served by the residence. An ecological view that considers the experiences of individuals during socialization potentially provides a useful common conceptual approach to all forms of residential care. We are presently attempting to apply this approach in a follow-up study of the transition from childhood into adulthood of all mentally retarded children born in a given community over a 5-year period and still living in that community at ages 8 and 10 years (Richardson, 1978).

ACKNOWLEDGMENTS

The author gratefully acknowledges the support of the Foundation for Child Development and the Social Science Research Council of the United Kingdom in carrying out his research, and the assistance of Helene Koller in the preparation of this chapter.

REFERENCES

Binda, R. 1975. Residential services for the mentally retarded. In: D. A. Primrose (ed.), Proceedings of the Third Congress of the International Association for the Scientific Study of Mental Deficiency. Polish Medical Publishers, Warsaw.

Birenbaum, A., and Seiffer, S. 1976. Resettling Retarded Adults in a Managed Community. Praeger Publishers, New York.

Cohen, H. J. 1975. Obstacles to developing community services for the mentally retarded. In: M. J. Begab and S. A. Richardson (eds.), The Mentally Retarded and Society: A Social Science Perspective. University Park Press, Baltimore.

Damen, P. C. 1975. Organizations and treatment. In: D. A. Primrose (ed.), Proceedings of the Third Congress of the International Association for the Scientific Study of Mental Deficiency. Polish Medical Publishers, Warsaw.

Dentler, R. A., and Mackler, B. 1961. The socialization of retarded children in an institution. J. Health Hum. Behav. 2:243–252.

Goffman, E. 1961. Asylums. Anchor Books, Garden City, N.Y.

Innes, G. 1975. A multi-disciplinary study of mental subnormality in northeast Scotland. In: D. A. Primrose (ed.), Proceedings of the Third Congress of the International Association for the Scientific Study of Mental Deficiency. Polish Medical Publishers, Warsaw.

King, R. D., Raynes, N. V., and Tizard, J. 1971. Patterns of Residential Care. Routledge and Kegan Paul, London.

Kushlick, A. 1975. Epidemiology and evaluation of services. In: M. J. Begab and S. A. Richardson (eds.), The Mentally Retarded and Society: A Social Science Perspective. University Park Press, Baltimore.

Morris, P. 1969. Put Away. Atherton Press, New York.

Nemeth, S. M. 1975. The organizational dimension of care. In: D. A. Primrose (ed.), Proceedings of the Third Congress of the International Association for the Scientific Study of Mental Deficiency. Polish Medical Publishers, Warsaw.

Pratt, M. W., Raynes, N. V., and Roses, S. 1977. Organizational characteristics and their relationship to the quality of care. In: P. Mittler (ed.), Research to Practice in Mental Retardation, Vol. 1. Care and Intervention. University Park Press, Baltimore.

Primrose, D. A. 1977. Asylum. In: P. Mittler (ed.), Research to Practice in Mental Retardation, Vol. 1. Care and Intervention. University Park Press, Baltimore.

Richardson, S. A. 1978. Careers of mentally retarded young persons: Services, jobs and interpersonal relations. A preliminary report. Am. J. Ment. Defic. 82:349–358.

Thormahlen, P. W. 1965. A study of on-the-ward training of trainable mentally retarded children in a state institution. Cal. Ment. Health Res. Monogr., No. 4.

Zigler, E., and Balla, D. A. 1977. Impact of institutional experience on the behavior and development of retarded persons. Am. J. Ment. Defic. 82:1–11.

Living Environments for Developmentally Retarded Persons
Edited by H. Carl Haywood and J. R. Newbrough
Copyright 1981   University Park Press   Baltimore

Mental Health of Mentally Retarded Persons
Social-Ecological Considerations

Paul E. Stucky, B.A.

Department of Psychology and Human Development
Box 319, Peabody College
Vanderbilt University
Nashville, Tennessee 37203

J.R. Newbrough, Ph.D.

Coordinator, Center for Community Studies
John F. Kennedy Center for Research on
    Education and Human Development
Box 319, Peabody College
Vanderbilt University
Nashville, Tennessee 37203

A major objective of the deinstitutionalization movement has been the placement of retarded persons in community settings that are designed to enhance independent functioning and to increase participation in everyday community life. The implementation of this objective has made it apparent that consideration has to be given to the character- istics of persons (what they can and cannot do) and of settings (what behavioral skills are necessary in order to function in them).

   We have considered community placement within the context of social ecology theory because it offers a way of considering the every- day living system of retarded people (Stucky and Newbrough, 1981). Our approach to ecological theory derives from Lewin's notion of the life space, which he described as a single dynamic entity made up of the person and the environment as it exists for that person (Lewin and

Cartwright, 1976). John R. P. French, one of Lewin's students, extended thinking about life space with the idea of person-environment fit. He developed a way of measuring fit in terms of discrepancy between the person's needs and the environmental supply available to meet those needs, as well as the discrepancy between the demands of the environment and the person's ability to meet (supply) those demands (French, 1968). Within this framework, mental health can be understood in terms of optimal person-environment fit (French, Rodgers, and Cobb, 1974).

Mental health as a social movement has had two main streams of concern within it: 1) the care of behaviorally deviant persons who may be dangerous to themselves and others, and 2) the treatment and cure of disordered self-identities when persons experience strange thoughts, sensations, and feelings. The first concern has commonality with the mental retardation field, but the second has been less salient in that field. Basic behavioral and personality disorders have often been seen as inherent elements of the deficits in cognitive and intellectual functioning of retarded persons (Sternlicht, 1976). Thus, considerations for the treatment of disorder and the promotion of mental health have been secondary to concern for cognitive development.

As part of the mental health movement, the advent of community placement of mentally disordered persons brought with it an emphasis on living patterns in daily rounds (Klein, 1968). The major theories underlying the movement have been ecological, with emphases on both individual and environmental characteristics (Caplan, 1964; Leighton, 1959, Srole et al., 1961). We have chosen to consider the mental health of retarded persons from the ecological perspective, and have postulated three dimensions: 1) adequate task performance, 2) maintenance of social relationships, and 3) a sense of well-being. We see these dimensions as necessary and sufficient elements in the definition of mental health within a social ecology framework.

A PERSON-ENVIRONMENT APPROACH TO MENTAL RETARDATION

The diagnosis of mental retardation seems primarily based on the inability to perform tasks adequately and the attendant difficulties that persons have in acquiring new behavior patterns. The most commonly accepted definition of mental retardation refers to significantly subaverage intellectual functioning, together with personal behavior that does not exhibit as much independence and social responsibility as is displayed by age and social class peers (Grossman, 1977). These criteria are used in the clinical process whereby people are classified and labeled as retarded.

Labeling theory and work in the area of deviance have been helpful in pointing out that both behavioral acts and the perception of important and dominant social others constitute the mechanism for labeling (Newbrough, 1968, 1972; Rains et al., 1975; Rhodes, 1975; Rhodes and Sagor, 1975). A label applies only to an individual in a particular social context, and it says as much about the values and competency requirements of the setting and the people around the individual as it says about the individual's behavior. Thus, in a school context, both the behavioral requirements of the school and the level of individual performance contribute to the assignment of a label of mentally retarded to many children who would not be so identified outside of school (Mercer, 1975) or once they were beyond school age (Gruenberg, 1964; Richardson, 1978). Rhodes and Sagor (1975) indicate that, even though individual behavioral differences do exist, it is the collective interpretation that determines whether these differences will have a positive or negative impact on the community.

Labels like "mentally retarded" have made labeled people seem qualitatively different from average citizens (Edgerton, 1970), often leading to less than equal treatment and to violations of human and constitutional rights. The label "mentally retarded" has led to assumptions of ineducability and inability to cope socially. Yet the very existence of a label denies special persons any socially sanctioned way of coping with their difference from others, and these persons are forced either to accept the social assumptions and expectations or to invent fictitious histories in order to "pass" (Goldschmidt, 1974). Labels and categorizations have been used to channel persons to the appropriate service resources. Unfortunately, the labels have also served to designate the recipients of them as victims. Because the focus has been on the individual person, the need for change in the social context or life-space has not been seen as essential.

From a person-environment perspective, there is a different way of thinking about mental retardation and about persons called mentally retarded. A separation is not made between such individuals and their living environments. Attention is given to the qualities of the individual, as well as those of the other persons and the setting that characterize retardation. Ecological assessment techniques, which serve to evaluate the context and persons in the context, then become useful (Dokecki, 1977; Hobbs, 1975; Newbrough, 1977; Williams, 1977). Change is seen as a basic human characteristic, and focus is centered on the potential for growth (Feuerstein, Rand, and Hoffman, 1979; Feuerstein et al., 1980; Haywood, 1977). Intervention is focused as much on the conditions and changes in the caregivers and settings as on the special persons themselves. There is the recognition that the unique qualities of the individual and the context can be oriented to promote a person-environment congruence that optimizes the functioning of all concerned. From the person-environment perspective, the mental health of retarded persons becomes inseparable from their living environments.

A PERSON-ENVIRONMENT APPROACH TO
THE MENTAL HEALTH OF RETARDED PERSONS

Traditional approaches to the promotion of the mental health of retarded persons have, in fact, been largely limited to the identification and treatment of psychological and behavioral disturbances (Balthazar and Stevens, 1975; Haracopos and Kelstrup, 1978; Heaton-Ward, 1977; Katz, 1972; Menolascino, 1970). All of the identified behavioral disturbances (major and minor) have been found to occur in association with mental retardation (Beier, 1964; Singh, 1972). The incidence of disturbance is higher among retarded persons than it is in the general population (Beier, 1964). However, it can be misleading to generalize this finding to all types of retardation, given the variety of etiological and behavioral characteristics that are included in the retardation category. In addition, the diagnosis of disturbance can itself prove problematical, especially with profoundly retarded persons and some severely retarded persons who lack intelligible speech (Heaton-Ward, 1977). Nevertheless, behavioral problems, second to intellectual deficiency, are the most important cause of initial institutionalization (Beier, 1964) and the major cause of reinstitutionalization after discharge to the community (Eagle, 1967; Gollay et al., 1978; Maney, Pace, and Morrison, 1964; Windle, 1962; Windle, Stewart, and Brown, 1961).

Psychotherapy has been a major approach to treatment. An array of therapeutic techniques has been adapted, including individual and group therapy, art, music, and recreational therapy and counseling (Bialer, 1967; Sternlicht, 1977). Behavior modification has represented an alternative approach. Practitioners within this orientation have tended to ignore the diagnostic labels. Instead, they intervene directly to change the particular behavior patterns deemed undesirable.

From a person-environment perspective, both psychotherapy and behavior modification are useful, but limited. First, there has been a lack of understanding of the phenomenology of mental retardation, and of the ways retarded persons see and experience their daily lives (Edgerton, 1977). Both the descriptive studies of retarded persons (Edgerton, 1967, 1977; Edgerton and Bercovici, 1976) and the autobiographical histories of retarded persons themselves (Bogdan, 1980; Turner, 1980) have been helpful to improve understanding and to underline the fact that professional perceptions of retarded persons and what makes for their well-being are not always close to those perceptions that retarded persons have of themselves. Second, the approaches mentioned are primarily based on the assumption that mental health results from the remediation of individual disorder or lack of competence. This assumption has led to a focus on individual change and skill acquisition, which includes the expectation that retarded people will generalize their experience to new situations and will carry their social skills and mental health with them wherever they go. The inadequacy of this assumption is suggested by situations, like those described by Rosen, Clark, and Kivitz (1977), in which some retarded persons who settled in the community functioned adequately, paid their bills, went to work, and stayed out of trouble, but nevertheless were withdrawn, lonely, uncomfortable in social situations, and generally unhappy.

From a person-environment perspective, the mental health of retarded persons is a joint function of person characteristics and setting characteristics. It is more than the absence of behavioral disorders and mental illness. In addition, it represents a quality of life that is reflected in task performance, social relationships, and well-being, not only in retarded people, but also in caregivers, family members, and neighbors.

Task Performance

Adequate performance requires that persons meet the demands of the environment, while at the same time obtaining from it satisfaction of their own needs. French et al. (1974) have described this performance in terms of achieving a balance between supply and demand. When there is an imbalance, persons seek to cope, either by changing the environment so that it better supplies their needs or by changing themselves to adjust better to the environment. Change in one leads to change in the other, until a balance is reached.

In order to cope successfully, the ability that people have must be translated into skills and resources that are adequate for fitting or changing their environments. Skills are largely acquired and given specific form by the social structure and institutions within which people learn and develop. Thus, as Mechanic (1974) stressed, individual ability to cope is greatly affected by the degree of fit between the social structure and the environment. If social institutions do not provide retarded people or their caregivers with opportunities to acquire the social and technical skills that are appropriate to the demands of their jobs, they will have difficulty coping. Similarly, if the environment does not supply necessary information, social support, and economic stability to retarded persons, caregivers, neighbors, and professionals, they will have trouble coping.

We mentioned above the frequency with which maladaptive or problematic behavior is cited as a cause of institutionalization. This indicates the extent of difficulty retarded persons have in coping and maintaining an adequate fit between themselves and their environments. Edgerton and Bercovici (1976), in their study of retarded persons discharged from Pacific State Hospital (now Lanterman State Hospital), found that their subjects experienced instability and fluctuation in their adjustment. The findings of a subsequent study of the community adjustment of retarded persons led Edgerton (1977) to note that change was the most conspicuous feature of their daily lives. Change and instability can lead to growth, if retarded persons have the ability to cope, but if they are without that ability, the situation becomes stressful and overwhelming.

Retarded persons encounter numerous barriers when trying to cope with community settings. They frequently lack both social skills and a familiarity with the behavioral cues and values of the dominant culture. The retarded person's experience has been compared to the transition or culture shock of returning expatriates (Coffman and Harris, 1980). They are threatened by economic instability as a result of their own limited marketable skills and a shortage of alternative work possibilities (Edgerton and Bercovici, 1976; Gollay et al., 1978; Koegel and Kernan, 1981). Retarded persons may not have supportive relationships, i.e., people who will stand by, but not interfere too much. Ferrara (1979) and Wolfensberger (1967a) have noted the tendency of parents to be overprotective, thus perpetuating dependency and limiting possibilities for risk-taking and growth (Perske, 1974). Finally, retarded persons are often faced with inappropriate expectations of others, lack of self-acceptance, and lack of acceptance by others—all of which result from labels and societal processes of exclusion.

The issue of adequate task performance is also important for caregivers. Their ability to cope is affected: 1) by lack of information about, access to, or availability of supportive services for the retarded persons in their care (Gorham et al., 1975; Willer, Scheerenberger, and Intagliata, 1978) and 2) by lack of adequate funding, both for residences (Bruininks et al., 1980a; Willer et al., 1978) and for natural families (Bruininks et al., 1980b). Lack of information about and understanding of the people being cared for can also be a handicap. The conflict between the societal valuation of achievement and intelligence and the unique characteristics of retarded persons can lead to community rejection and can affect the attitudes of the caregivers (Wolfensberger, 1967a).

Environments That Enhance   Just as environments can pose real barriers to coping, they can also serve to enhance people's efforts to function adequately. The elements of enhancing environments include formal and informal social supports and provisions for social and economic stability.

Formal and informal human relationships enhance coping when

they are based on acceptance and understanding, and they are ongoing, dependable, and readily accessible. The self-help and advocacy groups of parents and of retarded persons are important sources of informal support. Through such groups, many parents have experienced the support and understanding of other parents with retarded family members. Gorham et al. (1975) noted that parent organizations are probably the major organized providers of information about the services needed by retarded persons. People First, a self-advocacy organization of retarded persons (Posner, 1977; Schaaf et al., 1977; Cunio et al., 1978; Heath, Schaaf, and Talkington, 1975), represents a major breakthrough in self-help for retarded persons. Through People First, they are able to provide each other with support and understanding, to obtain more public awareness and recognition of their rights, and to have a basis for identity and self-esteem.

A second type of informal support, described by Bayley (1973) in his study of retarded persons in Sheffield, consists of relatives, friends, and neighbors of the retarded persons and their families. The assistance of this informal network was often found to be much more vital to coping than was professional social-work help. A third type of informal support, particularly for retarded persons, is the benefactor, described by Edgerton (1967) as a person without stigma in the community who could vouch for the retarded person and be of assistance in coping with daily life.

The main source of formal supportive relationships is service professionals. In spite of frequent low ratings in helpfulness and considerateness (Gorham et al., 1975; Wolfensberger, 1967a), they have a useful role to play in providing information, supervision, and specialized care. Two newer approaches to formal support have come from Project Re-ED, an educational and ecological approach to the treatment of emotionally disturbed children, started in 1962 in Nashville, Tennessee, and Durham, North Carolina (Hobbs, 1966, 1975, 1979; Lewis, 1971; Weinstein, 1969). In Project Re-ED, the first source of support is the teacher-counselor. Teacher-counselors are specially trained educators who are also skilled in counseling and in using consultants in mental health and education. Their work is not confined to classroom teaching. Instead, they are part of a team that seeks to design all the daily activities of its children so that they will learn to function in ways that are satisfying to themselves and to the people who are important to them.

A second source of formal support drawn from the Re-ED model is the liaison member of the Re-ED team. The liaison teacher-counselor facilitates linkages between the disturbed children and their social-environmental system, and facilitates the efforts of key persons in the system to achieve a quality of person-environment fit that allows for the development of the child as well as of the family, neighbors, and friends (Dokecki, 1977; Williams, 1977).

A second way in which the social environment can contribute to individual coping is through the establishment of provisions for social and economic stability and integration. The need for adequate funding for caregivers has already been noted. There is also need for appropriate economic options for retarded persons. Gollay et al. (1978), in their study of deinstitutionalized community residents, found that many problems were related to work. Finding a job and keeping it were among the problems most frequently mentioned. Retarded persons are among the first to suffer from slowdowns in the economy or rising unemployment. One of the most common options is sheltered workshops. Although the importance of workshops should not be minimized, their economic situation is tenuous, they provide a restricted range of settings and activities, and there are simply not enough of them. Far more options could be created through diversification of the competitive sector by establishing small business and manufacturing enterprises at the local level (Koegel and Kernan, 1981; Rusch, Schutz, and Heal, 1981). These enterprises would provide a broader range of job opportunities and increased possibilities for economic stability. They would also allow for increased social contacts between retarded persons and their nonretarded neighbors, thus helping to meet relational needs and adding to a sense of community.

Social Relationships

Social relationships represent the fit between persons. The ability to establish and maintain social relationships enables people to go successfully about their daily rounds. McCarver and Craig (1974) reported a number of studies that indicated that the success of deinstitutionalized residents in the community was related to their having adequate social skills. On a more intimate level, relationships are a vehicle for the friendship and acceptance that can bring satisfaction and security to life. Friendship and acceptance are also the basis for growth and increased self-acceptance (Rogers, 1961).

When retarded persons are moved to community settings, it is often done without regard for personal friendships (Berkson, personal communication, September 25, 1979). They seem to have few friends and do not make new ones readily. Richardson (1978) compared retarded persons to a matched sample of nonretarded persons and reported that fewer retarded persons could claim two best friends or could feel that they had gotten along very well with people since leaving school. Baker, Seltzer, and Seltzer (1977) and Rosen et al. (1977) found that some retarded persons in the community had attained independence, yet led meaningless and lonely lives. Gollay et al. (1978), in their study of 440 deinstitutionalized community residents, found that 80% of the group said they had good friends, but many had no friends in the community, and, for about 20% of those interviewed, loneliness and social relationships were problems. In the same study, 74% of the group reported having a nonprofessional friend or relative to whom they could turn for informal guidance and personal support. However, one-quarter of the group had no one, and one-third of the severely retarded adults and nearly one-half of the children also reported having no one to turn to in the community.

The establishment of relationships requires the ability to respond appropriately to the behavior of others, and to recognize and to give the often subtle cues of everyday interactions. This may require special training and experience in normal settings, especially for retarded persons with a long history of institutional living. Life in an institution often contributes to the acquisition or perpetuation of stereotypic, aggressive, or even affectionate behavior that is not acceptable in non-institutionalized settings (Rosen et al., 1977). Similarly, years of living in an institution may make people unaware of their expressions and require that they learn the gestures and meanings of social relationships (Birenbaum and Seiffer, 1976).

The settings of people's daily rounds can provide opportunities for interaction. Deinstitutionalization has contributed to the decrease of some of the physical barriers to relationships between retarded and nonretarded persons by reducing the distance that isolated many formerly institutionalized retarded persons and their caregivers from neighborhoods and noninstitutional settings. Social barriers to interaction also diminish as the differences between retarded and nonretarded persons become less evident or less important. Edgerton and Bercovici (1976), in reviewing the findings of their study of deinstitutionalized community residents, stated that, as retarded persons grew older and less healthy, less could be expected of them and their relative incompetence became less noticeable. Similarly, when unemployment in the area went up, so that the criteria of normality changed, the perceived normality of the retarded subjects increased.

Lewin focused much of his work on interpersonal relationships. He found that, if social relationships are to be maintained and to contribute to self-esteem, they need to be based on participation in decision-making, on genuine interdependence, on mutual giving and receiving, and on the establishment of attainable goals for each member (Lewin and Cartwright, 1976). These are qualities of a social setting that can be found, in part, in sheltered villages, such as Camphill (Baker et al., 1977; Davis, 1978; Zipperlen, 1975). Camphill Village is a partially self-supporting community in which staff members (called co-workers) and their families represent between 30% and 50% of the population. At Camphill, retarded adults (called villagers), co-workers, and their families live together in homes and share household tasks. Work in the village is assigned daily by a work group to co-workers and villagers alike, on the basis of individual abilities and community needs. Work is generally done by small teams of retarded villagers and co-workers whose varying skills must be brought together to produce a high quality result. In the evenings there are dramatic events and discussion groups that involve villagers and co-workers alike. Through this variety of levels of participation, a strong basis for relationships is established.

Similar types of interdependence could take place in conventional neighborhoods through community activities and projects, both economic and social, that would meet specific needs in the community and that would require the diversity of skills of both retarded and nonretarded persons. Given a base of interdependence, a liaison person could work to enhance the possibilities for all persons to be given fair treatment and for interactions to be based on mutual respect and caring.

Well-being

A sense of well-being arises out of the satisfaction of basic physiological needs and of needs for love, for safety, for esteem, and for knowing (Maslow, 1970). It is not an end state of happiness, but a process of continued growth (Allport, 1955; Rogers, 1961). Cobb (1971) looked at individual joy and satisfaction and showed that they were best understood as transient states affected by each individual's relationship with the environment.

Environments that contribute to well-being provide opportunities for experiencing interest and enjoyment in the course of daily living. For many deinstitutionalized and noninstitutionalized persons, community living has provided access to a whole range of new activities and experiences (Baker et al., 1977; Gollay et al., 1978). There is often a variety of options for recreational activities, for meeting new people, and for going to different places. Yet retarded persons often assume a dependent behavioral stance. They have learned not to initiate and may remain in a quiescent state of boredom unless someone takes the initiative to activate them. This background state of passivity and boredom needs to be taken into account in programming for deinstitutionalized persons, as well as for severely and profoundly retarded residents in restricted home and institutional settings.

Considerable attention has been focused on the quality of relationships and care offered to retarded persons in various types of residential environments (Balla, 1976; Baroff, 1980; Begab, this volume; Berkson, this volume; Bjaanes and Butler, 1974; Butler and Bjaanes, 1977, 1980; Butterfield, 1967; Edgerton, Eyman, and Silverstein, 1975;

Haywood, this volume; Howell and May, 1980; Kiernan, this volume; King, Raynes, and Tizard, 1971; McCormick, Balla, and Zigler, 1975; Raynes, Pratt, and Roses, 1977; Tizard, 1970; Zigler and Balla, 1977). Conclusions from this line of research are still rather tentative. There are great differences between large institutions and a lack of uniformity among them, and the same problem occurs with the various types of community residential options. Variations in organizational structure, service programming and utilization, staff attitudes and training, and staff participation in decision-making are some of the factors that have been found to affect the quality and orientation of care offered to residents. A tentative conclusion is that care is more likely to be oriented toward residents in group homes than toward residents in large institutions. Small group homes tend to provide privacy, to treat residents more like individuals, and to offer greater contact between staff and residents.

The well-being of the caregivers is essential for achieving an atmosphere in which retarded persons can experience love and esteem and receive the personal attention they need to develop and pursue their interests. Therefore, caregivers must derive satisfaction from their work. Staff members at institutions and group homes generally have no familial or outside personal connection with the residents, hence they often lack the intrinsic pleasure and motivation that most parents have in teaching and caring for their children. Because caregivers may lack this involvement, it becomes vital to design working conditions in which they can become interested and excited and find pleasure and joy in their work.

Zaharia and Baumeister (1979a, 1979b) studied job satisfaction and turnover among technician level staff members in public residential institutions. Technicians constitute the largest group of the staff and are responsible for direct services to residents, including training, recreation, and discipline. Absenteeism and turnover are considered indications of dissatisfaction as well as of organizational dysfunction, and they clearly reflect and affect the quality of care being provided. Zaharia and Baumeister (1979b) found a monthly controllable absenteeism rate of 2.4% and a monthly controllable turnover rate of 6.7%, for an annual average of 29%, almost one-third of the staff. In their review of the literature, Zaharia and Baumeister (1978) found the following factors reported as contributing to technician turnover: low pay, low job status, the availability of other jobs, administrative and organizational deficiencies, lack of job satisfaction (which may be affected by repetitiveness and lack of autonomy), and personal factors of employees. In a study conducted in three large public residential facilities in Tennessee, Zaharia and Baumeister (1979a) found technician job satisfaction to be associated with smaller staff size, appropriate staffing patterns (which motivate and do not overtax), and assignment to work in coed residential units. However, it is noteworthy that in all areas of satisfaction, particularly with respect to pay, average scores for technicians were lower than those of industrial workers.

A major conclusion in the work of Zaharia and Baumeister (1978, 1979a, 1979b) is that organizational patterns and management practices play a crucial role in the reduction of turnover and the enhancement of employee satisfaction in institutional settings. Some possible strategies include 1) forming small work groups and coed work groups, 2) rapidly integrating new employees, 3) increasing staff autonomy, 4) increasing provisions for task variation and ongoing education in order to avoid social deprivation from institutional work, and 5) improving the pay scale and job status.

The experience of caregivers in noninstitutionalized settings, such as community residential facilities with live-in house parents, foster homes, and natural homes, is somewhat different from that of institutionalized staff. They frequently experience continuous demands on their time and patience, often without the chance for relief. Even when there is some respite during the day, main caregivers typically feel responsible for the provision of care and may feel guilty when they are not actually present. All joy can easily be lost. Bruininks et al., (1980b), in reviewing studies of family care, reported that the main problems cited by family caregivers were 1) lack of free time to go out, 2) neglect of other family members, and 3) adverse reactions from other relatives. Willer et al. (1978), as well as Bruininks and co-workers (1980a, 1980b), cited the lack of availability or adequate access to supportive services as a major problem for residential caregivers and residents. Thus, the well-being of community-based caregivers depends on finding ways of sharing their responsibilities and of maintaining outside interests and contacts. Organized support services, such as volunteer programs and formal respite workers, can play an important role. In addition, community integration and involvement can provide the kind of support caregivers need. In an integrated community, relatives and neighbors are more readily available than formal support personnel to assist in the large, and particularly in the small, ways that would not warrant a formal request for help. In addition, caring neighbors offer signs and expressions of friendship to caregivers and residents as they go about their daily rounds, which can be essential to their experience of well-being.

IMPLICATIONS OF A PERSON-ENVIRONMENT APPROACH

A primary implication of the person-environment approach is that the mental health of retarded persons is a reflection of the living environments in which they go about their daily rounds. The vast majority of living environments for retarded persons are in an urban community. Partially as a result of deinstitutionalization, the number of retarded people isolated in institutions has decreased substantially (Bruininks et al., 1980b), and the number and types of alternative living arrangements in the community have greatly increased (Baker et al., 1977; Bruininks, Hauber, and Kudla, 1980). What deinstitutionalization has not done is promote change in communities, so that neighborhoods can create meaningful social roles, or niches (Mills and Kelly, 1972), through which retarded persons can become integrated to their environments. The underlying assumption may have been that neighbors would react positively and integration would occur naturally. In fact, deinstitutionalization has not promoted a process of person-environment fit (Butler and Bjaanes, 1977, 1980). As it stands, retarded persons are a sort of surplus population and communities do not need them. They are considered people to be served, a burden to be borne.

Normalization, as described by Nirje (1969), means the process of making available to retarded persons conditions of daily life that are as similar as possible to those of the mainstream of society. Wolfensberger (1972) defined it as the use of culturally normative means to elicit (in retarded persons) behavior patterns as similar as possible to those of everyone else. The hope is that by going about daily rounds in ordinary settings, retarded persons will learn to fit in. This process places important emphasis on acquiring skills that will enable retarded persons to find jobs and to travel around town. It also indicates the need to develop social skills in order to interact with people, and to learn the correct gestures and cues that will allow them to act appropriately and not call attention to their retardation (Birenbaum and Seiffer, 1976). As a result, researchers recognize the need for persons to observe retarded people in their daily rounds, to encourage appropriateness of behavior, and to facilitate the process of normalization.

An implicit assumption of normalization is that what is normal is best, and adaptive behavior is evaluated in terms of the dominant societal values of independence and social responsibility. Thus, normalization brings with it the risk of focusing on adapting the individual, rather than emphasizing diversity and fashioning special arrangements to enhance individual strengths and uniqueness.

The Ecology of Person-Environment Fit

Persons and their environments or life-spaces can be understood as systems that include the persons, the settings of their daily rounds, and other persons who directly or indirectly enter the settings. The persons and settings that compose a system are interrelated, so that a change in one component can alter the relationships of all the rest and affect the functioning of the entire system. Problems reside in the system and reflect not only individual behavior, but also the way each person's behavior affects other persons in particular settings. Behavior may be functional in one context and dysfunctional in another. Planning for intervention must include an evaluation to determine whether changes in particular persons are needed, and how such changes will affect the other components of the system. Interventions may require changes in particular persons, in settings, and in the ways they interact with each other, so that the system will finally function in ways that enhance the well-being and development of all.

People have unique strengths and weaknesses that enable them to cope better in certain environments than in others. Consequently, we look for the best fit between persons and environments in general, not just the fit between a particular person and the best environment. This means that sometimes environments have to be changed to create meaningful and appropriate roles and ways of interacting. Coping describes a person's competency in particular settings. Hobbs (1975) pointed out that, if the demands of setting or environment are too great, a person may not respond, or may respond inappropriately; if the demands are too small, a person will get bored. Personal growth and interest are fostered by maintaining a just-manageable discrepancy between what the person knows and can do, and what is necessary for the environment.

Implications for Intervention

An ecological approach to intervention was described above in considering Project Re-ED. In Re-ED, the problem of a disturbed child is not regarded only as a symptom of individual pathology, as something the child has. Rather, it is considered to be a breakdown of an ecological system that includes the child, the family, the school, the neighborhood, and the larger community, including social agencies. The objective of intervention is not simply to cure the child, but also to enable the system to function. Thus, assessment and intervention are focused on the individual strengths of the child and on the resources of the community. The goal is to get each component of the system—the child, parents, neighborhood—to attain a level of functioning that allows the rest to function also. The Re-ED interveners stay in the picture until the system becomes functional on its own resources and stabilizes sufficiently.

Crucial to the ecological approach illustrated by Project Re-ED is the function of the liaison worker (Williams, 1977). The liaison worker 1) gathers information on the child and the system, identifying resources and liabilities; 2) establishes linkages among key members of the system, including parents, teachers, other professionals, friends, Re-ED staff, and, at times, the child; 3) facilitates agreement on common strategies; and 4) monitors the process. As the system begins to function more adequately, and the original disturbance fades, the liaison person phases out of the process.

An important dimension of ecological intervention is the establishment of an appropriate definition of success, because this will determine the direction of the intervention. At the individual level, success for retarded persons in the community is frequently defined in terms of independence and adaptive functioning. The criteria for success include holding a job, properly carrying out household duties, staying out of trouble, and not returning to an institution or another public agency. These definitional terms and criteria may not be adequate. Edgerton and Bercovici (1976), in a follow-up study of residents discharged from Pacific State Hospital (Lanterman State Hospital), found that the retarded persons who were interviewed rated confidence higher than competence, and well-being over independence. These findings underline the importance of allowing retarded persons to help define what success is for them.

In considering success at the level of the entire system or community, it may be useful to study the quality of life of retarded persons in low-income neighborhoods. Research literature is relatively scant and inconclusive in this area, although Wolfensberger (1967a) did cite a number of studies that suggested greater acceptance of mentally retarded persons in low-income families. He proposed that mildly retarded persons might be more readily integrated into families of lower socioeconomic classes, because in such families breadwinning may be valued more highly than achievement, and retarded behavior may not be so readily recognized. In low-income neighborhoods there is often interdependence and diversification of roles and functions as well as an acceptance of diverse behavioral styles. Research is needed to determine the extent to which these are characteristics of successful communities.

Implications for Training

If training is to enhance person-environment fit, it should be appropriate to the particular strengths and needs of retarded persons. Willems (1977) discussed the implications of an ecological perspective for the use of behavior modification techniques, which are so frequently employed with retarded persons. He made the point that, in order to be able to plan and to use operant approaches rationally, it is necessary to understand the properties of the system and the ways in which the people, places, and situations interact. Changes in certain kinds of behavior can lead to alterations in the entire system of contingencies, resulting in unexpected outcomes and side effects. Therefore, it is important 1) to use research methods that elucidate interdependencies, 2) to study the linkages between settings and behavior, and 3) to collect long-term data with which to evaluate success and the causes of unwanted side effects.

An implicit assumption of normalization is that skills are best learned in the contexts in which they are to be used, an idea that concurs with an ecological approach to training. In an ecological approach, the objective is to use cues and reinforcers that are functionally related to the desired behavior and that are likely to occur in the criterion settings (Rogers-Warren, 1976). Although this might take more time and be less efficient for staff members than the use of strictly artificial reinforcers, it can more realistically teach retarded persons the contexts in which skills are used and the consequences of their acts.

It is also important to use as trainers those persons, including relatives, neighbors, and co-workers, whom retarded persons are likely to encounter in the course of using the skills they are acquiring. Therefore, on-the-job training is important. In addition, by involving retarded people themselves in the training process, a valuable feedback loop can be incorporated into the system. Matson, Marchetti, and Adkins (1980) found that involvement of the residents in their training program, through self-evaluation and self-monitoring, not only improved performance but also pleased the residents.

Implications for Employment

Satisfactory employment requires a match between the skills and preferences of the employee and the requirements of the job. This calls for training in skills that are marketable, as well as an increase in the range of available job opportunities. Wolfensberger (1967b) has noted the relationship between the types of employment available in a community and the number of inadequately functioning individuals. Increased automation and specialization can be expected to lead to increased frequency of dysfunction.

Earlier we alluded to the potentially beneficial effect of more small-sized production and marketing units, which would create demand for labor at the local level. A second factor affecting work possibilities for retarded persons is what Barker and Schoggen (1973) described as "undermanned" settings, in which there were not enough people to fill all the roles. They found that when behavior settings, such as work sites, were understaffed, there was increased pressure drawing people in, and they were required to perform at a higher level of responsibility, thus giving them the opportunity for growing and acquiring new skills and competencies. These growth effects of understaffing are more likely to occur in smaller, local settings.

If an employment relationship is to represent an appropriate fit, it must fulfill the expectations of the employer and community as well as of the employees. For the former, it often requires that the work performed be economically productive or in some other way contribute to the defined social and economic objectives. For retarded employees, it means that the work should provide satisfying activity as well as adequate income. However, this is not always the case. Although studies have shown that a majority of retarded people tend to express contentment with their work, Baker et al. (1977) found that one-third of those interviewed did not like their placements, and Gollay et al. (1978) reported that only two-thirds of the study subjects were satisfied, and satisfaction was lower among the severely retarded. Often, retarded persons are assigned to jobs that require few interpersonal skills or opportunities. They have been found to earn less than nonretarded persons of the same age (Richardson, 1978) and sometimes less than nonretarded persons within the same occupational categories (Skaarbrevik, 1971). A liaison person could help to enhance fit and to ensure fair treatment for retarded employees.

Implications for the Residential Environment

From an ecological perspective, the residence and home experiences are viewed as parts of the unique life-space of each person. We would not expect that a single type of architectural design would be best for all, but that it would be part of a larger environment that either enhances or detracts from person-environment fit. Bednar (1973) makes the point that there is a reciprocity of influence between people and their environments that is key to the planning of new, responsive dwellings. Architectural planning must begin by understanding how staff members and handicapped persons interact with the physical environment, including the buildings and spaces that make up the built environment. Similarly, it is important to know how various features of the built environment relate to resident and staff functioning.

Knight, Zimring, and Kent (1976) and Knight et al. (1977) have studied the role of the built environment in promoting the acquisition of appropriate social behavior and in enhancing the satisfaction of the individual's personal needs for control of stimulation/arousal, information, and privacy. The researchers believed that normal and variegated living environments, which include public, semi-public, semi-private, and private rooms (with doors that can be locked), maximize the choices and controls that retarded people can exercise over their environment and behavior. A variety of choices is particularly needed by handicapped persons, who often lack the social skills by which we seek aloneness and establish control. Most people seek to create a home base in which they can feel safe and relax, the classic function of the private home. The home typically includes various spaces in which one can be alone, arrange objects as one may please, and collect and keep objects and materials that have personal meaning. Persons who require special care often are not able to have these spaces and are not able to meet the needs of privacy and personal meaning.

Knight et al. (1977) and Knight, Zimring, and Kent (1976) examined the effect of normalized physical environments that provided for personal spaces on the institutionalized population at Belchertown State School, in a group of predominantly severely and profoundly retarded persons. The investigators found that, when such an environment was part of a normalized social system in which residents could choose privacy, and staff and other residents respected the choices, social interactions of the residents, particularly with other residents, increased and became more positive. The significance of their finding is not that a more compartmentalized plant is best for all, but that an appropriate physical environment, as part of a larger ecological fit, can promote greater and more positive social interaction.

Wandersman (1979a, 1979b) has argued that participation in the design and control of environments has salutary effects on various groups of people. In one study, Wandersman (1979b) used planning or selection among alternative environments as measures of participation. He found that when subjects participated, they experienced more satisfaction with their environments and felt more creative, helpful, and responsible and less alienated and anonymous than subjects who did not participate. His findings also indicate that persons prefer to participate in environments that are important to them and about which they have opinions. Barker and Gump (1964), in their study of small and large schools, found that the size of environmental units affects participation. In small schools, there is greater participation by more students, students feel more responsibility, and they have a sense that they matter.

Generalizing the larger findings to include retarded people, we would expect that opportunities for participating and assuming responsibility would be enhanced in smaller residences, and especially those that, as a part of daily events, include the presentation of choices and the process of consultation between the caregivers and retarded persons (a meaningful social exchange in which retarded persons can experience themselves as listened to and needed). Choices, once made, would be allowed to run their course so that the retarded person could develop personal judgment.

External features of a residence, as well as its location, also influence the possibilities for social integration and fit. Wolfensberger (1972) observed that inordinately large size or institutional appearance can reinforce community expectations of deviant behavior, making integration more difficult. Locations close to stores and centers of entertainment, allowing for access to community services and activities, can contribute to self-sufficiency and decreased dependency on the staff (Bjaanes and Butler, 1974; Eyman, Demain, and Lei, 1979). Finally, looking at the larger context, there has been consideration of the relative merits of rural versus urban placement (Edgerton et al., 1975; Krischef, 1959; Scheerenberger and Felsenthal, 1977; Windle, 1962). The issue may not be one of a choice between rural or urban environments, but rather one of the extent to which the location offers access to a diversity of roles, a variety of places to meet and interact with other people, and understaffed settings into which retarded people will be drawn. It is generally the case that rural communities and lower income neighborhoods have more small shops, informal meeting places, and nonspecialized tasks that may increase the opportunities of retarded people to cope independently and to interact with others.

CONCLUSION

An underlying assumption of the ecological approach is that the individual experience of mental health is inextricably linked to the qualities of life afforded by the environment. A focus is placed on the community environment within which (to a greater or lesser extent) retarded people go about their daily rounds. An ecological approach provides a framework for understanding and fostering changes at the community level that can enhance task performance, the quality of relationships, and the individual experience of well-being.

The community can be viewed as a habitat that promotes the development of its residents and serves as a support system for improving the quality of life (Newbrough, 1974). From this perspective, recent attention to enhancing community through local empowerment and participation is important (Berger and Neuhaus, 1977; Etzioni, 1976; Kaswan, 1977; Ryan, 1972). There is increasing awareness of the mutual support and caring that can be offered by extended family networks and self-help groups. The neighborhood revitalization movement (Ahlbrandt and Brophy, 1975; Yates, 1973) has contributed to the recovery of the physical environment and to increased participation and interaction by local citizens. Through the Community Education Act of 1974, local schools are being transformed into centers of community activity and ongoing education. Movements like these are helping to make neighborhoods better places in which to live. They also represent special opportunities for greater involvement of retarded people in the community and for the creation of settings and roles that best fit their needs. However, as Butler and Bjaanes (1980) have pointed out, mere placement in community care facilities does not ensure utilization of community services or participation in a variety of community settings and activities. Conscious effort must be made to promote integration through attention to the characteristics of the living environments and of the retarded residents. Liaison workers can be of crucial importance, as advocates for retarded persons, and as links that help make integration possible.

Because the local community exists within the framework of the larger society, quality of life is affected by national economic structures, priorities, and policies. It is important for retarded persons to have a safe environment, to have provisions for adequate income, housing, and health care, to have a comprehensive public transportation system, and to have full employment. These goals stand as the appropriate criteria of a good community for all citizens.

An ecological approach to the mental health of retarded persons calls for intervention at the individual level that is supportive when there is suffering, and that promotes individual competence. At the local level, intervention should promote living environments that allow for a diversity of roles and encourage social and economic integration. Finally, at the societal level, intervention should promote policy and structural changes that lead to distributive justice, local empowerment, and respect for individual rights.

REFERENCES

Ahlbrandt, R. S., and Brophy, P. C. 1975. Neighborhood Revitalization. Lexington Books, Lexington, Massachusetts.
Allport, G. W. 1955. Becoming: Basic Considerations for a Psychology of Personality. Yale University Press, New Haven.
Baker, B. L., Seltzer, G. B., and Seltzer, M. M. 1977. As Close as Possible: Community Residences for Retarded Adults. Little, Brown and Company, Boston.
Balla, D. A. 1976. Relationships of institution size to quality of care: A review of the literature. Am. J. Ment. Defic. 81:117–124.
Balthazar, E. E., and Stevens, H. A. 1975. The Emotionally Disturbed, Mentally Retarded: A Historical and Contemporary Perspective. Prentice-Hall Inc., Englewood Cliffs, N.J.
Barker, R. G., and Gump, P. V. 1964. Big School, Small School: High School Size and Student Behavior. Stanford University Press, Stanford.

Barker, R. B., and Schoggen, P. 1973. Qualities of Community Life. Jossey-Bass, Inc., Pubs., San Francisco.

Baroff, G. S. 1980. On "size" and the quality of residential care: A second look. Ment. Retard. 18:113–118.

Bayley, M. 1973. Mental Handicap and Community Care. Routledge and Kegan Paul, London.

Bednar, M. J. 1973. Planning environments responsive to new program concepts. In: R. M. Gettings (ed.), Synergism for the Seventies: Conference Proceedings of the National Conference for State Planning and Advisory Councils on Services and Facilities for the Developmentally Disabled. The Council for Exceptional Children, Reston, Va.

Beier, D. C. 1964. Behavioral disturbances in the mentally retarded. In: H. A. Stevens and R. Heber (eds.), Mental Retardation: A Review of Research. University of Chicago Press, Chicago.

Berger, P. L., and Neuhaus, R. J. 1977. To Empower People: The Role of Mediating Structures in Public Policy. American Enterprise Institute for Public Policy Research, Washington, D.C.

Bialer, I. 1967. Psychotherapy and other adjustment techniques with the mentally retarded. In: A. A. Baumeister (ed.), Mental Retardation: Appraisal, Education, and Rehabilitation. Aldine Publishing Company, Chicago.

Birenbaum, A., and Seiffer, S. 1976. Resettling Retarded Adults in a Managed Community. Praeger Publishers, New York.

Bjaanes, A. T., and Butler, E. W. 1974. Environmental variation in community care facilities for mentally retarded persons. Am. J. Ment. Defic. 78:429–439.

Bogdan, R. 1980. What does it mean when a person says "I am not retarded"? Educ. Train. Ment. Retard. 15:74–79.

Bruininks, R. H., Hauber, F. A., and Kudla, M. J. 1980. National survey of community residential facilities: A profile of facilities and residents in 1977. Am. J. Ment. Defic. 84:470–478.

Bruininks, R. H., Kudla, M. J., Wieck, C. A., and Hauber, F. A. 1980a. Management problems in community residential facilities. Ment. Retard. 18:125–130.

Bruininks, R. H., Thurlow, M. L., Thurman, S. K., and Fiorelli, J. S. 1980b. Deinstitutionalization and community services. In: J. Wortis (ed.), Mental Retardation and Developmental Disabilities: An Annual Review, Vol. 11. Brunner/Mazel Inc., New York.

Butler, E. W., and Bjaanes, A. T. 1977. A typology of community care facilities and differential normalization outcomes. In: P. Mittler (ed.), Research to Practice in Mental Retardation, Vol. 1. Care and Intervention. University Park Press, Baltimore.

Butler, E. W., and Bjaanes, A. T. 1980. Deinstitutionalization, environmental normalization and client normalization. Paper presented at the meeting of the American Association on Mental Deficiency, May 14, San Francisco, California.

Butterfield, E. C. 1967. The role of environmental factors in the treatment of institutionalized mental retardation. In: A. A. Baumeister (ed.), Mental Retardation: Appraisal, Education, and Rehabilitation. Aldine Publishing Company, Chicago.

Caplan, G. 1964. Principles of Preventive Psychiatry. Basic Books, Inc., New York.

Cobb, S. 1971. A community level model for depression (Working Paper 3). Unpublished manuscript, Center for Community Studies, George Peabody College for Teachers, Nashville, Tennessee.

Coffman, T. L., and Harris, M. C., Jr. 1980. Transition shock and adjustments of mentally retarded persons. Ment. Retard. 18:3–7.

Cunio J., Heath, D., Kaplan, S., Scott, R., Price, D. W., and Schaaf, V. 1978. People first. Unpublished manuscript. (Available from People First International, Inc., P.O. Box 12642, Salem, Oregon 97209.)

Davis, S. 1978. The life and times of Rudolf Steiner, part 3: Notes from Camphill Village. New Age 4:56–59.

Dokecki, P. 1977. The liaison perspective on the enhancement of human development: Theoretical, historical, and experiential background. J. Community Psychol. 5:13–17.

Eagle, E. 1967. Programs and outcome of community placement of institutionalized retardates. Am. J. Ment. Defic. 72:232–243.

Edgerton, R. B. 1967. The Cloak of Competence: Stigma in the Lives of the Mentally Retarded. University of California Press, Berkeley.

Edgerton, R. B. 1970. Mental retardation in non-Western societies: Toward a cross-cultural perspective on incompetence. In: H. C. Haywood (ed.), Social-Cultural Aspects of Mental Retardation. Appleton-Century-Crofts, New York.

Edgerton, R. B. 1977. The study of community adaptation: Toward an understanding of lives in process. In: P. Mittler (ed.), Research to Practice in Mental Retardation, Vol. 1. Care and Intervention. University Park Press, Baltimore.

Edgerton, R. B., and Bercovici, S. M. 1976. The cloak of competence: Years later. Am. J. Ment. Defic. 80:485–497.

Edgerton, R. B., Eyman, R. K., and Silverstein, A. B. 1975. Mental retardation system. In: N. Hobbs (ed.), Issues in the Classification of Children, Vol. 2. Jossey-Bass, Inc., Pubs., San Francisco.

Etzioni, A. 1976. Social Problems. Prentice-Hall, Inc., Englewood Cliffs, New Jersey.

Eyman, R. K., Demaine, G. C., and Lei, T. 1979. Relationship between community environments and resident changes in adaptive behavior: A path model. Am. J. Ment. Defic. 83:330–338.

Ferrara, D. M. 1979. Attitudes of parents of mentally retarded children toward normalization activities. Am. J Ment. Defic. 84:145–151.

Feuerstein, R., Rand, Y., and Hoffman, M. B. 1979. The Dynamic Assessment of Performers: The Learning Potential Assessment Device, Theory, Instruments, and Techniques. University Park Press, Baltimore.

Feuerstein, R., Rand, Y., Hoffman, M. B., and Miller, R. 1980. Instrumental Enrichment: An Intervention Program for Cognitive Modifiability. University Park Press, Baltimore.

French, J. R. P., Jr. 1968. The conceptualization and measurement of mental health in terms of self-identify theory. In: S. B. Sells (ed.), The Definition and Measurement of Mental Health. U.S. Government Printing Office, Washington, D.C.

French, J. R. P., Jr., Rodgers, W., and Cobb, S. 1974. Adjustment as person-environment fit. In: G. V. Coelho, D. A. Hamburg, and J. E. Adams (eds.), Coping and Adaptation. Basic Books, Inc., New York.

Goldschmidt, W. 1974. Ethology, ecology, and ethnological relations. In: G. V. Coelho, D. A. Hamburg, and J. E. Adams (eds.), Coping and Adaptation. Basic Books, Inc., New York.

Gollay, E., Freedman, R., Wyngaarden, M., and Kurtz, N. R. 1978. Coming Back: The Community Experience of Deinstitutionalized Mentally Retarded People. Abt Books, Cambridge, Massachusetts.

Gorham, K. A., Des Jardins, C., Page, R., Pettis, E., and Scheiber, B. 1975. Effect on parents. In: N. Hobbs (ed.), Issues in the Classification of Children, Vol. 2. Jossey-Bass, Inc., Pubs., San Francisco.

Grossman, H. J. (ed.). 1977. Manual on Terminology and Classification in Mental Retardation. Revised Ed. American Association of Mental Deficiency, Washington, D.C.

Gruenberg, E. M. 1964. Epidemiology. In: H. A. Stevens and R. Heber (eds.), Mental Retardation: A Review of Research. University of Chicago Press, Chicago.

Haracopos, D., and Kelstrup, A. 1978. Psychotic behavior in children under the institutions for the mentally retarded in Denmark. J. Autism Child. Schizophr. 8:1–12.

Haywood, H. C. 1977. Alternatives to normative assessment. In: P. Mittler (ed.), Research to Practice in Mental Retardation, Vol. 2. Education and Training. University Park Press, Baltimore.

Heath, D. L., Schaaf, V., and Talkington, L. W. 1975. People First: Evolution Toward Self-advocacy. Developmental Disabilities Research Series, No. 43. State of Oregon.

Heaton-Ward, A. 1977. Psychosis in mental handicap. Br. J. Psychiatry 130:525–533.

Hobbs, N. 1966. Helping disturbed children: Psychological and ecological strategies. Am. Psychol. 21:1105–1115.

Hobbs, N. 1975. The Futures of Children. Jossey-Bass, Inc., Pubs., San Francisco.

Hobbs, N. June, 1979. Helping disturbed children: Psychological and ecological strategies, II: Project Re-ED, twenty years later. Unpublished manuscript, Center for Study of Families and Children, Institute for Public Policy Studies, Vanderbilt University, Nashville, Tennessee.

Howell, H. H., and May, A. E. 1980. Resident-care practices in the county of Somerset, England. Am. J. Ment. Defic. 84:393–396.

Kaswan, J. W. 1977. Quandaries of psychological services. Unpublished manuscript. (Available from 3475 Margarita Avenue, Oakland, California 94605.)

Katz, E. (ed.) 1972. Mental Health Services for the Mentally Retarded. Charles C Thomas, Publisher, Springfield, Ill.

King, R. D., Raynes, N. V., and Tizard, J. 1971. Patterns of Residential Care: Sociological Studies in Institutions for Handicapped Children. Routledge and Kegan Paul, London.

Klein, D. C. 1968. Community Dynamics and Mental Health. John Wiley and Sons, Inc., New York.

Knight, R. C., Zimring, C. M., and Kent, M. J. 1976. Normalization as a social-physical system, Technical Report 3. Institute for Man and Environment, University of Massachusetts, Amherst.

Knight, R. C., Zimring, C. M., Weitzer, W. H., and Wheeler, H. C. (eds.), February, 1977. Social development and normalized institutional settings: A preliminary research report. Institute for Man and Environment, University of Massachusetts, Amherst.

Koegel, P., and Kernan, K. T. 1981. Issues affecting the involvement of mildly retarded individuals in competitive employment. In: M. J. Begab, K. T. Kernan, and R. B. Edgerton (eds.), The Impact of Specific Settings on the Development and Behavior of Retarded Persons. University Park Press, Baltimore.

Krischef, C. H. 1959. The influence of rural-urban environment upon adjustment of dischargees from the Owatonna State School. Am. J. Ment. Defic. 63:860–865.

Leighton, A. H. 1959. My Name is Legion. Basic Books, Inc., New York.

Lewin, K. and Cartwright, D. (ed.), 1976. Field Theory in Social Science. University of Chicago Press, Chicago.

Lewis, W. W. 1971. Project Re-ED: The program and a preliminary evaluation. In: H. C. Rickard (ed.), Behavioral Intervention in Human Problems. Pergamon Press, Inc., New York.

McCarver, R. B., and Craig, E. M. 1974. Placement of the retarded in the community: Prognosis and outcome. In: N. R. Ellis (ed.), International Review of Research in Mental Retardation. Academic Press, Inc., New York.

McCormick, M., Balla, D., and Zigler, E. 1975. Resident-care practices in institutions for retarded persons: A cross-institutional, cross-cultural study. Am. J. Ment. Defic. 80:1–17.

Maney, A. C., Pace, R., and Morrison, D. F. 1964. A factor analytic study of the need for institutionalization: Problems and populations for programs development. Am. J. Ment. Defic. 69:372–384.

Maslow, A. H. 1970. Motivation and Personality. Harper and Row Pubs., Inc., New York.

Matson, J. L. Marchetti, A., and Adkins, J. A. 1980. Comparison of operant- and independence-training procedures for mentally retarded adults. Am. J. Ment. Defic. 84:487–494.

Mechanic, D. 1974. Social structure and personal adaptation: Some neglected dimensions. In: G. V. Coelho, D. A. Hamburg, and J. E. Adams (eds.), Coping and Adaptation. Basic Books, Inc., New York.

Menolascino, F. J. (ed.), 1970. Psychiatric Approaches to Mental Retardation. Basic Books, Inc., New York.

Mercer, J. R. 1975. Psychological assessment and the rights of children. In: N. Hobbs (ed.), Issues in the Classification of Children, Vol. 1. Jossey-Bass, Inc., Pubs., San Francisco.

Mills, R. C., and Kelly, J. G. 1972. Cultural adaptation and ecological analogies: Analysis of three Mexican villages. In: S. E. Golann and C. Eisdorfer (eds.), Handbook of Community Mental Health. Appleton-Century-Crofts, New York.

Newbrough, J. R. 1968. Working papers and reading notes: Seminar on conformity and deviance. Unpublished manuscript. Center for Community Studies, George Peabody College for Teachers, Nashville, Tennessee.

Newbrough, J. R. 1972. Concepts of behavior disorder. In: S. E. Golann and C. Eisdorfer (eds.), Handbook of Community Psychology. Appleton-Century-Crofts, New York.

Newbrough, J. R. 1974. Community psychology: Some perspectives. J. Community Psychol. 2:204–206.

Newbrough, J. R. 1977. Liaison services in the community context. J. Community Psychol. 5:24–27.

Nirje, B. 1969. The normalization principle and its human management implications. In: R. B. Kugel and W. Wolfensberger (eds.), Changing Patterns in Residential Services for the Mentally Retarded. President's Committee on Mental Retardation, Washington, D.C.

Perske, R. 1974. The dignity of risk. In: W. Wolfensberger(ed.), The Principle of Normalization in Human Services. National Institute on Mental Retardation, Toronto.

Posner, B. 1977. The pride of work, the pride of being. In: P. Mittler (ed.), Research to Practice in Mental Retardation, Vol. 2. Education and Training. University Park Press, Baltimore.

Rains, P. M., Kitsuse, J. I., Duster, T., and Freidson, E. 1975. The labeling approach to deviance. In: N. Hobbs (ed.), Issues in the Classification of Children, Vol. 1. Jossey-Bass, Inc., Pubs., San Francisco.

Raynes, N. V., Pratt, M. W., and Roses, S. 1977. Aides' involvement in decision-making and the quality of care in institutional settings. Am. J. Ment. Defic. 81:570–577.

Rhodes, W. C. 1975. A Study of Child Variance, Vol. 4. The Future. University of Michigan Press, Ann Arbor.

Rhodes, W. C., and Sagor, M. 1975. Community perspectives. In: N. Hobbs (ed.), Issues in the Classification of Children, Vol. 1. Jossey-Bass, Inc., Pubs., San Francisco.

Richardson, S. A. 1978. Careers of mentally retarded young persons: Services, jobs, and interpersonal relations. Am. J. Ment. Defic. 82:349–358.

Rogers, C. R. 1961. On Becoming a Person: A Therapist's View of Psychotherapy. Houghton Mifflin Company, Boston.

Rogers-Warren, A. 1976. Planned change: Ecobehaviorally based interventions. In: A. Rogers-Warren, and S. F. Warren (eds.), Ecological Perspectives in Behavioral Analysis. University Park Press, Baltimore.

Rosen, M., Clark, G. R., and Kivitz, M. S. 1977. Habilitation of the Handicapped: New Dimensions in Programs for the Developmentally Disabled. University Park Press, Baltimore.

Rusch, F. R., Schutz, R. P., and Heal, L. W. 1981. The impact of setting on nonsheltered work behavior: A recommendation. In: M. J. Begab, K. T. Kernan, and R. B. Edgerton (eds.), The Impact of Specific Settings on the Development and Behavior of Retarded Persons. University Park Press, Baltimore.

Ryan, W. 1972. Blaming the Victim. Vintage, New York.

Scheerenberger, R. C., and Felsenthal, D. 1977. Community settings in mentally retarded persons: Satisfaction and activities. Ment. Retardation, 15(4):3–7.

Schaaf, W., Hooten, T., Schwartz, T., Young, C., Kerron, J., and Heath, D. 1977. People First: A self-help organization of the retarded. In: J. Wortis (ed.), Mental Retardation and Developmental Disabilities, Vol. 9. Brunner/Mazel, Inc., New York.

Singh, R. K. J. 1972. Psychotherapy with behaviorally disturbed mentally retarded. In: E. Katz (ed.), Mental Health Services for the Mentally Retarded. Charles C Thomas, Publishers, Springfield, Ill.

Skaarbrevik, K. J. 1971. A follow-up study of educable mentally retarded in Norway. Am. J. Ment. Defic. 75:560–565.

Srole, L., Langner, T. S., Michael, S. T., Opler, M. K., and Rennie, T. A. C. 1961. Mental Health in the Metropolis: The Midtown Manhattan Study, Vol. 1. McGraw-Hill Book Company, New York.

Sternlicht, M. 1976. Personality: One view. In: J. Wortis, (ed.), Mental Retardation and Developmental Disabilities: An Annual Review, Vol. 8. Brunner/Mazel, Inc., New York.

Sternlicht, M. 1977. Issues in counseling and psychotherapy with mentally retarded individuals. In: I. Bialer and M. Sternlicht (eds.), The Psychology of Mental Retardation: Issues and Approaches. Psychological Dimensions, New York.

Stucky, P. E., and Newbrough, J. R. 1981. Mentally retarded persons in the community. In: M. J. Begab, K. T. Kernan, and R. B. Edgerton (eds.), The Impact of Specific Settings on the Development and Behavior of Retarded Persons. University Park Press, Baltimore.

Tizard, J. 1970. The role of social institutions in the causation, prevention, and alleviation of mental retardation. In: H. C. Haywood (ed.), Socio-Cultural Aspects of Mental Retardation. Appleton-Century-Crofts, New York.

Turner, J. L. 1980. Yes, I am human: Autobiography of a "retarded career." J. Community Psychol. 8:3–8.

Wandersman, A. 1979a. User participation: A study of types of participation, effects, mediators, and individual differences. Environ. Behav. 11:185–208.

Wandersman, A. 1979b. User participation in planning environments: A conceptual framework. Environ. Behav. 11:465–482.

Weinstein, L. 1969. Project Re-ED schools for emotionally disturbed children: Effectiveness as viewed by referral agencies, parents, and teachers. Except. Child. 35:703–711.

Willems, E. P. 1977. Behavioral technology and behavioral ecology. In: A. Rogers-Warren, and S. F. Warren (eds.), Ecological Perspectives in Behavioral Analysis. University Park Press, Baltimore.

Willer, B., Scheerenberger, R. C., and Intagliata, J. 1978. Deinstitutionalization and mentally retarded persons. Community Ment. Health Rev. 3:1–12.

Williams, J. 1977. Liaison functions as reflected in a case study. J. Community Psychol. 5:18–23.

Windle, C. D. 1962. Prognosis of mental subnormals. Monograph Supplement. Am. J. Ment. Defic. 66:1–180.

Windle, C. D., Stewart, E., and Brown, S. J. 1961. Reasons for community failure of released patients. Am. J. Ment. Defic. 66:213–217.

Wolfensberger, W. 1967a. Counseling parents of the retarded. In: A. A. Baumeister (ed.), Mental Retardation: Appraisal, Education, and Rehabilitation. Aldine Publishing Company, Chicago.

Wolfensberger, W. 1967b. Vocational preparation and occupation. In: A. A. Baumeister (ed.), Mental Retardation: Appraisal, Education, and Rehabilitation. Aldine Publishing Company, Chicago.

Wolfensberger, W. 1972. Normalization: The Principle of Normalization in Human Services. National Institute on Mental Retardation, Toronto.

Yates, D. 1973. Neighborhood Democracy: The Politics and Impacts of Decentralization. Lexington Books, Lexington, Massachusetts.

Zaharia, E. S., and Baumeister, A. A. 1978. Technician turnover and absenteeism in public residential facilities. Am. J. Ment. Defic. 82:580–593.

Zaharia, E. S., and Baumeister, A. A. 1979a. Cross-organizational job satisfactions of technician-level staff members. Am. J. Ment. Defic. 84:30–35.

Zaharia, E. S., and Baumeister, A. A. 1979b. Technician losses in public residential facilities. Am. J. Ment. Defic. 84:36–39.

Zigler, E., and Balla, D. A. 1977. Impact of institutional experience on the behavior and development of retarded persons. Am. J. Ment. Defic. 1977. 82:1–11.

Zipperlen, H. R. 1975. Normalization. In: J. Wortis (ed.), Mental Retardation and Developmental Disabilities, Vol. 7. Brunner/Mazel, Inc., New York.

THE COMMUNITY
ORIENTATION

Living Environments for Developmentally Retarded Persons
Edited by H. Carl Haywood and J. R. Newbrough
Copyright 1981 University Park Press Baltimore

Personal Growth and Community Residence Environments
A Review

Matthew P. Janicki, Ph.D.
Director, Bureau of Program Research and Planning
State of New York Office of Mental Retardation
  and Developmental Disabilities
44 Holland Avenue
Albany, New York 12229

The literature addressing the rehabilitative process of physically and/ or developmentally disabled persons after deinstitutionalization is replete with reports that attempt to identify personal characteristics and placement process artifacts associated with success or failure following admission to a community-care setting. In most cases, the institution is still considered the normative residential setting; anecdotal and research reports attempt to relate to the phenomenon of the institutional rather than the cultural norm, which is the setting most like a natural home. However, the residual developmentally disabled population in the nation's institutions, although representing a substantial number of persons, is dwarfed by the overall number of persons similarly disabled, but residing in a home with parents or kin, or in a variety of community residential facilities (Bruininks, Hauber, and Kudla, 1980; DDPRSCA, 1979). To better understand the living environment of the majority of disabled persons, an examination of the effects of the environments associated with community living alternative settings is warranted.

Much has been written reviewing the differences within institutional settings (Balla, Butterfield, and Zigler, 1974) and between institutional and community settings (Eyman et al., 1977), and, to a lesser degree, the differences between certain types of community-care settings (Bjaanes and Butler, 1974; Willer and Intagliata, 1979). However, little systematic research has been conducted to identify characteristics

59

within same-category community living alternative settings (Crawford, Aiello, and Thompson, 1979; Landesman-Dwyer, Stein, and Sackett, 1978). Many anecdotal reports appear that address particular activities of persons living within community residences (Rodman and Collins, 1974; Thakur, 1974) and foster family care settings (Intagliata, 1979; Newman and Sherman, 1979–80), but only a few empirical investigations are found in the research literature that attempt to identify the variables associated with those settings that effect change—whether rehabilitative or dehabilitative. Community residences emerge as a community living alternative for persons who do not need the structure or restrictive nature of services as provided in institutional settings, or who no longer have a viable living arrangement and need some supervision and training other than institutional care (Dunn, 1969). This investigator intends to identify those factors that encourage growth and that promote the highest development of independence and competence within an emergent type of community living alternative setting: group home community residences.

THE COMMUNITY RESIDENCE
AS A COMMUNITY LIVING ALTERNATIVE

The community residence and its place in the continuum of residential services have been described elsewhere (Gardner, 1977; Glenn, 1976; Lensink, 1974; Madle, 1978; Wolfensberger, 1972). However, the community residence as a community living alternative bears definition. A community residence is defined as a community-based residential facility that operates 24 hours a day to provide services to a small group of disabled people who are presently or potentially capable of functioning in a community setting with some degree of independence (O'Connor and Sitkei, 1975). Although the community residence operates on a 24-hour basis, its inherent design separates the home function aspect from the workshop, training center, or school aspects of a person's life (Wolfensberger, 1972). The purpose of a community residence is to provide a home. The setting promotes the idea that persons who are disabled should live among people who are not disabled and should be treated as much like nondisabled persons as possible (Madle, 1978).

A community residence, however, like any other home, must be an environment oriented toward personal growth. It not only should provide the ingredients for learning basic self-care and independent support skills, but also should provide a diversity of activities that permit exposure to a variety of capabilities. Tizard (1964) notes that a home must supply: affection and interpersonal interest, a positive regard and understanding of the disability and its effects upon the individual, a sense of stability and feeling of welcomeness for the individual until he or she decides to or can leave the home for a more independent living pattern, a range of opportunities for making the best of abilities and aptitudes, and a share in the common life of a small, family-like group of people. Consequently, the model for the community residence is cooperative household living. Within this context, individuals reside in a cooperative group living situation, sharing work, responsibilities, and friendships. Nurturance is provided both by the interpersonal milieu, created by the interactions among residents and staff, and by the ambiance of the home environment.

Within this context, a home must also be designed to promote a normal life and the development of individual skills. This approach to human management is widely called "normalization." Inherent in this approach is a belief in developmental growth throughout one's life. "Normalization," Wolfensberger (1980) notes, is the use "of means which are as culturally normative as possible, in order to establish, enable, or support behaviors, appearances and interpretations which are as culturally normative as possible" (p. 80). It is a process that involves using progressively normalized procedures to bring about greater levels of normal functioning. The intent of any community residence program is intimately related to a system of rehabilitative technology that provides the process for, and outcome objectives of, an individual's growth. Community residences, in large measure, are homes for people making a transition. Persons can enter these homes, increase their independence and skill competence, and then move on to other settings. Some individuals, however, live permanently in community residences. Each year these people gain greater ability in cooperative living, test their capabilities, and receive the guidance and supervision they need.

The community residence has a number of constructs that define its operation. Janicki and Reynolds (1979) have identified three constructs for defining and analyzing community residences: the residence environment, the rehabilitative intent, and the management system. These three factors, operating in effective community residences, are connected by a single philosophical strand—normalization. In other words, an effective community residence uses and manages techniques of intervention that are as culturally normative as possible, and develops and maintains appropriate personal characteristics and normal behaviors in the people living there. Therefore, it is necessary to focus both on the normalized methods of intervention and on the extent to which these methods effectuate normal behaviors. The residence environment and rehabilitative intent reflect, respectively, the extrinsic and intrinsic considerations of a cooperative household living model.

Residence Environment

In their report, Janicki and Reynolds (1979) first consider the residence environment. The residence environment is defined by all the factors that contribute to the residence, including its physical design and use, the staff that supports its existence, and the manner in which it provides for its occupants. The appropriate residential alternative for an individual should be defined by comparing it with a normal domicile environment. A community living alternative should not be measured against a more restrictive setting, such as an institution, but rather against the kind of home the individual would have had in a normal family or cooperative living setting. Therefore, a community residence should be defined in terms of how well it approximates or moves toward an idealized normal environment. Moreover, the community residence must promote integration, not segregation, of its members and the general community. Integration means that people are given the opportunity to move and communicate in age-appropriate ways, and to use typical community services, such as schools, stores, churches, transportation, and health services. However, physical integration is only relevant if it leads to increased social interaction in the general community. Hence, the appearance and/or location of a community residence affects the perceptions that the community has of the residence (and its occupants), and also affects the rate of social assimilation consequently experienced by the persons living there.

According to the normalization principle, two important integration considerations apply to the design of a residence environment: physical and social integration. The first consideration, physical integration, is a crucial design prerequisite for a community residence to reach its goal. Location, context, accessibility, and size are four critical variables that promote physical integration, the first two of which have paramount importance. A community residence must be designed as one among many services used by a community. In any community there are people who need special services to cater to their individual situations. In many cases, a disabled person may need special housing assistance or a special living arrangement. Consequently, communities need to have residences that are located within normal neighborhoods, provide homelike environments, and are easily accessible. In this manner, the community is accessible to its residents, their families and friends, and to the people who work in the residence. The residence must be near transportation, stores, and day programs or employment situations. It must reflect the character of its surroundings, neither overshadowing its neighbors in size, nor providing services that upset the neighborhood's natural balance.

The second consideration, social integration, relates to the assimilation of the disabled person into the community. Individuals residing in a community residence should be encouraged to become members of the greater community. Similarly, citizens in the normal community should be encouraged not to view or to react to these, albeit disabled, members of the general community as transient consumers. Several facets of social integration that fall within the area of program services have relevance here. Three major variables are critical: program features, service and user labels, and building perception. The residence environment has the burden of providing a mechanism for totally integrating the residents into the neighborhood. Care must be taken that rules, regulations, policies, or other artifacts are not created that conflict with the character of the community, and that consequently impede integration. Consumer labels should not be used to identify the environment. For example, a name for the residence could easily provide a differentiation from the other houses in the neighborhood. Additionally, the building's appearance must be consistent with the intended function of the environment; thus, a home should look like a home. Extrinsic environmental considerations are important in the process of defining a residence within the context of its intended purpose.

Rehabilitative Intent

Janicki and Reynolds cite rehabilitative intent as their second construct. Rehabilitative intent defines the goals of behavior change and the process of applying rehabilitative technology to the attainment of those goals. The program services of a residential alternative must have a rehabilitative intent. Such a rehabilitative orientation must be tailored to an individual's self-perceptions, his abilities for self-sustained living activities, and his relationships with the community at large. Furthermore, it is essential that the community residence approximates the learning and living experiences that would have enhanced the person's abilities to attain competence if he or she had grown up normally in a natural home setting. The rehabilitative intent can also be a function of the intensity with which the program provides these experiences. Essentially, the rehabilitative intent accounts for the intrinsic qualities of a home, with all the accoutrements of a cooperative household living environment. The design fosters growth in skills corresponding to the model.

As part of the rehabilitative intent of program services, several other factors should be considered. The developmental model should provide for the design of skill development programs and should consider all disabled persons as capable of growing and acquiring new skills. The model serves as a foundation for the rehabilitative technology that is used in designing conditions that will facilitate growth. Rehabilitative technology should be inherent in the design of each resident's individual program plan and should provide for options that take into account the individual's 1) personal growth through a progressive modification of structure, 2) greater involvement with and integration into community activities, and 3) ready access to more normalized conditions in which to function. Behavioral methodology, which has been recognized as a viable means of maximizing rehabilitative intent, is consistent with the belief system inherent in normalization (Roos, 1972).

Much has been said about the lack of understanding among service planners about the importance of a systems approach to rehabilitation (Anthony, 1977). It is essential that the residential environment and program services employ a holistic approach to need or gain planning. The technology associated with rehabilitative intent specifies, to some degree, the parameters of the individual's activities and the intensity with which staff attend directly to shaping new skills.

Another component that defines the design of the program system is the use of the residence within the following four factors: specialization, continuity, integration, and dispersal (Wolfensberger, 1972). The community residence should be designed as a small specialized setting in which the individual needs of a relatively homogeneous group of individuals can be served. The environment must reflect harmony, personal satisfaction, and growth among the members of the household. The community residence is first a home, and secondly a service environment. Only services related to household activities, daily living skills, health care, recreation, and socialization should be provided. Vocational and educational activities should be provided in other nonresidential environments.

The program must fit into a general continuum of services so that the overall plan for the residence's services and activities reflects the dimension of the community's residential alternatives. Movement and access to other residential alternatives within the continuum must be integral to program design so that as each individual's needs change, the access to more appropriate services is present. To promote integration, residents should be encouraged to use community services to meet their health, vocational, recreation, and other generic needs. The residence program should not create a perception in the community that it is less than homelike; labels and terms and activities projecting a negative image should not be present. The community residence should develop community experiences for each person living in the residence in order to enhance the individual's use of generic community resources, but the program's activities should not overwhelm any one public or private generic provider.

Management Systems

According to Janicki and Reynolds, the third construct, the management system of the community residence, has essentially two defining processes: the administration's understanding of the residence's purpose (which determines the character of each community living alternative), and the manner in which management administrates.

The first process is crucial; management must be aware of the environmental and services issues essential to the community residence model. If management is aware of the basic thrust of the community residence approach, then the probability is heightened that, notwithstanding fiscal constraints and political realities, the program will be sound and provide the developmental methodology for services and a homelike environment. Moreover, other artifacts are found within the management system, such as a capacity to deliberately and carefully plan each disabled person's individual program plan. The results of this system can better be measured by the activities and interactions of residents, staff, and community than by carefully scribed records. However, a balance struck between thoughtful reflection on 1) the process of change, documented by the individual program plan, and 2) the outcome of change, measured by resident gains, is optimal. Fundamentally, management must accept the belief system underlying a community residence (management's administrative practices must support both the physical characteristics that go into making a home, and the rehabilitative and normalizing intents of its services and programs).

The second process is related to the administrative nuances of management style and attitudes. Both residents and those employed within the community residences should be treated in a like manner—with respect and positive regard. The attitudes shown by management toward the residents, their guests, and the staff will be reflected in the overall character of the program. The program should be devoid of rules and restrictions that are either demeaning or not age-appropriate. A democratic leadership process based upon participatory procedures should be evident; openness and an active self-renewal process must be present, along with clearly stated expectations of staff roles and functions. Management must have the competence with which to manage a number of often competing and pressing demands; the strength and durability of the community residence will be reflected in how well, and in the manner in which, these demands are met.

Within these constructs, the measurement of any community residence environment should focus on how well it satisfies its goals.
Several questions must be asked: Is the residence what it purports
to be—a home? Does it provide services that are directed toward
enhancing the image and personal growth of the persons living in it?
Does it provide for change; do people grow and profit from having
lived in it?

The concepts of the community residence model support its use
as a viable alternative care environment. However, O'Connor (1976)
notes that only about 69% of the community living alternatives she
surveyed in the early 1970s provided conditions associated with normalization. The variability of the community residential facilities surveyed indicate a lack of consistency in environmental and program
design. Several authors have attempted to address this issue. Baker,
Seltzer, and Seltzer (1979) and Seltzer and Seltzer (1977), in reporting
the results of a subsequent survey, identified the community living
alternatives dimension. One of the elements within this dimension,
identified as small group homes, housed up to ten persons. The researchers noted that typical small group home programs appeared to
be normalized, with residents having high autonomy, extensive responsibilities, and work-oriented day activities. Other facilities were
of greater size or of specialized nature and offered less normalizing
characteristics. Although this characterization helps to define the community residence within a dimensional approach, it does not offer a
typology within the model itself. However, Bjaanes and his colleagues
(Bjaanes and Butler 1974; Butler and Bjaanes, 1977, 1978) presented
a typology that characterized community residences within three categories: custodial, maintaining, and therapeutic. They defined custodial environments as those in which little or nothing is done to facilitate
the normalization process; there is little supervision and only minimal
activities for residents. Therapeutic care environments, on the other
hand, are those in which there are active, ongoing attempts to enhance
the normalization process. These residences foster rehabilitative services and provide support and guidance for residents. Extensive community contacts and well-organized and varied activities are also provided. The maintaining environments fall in between; residents remain
more or less at an unchanging level of competence. These environments
have some habilitative programs, community contact, activities, and
caregiver involvement, but not at the level or to the degree of intensity
of the therapeutic environments.

Based on this background, this chapter examines the character of
available research in community residences and related areas. The

underlying assumption is that certain factors within residences lead to optimal growth and meet the rehabilitative intent of the model.

RESEARCH RELATED TO RESIDENCE CHARACTERISTICS

The research literature that addresses the characteristics of community residences can be divided into two categories: those studies that review the strengths and weaknesses of the disabled individual, and those studies that evaluate environmental factors. Both categories are crucial to a full analysis of the conceptual integrity of the community residence model. The variables that are resident-oriented include age, conceptual development level (IQ), extent or severity of disability, and adaptive behavior strengths or weaknesses. The measures of the resident-oriented variables are usually demographic descriptors and measures of intelligence and adaptive behavior; the research on these resident-oriented variables has been reviewed elsewhere (Jacobson and Schwartz, 1979). The environment-oriented variables include size, character of caregivers, staff competence, physical and social integration characteristics, individualization, and character and intensity of program. Environment-oriented variables are measured by instruments assessing management practices, home environment characteristics, staff knowledge and skills, and program- adherence to normalization practices. Environments not only are evaluated for physical and social integrative aspects but also are assessed in terms of the psychosocial milieu created by the actions and personalities of the staff.

A number of instruments that assess environmental characteristics have been used (McLain et al., 1979); however, only one exists that is paired with an underlying ideology. An environmental evaluation instrument, which also contains the conceptual framework for evaluating normalization practices, is the Program Assessment of Service Systems (PASS). Developed by Wolfensberger and Glenn (1975b), PASS-3, as the current version is known, was designed to have the following characteristics: 1) ability to quantitatively assess and compare the quality of the widest range of human services, regardless of particular type of service involved; 2) ability to incorporate normalization principles as major criteria of program evaluation; 3) sufficient objectivity to ensure reasonable reliability across raters; and 4) adaptability, to permit additions, deletions, or other changes without impairing the total assessment schema and without losing comparability with other assessments performed at a different time or on a different service.

PASS is comprised of 50 rating scales that can be used to assess a service in terms of its adherence to the human-management model associated with the principles of normalization. Programs receive scorings on a number of characteristics, including attitudes, staff capabilities, environment, funding, and administrative practices. As Wolfensberger (1972) notes, PASS was intended to provide an objective means of assessing (either by internal or external evaluation) both the quality of a human service and qualitative changes over a period of time. PASS can therefore offer a means for assessing the characteristics of community residences. Moreover, in lieu of available direct data from PASS, the PASS domain conceptual scheme can be applied and used as the framework through which other research can be reviewed and synthesized.

PASS has been applied to the evaluation of community residence environments in a number of studies (Eyman, DeMaine, and Lei, 1979; Flynn, 1980; Fiorelli, 1978). Two of the efforts produced a factoring of the ratings that may offer promise for conceptualizing residential environments. Flynn (1980) applied PASS to several community residences in Indiana of variable size and design, in an attempt to determine which PASS ratings would discriminate between four predominant types. He found that 18 of the 50 ratings (which produced three predominant factors: Normalization-Program, Normalization-Setting, and Adaptive Administration) also were able to discriminate among the settings.

Normalization-Program includes the following ratings: Access; Socially integrative social activities; Age-appropriate autonomy and rights; Culture-appropriate labels and forms of address; Culture-appropriate rights; Model coherency; Lack of social overprotection; and Individualization. The second, *Normalization-Setting*, includes Congregation and assimilation potential; Deviancy image juxtaposition; Deviancy program juxtaposition; Age-appropriate facilities, environmental design and appointments; Culture-appropriate internal design and appointment; and Physical comfort. The last, *Adaptive Administration*, includes Ties to academia; Staff development; Administrative control and structure; and Program evaluation and renewal mechanisms.

Tad Mayeda and his colleagues (DeMain, 1978; Eyman, DeMaine, and Lei, 1979; Mayeda, 1979) examined PASS for its empirical applications to residential environments. DeMaine (1978) further attempted to determine whether PASS-3 was fulfilling its purpose of quantitatively evaluating the quality of human service programs. She reported that PASS-3 produces six mutually exclusive factors that evolve different scores to achieve a composite assessment. The analysis isolated the six factors: Normalization, Administrative Policies, General Environment, Administrative Ideology, Location and Accessibility, and Comfort and Physical Setting. These six factors, when compared with data from the Adaptive Behavior Scale scores on occupants of over 200 California community living alternatives, were able to discriminate growth contingent upon adherence to normalizing practices.

Because the work of DeMaine et al. also included a qualitative measure of adaptive behavior, the factors derived better lend themselves to a more detailed analysis of the research literature related to community living alternatives. Consequently, the following review uses the organized framework of the six factors of the DeMaine analysis, but also incorporates the constructs of the three critical components of the community residence model: residence environment, rehabilitative intent, and management systems.

Normalization

The Normalization factor, which Mayeda (1979) considers the most potent, ties together a number of PASS ratings that offer the most powerful mechanisms for making the normalization principle operational. Wolfensberger and Glenn (1975a) noted that PASS, although serving as a tool for evaluating the quality and adequacy of a human service program, is also designed in a manner that provides for ratings and rating clusters to be discrete and interrelated at the same time. Because of this, subareas or item areas are not necessarily independent of each other. The design of PASS produces a variability in the elements that are drawn across domains, yet many elements seem to address similar parts of a program. Eyman, DeMaine, and Lei (1979) note that there was not a discernible relationship between this factor and developmental change in any of the adaptive behavior domains. However, this may be an artifact of the very nature of the design of PASS, so that noncoherence within a domain is not unexpected.

Mayeda notes that the ratings comprising the normalization factor assess compliance with normalization principles. Normalization elements also seem to be most associated with those design characteristics inherent in a community residence as a living situation that maximizes learning, acceptance, and assimilation. The factor is comprised of the following 17 loadings: Autonomy and rights; Intensity of relevant programming; Labels and forms of address (age-appropriate); Social over-protection; Activities, routine, and rhythms; Possessions; Rights; Sex behavior; Facilities, environmental design, and appointments; Interactions; Socially integrative social activities; Personal appearance (age-appropriate); Individualization; Personal appearance (culturally appropriate); Physical overprotection; Labels and forms of address (culturally appropriate); and Staff development.

The aggregate of these ratings is the human rights or normalization factor. Normalization defines the character of each program and addresses such issues as the nature of a residence's policies, practices, and design. Consequently, to receive a high number of points on PASS, the residence should have and practice policies that enhance the individual, that permit individual decision making, and that provide the individual with a level of challenge and a temporal massing of that challenge that facilitates the rehabilitative intent. Moreover, the community residence cannot have administrative controls that thwart the residents' everyday experiences and that prevent the residents from being involved in out-of-residence activities. The staff interactions with residents should be age-appropriate and should follow sound interpersonal relationship practices. The residents should dress according to age and contemporary dress standards and should participate in community activities. The staff should be trained and should possess a level of competence and an attitude that facilitate growth in the residents. The aggregate of these factors produces a program environment that facilitates skill gain and movement toward independent living.

Within the broad use of the term normalization, Bjaanes, Butler, and Kelly (1980) have postulated a distinction. They suggest that the study of conditions for enhancing growth should be dichotomized into environmental and client normalization. Environmental normalization, the authors note, is the "process of developing culturally normative and appropriate residences and services, devoid of the dehumanizing stigma so often attached to being mentally retarded" (p. 2). Client normalization, they further note, is the "acquisition of necessary skills for . . . assuming culturally normative social roles and responsibilities" (p. 2).

The subtleties of these distinctions can only be picked up by a formal evaluative measure, such as PASS, or by some other instrument that is designed to measure elements of the environment, such as resident practices or staff orientation. The research literature does not provide specific information on each rating of PASS that would be needed for a comprehensive review. However, a number of the ratings within the normalization factor can be synthesized, matched against specific constructs, and culled from the available literature. The major ratings include autonomy and rights; intensity of relevant programming; social overprotection; activities, routine, and rhythms; interactions; socially integrative activities; and staff development. These ratings can be collapsed within the following normalization-oriented variables, which collectively have impact upon a program: staff behavior, program orientation, program process, and social integration.

Staff Behavior   Because the environment of, and the resident behavior within, a community residence is governed to a great degree by the character and activities of the staff, studies and reports that comment upon staff behavior were evaluated for evidence or absence of support as it related to resident growth. A number of studies and/or anecdotal reports comment upon staff behavior as related to interactions, protective practices, and program intensity effects upon the acquisition of new adaptive behaviors (Aanes and Moen, 1976; Bjaanes and Butler, 1974; Browder, Ellis, and Neal, 1974; Campbell, 1971; Gunzburg, 1977; Intagliata, 1979; Johnson and Bailey, 1977; Stacy, Doleys, and Malcolm, 1979). Both Campbell (1971) and Gunzburg (1977) noted that initial gains upon entry to a community residence setting were seemingly heightened when the residence staff did things for the individuals. However, staff actions tended to foster dependence rather than the rehabilitative intent—independence skills acquisition.

Gunzburg noted that individuals in directive programs (i.e., those with goal-oriented rehabilitative intent and concomitant staff training models) showed greater gains in adaptive behavior than those individuals in programs merely providing what Bjaanes and Butler (1974) would term "maintaining environments." Of the five residences Gunzburg cited, the three with directive practices had measured change, documented by gains on the Progress Assessment Chart, of 46%, 39%, and 56%, as opposed to only 17% and 8% for the maintaining environments.

One of the factors in investment of effort, as measured by the over-protective, labeling, and program intensity ratings, is the degree to which staff have "worked out" their feelings toward disability and have accepted "stigmatized" individuals. Browder, Ellis, and Neal (1974) found that those foster home parents[1] who accepted the disability of persons under their care were more adequate at meeting in-home and out-of-home needs. These parents also maintained good

---

[1] Although foster care homes operate from a different model [i.e., surrogate family (Newman and Sherman, 1979–80; Provencal and MacCormack, 1979)] in comparison to most community residences, which use a cooperative household living model, the literature examining this type of residence is included because similar factors (e.g., staff attitudes, rehabilitation intent) affect both. Bruininks, Hill, and Thorsheim's (1980) definition illustrates this difference: "A foster home is a family residence owned or rented by one or more persons who constitute what is commonly called a family, in which the family incorporates generally no more than six (disabled) children or adults into their family group. These (disabled) persons live with the family as family members sharing the same home and participating in the same activities as other family members do, within the limits of their ability" (p. 4). These model distinctions have been further addressed by Janicki, Jacobson, and Schwartz (1980).

relationships with host agencies and had residents who showed greater improvement in, or positive acquisition of, appropriate behaviors.

The most detailed work examining homes that have different types of caregivers is the work of Willer, Intagliata, and their colleagues (Intagliata, 1979; Willer and Intagliata, 1979). They identified a number of staff characteristics that differentiated high-quality (HQ) foster care homes from low-quality (LQ) foster care homes. Findings indicated that residents of LQ homes showed more inappropriate behavior than did the residents of HQ homes. Both groups, however, showed the same number of problems prior to discharge from state institutions. The researchers attributed these differences to the style in which the care providers managed the homes. HQ homes were better with behavioral changes, use of time, level of independence, and social supports. HQ providers were also active in treatment planning, encouraging client independence and use of services, having residents improve in levels of behavioral functioning, having residents actively use community resources, and allowing residents to behave as independently as they are able.

The authors felt that the differences observed between HQ and LQ homes in residents' behavior change and overall quality of life could not be attributed to the differences in the residents. Willer and Intagliata noted that there were significant differences between the two types of foster family caregivers. HQ home caregivers generally were better educated, had health-related training, were motivated to be in their role because of previous experience with mental retardation, lived in urban areas, more readily sought out services and activities for their residents, were actively involved themselves in resident program planning, had established and maintained stable and well-organized homes, had established warm, supportive, but *not* dependent, relationships with residents, and had encouraged residents to use community resources and to develop new skills. The LQ caregivers generally were less educated, had experience raising only their own children, were motivated for their role because they wanted to care for other people or needed a means of extra income, lived in rural areas, were less likely to use community services (even when available) for residents, were less involved in resident treatment planning, had unstable and less organized homes, established dependent relationships with the residents to avoid loneliness, and were more concerned with managing unruly behavior than with developing the residents' new living skills.

Using the Adaptive Behavior Scale, Aanes and Moen (1976) rated changes in a number of group home residents in Minnesota over a period of one year after placement. Although finding some gains in certain behaviors, they noted that residents did not show the gains in self-direction that were expected. They hypothesized that group home parents (using a foster family care model) did not promote self-direction because it would have "created more time demands." They interpreted this as meaning that highly independent residents—those displaying initiative and persistence—would make more work. Bjaanes and Butler (1974) indicated that the development of independent functioning (which is incompatible with over-protectiveness and with low intensity of programming practices) appeared to be related to the involvement of caregivers in the ongoing stream of behavior.

Several references relate staff development to outcome in rehabilitative intent within a community residence program. Both Close (1977) and Nihira and Nihira (1975) note that caregivers needed training in behavior modification and skill acquisition techniques to provide greater gain in behavior competence in residents. Close (1977), in a comparative study, showed that staff who were trained were able to effect gains in acquisition of self-care skills and appropriate social behavior among a group of severely and profoundly retarded adults in a community residence (as compared to a control group of matched subjects who remained in an institutional setting). Schinke and Wong (1977) found that, among different group homes, those with staff trained to use behavior modification methodology showed significantly greater increases in the frequency and duration of positive staff and resident behaviors. Staff so trained also showed less decline in job satisfaction and gave more positive evaluations of their residents. Schalock and Harper (1979) have shown that staff trained to use behavioral methodology were able to produce skill acquisition in those individuals targeted to move from group homes to independent living apartments.

Staff attitudes, orientation, development, and competence do have an effect upon resident gains. It would seem that those homes receiving high PASS scores on staff development, intensity of relevant programming, and absence of social over-protection also show gains in residents' independent living skill acquisition.

Program Orientation   Another relevant factor is the extent to which the program is resident-centered, involving ratings related to autonomy and rights; activities, routines, and rhythms; and a number of other individual-oriented ratings. A number of researchers have delved into the resident- versus staff-centered issue (Gilbert and Hemming, 1979; King and Raynes, 1968; McLain et al., 1975, 1977b), a notion first applied by King and Raynes when they investigated whether there was a continuum from institution-centered to resident-centered practices in institutional settings. Institution-centered practices were seen to consist of rigidity of routine, regimentation of residents, depersonalization, and limitation of staff-resident interactions—those practices that were intended to ease the operation of the institution. Resident-oriented practices were those that dealt with residents as individuals and gave each individual greater choice and autonomy in personal needs and rights. It is expected that the more resident-centered a program is, the more normalizing the environment, and research literature seems to bear this out.

Two scales that address treatment practices and that reflect this orientation distinction are the Resident Management Practices Scale (RMPS) and the Characteristics of the Treatment Environment scale (CTE). Both scales show that resident-oriented practices are more highly associated with autonomy, individualization, rights, and other normalization elements. Gilbert and Hemming (1979) found that, in general, small group bungalows had more resident-oriented practices and more positive staff-resident interactions than institutional ward settings. McLain et al. (1977b) found higher autonomy and activities scores, using both the CTE and RMPS, among family care homes and resident facilities than in ward settings of an institution. McLain and his colleagues also discovered that, of the two community living alternatives, the autonomy and activity scores were higher in resident facilities that had more than six residents and a specially trained staff.

Using the CTE, Brown and Guard (1979) examined the characteristics of a group of community nursing facilities housing mentally retarded persons in Washington State. They noted that the programs they studied were not ideal settings, because of program design, size, and character. Because the eight facilities examined had a mean of 77 residents, neither the program character nor the staff patterns could be described as homelike. Defining autonomy as having freedom of choice, privacy, and responsibility, the investigators noted that the presence of both autonomy and activity were conducive to self-esteem, growth, and competence. Conversely, the authors posited that the lack of activity led to passivity, apathy, and alienation, contributed to dehumanization, and structured staff-resident relations along an authoritarian-submission dimension. Findings showed that the programs that provided the most autonomy and activity for their residents were those that had a younger staff, hired a greater proportion of supervisory personnel, and included the residents and their families in the treatment goal-setting process.

Resident-centered programs are associated with measurable gains in residence occupants. Mayeda's (1979) comments bear witness to a paradoxical finding: the more concerned the program is with adherence to normalization, and the less concerned it is with direct staff involvement, the fewer the gains demonstrated in program residents.

Program Process   Several notions are subsumed under the variable of the program process, including the program's character and the effects of the program upon its occupants, and the intrinsic elements within the program that contribute to cooperative living. The inherent nature of cooperative household living demands a sharing of the household responsibilities that contribute to the general welfare of the group, an interplay among the group members that promotes growth in personal attributes and compensates for liabilities, a development of affiliative patterns that promote harmony, and a demonstration of resident activities that are socially oriented.

The effects of the residence process within the context of its character have been noted by several researchers (Campbell, 1971; Diller et al., 1978; Fiorelli, 1978; Mulvihill, 1978; Rodman and Collins, 1974). Furthermore, a number of studies have looked at differences between individuals within different settings (Eyman et al., 1977) and between individuals who have moved to community settings (Fiorelli and Thurman, 1979; Schroeder and Henes, 1978).

Eyman et al. (1977) compared changes in Adaptive Behavior Scale scores across several institutional and community settings. The authors noted: "the relationships between change on the three adaptive behavior factors and environmental measures on programs were generally higher in the community facilities than in the institutions" (p. 312). The researchers concluded that their results confirmed earlier findings that the social-psychological characteristics of a residence do, in fact, influence the behavior of its residents.

Thurman and Fiorelli (1979) reported that generally favorable changes occurred in the patterns of behaviors and styles of interactions among a number of retarded adults following their move from an institutional to a community setting. The authors felt that their results were consistent with other anecdotal accounts and research surveys that discussed favorable behavioral changes manifested by formerly institutionalized individuals. Because the researchers only assessed the individuals six weeks prior to and six weeks following movement, their comments were restricted to the short-term benefits of movement to community living. They did not specifically study either the interaction of environmental variables or the effects of novel situations (i.e., the abilities of individuals to adapt to new environments). However, as they later reported (Thurman and Fiorelli, 1979), initial changes "seemed to occur more as a function of broad ecological differences rather than of specific programmatic differences or types of residential setting per se" (p. 340).

The fact that changes do occur within a residence environment is obvious; however, what contributes to change within the program process is not. Gunzburg (1977) has postulated that persons living in community residences need to demonstrate growth in five areas: social knowledge, social habits, emotional attitudes, independence, and maturity. The use of a cooperative living model with rehabilitative intent can contribute to the development of this behavior. Within this context, Provencal and MacCormack (1979) criticized the use of foster care for adults and posed a distinction between the foster care concept and the community home. They noted that the community home becomes a "highly desirable environment created for adults from a combination of carefully selected age-appropriate elements of foster care as well as other habilitative concepts" (p. 4). The authors further noted that staff in community homes had to lean away from a parenting role toward one that promoted growth, development, and encouragement. With this basis, the community home places an emphasis upon the acquisition of skills and attributes that facilitate independence and self-reliance. The means for reaching this goal are carefully articulated behavioral objectives; however, the intrinsic qualities lack definition.

Research literature indicates that some authors have attempted to define the characteristics of the development process. Newman and Sherman (1979–80) identified four indicators (social interaction, affection, ritual, and social distance) in an attempt to define the idea of "familishness" or "familism." Their study, although applied to a surrogate family model, examined variables that have application to community residences as well. In an examination of over 100 foster family care homes, the authors found that most of the homes studied did indicate family integration, but that the adults in the homes were more affiliated with their surrogate parents than with other members of the household. These results could support the notions presented by Provencal and MacCormack (1979) that the factors associated with adult family care may not lead to the most normalizing adult environment. In addition, the interaction patterns measured by the indicators identified by Newman and Sherman could be applied to cooperative household living.

In a study examining the differences between cooperative household living and surrogate family residences, Butler and Bjaanes (1977) reported that the home care environments were "not providing the occupants with those activities considered necessary for individual development" (p. 342). The authors identified five specific types of behaviors participated in by residents in both environments: active leisure, passive leisure, work and chores, personal activities, and interactive activities. They also noted that there were variations within types of behaviors found in residences, but that across types the majority of behaviors were interactive. Because the size of the cooperative living facilities ($N = 30$) confounded the use of small group living, it is difficult to equate the board-and-care facilities with average community residences under this model. In addition, the home care programs studied were not necessarily representative of the population, because inconsistencies were noted within the same types of programs. However, the research data do illustrate that activities participated in by residents varied within as well as between those two types of residential options.

Another component of the process, resident interactions, was evaluated by Landesman-Dwyer, Berkson, and Romer (1979). They observed friendship patterns in 18 group homes and found that group home variables, rather than individual characteristics of residents, were significant predictors of affiliative behavior. The authors noted that the character of a group home could be measured and could be related to the social behavior of its residents. They also found that in homes with less intellectually disabled residents, the friendships were more intense, and that the larger the home, the more extensive the friendship groups. Although Landesman-Dwyer et al. were evaluating the extent to which environment and individual variables influenced social relationships, they did not, except for size, report other process characteristics of the homes or staff. To what extent these other variables could have influenced their results is not known.

One concept related to program process, the effects of programs, appears to be well substantiated; the other, the process characteristics, has yet to be fully examined. The work of several investigators (Bjaanes and Butler, 1974; Landesman-Dwyer et al., 1979; Newman and Sherman, 1979–80) has identified some of the process variables, but further research is needed to draw these variables together.

Social Integration   Involvement of residents in their community and involvement of others with the residents have been studied by a number of researchers. Balla (1976) states that "parental and community involvement may be enhanced in community-based facilities" (p. 117). Campbell (1971) found that group home residents were more apt to visit their parents' homes than were institutionalized persons. Intagliata (1979) found that residents of high-quality homes were visited more frequently by parents and/or relatives and that they made more use of social supports. Brown and Guard (1979) found a positive relationship between residences that involved families in treatment planning and residences that showed greater autonomy and activity of the residents. Conversely, Birenbaum and Re (1979) found a decline in the use of community leisure resources by the residents of the community facility they studied over a period of four years. The investigators felt that, after a period of intense involvement in community recreation, the residents had adopted normal recreation patterns; however, they reported that community recreation was also affected by constraints derived from staff attitudes.

Bjaanes and Butler (1974) contrasted board-and-care facilities with home care facilities and found that the proximity of the board-and-care facilities to a city business district facilitated the resident's use of neighborhood services. The board-and-care residents apparently did use these services to a greater degree than the residents of the home care facilities. The authors noted that proximity of and exposure to community resources were important normalizing ingredients. In another study, Butler, Bjaanes, and Hofacre (1975) observed the use of community resources in a number of southern California facilities ranging in size from three to 95 residents. They noted that facility location, facility size, resident characteristics, and caregiver education, experience, and attitudes were all believed to contribute to a facility's use of community resources. The researchers also noted that facilities with more than seven residents appeared to have a broader range of contact with community services and programs.

Socially integrative experiences have been found to produce greater levels of social behaviors (Brody and Stoneman, 1977; Marbolin et al., 1979; May, 1976; Stacy, Doleys, and Malcolm, 1979). Marbolin and his colleagues noted that riding on buses, eating in restaurants, and other such experiences stemming from social interactions maximized learning of community-use behaviors. Stacy, Doleys, and Malcolm (1979) noted that "social-skills training is required not only for the development of appropriate behavior, but that without such training exposure to community living may result in diminished assertive behavior" (p. 157). Brody and Stoneman noted that effective social functioning must be preceded by the acquisition of social behavior patterns. Accordingly, developmentally disabled adults moving into community group homes must be encouraged to use community resources to gain and maintain acceptable social skills. Gump (cited in Brody and Stoneman, 1977) emphasized this point and stressed that environmental settings have a major role in determining the appropriateness of social responses.

The research literature appears to support the notion that there is a positive relationship between growth in resident skills and 1) staff competence, 2) resident-centered programs, 3) intensity of relevant programming, and 4) social integration. In general, the ratings that Mayeda identified as comprising the Normalization factor do appear to be associated with the way in which new behaviors and skills are gained.

Administrative Policies
DeMaine (1978) notes that the second factor of PASS emphasizes Administrative Policies, particularly as they pertain to normalization principles. Mayeda (1979) further reports a statistically significant positive correlation between improved client behavior, particularly in community self-sufficiency, and PASS scores on this factor. Eyman, DeMaine, and Lei (1979) found that, within the specific community residence population they studied, improvement was not associated with age, but with IQ and with initial scores on the Behavior Development Scale (BDS). They also found that Administrative Policies was one of the PASS factors (along with General Environment, Location and Accessibility, and Comfort and Physical Setting) that was associated with growth in adaptive behavior.

The PASS ratings that comprise this factor are: Ties to academia; Age group priorities; Deinstitutionalization; Research climate; Planning process; Activities, routines, and rhythms (culture-appropriate); Utilization of generic resources; and Budget economy. These individual ratings can be made operational when administrative policies translate into administrative practices.

Administrative practices within community residences have not been found to be the focus of studies in the management literature. However, indicators such as treatment practices, management policies, and job satisfaction can be used to draw inferences from such practices. Because it can be inferred that treatment practices are a reflection of management orientation, some extraction can be made from those clinical studies that comment upon administrative practices. Clinically oriented reports show 1) the loss of behavioral gains or lack of development of new behaviors when management policies do not correspond to rehabilitative intent (Aninger and Bolinsky, 1977; Bernstein and Karan, 1979; Campbell, 1971; Gunzburg, 1977), and 2) significant acquisition of new behaviors when there is correspondence to rehabilitative intent (Bjaanes and Butler, 1974; Brown and Guard, 1979; Close, 1977; Gunzburg, 1977; Intagliata, 1979; Tizard, 1964). In addition, ecological measures, such as the Characteristics of the Treatment Environment (CTE), used by Brown and Guard (1979) and McLain et al. (1975), indicate that desirable management-supported treatment practices were evident in those program units where high CTE Autonomy and Activity scores were found.

Treatment practices can also reflect the presence of or lack of flexibility within a program's design. Lack of flexibility can keep individuals from experiencing personal growth. However, as Bernstein and Karan (1979, p. 44) note, "failure should not be the client's; instead, the habilitation program in which the client is involved must be capable and willing to re-program as needed, or else acknowledge that it may not be the appropriate training program for the client."

The effects of various management policies can be seen in a contrast between two reports in which size of the residence was considered. Bjaanes and Butler (1974) noted that board-and-care facilities (which housed over 30 residents) were closer to the objective of normalization than were home care facilities. They felt that this was partly caused by the size and location of the residence and by the level of competence of the residents, but primarily by the method of supervision. Conversely, Birenbaum and Re (1979) noted that residents in a community facility equivalent in size to the board-and-care type were less active in leisure activities in the community and were more restricted in personal decision making at home because management policies directed staff members to stress conformity to house rules.

Welch and Iaquinta (1979) found that adverse administrative practices contributed significantly to residence staff's perceptions of what caused burn-out. Kerr (1977) found that most managers of British hostels expressed satisfaction with their jobs because they were permitted to plan and develop policies, to have direct responsibility for day-to-day operations, to select staff, and to provide inservice training. However, the managers reported that their staff showed a high turnover rate, which they attributed to, among other things, inadequate pay and lack of career opportunities—conditions outside of their control. Consequently, if staff perceive working conditions as adverse, negative staff attitudes and behaviors will, as Welch and Iaquinta note, "result in lowered quality of resident life experiences."

General Environment

According to Mayeda (1979), General Environment addresses issues of normalization with regard to programming and physical setting. DeMaine (1978) related the following ratings to this factor: Model coherency; Program-neighborhood harmony; Function congruity image; Deviant client and other juxtaposition; Building-neighborhood harmony; Deviancy program juxtaposition; Congregation and assimilation potential; and Program, facility, and location names. These ratings can be reflected in three general variables; size, model coherency, and harmony and function.

Size   The variable of size has been the focus of much controversy in the literature related to community residences (Balla, Butterfield, and Zigler, 1974; Fanning, 1978; Landesman-Dwyer, Sackett, and Kleinman, unpublished manuscript). A number of authors note that the size of a community facility is not a factor in personal development, while others cite an optimal range that produces gain in residents. Investigators have addressed the size variable in a number of ways: 1) research or anecdotal reports that relate programmatic factors and the number of residents; 2) commentaries on size as a factor in community acceptance and resident assimilation; and 3) architectural studies investigating size and design variables. Wolfensberger and Glenn (1975a) note that size has some internal absolute limits and that two factors contribute to these: 1) the complexity that comes with group size, and 2) the decline of individualization. The first factor relates to an eventual loss of supervisory and administrative control as size exceeds manageable limits. The second factor, the decline of individualization, is associated with a withdrawal from meaningful interactions and with a loss of group identity.

Balla, Butterfield, and Zigler (1974) indicated that size of a residential facility was not a factor in resident change. However, as these authors note, their inquiry did not address community residences. Instead, their conclusions were based upon an examination of the behavioral growth of institutionalized children (between the ages of 10 and 15) residing in a number of campus facilities of an aggregate size of at least 300 persons. Balla (1976) subsequently noted that care was more adequate in smaller institutions; however, he felt that it was the type of institution rather than the size that influenced care. Brown and Guard (1979), in examining Washington State nursing homes, noted that size was not a factor in their findings of individual development, even though the eight settings studied had a mean resident population of 77. Bjaanes and Butler (1974) and Birenbaum and Re (1979) examined facilities that were in excess of 50 beds and noted gain in their residents. Bjaanes and Butler concluded that the larger facilities provided far more normalizing experiences than did the smaller ones they studied. In a subsequent study, they reported that residents of community residences with more than seven occupants had a greater rate of individual independence (Butler, Bjaanes, and Hofacre, 1975).

Conversely, a number of reports note that size is a variable that affects treatment practices. Balla (1976) postulated that quality of life was better in small community-based facilities. Balla's analysis, however, was devoid of the use of any standardized behavioral scales that measure skill attainment. Both King, Raynes, and Tizard (1971) and McCormick, Balla, and Zigler (1975) found that group homes had the most resident-oriented care practices when compared to other congregate living arrangements. Campbell (1971) found that group home residents showed significantly greater personal independence than persons residing in institutions. Edgerton (1975) noted that the quality of life varied in the alternative care facilities he studied, with evidence "here and there of exciting progress toward the goal of normalization." O'Connor (1976) reported that facilities with fewer than 20 persons were more likely to be normalized than those with over 20 persons. O'Connor defined "normalized" as the absence of security features, the existence of personal effects, and the enhancement of privacy. Gilbert and Hemming (1979), Race and Race (1978), Schroeder and Henes (1978), and Tizard (1964) found that smaller residences promoted growth in language skills. Gilbert and Hemming also noted that the stimulating environment within small residences has an effect upon staff behavior that makes it more resident-oriented. McLain et al. (1977b) found that foster family home situations (fewer than six persons) and residence facilities (more than six persons) had higher autonomy and activity scores on the CTE II than did retardation institutions and skilled nursing facilities. Harris et al. (1974) noted that the smaller the number of residents, the more functional and accountable the activities of the staff were.

Landesman-Dwyer and her colleagues (Landesman-Dwyer, Stein, and Sackett, 1976, 1978; Landesman-Dwyer, Sackett, and Kleinman, unpublished manuscript) conducted an observational study within Washington State's community residences to determine whether the size of the group home had any significant effect upon residents. They studied whether group home size (ranging from six to 20 persons) was correlated with patterns of daily activities for residents and staff members and found that, although staff behavior did not differ across the homes, resident behavior did. The researchers also noted that group home size was not the most important factor in accounting for behavioral differences. When within-home interactions were observed, Landesman-Dwyer, Berkson, and Romer (1979) reported a relationship between size of home and residents' affiliative behaviors. The residents of smaller group homes (those with six to nine residents) spent less time in dyadic peer interactions, associated with fewer peers per day, and had lower probability of having a reciprocated or mutual "best" friendship than residents of large group homes (18–20 persons). It has been reported elsewhere that too small a group size may interfere with interpersonal interactions (Wolfe, 1975). Correspondingly, Landesman-Dwyer and her colleagues felt that social relationships were enhanced as the number of peers increased; however, staff-resident interactions did not increase as size became smaller. Landesman-Dwyer, Sackett, and Kleinman (unpublished manuscript) concluded that they did not find any dramatic effects related to group home size in community residences when size varied from six to 20 residents.

Race and Race (1978) observed that for individuals in a 12-bed residence, "the group as a whole compensates for the individual practical shortcomings of its members" (p. 60). They noted that they could not deny the importance of practical abilities for a group as a whole to function, but that it was not necessary for every member to have all the skills necessary to survive as an individual. "After all," they noted, "how many 'normal people' exist completely independently?" (p. 60). Consequently, within a cooperative household living model, minimum size is crucial to facilitating group process; obversely, excessive size will deter group process.

Model Coherency The ratings that comprise model coherency relate to program design; model coherency is an internal consistency measure reflecting specialization of function and program content. For example, if the program is a home with a rehabilitative intent, consistency would relate the structure of the home with the integrity of the program design. Researchers, for the most part, have not sufficiently identified the residential alternative model under study to correspond intent with coherency. Gunzburg (1977) noted that the five programs he reviewed had differing designs. Because, in his assessment, he was interested in client outcome, he questioned whether each program was designed in a manner to achieve the desired outcome, i.e., resident growth. He noted that three of the five residences cited appeared to be consistent with a rehabilitative-residence model—a small group home matched with directive programming. The outcome, skills related to independent living, showed significant gains over the period studied.

Bjaanes and Butler (1974) examined two types of California community living alternatives: board-and-care facilities and home care facilities. Although they reasonably expected the smaller (four to six persons) home care facilities to offer more normalizing experiences, the authors found that the larger (30 to 50 persons) board-and-care facilities provided more consistent conditions corresponding with normalization. However, the authors did not find a consistent pattern of conditions within the home care facilities. The two home care facilities examined differed sufficiently enough to make it difficult to generalize findings. The variability in the results can be attributed to 1) a lack of rationale for the design and intent of each type of community living alternative, and 2) the study's lack of a randomly selected sample of home care facilities.

The difficulty in understanding the correspondence between design and intent can be seen in the study reported by Aninger and Bolinsky (1977), who examined growth in several adults following transfer from an institutional setting to an apartment living situation. Their investigation lacked a model; consequently, their lack of findings of gain of independent skill behaviors could be attributed to the lack of rehabilitative intent within the apartment program. The authors assumed that movement into an apartment setting was all that was needed to produce new behaviors. Although lack of model coherency is pervasive in the research examined, some exceptions do appear (Brody and Stoneman, 1977; Campbell, 1971; Close, 1977; Johnson and Bailey, 1977; Rodman and Collins, 1974). For example, Campbell (1971) acknowledged the lack of rehabilitative intent in the residence he studied and noted that changes over time were not maintained because staff were doing things for the residents and consequently fostering dependency.

Harmony and Function   Harmony and function, the variable most intimately associated with the General Environment factor, addresses the appropriateness of a service within the context of its neighborhood. For the most part, references to program-neighborhood and building-neighborhood harmony, apparent design features, and other related issues, are not cited in the clinical literature. There is, however, a growing body of literature that approaches the subject from the perspective of environmental design and physical integration. These design issues relate size to environmental harmony and function, not to programming intent.

Although size was discussed previously in relation to rehabilitative intent, its inclusion here is relevant from a different perspective: physical integration and design. A number of authors address size from this perspective (Butler, Bjaanes, and Hofacre, 1975; Gerry, 1975; Golub, 1979). Golub notes that the "common home-care facility is a group home—an independent housing unit, typically accommodating between eight and twelve persons," and that physically, the typical group home is a "large single-family residence in a residential neighborhood having a minimum of five bedrooms, a living room and a play room, a large dining room, and what usually would be considered superadequate kitchen and bathroom facilities" (p. 326). Gerry (1975) notes that the most appropriate number of people in a residence seems to be eight to ten and that assimilation is heightened by location within "a mixed neighborhood—one with apartments, one-family dwellings, older and younger people, and transient as well as permanent neighbors . . ." (p. 31). He further notes that internal appointments should lean toward warm colors, dark woods, fabrics rather than plastic, and carpeting rather than tile. Golub indicates that a conversion of an existing residence is usually easier, cheaper, and faster than developing purpose-built housing, a notion supported programmatically by Landesman-Dwyer, Stein, and Sackett (1978), who found that specially designed new group homes were related to decreased community interaction.

Wolfensberger and Glenn (1975a) propose that 15 to 20 persons should be the upper limit for a residential setting; in fact, a group home designed to accommodate this number should look no larger than a large family house. Consequently, it is not surprising that Thakur (1974) reported initial adverse community reaction to the development of a hostel that housed 28 persons. Conversely, Ziemianski (1977) observed that the three 6–12-bed community residences she studied had a high assimilation rate measured by neighborhood and community acceptance. Other attitudinal changes of persons living near community residences have also been noted (Kastner, Reppucci, and Pezzoli, 1979; Willms, 1979). In fact, it has been reported that "the experience of living in a community with retarded people promotes more positive attitudes toward them" (Kastner, Reppucci, and Pezzoli, 1979, p. 143). Scheerenberger (1977) related the question of zoning to single-family dwellings, noting that a recent court decision in New York State reinforced the harmony and function concept by asserting that the purpose of a group home is to be the opposite of an institution—it is to be a home like other homes. The homelike character is strengthened because the group home is a "relatively permanent household and is not a framework for a transience or transient living" (p. 7).

The research literature appears to indicate that size, model coherency, and harmony and function all have an effect upon program intent, environmental design, and management. Presupposing that community residences use a cooperative living model, a minimum of persons should be present to promote interaction and skill learning. Research supports the idea that four to six persons is within a lower group limit. However, homelike atmosphere cannot be achieved when the group becomes unwieldy and individuality is hampered. The upper limit appears to fall in the 10 to 14 persons range, inasmuch as neighborhood acceptance and assimilation are heightened by a group size that is not seen as deviant for the neighborhood. It seems that research literature reinforces both common practice and federal policy (*Federal Register*, 1978; 1979), supporting the use of group homes in the six to 14 persons range. However, further research is needed to examine all the rating interactions within this factor.

Administrative Ideology

DeMaine (1978) indicated that Administrative Ideology emphasizes issues related to the administration of services, including such issues as administrative structure and program evaluation mechanisms. This general factor addresses processes associated with nondirect service orientations, such as organizational structure, support for students, evaluation of methods, and involvement in outside interests. Administrative Ideology is comprised of the following program administrative ratings: Education of the public; Program planning and renewal mechanisms; Administrative control and structures; Consumer and public participation; Manpower development; Comprehensiveness; and Innovativeness.

Eyman, DeMaine, and Lei (1979) found that this factor had an inverse relationship to adaptive behavior gains in California's group home residents. Residents showed most improvement in the Behavior Development Scale's personal self-sufficiency factor when homes received low PASS scores on education of the public and manpower development. Mayeda (1979), puzzled by this finding, noted similar observations by Nebraska's ENCOR. He posited that, because the sample of California facilities consisted exclusively of small residences, "the inverse correlation could be interpreted as showing that with limited staffing, if more time and energy are spent on administrative chores, less time and energy are spent in direct client care" (p. 105).

It is conceivable that the findings of Landesman-Dwyer, Berkson, and Romer (1979) could be interpreted in a like manner. Because between-resident affiliations were found to be more highly developed in larger group homes, one explanation might be that more staff-resident interactions took place in the smaller homes, hence the differences. However, Landesman-Dwyer, Sackett, and Kleinman (unpublished manuscript) have indicated in a subsequent report that staff-resident interactions did not increase as size became smaller; therefore, some other variable (such as severity of resident's disability) has contributed to this effect. Mayeda (1979) does note that he expects that the opposite is true in larger settings. This expectation can be borne out by Brown and Guard (1979), who found that there was a positive association between a larger supervisory staff, high scores on autonomy and activity on the CTE, and greater involvement of the family in treatment planning.

Location and Accessibility

The fifth factor, according to DeMaine (1978), gives an indication of physical location and availability of service and contains the following ratings: Access; Local proximity; Physical resources; and Regional proximity. Location and Accessibility can be defined in terms of the physical closeness of the residence to the population cluster, the residents' abilities to gain access to generic services, and the representation of the general area's own population among the occupants of the residence.

Eyman, DeMaine, and Lei (1979) note that gains in skills related to community self-sufficiency, personal self-sufficiency, and personal-social responsibility (as measured by the Behavior Development Scale) are associated with high scores on the ratings in Location and Accessibility, especially for older and less impaired individuals. The authors note that this is one of the four PASS factors that seems to contribute most to growth in adaptive behavior.

Butler, Bjaanes, and Hofacre (1975), although not specifically controlling for location, did observe that the use of community resources by residents of the community residences they studied was associated with the education and previous experience of service providers, the size and location of the facility, and the characteristics of the surrounding neighborhood. They observed that facilities located close to a metropolitan center demonstrated greater use of resources than did those in suburban or rural settings. In fact, the authors have subsequently noted (Butler and Bjaanes, 1977) that their collective research shows that "if community-care facilities are to provide normalizing environments, attention must be paid to the location and qualifications of service providers, the nature and extent of internal programs, and exchange with the community and utilization of community programs" (p. 346).

Comfort and Physical Setting

The sixth factor deals primarily with the comfort and functional nature of the physical setting in which services are provided (Mayeda, 1979). Eyman, DeMaine, and Lei (1979) note that this is another of the factors highly associated with growth in adaptive behaviors. High PASS facility scores in environmental blending, location of services, and comfort and appearance seem to produce positive change, to a significant degree, in elements of behavior associated with improvements in self-help skills, regardless of age or level of impairment. This factor was also significantly related to increases in behavior associated with personal-social responsibilties. Comfort and Physical Setting are comprised of the following ratings: Environmental beauty; Physical comfort; Internal design and appointment; and Deviant staff juxtaposition.

Because several of the ratings that comprise this factor address the environmental design of the community residence in terms of its homelike atmosphere, commentary derived from the environmental design literature is relevant. As Kennedy (1978) has noted, "if the building becomes a symbol of normality, the residence-community gap can be bridged" (p. 6).

A number of reports have appeared that examine the design characteristics of residential alternatives. However, none directly answers the challenge posed by Dybwab (1970) when he noted that "unfortunately there have been practically no instances where, in the designing of new facilities, a deliberate effort is made to create parallel settings differing in important exterior and interior features of architectural design to permit ongoing comparative studies'' (p. 48). It must be recognized that one of the subtle mechanisms in rehabilitative intent is the manner in which 1) the environment is used to evolve change, and 2) the message is given by the environment to its occupants and about its occupants. A comparison design in purpose-built housing is found in housing for elderly persons. In a study published in the *Architectural Record* (Editorial, 1979), a group of design researchers described an evaluative study that tested basic pre-design assumptions against actual use. A control was introduced in which similar purpose-built housing was matched against size and structural design. The authors noted several findings that are relevant: 1) privacy, coupled with a feeling of shared community, was very important to the residents; and 2) the residents needed a means of bringing with them enough of their former lives to "feel emotionally whole." Both these findings are consistent with the PASS notions of individualization and possessions.

Some aspects of the literature on residential crowding are relevant to this factor. Size, as an artifact of community residence character, interacts with individual space; physical comfort is the sum of this interaction. Hopstock, Aiello, and Baum (1979) note that physical density is an important consideration. Physical density, defined as the ratio of the amount of space available to the number of people occupying that space, can be varied in two ways: 1) by changing the amount of space available (spatial density variations); and 2) by changing the number of people in the space (social density variations). Consequently, another artifact of comfort and size is the number of persons a home can ideally sustain without crowding and having negative effect on rehabilitative intent. The extensive use of the community by the board-and-care facility residents studied by Bjaanes and Butler (1974) seems to be linked to the social and spatial density of the facilities.

Reizenstein and McBride (1978) evaluated a cluster of three purpose-built residences, each housing eight adult residents and two staff. The evaluation was based upon three design issues: social contact, activity support, and symbolic identification. Social contact was defined as the degree to which the physical environment affects the amount and quality of social interaction. Activity support was defined as the degree to which the physical environment allows a normal range of daily activities and facilitates successful accomplishment of tasks associated with these activities. Finally, symbolic identification was defined as the information an environment conveys about the people associated with it. The assessment was directed toward three social-environment issues associated with the normalization principle: control over one's life, personal growth, and integration into society.

Reizenstein and McBride reported that comfort is compromised if no semi-public or semi-private spaces are available (either private space of bedroom or public space of the living room). They also noted that social contact is lessened if private spaces are unavailable for pairs or small groups who want to interact in isolation. Activity support reflects design for adequate kitchen, laundry, leisure activities, personal hygiene, and sleeping space. Houses must be like homes to provide symbolic identification; and they must provide security, comfort, and group membership. In terms of the three dwellings they studied, Reizenstein and McBride noted that, although the design flaws did not quite produce a home, the setting was not identified as an institution either.

Knight et al. (1978) noted that when private spaces are available, people recognize them and use them. Private space provision within living alternatives has been found by the authors to be associated with production of positive social behaviors. They note that private (single and double) bedrooms and a good hierarchy of spaces are best, because they offer residents the greatest opportunity to control their personal experiences.

The available information in the research literature supports the idea that the more a residence is like a home in context and in use, then the greater will be the development of behavior appropriate to the context of a home. Literature is just beginning to emerge that defines the process characteristics that address comfort and appearance; however, more direct research is still required.

RESEARCH RELATED TO RESIDENT GROWTH

The research literature contains only a few studies that examine the community residence as an experimental condition.

Two studies (Close, 1977; Schroeder and Henes, 1978) compared persons living in group homes with control subjects remaining in an institution. Schroeder and Henes examined the differences in Progress Assessment Chart (PAC) behavior gain scores between a group of 19 adults (12 males, 7 females) placed in four group homes and a group of control subjects chosen at random from a sample pool within an associated institution. The control subjects were matched against the characteristics of the experimental subjects on age, IQ, and PAC scores. The authors compared pre- and post-test scores on the PAC of group home residents who were deinstitutionalized with their matched control counterparts awaiting placement. The design of the study, although containing a pre- and post-test, did not offer selection prior to assignment to the experimental or to the control condition. Because the authors did not describe the group homes, no judgments can be made about the effects of home environment variations. From the findings that PAC-measured behaviors in the communication area showed significant gains and that there were "significant differences between scores for experimental and control groups," one can only infer that something *in the environment* of the noninstitutionalized persons surveyed produced some changes. Because no controls were held for day program, an alternative interpretation could be made that gains were the result of the residents' sheltered workshop experiences.

Close (1977) used a pre-test/post-test control group design with random assignment to evaluate post-institutional community adjustment of severely and profoundly retarded adults. From a pool of 15 subjects (8 women, 7 men) he randomly selected 8 subjects (4 men, 4 women) for admission to a group home. The program environment, according to the author, was conceptually consistent with normalization (i.e., a daily routine free from regimentation and a behaviorally designed rehabilitative program). The experimental condition was the group home environment with an accompanying intense behavioral shaping of community independent living skills.

Using an instrument called the Development Record, and taking observations in a standardized format, Close found no differences between his experimental and control subjects on the pre-test, but did report that the experimental group demonstrated statistically significant gains on the post-test after one year. He noted that a community residence can provide a specialized environment that promotes increases in self-care and social skill competence, but that this has to be accomplished through the existence of a positive philosophy, individualized skill training, and consistency in behavior management procedures. Although Close was able to demonstrate significant change, it is not clear whether the change was caused by the group home environment or by the intense program offered by the staff. A reasonable alternative to the design would have been also to institute a control group in which only the residential component in a group home (devoid of the intense behavior shaping) was offered, or to institute a control group receiving the equivalent intensity of program but remaining within the institutional setting.

One of the studies most often cited as an example of gain in community residences is the one conducted by Bjaanes and Butler (1974) in California. Although their report contains a significant model base for their research, their concluding discussions do not associate the outcome with their model or with their assumptions. Using a naturalistic observation approach with no controls, the researchers examined the behavioral environments of two different types of California community living alternatives, board-and-care facilities and home care facilities, but their design did not include matching or randomization. The geographic catchment areas of interest had only two board-and-care facilities; however, out of 18 home care facilities, the investigators chose two, but did not do so randomly or out of consideration for matching location, character, or any other variable.

Bjaanes and Butler divided their assessment into four areas: physical, supportive, attitudinal, and behavioral, but did not report what specific instrumentation was used for the first three, except to refer to the "use of questionnaire." The behavioral variable, however, was examined by detailed observation and by a reporting technique "using modal behavior and modal characteristics as a means of describing behavioral components of life space in community care facilities" (p. 431).

Bjaanes and Butler report descriptive differences between the two types of facilities, not only in program but also in location and assimilation potential. The two board-and-care homes were dormitory-type community residences, one with 30 men, the other with 50 men (24 of whom were mentally retarded and part of the study). The residences were located in an urban transitional area close to the central business district. Their immediate vicinity, an area of older homes, apartments, and businesses, was within walking distance of a park, the bus depot, movie houses, and a city shopping mall. The caregivers (an owner and two to three assistants) exercised little control over where the residents went, and extensive contact with the community was evident. The residents were predominantly in their twenties and thirties, and they tested generally in the mildly retarded range.

On the other hand, the two home care facilities (foster family care type residences) were in a suburban setting. Neither was within walking distance of parks, recreation facilities, transportation, or businesses. The residents were limited in terms of where they could go; in fact, they were rarely permitted to go anywhere by themselves. The residents were generally in their thirties and forties; they functioned in the mildly to moderately retarded range of intellectual functioning.

The importance of this study is the extensive descriptive information generated that permitted the authors to comment on the differences in behavior, time-use patterns, and characteristics of the two groups. The investigators noted that, although the board-and-care facilities were closer to the objectives of the normalization principle and of the development of social competence, there were substantial variations within, as well as between, board-and-care facilities and home care facilities. The authors noted that more behavior was independent in board-and-care facilities than in home care facilities and that the development of independent functioning appeared to be related to the geographic location of the facility and to the involvement of the caregivers in the ongoing stream of behavior. These findings offer substantiation for the use of the normalization principle in program design;

however, the authors' conclusions on differences in the overall effects of the home environments must be evaluated cautiously because of the lack of suitable controls.

The other major study that specifically examines the effects of environment upon adaptive behavior is that of Eyman, DeMaine, and Lei (1979). They used a one-group pre-test/post-test design to investigate the relationship of factor-analyzed scores derived from PASS-3 with changes in the adaptive behavior of residents placed in community facilities. For a number of reasons, the authors had PASS evaluations on a great number of family care and board-and-care facilities, and they also had Adaptive Behavior Scale (ABS) scores as a result of three annual assessments on 245 persons living in 87 family care homes and 11 board-and-care homes (essentially group homes). Using a path analysis procedure, the researchers compared the ABS data derived on their subjects with the PASS data derived on the residences, and they concluded that the results of the study supported the assertion that some of the principles of normalization are related to the development of retarded individuals. Specifically, they found that high PASS facility scores on Environmental Blending, Location of Services, and Comfort and Appearance appeared to produce positive change, to a significant degree, on the subject's personal self-sufficiency scores. Additionally, the authors noted that PASS rating scores on Administrative Policies, Location of Services, and Comfort and Appearance showed a significant relationship with positive change in the community self-sufficiency domain of the ABS, and that PASS ratings on Location and Proximity of Services were significantly associated with improvement in the personal-social responsibility domain. In general, the authors noted that the characteristics of the residences, as measured by four PASS rating factors (i.e., Administrative Policies, Environmental Blending of Facility with Neighborhood, Location and Proximity of Services, and Comfort and Appearance) seemed to contribute significantly to growth in adaptive behavior. The implications of the study are that there are differences among community residences, that these differences can be measured (by an instrument like PASS 3), and that these differences do affect the rate and substance of new behavior acquisition.

SUMMARY

The intent of this chapter is to identify those factors within a predominant type of community-care setting—community residences—that encourage growth and that promote the highest development of independence and competence behaviors. There is not, as Bruininks,

Hauber, and Kudla (1980) indicate, a standard classification system that categorizes this residential alternative. However, it is generally accepted (and used for the purpose of this investigation) that a community residence is a small, community-based, sheltered, group home type of residential facility that operates 24 hours a day, 7 days a week, and provides room, board, supervision, and programming designed to enhance skill development for independent living.

Bruininks, Hauber, and Kudla (1979, 1980) indicated that, in 1977, there were nationally over 3,200 community living alternative programs in the 1–10-bed range providing housing to over 17,500 persons. An additional 9,700 persons were housed in some 670 community living alternatives that were in the 11–20-bed range. However, it should be noted that these figures include a variety of sheltered living arrangements and that they may not all be using the same model. Trends indicate that community residences represent a sizable living alternative and will continue to do so in the years to come. Indeed, the growth of community residences is well illustrated in New York: in 1969 only nine licensed community residences existed, but by 1979 the number of community residences was well over 400. Bruininks and his coworkers did not involve themselves in a typology, so that comparisons of their data with the posited typology developed by Bjaanes and Butler or with the dimensional perspective of Baker, Seltzer, and Seltzer (1979) are not possible.

It has been posited that a community residence is a therapeutic environment providing, in addition to room and board, the rehabilitative experiences designed to promote independent skill development. The terminal objective is movement to a less structured and more independent setting. However, the objective may also be long-term housing and supervised care. To facilitate the examination of this process, a triad of constructs (residence environment, rehabilitative intent, and management systems) exists that defines the residence model. The use of the framework of these constructs has permitted a number of conclusions to be drawn from the available community residence literature.

Residence Environment

Research literature confirms the residence model variables related to size, assimilation, and design. There seems to be more gain in resident skills in homes with between six and 14 persons than in homes with lesser numbers or in facilities with a greater number, but dependence can be fostered in homes below this size, and deindividualization can exist in homes above this size. Residences have the greatest assimilation potential when the dwelling design matches the surrounding neighborhood and when its resident size does not overly tax the community's generic resources and commercial enterprises. Various federal regulations pertaining to the definition of group living arrangements, food-stamp eligibility, and the distinction of small community ICF/MRs (all of which relate to an occupant census of less than 15) reinforce this idea.

Furthermore, residents show more gain when they comprise a reasonably matched and sized group. However, there are distinct differences between the milieu of residences that have more intellectually handicapped residents and the milieu of those that have minimally intellectually impaired but physically disabled persons. Furthermore, the use of residences for more severely intellectually disabled individuals may change the design and character of the model.[2] More specific research is still needed that will observe and define the residence-environment variables associated with cooperative household living.

Rehabilitative Intent

Research literature confirms some of the notions inherent in Bjaanes and Butler's typology, particularly in the instances where habilitation technologies are used and the program model for adults is cooperative group living rather than surrogate family living. In this regard, several conclusions seem apparent. A high degree of program intensity, when coupled with a sound behavioral methodology, seems to produce greater learning of new behaviors. Also, when residence staff are comfortable with their own feelings toward disability and correspondingly exert a high degree of effort, residents develop more appropriately. At the same time, those residences that encourage wider use of community resources facilitate development of independence in community-use skills in their occupants. Growth and the acquisition of new skills are also associated with residences that, even at the risk of failure, provide for individualization and autonomy.

Resident characteristics, such as degree of disability, affect rate of development, extent of interpersonal interactions, and rehabilitative methods used. The social character of residences, defined partially as a function of the disabling condition, has yet to be fully explored. However, it seems that the residence's group character and extent of socially integrative activities can affect friendship patterns among residents. As a greater number of more disabled persons use this living alternative, residence characteristics will take on greater import. Over-

---

[2] It would seem evident that certain variables, such as degree of cognitive impairment and physical and health status, would have an effect upon the nature of a community residential program designed to serve persons with profound disability. However, the model that best serves this population has yet to be empirically defined.

all, it can be concluded that rehabilitative intent is closely associated with outcome in the residence experience. Residences that carefully plan the intents of cooperative living experiences, and integrate these with a strong reliance on community resources, demonstrate more relevant gains among their occupants.

Management System

Although the research literature does not yet fully analyze management practices, it does indicate that administrative practices that promote a resident-centered environment also produce a more normative home, with greater resident gain. Administrative practices that permit the staff to focus their attention on providing a homelike atmosphere, and that promote staff initiative while at the same time designating specific accountability, are associated with greater gains in the areas of community and personal self-sufficiency. Management, perhaps, represents the greatest unknown in community residence literature, but as the use of community residences continues to grow, more research in variations in the management system is imperative.

An extensive body of knowledge seems to substantiate the program-oriented tenets inherent in normalization as it applies to community residences. However, the deficits in research that examines the environmental tenets are evident (e.g., too often the effects of the character of the home are not taken into account in comparison efforts). The work of Flynn, Mayeda, and others in meeting the research challenge offered by Wolfensberger and Glenn (1975a) is encouraging. Although requiring further substantiation, the preliminary findings of Mayeda and his colleagues that identify six factors, all but one positively correlated with gain, seem to represent encouraging support for the general tenets of the normalization ideology upon which a number of programs and developmental service systems are built. The current community residence literature would profit from a well-designed study examining the ratings inherent in Mayeda's General Environment, Location and Accessibility, and Comfort and Physical Setting factors. Such a study would also provide, in a systematic manner, a reliable measure of the effects of a normative environment and of the use of integrative methodologies.

Baker, Seltzer, and Seltzer (1979) have given us a dimensional perspective of community residences. Nevertheless, the development of validation mechanisms to determine the spread of a typology within one segment of a particular dimension of residence environments (similar to the mechanism posited by Bjaanes and Butler) is in order. Clinical judgment tells us that some homes have characteristics that make them more of a home than others; this intuitive factor now needs to be made operational. Furthermore, the vagaries of social policy are well known (Levine and Levine, 1970). It should also be considered that deinstitutionalization and communitization are derived from an ideologically based social policy, but are not yet fully substantiated by an exhaustive body of research. For, as Zigler and Meunchow (1979) note, "the problem with social policy based largely on good intentions is that the pendulum can swing very quickly in the opposite direction" (p. 994).

Several questions raised still need to be addressed. The character of the staff has been described, but differences attributed to gain have not been isolated within a research design. Normative practices are an abstraction that an instrument like PASS can measure; however, implementers of the residence model within any state's continuum of care need operational anchors upon which to base standards and design efforts. Therefore, more explicit research is necessary. The intent of research efforts would not be to produce a system of identical residences, because each residence is its own system and by design needs to be so. Instead, research should offer more concrete direction toward fulfilling the intent upon which the community residence model is based.

ACKNOWLEDGMENTS

The author is indebted to Robert Lubin and Howard Gold for their invaluable editorial comments.

REFERENCES

Aanes, D., and Moen, M. 1976. Adaptive behavior changes of group home residents. Ment. Retard. 14:36–40.

Aninger, M., and Bolinsky, K. 1977. Levels of independent functioning of retarded adults in apartments. Ment. Retard. 15:12–13.

Anthony, W. A. 1977. Psychological rehabilitation: A concept in need of a method. Am. Psychol. 32:658–662.

Baker, B. L., Seltzer, G., and Seltzer, M. M. 1979. As Close as Possible: Community Residences for Retarded Adults. Little, Brown, and Company, Boston.

Balla, D. A. 1976. Relationship of institution size to quality of care: A review of the literature. Am. J. Ment. Defic. 81:117–124.

Balla, D. A., Butterfield, E. C., and Zigler, E. 1974. Effects of institutionalization on retarded children: A longitudinal cross-institutional investigation. Am. J. Ment. Defic. 78:530–549.

Bernstein, G. S., and Karan, O. C. 1979. Obstacles to vocational normalization for the developmentally disabled. Rehabil. Lit. 40(3):66–71.

Birenbaum, A., and Re, M. A. 1979. Resettling mentally retarded adults in the community—about four years later. Am. J. Ment. Defic. 38:323–329.

Bjaanes, A. T., and Butler, E. W. 1974. Environmental variation in community care facilities for mentally retarded persons. Am. J Ment. Defic. 78:429–439.

Bjaanes, A. T., Butler, E. W., and Kelly, B. R. 1980. Placement type and client functional level factors in provision of sources aimed at increased adjustment. In: R. Bruininks, C. E. Meyers, B. B. Sigford, and K. C. Lakin (eds.), Deinstitutionalization and Community Adjustment of Developmentally Disabled Persons. AAMD Monograph, Washington, D.C.

Brody, G. H., and Stoneman, Z. 1977. Social competencies in the developmentally disabled: Some suggestions for research and training. Ment. Retard. 15:41–43.

Browder, J. A., Ellis, L., and Neal, J. 1974. Foster homes: Alternatives to institutions? Ment. Retard. 12:33–36.

Brown, J. S., and Guard, K. A., 1979. The treatment environment for retarded persons in nursing homes. Ment. Retard. 17:77–82.

Bruininks, R. H., Hauber, F. A., and Kudla, M. J. 1979. National Survey of Community Residential Facilities: A Profile of Facilities and Residents in 1977. Department of Psychoeducational Studies, University of Minnesota, Minneapolis.

Bruininks, R. H., Hauber, F. A., and Kudla, M. J. 1980. National survey of community residential facilities: A profile of facilities and residents in 1977. Am. J. Ment. Defic. 84:470–478.

Bruininks, R. H., Hill, B. K., and Thorsheim, M. J. 1980. A Profile of Specially Licensed Foster Homes for Mentally Retarded People in 1977. Department of Psychoeducational Studies, University of Minnesota, Minneapolis.

Butler, E. W., and Bjaanes, A. T. 1977. A typology of community care facilities and differential normalization outcomes. In: P. Mittler (ed.), Research to Practice in Mental Retardation, Vol. 1. Care and Intervention. University Park Press, Baltimore.

Butler, E. W., and Bjaanes, A. T. 1978. Activities on the use of time by retarded persons in community care facilities. In: G. P. Sackett (ed.), Observing Behavior, Vol. 1. Theory and Applications in Mental Retardation. University Park Press, Baltimore.

Butler, E. W., Bjaanes, A. T., and Hofacre, S. 1975. The normalization process and the utilization of community agencies, services, and programs by community care facilities. Paper presented at the 99th Annual Meeting of the American Association on Mental Deficiency, Portland, Oregon.

Campbell, A. C. 1971. Aspects of personal independence of mentally subnormal and severely subnormal adults in hospital and in local authority hostels. Int. J. Soc. Psychiatry 17:305–310.

Close, D. W. 1977. Community living for severely and profoundly retarded adults: A group home study. Educ. Train. Ment. Retard. 12:256–262.

Crawford, J. L., Aiello, J. R., and Thompson, E. D. 1979. Deinstitutionalization and community placement: Clinical and environmental factors. Ment. Retard. 17:59–63.

DDPRSCA. 1979. 1977 National summary between public and community residential findings: Brief no. 3. Developmental Disabilities Project on Residential Services and Community Adjustment, University of Minnesota, Minneapolis.

DeMaine, G. C. 1978. Empirical validation of PASS 3: A first step in service evaluation through environmental assessment. Unpublished manuscript, University of California, Los Angeles.

Diller, L., Fordyce, W., Jacobs, D., and Brown, M. 1978. Post-institutional placement project: Evaluation report. Unpublished manuscript, Rehabilitation Indicators Project, NYC Medical Center, New York.

Dunn, L. M. 1969. Small, special purpose residential facilities for the retarded.

98   Janicki

In: R. B. Kugel and W. Wolfensberger (eds.), Changing Patterns in Residential Services for the Mentally Retarded. President's Committee on Mental Retardation, Washington, D.C.

Dybwab, G. 1970. Architecture's role in revitalizing the field of mental retardation. J. Ment. Subnorm. 16:45–48.

Edgerton, R. B. 1975. Issues relating to the quality of life among mentally retarded persons. In: M. J. Begab and S. A. Richardson (eds.), The Mentally Retarded and Society: A Social Science Perspective. University Park Press, Baltimore.

Editorial. 1979. Post-occupancy study leads to insights on elderly housing. Architectural Record 166(4):69–76.

Eyman, R. K., DeMaine G. C., and Lei, T. 1979. Relationship between community environments and resident changes in adaptive behavior: A path model. Am. J. Ment. Defic. 83:330–338.

Eyman, R. K., Silverstein, A. B., McLain, R., and Miller, C. 1977. Effects of residential settings on development. In: P. Mittler (ed.), Research to Practice in Mental Retardation, Vol. 1. Care and Intervention. University Park Press, Baltimore.

Fanning, J. W. 1978. The more the merrier—community living arrangements in jeopardy. Unpublished manuscript, University of Alabama Management Training Center, Birmingham, Alabama.

Federal Register. 1978. 43(229), Tuesday, November 28.

Federal Register. 1979. 44(212), Wednesday, October 31.

Fiorelli, J. S. 1978. A comparison of selected categories of behavior in more and less normalized living environments. Developmental Disabilities Program Evaluation and Research Technical Report no. 78–10. Temple University, Philadelphia.

Fiorelli, J. S., and Thurman, S. K. 1979. Client behavior in more and less normalized residential settings. Educ. Train. Ment. Retard. 14:85–94.

Flynn, R. J. 1980. Normalization, PASS, and service quality assessment: How normalizing are current human services? In: R. J. Flynn and K. E. Nitsch (eds.), Normalization, Social Integration, and Community Services. University Park Press, Baltimore.

Gardner, J. M. 1977. Community residential alternatives for the developmentally disabled. Ment. Retard. 15:3–8.

Gerry, W. P. 1975. Selection of homes. In: J. S. Bergman (ed.), Community Homes for the Retarded. Lexington Books, Lexington, Mass.

Gilbert, K. A., and Hemming, H. 1979. Environmental change and psycholinguistic ability of mentally retarded adults. Am. J. Ment. Defic. 83:453–459.

Glenn, L. 1976. The least restrictive alternative in residential care and the principle of normalization. In: M. Kindred, J. Cohen, D. Penrod, and T. Shaffer (eds.), The Mentally Retarded Citizen and the Law. The Free Press, New York.

Golub, K. L. 1979. Valuation of leased group homes. Appraisal J. 47:325–331.

Gunzburg, H. C. 1977. Guided or unguided adjustment to life in the community: An evaluation. J. Practical Approaches Dev. Handicap 1(1):31–36.

Harris, J. M., Veit, S. W., Allen, G. J., and Chinsky, J. M. 1974. Aide-resident ratio and ward population density as mediators of social interaction. Am. J. Ment. Defic. 79:320–326.

Hopstock, P. J., Aiello, J. R., and Baum, A. 1979. Residential crowding research. In: J. R. Aiello and A. Baum (eds.), Residential Crowding and Design. Plenum Publishing Corp., New York.

Intagliata, J. 1979. Factors related to the quality of community adjustment in family care homes. Paper presented at the Conference on Community Adjustment, March 16, 1979, Minneapolis, Minnesota.

Jacobson, J. W., and Schwartz, A. S. 1979. The influence of behavioral, physical, and attitudinal factors on personal development of group home residents: A literature review. Unpublished manuscript, New York State Office of Mental Retardation and Developmental Disabilities, Albany, N.Y.

Janicki, M. P., Jacobson, J. W., and Schwartz, A. A. 1980. Community living alternatives: A demographic and model base for community consultation. Paper presented at the 38th Annual Meeting of the American Psychological Association, September, Montreal, P. Q.

Janicki, M. P., and Reynolds, W. M. 1979. Evaluation of community residential alternatives. In: R. Petersen (ed.), Report of the Community Living Alternatives Task Force. New York State Office of Mental Retardation and Developmental Disabilities, Albany, N.Y.

Johnson, M. S., and Bailey, J. S. 1977. The modification of leisure behavior in a half-way house for retarded women. J. Appl. Behav. Anal. 10:273–282.

Kastner, L. S., Reppucci, N. D., and Pezzoli, J. J. 1979. Assessing community attitudes toward mentally retarded persons. Am. J. Ment. Defic. 84:137–144.

Kennedy, R. 1978. Physical environment as an educational tool in work with the mentally handicapped: A review of current literature. J. Practical Approaches Dev. Handicap 2(2):4–8.

Kerr, G. 1977. Wardens in hostels for the mentally handicapped. Br. J. Ment. Subnorm. 23:70–75.

King, R. D., and Raynes, N. V. 1968. Patterns of institutional care for the severely subnormal. Am. J. Ment. Defic. 72:700–709.

King, R. D., Raynes, N. V., and Tizard, J. 1971. Patterns of Residential Care: Sociological Studies in Institutions for Handicapped Children. Routledge and Kegan Paul, London.

Knight, R. C., Zimring, C. M., Weitzer, W. H., and Wheeler, H. C. 1978. Effects of the living environment on the mentally retarded (ELEMR) project. In: A. Friedmann, C. Zimring, and E. Zube (eds.), Environmental Design Evaluation. Plenum Publishing Corp., New York.

Landesman-Dwyer, S., Berkson, G., and Romer, D. 1979. Affiliation and friendship of mentally retarded residents in group homes. Am. J. Ment. Defic. 83:571–580.

Landesman-Dwyer, S., Sackett, G. P., and Kleinman, J. S. Small community residences: Does size really matter? Unpublished manuscript, University of Washington, Seattle.

Landesman-Dwyer, S., Stein, J. G., and Sackett, G. P. 1976. Group homes for the mentally retarded: An ecological and behavioral study. Department of Social and Health Services, Olympia, Washington.

Landesman-Dwyer, S., Stein, J. G., and Sackett, G. P. 1978. A behavioral and ecological study of group homes. In: G. P. Sackett (ed.), Observing Behavior, Vol. 1. Theory and Applications in Mental Retardation. University Park Press, Baltimore.

Lensink, B. 1974. One service system at work. In: C. Cherington and G. Dybwab (eds.), New Neighbors: The Retarded Citizens in Quest of a Home. President's Committee on Mental Retardation, Washington, D.C.

Levine, M., and Levine, A. 1970. Social History of Helping Services: Clinic, Court, School, and Community. Appleton-Century-Crofts, New York.

McCormick, M., Balla, D., and Zigler, E. 1975. Resident-care practices in institutions for retarded persons: A cross-institutional, cross-cultural study. Am. J. Ment. Defic. 80:1–17.

McLain, R. E., Silverstein, A. B., Brownlee, L., and Hubbell, M. 1977a. Measuring differences in residential environments among institutions for retarded persons. Psychol. Rep. 41:264–266.

McLain, R. E., Silverstein, A. B., Brownlee, L., and Hubbell, M. 1979. Attitudinal versus ecological approaches to the characterization of institutional treatment environments. Am. J. Community Psychol. 7:159–165.

McLain, R. E., Silverstein, A. B., Hubbell, M., and Brownlee, L. 1975. The characterization of residential environments within a hospital for the mentally retarded. Ment. Retard. 13:24–27.

McLain, R. E., Silverstein, A. B., Hubbell, M., and Brownlee, L. 1977b. Comparison of the residential environments of a state hospital for retarded clients with those of various types of community facilities. J. Community Psychol. 5:282–289.

Madle, R. A. 1978. Alternative residential placements. In: J. T. Neisworth and R. M. Smith (eds.), Retardation: Issues, Assessment, and Intervention. McGraw-Hill Book Company, New York.

Marbolin, D., O'Toole, K. M., Touchette, P. E., Berger, P. L., and Doyle, D. A. 1979. "I'll have a Big Mac, large fries, large coke, and apple pie," . . . or teaching adaptive community skills. Behav. Ther. 10:236–248.

May, A. E. 1976. A new hostel for the mentally handicapped and its effects on social development. Br. J. Ment. Subnorm. 22:41–46.

Mayeda, T. 1979. The use of client data in program planning and analysis. In: P. Sanofsky (ed.), Evaluating Program Effectiveness: The Administrator's Dilemma. SPS Communications, Inc., Watertown, Mass.

Mulvihill, M. S. 1978. Bridging the gap between the group home and independent living. J. Practical Approaches Dev. Handicap 2(2):9–11.

Newman, E. S., and Sherman, S. R. 1979–80. Foster-family care for the elderly: Surrogate family or mini-institution? Int. J. Aging Hum. Dev. 10:165–176.

Nihira, L., and Nihira, K. 1975. Normalized behavior in community placement. Ment. Retard. 13:9–13.

O'Connor, G. 1976. Home is a Good Place: A National Perspective of Community Residential Facilities for Developmentally Disabled Persons. American Association on Mental Deficiency, Washington, D.C.

O'Connor, G., and Sitkei, E. G. 1975. Study of a new frontier in community services: Residential facilities for the developmentally disabled. Ment. Retard. 13:35–39.

Provencal, G., and MacCormack, J. P. 1979. Adult foster care: Paradox and possibility. DD Polestar 1(7):4.

Race, D. G., and Race, D. M. 1978. Evaluation of a group home for mentally handicapped adults. Br. J. Ment. Subnorm. 24:49–61.

Reizenstein, J., and McBride, W. 1978. Designing for mentally retarded people: A socio-environmental evaluation of New England Villages, Inc. In: A. Friedmann, C. Zimring, and E. Zube (eds.), Environmental Design Evaluation. Plenum Publishing Corp., New York.

Rodman, D. H., and Collins, M. J. 1974. A community residence program: An alternative to institutional living for the mentally retarded. Training School Bull. 71:52–61.

Roos, P. 1972. Reconciling behavior modification procedures with the normalization principle. In: W. Wolfensberger (ed.), Normalization: The Principle of Normalization in Human Services. National Institute on Mental Retardation, Toronto, Ontario.

Schalock, R. L., and Harper, R. S. 1979. Training in independent living can be done. J. Rehabil. Admin. 3:129–132.

Scheerenberger, R. C. 1977. Deinstitutionalization in perspective. In: J. L. Paul, D. J. Stedman, and G. R. Neufeld (eds.), Deinstitutionalization: Program and Policy Development. Syracuse University Press, Syracuse.

Schinke, S. P., and Wong, D. E. 1977. Evaluation of staff training in group homes for retarded persons. Am. J. Ment. Defic. 82:130–136.

Schroeder, S. R., and Henes, C. 1978. Assessment of progress of institutionalized and deinstitutionalized retarded adults: A matched-control comparison. Ment. Retard. 16:147–148.

Seltzer, M. M., and Seltzer, G. B. 1977. Community living: Accommodations and vocations. In: P. Mittler (ed.), Research to Practice in Mental Retardation, Vol. 1. Care and Intervention. University Park Press, Baltimore.

Stacy, D., Doleys, D. M., and Malcolm, R. 1979. Effects of social-skills training in a community-based program. Am. J. Ment. Defic. 84:152–158.

Thakur, P. K. 1974. Benefits of hostel care. APEX: J. Inst. Ment. Subnorm. 2(1):8–10.

Thurman, S. K., and Fiorelli, J. S. 1979. Perspectives on normalization. J. Spec. Educ. 13:339–346.

Tizard, J. 1964. Community Services for the Mentally Handicapped. Oxford University Press, New York.

Welch, E. L., and Iaquinta, M. R. 1979. Staff burn-out factors and their implications for interviewing, orienting, and training staff in community residences for mentally retarded adults. Paper presented at 26th Annual Conference, AAMD, Region X, Waterville Valley, N.H.

Willer, B., and Intagliata, J. 1979. Environment, characteristics, and effectiveness of community residences for the mentally retarded. Paper presented at the Conference on Impact of Specific Settings on Behavior and Development, September, University of California, Los Angeles.

Willms, D. 1979. An investigation of public attitudes and concerns. Deficience Mentale/Ment. Retard. 24(4):10–15.

Wolfe, M. 1975. Room size, group size, and density: Behavior patterns in a children's psychiatric facility. Environ. Behav. 7:199–224.

Wolfensberger, W. 1972. Normalization: The Principle of Normalization in Human Services. National Institute on Mental Retardation, Toronto, Ontario.

Wolfensberger, W. 1980. The definition of normalization: Update, problems, disagreements, and misunderstandings. In: R. J. Flynn and K. E. Nitsch (eds.), Normalization, Social Integration, and Community Services. University Park Press, Baltimore.

Wolfensberger, W., and Glenn, L. 1975a. PASS 3—Program Analysis of Service Systems; A Method for the Quantitative Evaluation of Human Services: Field Manual. National Institute on Mental Retardation, Toronto.

Wolfensberger, W., and Glenn, L. 1975b. PASS 3—Program Analysis of Service Systems: A Method for the Quantitative Evaluation of Human Services: Handbook. National Institute on Mental Retardation, Toronto.

Ziemianski, L. 1977. An exploratory survey of the interrelationships of community residences for the handicapped with their surrounding localities. Unpublished manuscript, Eleanor Roosevelt Developmental Services, Schenectady, N.Y.

Zigler, E., and Muenchow, S. 1979. Mainstreaming: The proof is in the implementation. Am. Psychol. 34:993–996.

Living Environments for Developmentally Retarded Persons
Edited by H. Carl Haywood and J. R. Newbrough
Copyright 1981 University Park Press Baltimore

Organizational Design and the Social Environment in Group Homes for Mentally Retarded Persons

Cary Cherniss, Ph.D.
Illinois Institute for Developmental Disabilities
1640 West Roosevelt Road
Chicago, Illinois 60608

In this chapter we present a model describing how the social environment of a group home for retarded individuals may be influenced by its organizational design. The model summarizes what is already known about the impact of organizational design on group homes and also suggests a number of potentially fruitful research issues. To the extent that the model is empirically valid, it should also be a valuable framework for designing, modifying, evaluating, or managing a group home for mentally retarded persons.

ORGANIZATIONAL DESIGN

"Organizational design" refers to those aspects of a setting's social organization that can be readily manipulated by planners, administrators, or staff, including the structure of roles, the lines of authority, the decision-making rules, and the patterns of communication. Moos (1973) has suggested that there are at least six distinct ways of conceptualizing a social environment, one of which was identified as organizational structure or design.

During the last two decades, there has been growing recognition that organizational structure and climate significantly affect the attitudes and behavior of both "keepers" and "kept" in residential treatment programs. In one early work, Colarelli and Siegel (1966) found that modifying the organizational structure of a psychiatric ward dra-

103

matically improved staff morale and patient care. Specifically, they changed the role structure on the ward, making the psychiatric attendants the primary therapists for the patients, and giving them complete responsibility for making decisions concerning a patient's treatment and care. To make the innovation successful, the researchers found that the roles of the professional staff (nurses, psychologists, psychiatrists) also had to be modified. Gradually, these professionals became consultants to the aides, providing training, technical assistance, and support to facilitate the aides' work.

In a more recent experiment, Goldenberg (1971) developed a community residential setting for hard-core unemployed, inner-city youth. Situated in a house located in a residential neighborhood, the Residential Youth Center served 20 youths, ages 17 to 21 years, and employed eight staff members. The residents had previously been incarcerated in jails, mental hospitals, and institutions for the mentally retarded. Several had been diagnosed as schizophrenic or mentally retarded. Like Colarelli and Siegel (1966), Goldenberg initially decided that the program's success would greatly depend on its organizational design. After much study and thought, he developed what he called "horizontal structure." In this organizational design, each staff member carried a case load and had sole responsibility for making decisions concerning those clients. Also, each staff member had the opportunity to develop a program of activity (e.g., karate lessons, wood work, group therapy) for the residents and other staff members. In order to break down barriers to communication, each staff member was required to perform other staff roles at least once each month. Thus, each staff member (including the house director and the secretary) was required to cook a meal each month, to live-in one or two nights, and to perform all other roles at some point. Finally, administrative tasks were distributed among the staff, blurring the distinction between staff and administration. Decisions affecting the program as a whole were made collectively by the entire staff. A House Council also was established through which the residents could participate in making important decisions.

The rationale for horizontal structure as implemented at the Residential Youth Center was that the structure of roles and decision-making in programs often undermines morale, creates barriers to communication, generates inter-group and inter-personal conflict that cannot be resolved, and ultimately diminishes the effectiveness and humaneness of programs. Even though morale, commitment, and cooperation may be high during the early period of a program, over time the motivation and excitement diminish, mistrust and apathy increase, and signs of institutionalism begin to appear. Goldenberg (1971) hoped that, by modifying the organizational design, the diseases of institutionalism and burn-out could be prevented.

Although there has been growing recognition that organizational design may significantly affect the social environment in group homes for mentally retarded persons, most consultants and administrators have lacked a coherent framework for designing or modifying the organizational structure. As psychotherapists or diagnosticians, they have been able to choose from a wide assortment of well-developed conceptual frameworks (e.g., psychoanalytic theory, behavior modification) that provided conceptual road maps for helping the professional navigate the complex process of helping a handicapped individual. However, when these same practitioners attempted to treat handicapped programs, there was no readily available framework to guide their efforts.

Potentially useful conceptual tools have existed for some time. Researchers in organizational science and social psychology have developed several constructs for representing the social organization of settings, and their studies have indicated some of the relationships between social organization and individual attitudes and behavior. However, two factors have made this knowledge inaccessible to consultants and administrators working in human service organizations: 1) most of the research was conducted in business or industrial organizations, which are different in certain important respects from human service organizations; and 2) no one involved in the human services has attempted to integrate all of this research into a single, practical conceptual model.

The next section of this chapter presents a model suggesting a number of organizational characteristics that significantly influence the social environment of group homes. The model is based on a good deal of relevant empirical research, but also suggests unanswered questions and issues requiring more research.

DESCRIPTION OF THE MODEL

Imagine a group home for mentally retarded persons situated in a residential community. There are a number of resident-clients and a smaller number of staff-helpers who may or may not live on the premises. Within this group home, certain tasks must be performed—some routine, others not. To ensure that the tasks are performed, roles are created, rules are evolved about who makes what decisions, and some procedure is developed for monitoring the status of the home environment and for making necessary changes. An organizational design emerges very soon after the group home becomes operational.

Organizational design can directly influence the social environment experienced by the residents; however, it can also influence residents indirectly through its impact on the staff. For instance, the decision-making structure may directly influence the residents. Jones (1976) and Fairweather and associates (Fairweather et al., 1969) have shown that involving residents directly in the decision-making process can improve the social climate of the setting and can contribute to growth and to improvement in the residents. On the other hand, the decision-making structure also affects the helpers. Goldenberg (1971) has argued that when the helpers (i.e., the staff members working directly with the residents most of the time) are allowed to participate more in making decisions concerning treatment, they make better-informed decisions and the helpers' commitment to the residents increases; both of these consequences are beneficial to the residents. Thus, any aspect of organizational design can influence the mentally retarded client either directly or indirectly, through its effect on the primary helpers.

This chapter concentrates on the second effect—the impact of organizational design on the helper. One rationale for this focus is that it tends to be the more neglected one in the field of mental retardation. Much more research and writing has been concerned with the effect of the social environment directly on the mentally retarded client.

In Figure 1, a working model is presented that suggests how a group home's organizational design influences the residents through its impact on the helper and the helping relationship. It should be emphasized that the model only indicates the impact of organizational design. There are many other factors in addition to organizational design that influence the attitudes and behavior of the helpers that are not shown in the model. These factors include any training or previous experience in which the helper may have been involved, the helper's personal life, and the helper's personality. Also omitted here is the group home's external environment, which includes a host of important variables, such as level of funding, bureaucratic rules and actions occurring at higher levels, and community attitudes toward the home and toward mentally retarded persons in general. The model also does not include other aspects of the home's social environment that may have a significant impact on the helpers, such as the physical design. Despite the model's limited scope, organizational design is nevertheless an important force influencing helpers.

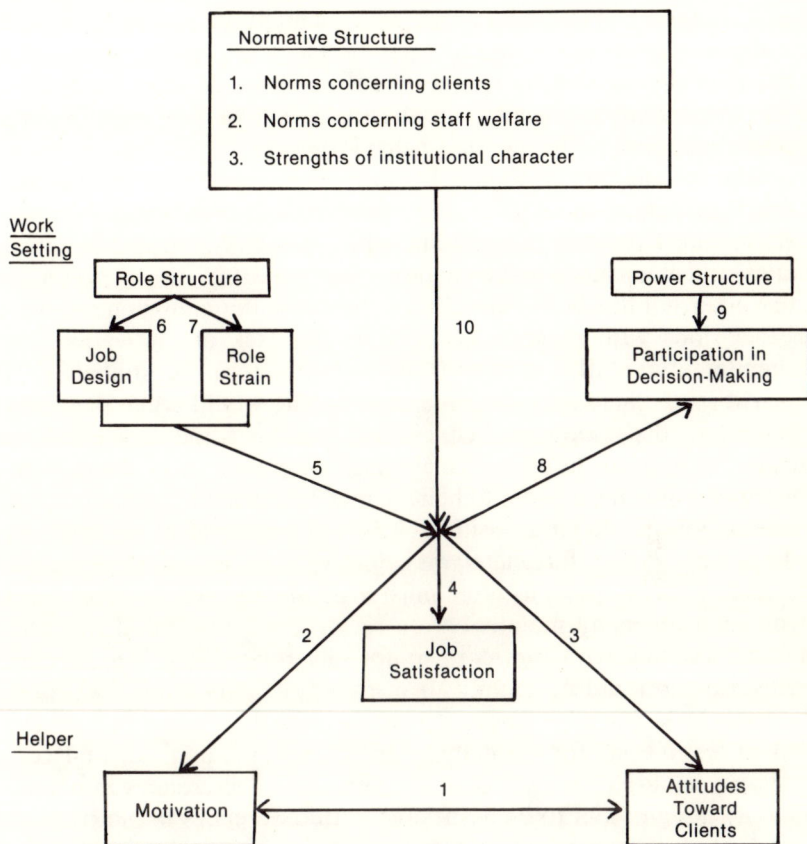

Figure 1.   A model of organizational design and its influence on the helper.

THE HELPER

On the bottom half of Figure 1, there are three boxes representing characteristics of the helper that are influenced by organizational design and that, in turn, influence the helper's treatment of residents in a group home. The box on the right, *Attitudes Toward Clients*, refers to attitudes, values, and beliefs concerning mentally retarded persons. What are mentally retarded persons capable of learning and doing? What are their needs? Are they different from nonretarded people, and if so, how? What methods of care and treatment are most desirable? When a resident acts up, what is the probable cause of his or her behavior? Is it caused by the retardation? By a perverse streak in his or her personality? Or is it more likely to be a reaction to the immediate social context? Those who work with mentally retarded persons in group homes on a day-to-day basis probably do not sit down and systematically answer these questions, but they do answer them at some level of consciousness, and these answers become attitudes and assumptions that influence their behavior.

The second box of Figure 1, *Motivation*, represents another important helper characteristic. Too often, staff in institutions for mentally retarded persons become apathetic, bored, careless about their duties, and mechanical in their actions. For these staff, the motto seems to be "Do as little as possible." They perform the minimum required of their jobs without enthusiasm. It is this lack of motivation and commitment in staff that often is meant by the term "custodial."

Although there may be some experts who would argue that mentally retarded persons are helpless and that no amount of effort by helpers in a group home will make any difference to profoundly retarded persons, most seem to believe that concerted human effort can eventually bring about a positive change in the world of the mentally retarded person. Unfortunately, a helper working in a group home for mentally retarded persons often must maintain a high level of zeal and dedication for many months before seeing even minimal change; for helpers working with the more profoundly retarded, a high level of motivation is required simply to maintain a humane level of care. Nevertheless, work by Sarata (1974) suggests that even in large residential institutions for mentally retarded persons, one can find considerable variation in level of staff motivation. Differences in organizational design seem to be associated with differences in motivation.

Attitudes and motivation can also each influence the other (Figure 1, Arrow 1). In an intensive study of a mental hospital, Stotland and Kobler (1965) found that when organizational problems led to a reduction in staff motivation, many staff members adopted more pessimistic attitudes about the patients and their chances of recovery. A similar phenomenon was observed in an earlier study by Schwartz and Will (1961). Conversely, Sarason et al. (1966) found that when public school teachers were told that a student in their class was emotionally disturbed, they often reduced the amount of effort expended to work with the student. Their attitude seemed to be, "If this student is disturbed, there's nothing I can do to help. In fact, if I persist in working with this student, I might even do real damage. This sort of problem is just over my head." In this case, a change in perception and attitude seemed to result in a reduction in motivation. Sarason et al. (1966) aptly called this the "Hands-Off Phenomenon."

The third box, in the bottom half of Figure 1, represents *Job Satisfaction*. This component of the model is based on a simple but important idea: Staff members in a group home for mentally retarded persons are essentially performing a job; thus, their attitudes and behavior will be influenced by the factors that influence any workers.

In many jobs, there is scant relationship among the elements of job satisfaction, motivation, and performance (Lawler, 1973). For instance, a dissatisfied worker on an assembly line who is closely supervised by a foreman will work as fast and as well as one who is satisfied. Job satisfaction in such a work setting may influence absenteeism and turnover, but performance on the job may not require a high level of motivation or job satisfaction. One important difference to consider when comparing those who weld fenders onto passing automobile frames and those who care for mentally retarded persons is that, in the latter job, motivation appears to make more difference in on-the-job performance. Thus, to the extent that job satisfaction influences a helper's motivational level, it also will influence his or her performance.

To what extent does helper job satisfaction influence helper motivation in group homes for mentally retarded persons? One probably can find instances in which moderate changes in satisfaction with the job have had no effect on a helper's motivation and performance. For example, McIntyre (1969) observed that classroom teachers in an elementary school did not seem to be affected when a new, highly authoritarian superintendent began making policy decisions that made the teachers angry and increasingly dissatisfied. The erosion in morale may have prompted some teachers to look for positions in other districts, but when they walked into the classroom, the organizational problems seemed to be left behind. Lower job satisfaction did not seem to affect motivation or performance in the helping role.

Conversely, one can also find instances in which staff members have been happy and satisfied, but minimally motivated to perform well in the helping aspects of their work. Staff working in group homes for mentally retarded persons may perform minimally while enjoying the security, the friendly relations with coworkers, and the salary associated with their jobs. Staff may become satisfied without any increase in motivation or effort. Thus, the satisfaction-motivation link cannot be assumed at this time, but must be carefully studied in future research. There may be a relationship, but it is a complicated one, contingent on the presence or absence of other, unknown factors.

Even if research eventually showed no direct link between helper job satisfaction and motivation on the job, there are other ways in which job satisfaction can influence the social environment and the residents' welfare. For instance, there seems to be a link between job satisfaction and physical illness in workers (Caplan et al., 1975). Workers who are more dissatisfied tend to lose more days of work because of sickness, which can seriously interfere with programming in a group home. Also, low job satisfaction may contribute to increases in staff turnover. Some administrators argue that high staff turnover is good because it ensures that the staff will be fresh, idealistic, and committed. Unfortunately, high turnover will not produce this effect. In fact, the less competent, less idealistic, and less motivated staff may be just the ones who stay when working conditions are adverse.

High staff turnover tends to carry with it high costs, both economic and psychological. Even in group homes that make a minimal investment in orientation and training of new staff, a certain amount of extra staff time is required to break in a new person, and the psychological costs for residents may be great. Balla (personal communication, 1977) noted that, in a study of seven institutions for the mentally retarded in Connecticut, higher staff turnover was associated with more wariness in the patients. It seems plausible to infer that when staff turnover is high, the retarded residents must deal with a highly turbulent environment—much more interpersonally turbulent than the environment experienced by people not in residential treatment. Such an environment is highly stressful and may adversely affect rehabilitation. Practitioners undoubtedly can point to instances when mentally retarded clients have regressed because of changes in caregivers, teachers, or some other aspect of their environment. Thus, even if low job satisfaction does not directly affect helper motivation during work hours, it eventually may adversely affect care in other, more subtle ways. Until research has clearly established the role of job satisfaction in the quality of care, any aspects of organizational design that seem to affect it should be considered. (See also Zaharia and Baumeister, 1978, 1979a, 1979b.)

THE WORK SETTING

In the top half of Figure 1 are the major components of organizational design that seem to influence a helper's job satisfaction, motivation, and attitudes toward clients. *Role Structure* refers to the way in which tasks and duties are allocated among staff and residents in a group home. Numerous tasks must be performed regularly, including cooking, cleaning, outside maintenance, the planning of activities, training and educational programming, individual counseling and support, as well as a host of administrative functions. To ensure that these tasks are performed adequately and efficiently, roles are created that combine a number of seemingly related tasks, and then the roles are assigned to particular individuals. The individuals are then evaluated primarily on how effectively they perform their assigned roles.

Although the way in which various tasks should be combined into roles may often be obvious to those in a particular group home, there is, in fact, a universe of alternatives. For instance, cooking is a necessary function. In some group homes, a special role, "cook," is created to perform the function. In other homes, no special role is created; instead, the staff on duty are expected to cook the meals in addition to performing their other duties. In still other group homes, cooking the meals is seen as something that the residents should do for themselves.

The way in which roles are defined has a direct impact upon residents. In one group home, all staff members were expected to sit down regularly with the residents assigned to them and to provide personal counseling (which was seen as a major part of the rehabilitation program). However, the staff found that so much of their time went into group supervision and crises (e.g., fights and accidents) that the important counseling work was being neglected. Thus, the house director decided to take one of the staff and designate her as "Treatment Specialist." She was relieved of other responsibilities and thus could ensure that all residents received approximately 90 minutes of personal counseling each week. In this case, a change in the role structure directly changed the amount and quality of individual attention provided to the residents.

The role structure of a home also affects the residents indirectly through its impact on the *Job Satisfaction* and *Motivation* of the staff (Arrows 4, 5, 6, 7, and 8 in Figure 1). Recent work by Hackman and Oldham (1975) has demonstrated how the role structure of a work setting determines the *Job Design* for the employee, which in turn influences the motivating potential of the job. A number of job design components that seem to influence the motivating potential have been identified, including the amount of variety, challenge, autonomy, feedback, task identity, contact with people, participation, information, and learning experienced in the job. (These components are listed and defined in Table 1.)

Sarata (1974) studied job design in three institutions for the mentally retarded and found that it did influence employee job satisfaction and did vary as a function of the institutional role structure. Two of the institutions were structured along traditional lines. Staff roles were specialized, clearly defined, and segregated in a rigid fashion. In these settings, variety, autonomy, learning, and several other job design dimensions tended to be low, and when these dimensions were low, staff job satisfaction tended to be low. In the third institution, an innovative administration had modified the traditional staff roles in a way that significantly increased variety and autonomy. All staff had

Table 1.   Dimensions of job design defined

Dimension	Definition
1. Variety	The extent to which the job involves change and variety in responsibilities and procedures.
2. Autonomy	The extent to which the job permits independent thinking and acting.
3. Challenge	The extent to which the job allows the worker to test his or her ability and to achieve optimally difficult tasks.
4. Task-Identity	The extent to which the job allows worker to work on a project from its planning until its completion, to work with a case or client from referral to termination, or to be involved in many aspects of service provided to client.
5. Feedback	The extent to which the job yields results that the worker can see.
6. Participation	Amount of worker involvement in planning future programs and in making administrative decisions affecting large parts of organization.
7. Information	The extent to which the worker is kept informed about decisions, plans, and activities affecting the job.
8. Learning	Amount of opportunity for worker to learn new techniques and approaches.
9. Contact	Opportunity for informal contact with other workers.

to work in more than one program, and, consequently, their work was more varied and challenging. They were more informed about what was happening in the institution because they came in contact with more parts of it, and they were given more opportunities for learning new skills and knowledge. Not surprisingly, staff job satisfaction was considerably higher in the institution where the role structure provided a more motivating job design.

ROLE STRAIN

A second line of research has examined the problem of *Role Strain* in organizational settings. Like job design, the level of role strain is a direct function of the setting's role structure. Early work in a variety of settings by Kahn et al. (1964) identified two types of role strain that affected worker job satisfaction: role conflict and role ambiguity. In jobs characterized by high role conflict, the worker is expected to do too many things or to do things that conflict. In an example described above, the staff in a group home initially were expected to do individual counseling and also to provide continuous group supervision. Given the number of staff on duty at any given time, staff found that they could not adequately perform both functions. Until the role structure was changed by creating a new role, the staff experienced a high level of role conflict and strain. The model depicted in Figure 1 suggests that, eventually, this high degree of strain could contribute to lower job satisfaction and reduced motivation (Arrows 5, 4, and 2).

The other type of role strain identified by Kahn et al. (1964), role ambiguity, refers to the extent to which role expectations are clearly communicated to the worker. When role occupants are not sure what they should be doing because they have not been told, or when the messages have been unclear, role strain occurs. If a worker in a group home is hired after a five-minute, pro forma interview, is given little orientation to the job, and is given unclear messages about what he or she should be doing while on duty, then the result is likely to be frustration, dissatisfaction, and a sense of hopelessness. The worker is likely to say, "Well, if no one can tell me what I'm supposed to be doing, why bother? I'll just lay low, take it easy, and look busy when one of the big wheels is around!"

Maslach (1976) has suggested some of the ways in which role strain can detrimentally influence staff working in human service programs. Her research has revealed that, in many instances, helpers are faced with impossible role demands. Case loads may be so large that helpers cannot possibly do what they should do for all of their clients, or they may be asked to do things for which they have had no training.

Impossible demands produce emotional strain in helpers, to which they respond in a variety of ways. Some simply quit; others somehow maintain a high level of commitment and personal involvement in their work, but their personal lives are adversely affected. Many others, however, cope with high role strain by emotionally withdrawing from their clients; often they stop thinking of their clients as people. Helpers may use jargon, labels, or humorous put-downs to maintain emotional distance between themselves and their clients, or they may respond to clients in a formal, detached, businesslike fashion, thereby discouraging clients from making demands on their time and energy. In some cases, the helper may even withdraw physically, as when workers in an institution for mentally retarded persons spend most of their time playing cards together in their glass-enclosed office. In all these instances, the result is ineffective and inhumane care.

Maslach has labeled this syndrome of role strain, emotional with-drawal, and impersonal care as "burn-out," and argues that it is a widespread problem in human service programs. To the extent that the role structure in a group home creates role strain, the helper will "burn out," and care and treatment of the mentally retarded client will deteriorate.

POWER STRUCTURE

Power Structure is a second element of organizational design that in-fluences helper job satisfaction, motivation, and performance in group homes for the retarded. Role structure refers to the way in which tasks, functions, and duties are allocated among members of a setting; power structure refers to the way in which power and authority are allocated among members. Many duties must be performed, and many decisions must be made (including decisions concerning who will perform the duties). How will these decisions be made? Who will participate in making these decisions? To whom is any given member of the program accountable? Who has authority over whom? The answers to these questions define the power structure of group homes and other settings.

Recent research by Cherniss and Egnatios (1978b) suggests that *Participation in Decision-Making* is a major concern of staff in community mental health programs, including programs for the mentally retarded. They examined a number of work-related decisions normally made in programs and found that, in every instance, staff wanted a greater voice than they currently had. Their research also suggested that the frustrated desire for more participation was con-tributing to unusually low job satisfaction in these staff (Cherniss and Egnatios, 1978a).

Staff participation in decision-making can influence the quality of group homes in many ways. Oppenheimer (1975) noted that unioni-zation of employees in public sector, human service organizations has become a major phenomenon during the last decade; a major impetus has been a growing sense of alienation and powerlessness in these workers. Although unions often do increase the collective power of employees, especially in areas like wages and fringe benefits, they may nevertheless further limit the employees' power in other ways. Col-lective bargaining agreements may become unwieldy, minutely spec-ifying what workers, as well as what management, can and cannot do on the job. Such restrictiveness limits flexibility; in educational or rehabilitative programs, reduced flexibility usually means reduced ef-fectiveness. Thus, when staff in mental retardation programs are denied a voice in making decisions concerning their work, the chances of unionization are increased. If staff unionize, the provision of care may be affected.

Staff participation in decision-making also may influence the quality of group homes through its effect on the quality of decisions made. Goldenberg (1971) indicated that, in the classical, pyramidal human service organization, those at the bottom tend to work most closely with the clients and thus possess the most information about the extent to which the organization is meeting clients' needs. However, the staff at the top of the pyramid, who make the decisions, have much less of this vital information. It is not surprising that administrators sometimes feel that they must make a decision in the dark, because they *are* in the dark much of the time, and this does affect the quality of those decisions. Goldenberg concluded that, by changing the power structure of the organization so that those who interact most with the clients also participate in decision-making, the quality of the decisions made will be improved.

Increasing staff participation in decision-making, however, is not an easy or a straightforward matter. There are many alternatives for the allocation of tasks and roles, as well as many alternatives for arranging a program for who makes what decisions and how. Who decides on the punishment when a resident in a group home breaks a rule? It could be the group home director, an individual staff member who is assigned to that resident, the staff as a group, or the residents themselves as a group, with or without the staff. Examples of each kind of decision-making arrangement probably occur in existing group homes.

Similarly, one could ask how the decisions concerning discipline and punishment are made. Is there a standard punishment for each type of rule infraction? In this case, the decision is made once and then is simply applied in a standard fashion in the future. On the other hand, the decision might be made on the basis of each individual case. The main point is that there are numerous decisions that are made daily in group homes. Each decision can be made in a number of different ways; how these decisions are made and who makes them constitute the power structure of a group home. The power structure is one aspect of the organizational design that can make or break a group home for mentally retarded persons. Although it is difficult and dangerous to generalize, research suggests that increasing staff and resident participation in decision-making tends to improve morale, motivation, and effectiveness. However, the extent to which this generalization is valid depends on the exact mechanisms developed for giving members a voice in the decision-making process. Some participatory structures could conceivably make matters worse rather than better.

NORMATIVE STRUCTURE

Normative Structure is the last component of organizational design depicted in the model. Although it may be referred to by different names (e.g., organizational climate), most organizational researchers have recognized the importance of the normative structure in defining the quality of life in a setting. Hasenfeld and English (1974) have suggested that, in human service organizations, the normative structure is especially important because the technology is not well-established empirically, outcomes are difficult to measure, and there is a strong moral component to the work, which involves the direct manipulation of people. To cope with the uncertainty and tension created by these factors, elaborate norms and values evolve. For instance, in mental retardation, normalization has become an important goal and value in many community programs. In the absence of hard data, staff working in the mental retardation field can feel more secure if their actions and decisions are somehow congruent with this norm. On the other hand, if normalization has become a strong value in a program, and a staff person acts in a way that violates this norm, strong pressure is often exerted to change the individual or his/her actions. In extreme cases, of course, those who question or oppose a norm may be forced out of the setting completely.

Thus, normative structure refers to the shared values, goals, beliefs, and norms that govern work and life in a group home. These norms and values may be either formal (written down as law) or informal. In larger settings, different groups probably will develop their own normative structure. Allen, Chinsky, and Veit (1974) have described how the aide culture in one institution for mentally retarded persons maintained a set of custodial values and norms that were discrepant with the institution's stated goals of humane treatment and rehabilitation, goals that other groups in the institution (e.g., professional staff) strongly supported. The authors described how one new aide who entered the setting attempted to defy the institution's normative structure, and how strong sanctions were directed against this deviant by other staff. Eventually, this particular aide quit. Undoubtedly, many others in his position who began with his orientation gradually changed and adopted the normative structure, eventually becoming staunch defenders of it. Arrows 10 and 3 of Figure 1 represent this process, in which a helper's attitudes about care and treatment are influenced by the normative structure. If the helper finds the normative structure to be incompatible with his or her attitudes, as in the case described above, job satisfaction may diminish to the point at which absenteeism increases and the person quits. (This effect is represented by Arrows 10 and 5 in Figure 1.)

Group homes for mentally retarded persons differ in the content of their normative structures. Some are primarily custodial, with an emphasis on control, predictability, and efficiency. Others emphasize treatment and rehabilitation. In these programs, staff effort and other program resources are directed toward changing residents' attitudes and toward increasing their skill and ability. In still other homes, the emphasis is on humane care. A high value is placed on the residents' welfare and comfort, without any concerted effort to change the residents. Butler (1977) has referred to these three types of programs as custodial, therapeutic, and maintaining. These terms refer to three types of normative structure that clearly influence staff attitudes and performances.

In addition to differences in norms and values concerning care of residents, group homes also differ in norms and values concerning staff welfare. In many settings, the implicit assumption seems to be that the staff, especially those who care for the residents on a day-to-day basis, are the most expendable resource. Staff are paid poorly, are made to work long hours, and are given little support, recognition, or encouragement. In these programs, administrators and professionals believe that the sole concern should be the care and rehabilitation of the residents. Staff who complain about their working conditions may be regarded simply as selfish and lazy deadbeats who should not be working in the field anyway. Such attitudes may actually be internalized by many of the staff themselves, who come to regard their roles and themselves as expendable and irrelevant. In this case, motivation and commitment will drop. Other staff may consider this lack of concern with their welfare offensive; as a result, their job satisfaction may drop and their performance also may be affected. Thus, the prevailing assumptions, expressed in word and action, about staff and their welfare are another important part of the normative structure of a group home.

Other important aspects of the normative structure in group homes are the strength of and the degree of articulation of a guiding philosophy. In many programs, there is no explicit underlying philosophy. Staff in these programs come to share certain vague norms and assumptions about the clients and how they should be treated. There may be a formal program written on paper somewhere, which is brought out for public relations purposes, but never discussed by staff nor used as a framework for their work. In general, there is little discussion of norms, values, or goals in these programs.

At the other extreme, there are programs with an explicit, frequently proclaimed and discussed ethos. Their philosophy of care or treatment has been carefully developed and articulated. It may be elaborate or simple, but some attempt has been made to translate it into operational guidelines that staff use on a day-to-day basis and refer to frequently. In these programs, staff are often selected on the basis of their demonstrated commitment to the accepted core values and methods. There probably are regular, ongoing orientation and educational programs that impress the guiding philosophy on all staff. Certain rituals and jargon often develop that come to symbolize the program's distinctive focus. Programs that fit this description can be thought of as having strong institutional character (Clark, 1970; Selznick, 1957).

INSTITUTIONAL CHARACTER

A number of writers on human service organizations have argued that strong institutional character enhances staff morale and motivation. Reppucci (1973) wrote: "A guiding idea or philosophy, which is understandable to, and provides hope for, all members of the institution, must be developed in conjunction with those members" (p. 333). In another context, Stotland and Kobler (1965) studied the history of a mental hospital and found that patient progress and welfare seemed to vary as a function of the strength of institutional character. When institutional character was strong, patients progressed in treatment, but when it weakened, patients regressed and attempted suicide more frequently. Because this study was of a single institution, it is impossible to conclude that there was a cause-effect relationship. Nevertheless, the authors were impressed with the consistency of the relationships between institutional character, staff morale and motivation, and treatment effectiveness.

Unfortunately, strong institutional character also can become a handicap for a group home. A single, uniform philosophy can interfere with flexibility, innovation, and autonomy. Programs with strong institutional character can be extremely resistant to change, even when confronted with strong evidence that they are failing or doing harm. A guiding philosophy may enhance morale, but it may also be a shared delusion. If the guiding philosophy is imposed on staff and residents from above, and they are allowed no voice in its development and are given no opportunity to modify it, it can be a source of conflict that eventually leads to lower job satisfaction and reduced motivation in staff.

To maintain strong institutional character while minimizing the potential abuses, two steps need to be taken. First, staff and residents should be involved in the development, implementation, and periodic evaluation of the guiding philosophy. Second, the experimental attitude should be made an important part of a program's guiding philosophy and normative structure. The experimental attitude recognizes that nothing is permanent; every decision, action, and policy must be regarded merely as an experiment, and change should occur continually, based on the results of these experiments. The experimental attitude insists that mistakes and problems are bad for a program only to the extent that the staff and residents do not learn from them.

The actual guiding philosophy that provides the basis for institutional character in human service programs can vary. For instance, some group homes may be organized on the basis of the token economy concept and may use this as the source of their distinctive character. Other group homes may emphasize a self-help concept and use this as the source of their distinctiveness. When institutional character is strong, most of a home's residents and staff may believe that their guiding philosophy is the only true way. However, it may be the case that few guiding philosophies are really better than any others. What does seem to be important and useful is the development of a single, unifying theme and a philosophy of practice that gives the program a strong, unique institutional character, a clear reason for being the way it is. Without a strong, distinct institutional character, there is no spark, no fire, no zeal; and without zeal, there is not sufficient confidence and motivation to sustain effective performance in the helping role.

To summarize, three components of organizational design have been discussed: normative structure, role structure, and power structure. In addition to directly influencing helper job satisfaction, attitudes toward treatment, and motivation, these components of organizational design also interact and influence each other.

QUESTIONS FOR FUTURE RESEARCH

The model presented in this chapter helps to summarize what already is known (with more or less certainty) about the probable effects of the organizational design of group homes for mentally retarded persons. The model also is useful for suggesting questions and issues for future research, some of which are discussed below.

On the most basic level, more research is needed to test and to validate the propositions already presented above. Virtually all of the research on which the model is based was conducted in other types of settings. Some of these research settings were other human service organizations that can be expected to function much like group homes for mentally retarded persons. Other settings under study were business and industrial organizations that might be very different from group homes. In any case, all of the propositions derived from previous research must be considered as being merely hypothetical and suggestive at this time. For instance, increasing staff participation in decision-making probably will improve job satisfaction, motivation, and performance in a group home, because it has had this effect in other settings. However, research in group homes should be conducted to confirm this generalization.

An especially important question concerns the ultimate significance of helper attitudes, motivation, and job satisfaction in group homes for mentally retarded persons. The model presupposes that motivational level, job satisfaction, and attitudes about treatment in staff substantially affect the quality of care and the effectiveness of treatment received by residents. Anecdotal evidence suggests that this is a plausible notion, but it could be argued that, in fact, staff members do not influence residents as much as has been supposed, and that employees in a group home will perform in much the same way no matter what their attitudes, motivation, or level of satisfaction. In any case, research is needed to resolve the issue.

Another important question concerns the relationship between role structure and role strain. There are different ways of assigning tasks and of structuring roles in group homes. The model suggests that different role structures will have different impacts on role strain. Data that could identify which role structures in group homes are associated with the least amount of role strain (especially role conflict) could be extremely useful. Similarly, variation in role structure is thought to be associated with variation in job design. Research is needed to determine if there are certain role structures that produce optimal levels of variety, autonomy, and task identity in staff jobs.

To aid this research, descriptive study of role structure and power structure in group homes should be conducted. What tasks are typically performed? Are there a few, general ways in which tasks are combined into roles? From the answers to these questions, a taxonomy of role structure in group homes for mentally retarded persons could be developed. Similar questions should be asked about power structure. What decisions must be made? Are there certain ways in which they are made in different group homes? In this way, a taxonomy of power structure could be generated as well. To develop these taxonomies, however, comparative study of a large number of group homes is necessary.

The concept of normative structure suggests a number of research questions. Butler (1977) already has suggested a typology based on norms and goals concerning the residents (therapeutic, maintenance, and custodial). Research is now needed to determine if this typology can be developed into valid and reliable measures.

A typology based on differences in norms concerning staff welfare could be developed in future research. Once this is done, the relationships between different aspects of normative structure relating to staff and residents can be examined. There is a maxim that staff should treat residents as staff themselves are treated by superiors. Thus, one possible hypothesis is that group homes that are perceived as supportive by residents are homes in which staff welfare is taken seriously.

Previous research on institutional character has tended to be based on studies of a very few settings. To what extent does strong character contribute to a positive social environment in group homes? What are the most common bases for creating institutional character in these sorts of settings? What are the most successful strategies used by administrators for developing strong institutional character in these settings? Future research employing larger samples could address these and other questions concerning institutional character.

In the long run, the most fruitful question to ask about organizational design in group homes for mentally retarded persons is, "How does it get to be the way it is?" Once a home has been established, most of what we have referred to as organizational design becomes part of the routine and is extremely difficult to change. At this point, we have no data concerning what percentage of existing group homes for the retarded are close to an optimal design. Epidemiological research on an organizational level is needed to determine this percentage. However, it seems safe to say that the percentage of group homes that resemble the optimal design is not very great, and that the care and rehabilitation of residents probably is suffering as a result. Therefore, it is crucial to study the developmental history of both good and bad homes, while focusing on the evolution of the organizational design. What factors contribute to the evolution of an optimal design in the good homes? How was the organizational design developed in the good homes? Were there consistent differences in the manner in which organizational design was developed in good homes as compared to bad homes?

Obviously, these questions are not easy to answer because they require an operational definition of good and bad homes. However, continuing controversy over desired outcomes, and over the most valid ways of measuring them, need not deter us from studying these sorts of questions. One can adopt a number of different, provisional measures of outcome (e.g., self-reported resident satisfaction and behavioral measures of the frequency and quality of staff-resident and resident-resident interaction) and one can roughly divide a sample of group homes into two groups (good and bad) based on these measures. Whatever the methodological constraints, we must begin studying how organizational design evolved in the good homes compared to the bad, for it is this kind of knowledge that will best help us to create more humane and effective programs in the future.

REFERENCES

Allen, G. J., Chinsky, J. M., and Veit, S. W. 1974. Pressures toward institutionalization within the aide culture: A behavioral-analytic case study. J. Community Psychol. 2:67–70.
Butler, E. W. 1977. A model for the evaluation of alternative community care facilities. Paper presented at the Conference on Alternative Living Environments for Mentally Retarded Persons, June, George Peabody College, Nashville, Tennessee.
Caplan, R. D., Cobb, S., French, J. R. P., Harrison, R. V., and Pinneau, S. R. 1975. Job Demands and Worker Health. U.S. Department of Health, Education, and Welfare, Public Health Service, Center for Disease Control, National Institute for Occupational Safety and Health, Washington, D.C.
Cherniss, C., and Egnatios, E. 1978a. Is there a job satisfaction problem in community mental health? Community Ment. Health J. 14:309–318.
Cherniss, C., and Egnatios, E. 1978b. Participation in decision-making by staff in community mental health programs. Am. J. Community Psychol. 6:171–190.
Clark, B. R. 1970. The Distinctive College. Aldine Publishing Company, Chicago.
Colarelli, N. O., and Siegel, S. M. 1966. Ward H: An Adventure in Innovation. Van Nostrand Reinhold Company, New York.
Fairweather, G. W., Sanders, D. H., Maynard, H., and Cressler, D. L. 1969. Community Life for the Mentally Ill: An Alternative to Institutional Care. Aldine Publishing Company, Chicago.
Goldenberg, I. I. 1971. Build Me a Mountain: Youth, Poverty, and the Creation of New Settings. MIT Press, Cambridge, Mass.
Hackman, J. R., and Oldham, G. R. 1975. Development of the job diagnostic survey. J. Appl. Psychol. 60:159–170.
Hasenfeld, Y., and English, R. A. (eds.). 1974. Human Service Organizations. University of Michigan Press, Ann Arbor.
Jones, M. 1976. Maturation of the Therapeutic Community: An Organic Approach to Health and Mental Health. Behavioral Publications, New York.
Kahn, R. L., Wolfe, D. M., Quinn, R. P., Snoek, J. D., and Rosenthal, R. H. 1964. Organizational Stress: Studies in Role Conflict and Ambiguity. John Wiley and Sons, Inc., New York.
Lawler, E. E. III. 1973. Motivation in Work Organizations. Brook/Cole, Monterey, Calif.
McIntyre, D. 1969. Two schools, one psychologist. In: F. Kaplan and S. B. Sarason (eds.), The Psycho-Educational Clinic: Papers and Research Studies. Community Mental Health Monograph Series, Vol. 4, pp. 21–90, Massachusetts Department of Mental Health.
Maslach, C. 1976. Burned-out. Hum. Behav. 5(9):16–22.
Moos, R. 1973. Conceptualizations of human environments. Am. Psychol. 28:652–665.
Oppenheimer, M. 1975. The unionization of the professional. Soc. Policy 5(5):34–40.
Reppucci, N. D. 1973. Social psychology of institutional change: General principles for intervention. Am. J. Community Psychol. 1:330–341.
Sarason, S. B., Levine, M., Goldenberg, I. I., Cherlin, D. L., and Bennett, E. M. 1966. Psychology in Community Settings: Clinical, Vocational, Educational, Social Aspects. John Wiley and Sons, Inc., New York.

Sarata, B. P. V. 1974. Employee satisfactions in agencies serving retarded persons. Am. J. Ment. Defic. 79:434–442.

Schwartz, M. S., and Will, G. T. 1961. Intervention and change on a mental hospital ward. In: W. G. Bennis, K. Benne, and R. Chin (eds.), The Planning of Change, pp. 564–583, Holt, Rinehart, and Winston, Inc., New York.

Selznick, P. 1957. Leadership in Administration. Harper and Row, Pubs., Inc., New York.

Stotland, E., and Kobler, A. L. 1965. Life and Death of a Mental Hospital. University of Washington Press, Seattle.

Zaharia, E. S., and Baumeister, A. A. 1978. Technician turnover and absenteeism in public residential facilities. Am. J. Ment. Defic. 82:580–593.

Zaharia, E. S., and Baumeister, A. A. 1979a. Cross-organizational job satisfactions of technician-level staff members. Am. J. Ment. Defic. 84:30–35.

Zaharia, E. S., and Baumeister, A. A. 1979b. Technician losses in public residential facilities. Am. J. Ment. Defic. 84:36–39.

Living Environments for Developmentally Retarded Persons
Edited by H. Carl Haywood and J. R. Newbrough
Copyright 1981 University Park Press Baltimore

Issues in the Community Adaptation of Mildly Retarded Adults

Keith T. Kernan, Ph.D.
Department of Psychiatry
Socio-Behavioral Research Group
Neuropsychiatric Institute
The Center for the Health Sciences
UCLA, 760 Westwood Plaza
Los Angeles, California 90024

Jim L. Turner, Ph.D.
Department of Psychiatry
Socio-Behavioral Research Group
Neuropsychiatric Institute
The Center for the Health Sciences
UCLA, 760 Westwood Plaza
Los Angeles, California 90024

L.L. Langness, Ph.D.
Departments of Psychiatry and Anthropology
Socio-Behavioral Research Group
Neuropsychiatric Institute
The Center for the Health Sciences
UCLA, 760 Westwood Plaza
Los Angeles, California 90024

Robert B. Edgerton, Ph.D.
Departments of Psychiatry and Anthropology
Socio-Behavioral Research Group
Neuropsychiatric Institute
The Center for Health Sciences
UCLA, 760 Westwood Plaza
Los Angeles, California 90024

125

The process called deinstitutionalization is, like mental retardation itself, not one thing but many. The term refers to a process during which a person labeled "mentally retarded" transfers residence from a large institution (e.g., hospital, training school, or colony) to a smaller residence (e.g., parental home, foster home, group home, halfway house, or independent apartment). The history of deinstitutionalization is long and complex, and the overwhelming bulk of what has been written about it is programmatic. Empirical research is in dreadfully short supply. There is the valuable research of Henshel (1972), O'Connor (1976), Birenbaum and Seiffer (1976), Bjaanes and Butler (1974), Muehlberger (1972), and Landesman-Dwyer and her colleagues (1978), but not very much more exists that tells us anything of significance about the lives of people who are undergoing deinstitutionalization. Indeed, there is virtually no research that describes the lives of mentally retarded persons in all their relevant environments over time.

RESEARCH METHODS AND ISSUES

We at UCLA have for some years been engaged in research that examines the lives of mildly retarded persons in community settings in the Los Angeles area. In this chapter we discuss very briefly how the research was done and then identify some of the issues that appear to be central to an improved understanding of mildly retarded persons, in all the settings of their lives.

Initial research in the early 1960s involved a 2-year study of some 50 mildly retarded persons who were discharged from a large state hospital after demonstrating what was considered by hospital officials to be satisfactory vocational and community adjustment (Edgerton, 1967). Although the results of this follow-up study suggested that most of these individuals had indeed made a viable adaptation to life outside the hospital, nevertheless most of them had required the assistance of a "normal" benefactor to do so. Furthermore, most were suffering from the adverse psychological effects of their institutionalization. Some years later, this same cohort was restudied with different results: after another 12 years of community adaptation, these individuals were both more competent and happier than they had been. Their reliance on benefactors was less, as was their suffering from the stigma of having

The preparation of this paper was made possible by the Mental Retardation Research Center, University of California at Los Angeles (USPHS Grant HD-04612-05) and by the Community Context of Normalization Study (NICHD Grant HD-09474-02), Robert B. Edgerton, Principal Investigator.

been labeled and subsequently hospitalized as mentally retarded (Edgerton and Bercovici, 1976).

At the same time, we undertook a study of the quality of life available to mildly retarded adults in community residential facilities (e.g., group homes). In this research, like that conducted earlier, we used a variety of methods, including survey interviews and systematic observation, but we relied primarily on participant-observation conducted over long periods of time. For example, in research on group homes, our participant-observers spent as many as 4 years in the study of a limited number of retarded persons in the settings that bounded their everyday lives. In addition to group homes, these settings included workshops, parental homes, buses, recreational places, and shopping excursions.

This research led to the conclusion that the community lives of such retarded persons were unnecessarily restricted (Edgerton, 1975). Rather than being allowed to experience more normal lives in the community, most of the persons in our sample were prevented from taking normal risks, were denied the right to make consequential decisions, and were systematically deprived of the right to come and go, to experience normal social relationships, and to move toward greater independence and competence. Instead, they were often held in dependent relationships, were over-medicated with tranquilizing drugs, and were punished for assuming normal adult prerogatives.

The findings of this research led in 1976 to a more ambitious project focused on the community context of normalization. The research (which continues as of this writing) focuses on the lives of 54 young adults who were labeled as mentally retarded, but who were also identified by professionals in the community service delivery system as possessing the potential for independent community living.[1] This sam-

---

[1] This sample, although subject to minor fluctuations from time to time, is constituted as follows:

Age:	18–30	30–40	40+
N:	39	12	3

Sex:	Male	Female
N:	25	29

Marital Status:	Single	Married
N:	34	20

Residence:	Parents	FC/BC	Independent
N:	14	13	27

Employment	None	Workshop	Competitively
N:	24	17	13

ple's potential for normalization permits us to ask whether such persons are, in fact, making progress toward more normal lives. If they are not, as is often the case, we have reason to ask "Why not?" Again, intense qualitative methods are used, not only participant-observation but also life history recordings and a kind of critical-incident analysis we have called "normalization incident" analysis (Edgerton and Langness, 1978). As before, we look intensively at the persons in our sample, seeing each one every 10 days or so for the duration of the research.

This research is concerned with all aspects of life in the community for the individuals under study. These aspects include employment; leisure-time activities; relationships with family members, caregivers, and spouses; encounters with the legal system; behavior in public places; self-maintenance activities and skills; sex and dating; and so on. Our goals are to understand and to describe the quality of the lives of mildly retarded people who reside in the community. In addition, we try to identify any problems such people may have and to identify the resources available for dealing with those problems.

As a result of our research experiences and concerns, we have identified a number of issues in the study of deinstitutionalization. Some of the more general of these are:

1.   The social competence of mildly retarded persons, like that of normal persons, varies from place to place. Without assuming that social competence is radically setting-specific for all persons, we believe that it is important to determine the extent to which the competence of retarded persons varies from home, to work, to public transactions, to recreation, to personal relationships. It is also important to determine how (or if) the judgments of delivery system personnel consider variations in competence when determining the potential, progress, or success of their retarded clients.

2.   The social competence of retarded persons also changes over time. Not only does it change over a period of years, as has so often been reported (Cobb, 1972), but it changes—sometimes markedly—in a period of weeks or even days. How fluctuations in their lives, as well as fluctuations in the process by which their lives are judged by others, affect retarded persons is a critical research issue. If even the most successful (i.e., competent and independent) mentally retarded persons living in community settings experience major ups and downs, not only in mood, but also in actual adaptive level, then this pattern is important to document and to understand, because most plans for monitoring and directing the lives of such persons presume greater stability in adaptation than we believe actually exists.

3.   Any perspective on the community adaptation of retarded persons must be sensitive to variations in class and subculture. Our

research clearly indicates that there is a pervasive middle-class bias on the part of delivery service personnel that often works to the disadvantage of retarded persons whose backgrounds and/or current levels of adaptation are typically not middle-class (Edgerton, 1975). The same bias exists with subculture, as we are beginning to find out with regard to Afro-Americans and Chicanos. Thus, middle-class standards of speech, housing, dress, hygiene, and general lifestyles are questionable but commonly used criteria for assessing community adaptation. Other legitimate standards by which adaptation can be assessed seem to be unacceptable to many delivery system professionals, a problem that works against retarded persons whose backgrounds or preferences lead them to different values and different behavior. The knowledge gained through an examination of the lives of mentally retarded people from a number of subcultures will provide a comparative point of view that may shed light on mental retardation as a social phenomenon.

4. With growing emphasis (usually mandated by legislation) on measuring individual progress toward normalization, it is essential that currently proposed evaluation devices be tempered by the realization that neither competence nor independence can be adequately assessed by a standard instrument based on brief contact with a client. As we have already asserted, competence and independence vary from time to time and place to place. Any assessment approach that fails to take those changes into account will assuredly distort reality. Therefore, we use a research approach that emphasizes multiple perspectives. Various persons—parents, employers, social workers, neighbors, friends—have differing views and interpretations concerning a retarded person's abilities and behaviors. These views may not agree with our own or with those of the retarded person. What matters in this approach is not the procrustean effort to determine who is "right." Rather, it is important to recognize that persons often disagree, but their various interpretations all become part of the essential reality that we strive to understand. Failing to recognize that the lives of retarded persons are complex and changing and that people often differ in their assessments of these lives does mentally retarded individuals yet another disservice.

In our research, we study the competence of mentally retarded persons as it varies across time and setting, as it differs with variations in class and subculture, and as it is perceived from multiple points of view. These general issues and the methodologies employed to study them are relevant to all aspects of the lives of mildly mentally retarded persons in the naturally occurring contexts of their lives. We focus especially on three areas of competence and behavior, the study of which is central to an understanding of human behavior in general and of mental retardation in particular: the language, the thought, and the personal and emotional adjustment of the mentally retarded. Indeed, these are three elements that have been of traditional concern to researchers. As essential aspects of human existence, and as important areas of potential difficulty for the mentally retarded, these topics must be considered to be central areas of concern in the study of deinstitutionalization. Presented below are brief overviews of what has been accomplished, what work we are presently engaged in, and what directions we believe future research should take in these areas.

REASONING AND JUDGMENT OF THE
MILDLY RETARDED IN COMMUNITY SETTINGS

There is considerable agreement now that IQ tests are not completely satisfactory for diagnosing mental retardation, and that attempts to devise adaptive behavior scales have been mostly unsuccessful (Langness, 1964). Even so, it appears that dependence upon IQ scores still predominates in diagnosis and, in fact, will even take precedence over all other information (Adams, 1973). At the same time, there is evidence that IQ scores will not predict success in adjusting to community living, work, and other such normal everyday activities. The scores also fail to account for the relatively large numbers of mentally retarded persons who disappear every year into the community (Cobb, 1972; Dingman and Tarjan, 1960; Henshel, 1972; Mercer, 1973; Tarjan, 1964). This would seem to indicate a level of intellectual functioning that is adequate for day-to-day community life but incongruent with IQ performance. This finding is also consistent with other evidence that mentally retarded persons act intelligently or at least reasonably in some contexts and for certain purposes (Braginsky and Braginsky, 1971; Edgerton, 1967; Linder, 1978).

There is, however, very little information on the cognitive abilities of mentally retarded persons in naturalistic settings. Virtually nothing is known about their ability to reason and to make judgments and inferences in such settings because the overwhelming bulk of information on the intellectual functioning of such individuals comes from IQ tests, clinical settings, and Piagetian-type experiments. We are unwilling to accept these as adequate or definitive measures of normal everyday intellectual functioning, and therefore propose to accumulate data on the mildly retarded in a variety of naturalistic situations and to analyze these data with respect to processes of reasoning and judgment. We are commencing research that seeks answers to such questions as: Do mildly retarded persons make mistakes in logic? Do they reason from incorrect premises? Do they hold irrational beliefs? What kinds of judgments are they actually required to make? Do they utilize the same kinds and range of information in making judgments that other (presumably normal) people do? Do they make similar inferences? Do they cope differently than others when presented with unique or novel situations? Do they, in short, seem to utilize the same strategies and rules of thought and logic as the investigator does?

The questions involved in conducting research are twofold: 1) How do you acquire pertinent data? and 2) How do you analyze them once you have them?

The primary data-gathering technique involves naturalistic observations of the everyday lives of mildly retarded persons. Participant-observers (Bogdan and Taylor, 1975; Edgerton and Langness, 1978; Madge, 1953; Schatzman and Strauss, 1973) can acquire data that are not otherwise obtainable. John Madge (1953) has summarized the goals of this approach: "The primary task of the participant-observer is to enter into the life of the community being studied. If this task is achieved, there will be two consequences: his subjects will learn to take him for granted and thus to behave almost as though he were not there, and he will learn to think almost as they think" (p. 131). This approach has served anthropologists well, and our research personnel do, in fact, enter into the life of the community by joining subjects in their homes, in sheltered workshops, in schools, in bowling alleys, in churches, in buses, and wherever else their lives take them.[2] This allows the researchers to observe how retarded persons behave in a variety of situations: solving problems; dealing with merchants, teachers, and bureaucrats; and coping with the logic and illogic of everyday life.

We are also doing intensive life history work with a number of mildly retarded persons. Like participant-observation, life histories have long been utilized by anthropologists (Langness, 1965), and they, too, can provide much more detailed information than is otherwise obtainable. This is particularly true for one of the current samples of retarded persons under study, in which some persons have been followed for more than 10 years, starting with Edgerton's work, *The*

---

[2] These persons include the 54 mildly mentally retarded adults of the Community Context of Normalization Study. We are also doing ethnographic work in a school for trainable mentally retarded (TMR) children. This school population consists of approximately 144 children ranging in age from 6 to 14.9 years. They are mostly Caucasian, but also include some Blacks and Hispanic-surnamed children. The children are bused to and from school, and most live with their natural or adoptive parents.

Cloak of Competence (1967). Not only have their own accounts of their lives been collected, but also corroborating and sometimes inconsistent accounts have been gathered from others who know them well. The rapport required for life history work, coupled with the personal feelings, attitudes, and beliefs that are exposed through intensive and probing interviewing, often reveal dimensions of personality and competence that would otherwise remain totally hidden.

Our approach to the competence of retarded persons is not exclusively naturalistic. Quasi-experimental procedures that combine intensive ethnographic field work and experience with the experimental procedures of cross-cultural psychologists are being tested. Recent work in cross-cultural psychology, attempting to overcome the biases and abuses of ordinary testing procedures (Kamin, 1974), has featured an entirely new approach to questions of intelligence and competence (Cole, Gay, and Sharp, 1971; Cole and Scribner, 1974; Price-Williams, 1975). This approach attempts to utilize naturally occurring events and culturally salient skills. Rather than using what are presumptively (but never truly) culture-free tests to measure differences in performance, this approach utilizes culturally specific tasks and materials that will reveal underlying similarities in process. Although we categorically deny any similarities between mildly retarded persons and the falsely labeled "primitive" societies on which most of this work to date has been attempted, these methods can be adapted to research on mentally retarded persons in their natural settings.[3]

Propositional Reasoning

Virtually no studies of propositional reasoning have been undertaken with retarded populations. This is an oversight of some significance, because the cognitive competence of the mildly retarded, like that of children, has been called into question primarily on the basis of their relatively poor performance on Piagetian tasks, as well as on their IQ scores (Inhelder, 1968). This conclusion itself has recently been questioned. Consider the following argument quoted from Falmagne (1975):

> There are two traditions in the study of logical reasoning. One is the Piagetian tradition; the other is the study of propositional reasoning . . . . Since its impoundment by psychology (and, evidently, before then) the "propositional" tradition has mostly focused on adult reasoning. This, in my opinion, stems from an unsupported prejudice. Historically, it is

---

[3] We have attempted this only with the school population and only in a very preliminary manner. Although we have so far employed only simple box-filing and tarpaulin-folding experiments utilizing naturally recurring situations, the potential for adapting and analyzing recurring school tasks is enormous.

due to the fact that the recent explosion in developmental research has coincided with the sudden recognition on this side of the Atlantic of Piaget's theory, its enormous scope and its unifying integrative quality as a general theory of intelligence. The prejudice concerning children's ability to handle verbal logical problems such as syllogisms or other forms of propositional inference, is founded on Piaget's assertion that children's logic, prior to the stage of formal operations, is structurally adequate for dealing with objects and their properties but is inadequate for fully competent propositional reasoning. The claim made here that this prejudice is unsupported, at least in the radical form in which it is often expressed is based on three considerations . . . . The first one is that the data base on which Piaget's theory has been developed comes from an empirical task domain different from the "propositional" situations mentioned above, and therefore cannot a priori be generalized to these situations . . . . The second, closely related consideration is that whether such a generalization is valid can only be answered in empirical grounds, that are as yet lacking, precisely because of the scarcity of empirical developmental work in the "propositional" area. Finally, the fact that adult reasoning in propositional situations is notoriously only in loose correspondence with what the ideal logical model would prescribe, calls for qualifications of what is meant by saying that the individual, from adolescence on, is in the stage of formal operations in contrast to his previous inadequacies in that respect. What is referred to here, of course, are the problems facing the validation of a competence model when its actualization at the behavioral level is imperfect; but much more crucially, the difficulty of denying such competence to other individuals whose inadequacy in performance only differs from the former by a matter of degree. (pp. 1–2)

Although Falmagne is referring here to the reasoning abilities of children, and although we absolutely deny any real similarities between children and mentally retarded adults, we do believe that her criticisms apply to our knowledge of mentally retarded adults as well as to children. It is not self-evident that mildly retarded individuals are incapable of reasoning at the same level as ordinary adults, although there are methodological problems involved in attempting to pursue such research with mentally retarded persons. (One problem, for example, has to do with the tendency of our retarded subjects to simply withdraw from further discussion when challenged in any way, no matter how logical, reasonable, or strong their position may be. Similarly, we find that they become inhibited when presented directly with what they perceive as any kind of formal test.) It has recently been suggested that logical reasoning should be part of the normal curriculum for the mentally handicapped, a position that obviously assumes that these persons are potentially competent in this respect (Cherkes, unpublished manuscript). Because of the difficulties we have encountered, we are attempting to find ways to avoid giving propositional reasoning problems as such and to utilize naturally occurring situations and conversations. The rather copious field notes that come in from participant-observers contain many examples of the reasoning abilities (or lack of them) of our sample population. Methods are being developed for analyzing audio- and videotaped spontaneous speech for this purpose as well (Cherkes, unpublished manuscript).[4]

Because no one knows what constitutes normal thought or reasoning (Henle, 1962), there are obvious problems in comparing the cognitive performance of mildly retarded persons with that of other individuals. Nonetheless, certain kinds of judgments can be made. To begin with, according to Spiro (1964), it is possible to characterize beliefs as either rational or irrational. A belief can be seen as irrational in the following ways:

1. The conclusion is invalidly deduced from some axiom or premise—that is, it rests on a fallacy in deductive logic.
2. The belief is an empirical generalization that is invalidly derived from available evidence—that is, it is irrational because it rests on a fallacy in inductive logic.
3. The belief asserts some proposition that is inconsistent with, or in contravention of, some other belief—that is, it is irrational because it violates the law of contradiction: A and non-A cannot be held simultaneously.
4. The belief asserts something about the universe that is inconsistent with, or in contravention of, reliable knowledge. To hold the belief is irrational because it is empirically absurd.

Although we know that even logicians do not think syllogistically in everyday life, the rules of logic do provide a convenient standard by which to measure certain kinds of thought (Henle, 1962). It is as unlikely to find certain logical fallacies among mentally retarded persons as it is to find them among anyone else. Following Wallace's (1962) suggestion, again with reference to "primitives," it is doubtful

---

[4] Consider, for example, the following verbatim excerpt from field notes:
The thing is, I am going to be living in an apartment where I can get job training. It will be very hard for me to find a job on my own right now even if I looked for ads in the paper because they only want experienced workers and I am not an experienced worker because I never held down a job. And there is nothing I can do about the fact that they only want experienced workers, just like there is nothing I can do about the fact that it is a cold windy morning.
At another extreme:
In here they have people who cook for you. This is a place for famous people. All famous people live here and the people in the office manage their money. The cook is to cook for the famous people who live here. So the people you see here are famous.

that the mildly retarded person would perform the following bit of fallacious reasoning:

A rabbit has four legs.
That animal has four legs.
Therefore that animal is a rabbit.[5]

Similarly, there is little reason to suppose that the mildly retarded systematically violate the basic schema:[6]

$$\frac{\text{A or B} \qquad \text{not A}}{\therefore \text{B}}$$

By utilizing the rules of logic, errors of reasoning can be identified. An argument that violates a rule of logic is said to be fallacious. It can be fallacious in three different ways: 1) in its material content, through a misstatement of facts; 2) in its wording, through incorrect use of terms; or 3) in its structure. These are called material, verbal, and formal fallacies. Arguments can be categorized as either logically correct or logically incorrect in terms of the particular fallacies that render the argument defective. This raises another question: Do mildly retarded persons tend to argue fallaciously in one of these modes more than in another?

Finally, studies of propositional reasoning have demonstrated very clearly that the role of content is often crucial to reasoning and judgment (Falmagne, 1975). Often the relation between the terms of a proposition, as specified by its meaning, is different from the relation specified by the rules of formal logic. For example, the conversion of the proposition "some b are not a" to "some a are not b" is incorrect according to the rules of formal logic. The material content of the propositions, however, may permit their joint truth. For example:

Some blondes are not German.
Some Germans are not blondes.

Some dogs are not poodles.
Some poodles are not dogs.

In the latter two propositions there is a contradiction, but both conversions—judged in terms of formal logic—are incorrect. Notice, however, that to fully understand this, it is necessary to share certain

---

[5] This follows the so-called Law of Von Domarus, which says that subjects are identical if they have a common predicate.
[6] According to Johnson-Laird (1975), 82% of a sample of 6-year-old children were able to make this inference correctly (p. 19). Although we have presented it to only a few of our slightly older school children (to see if it was possible at all), we have yet to get an incorrect response on the first trial.

assumptions or understandings with others about set inclusion—in this case, assumptions and understandings having to do with "blondness," "Germanness," "dogness," and "poodleness." It is because people tend to exploit such a communal base of knowledge that they can make inferences that are, if not always valid, at least plausible (Johnson-Laird, 1975, p. 51). From an anthropologist's point of view, this raises basic questions about the cultural transmission of knowledge. It may well be that many of the errors of mentally retarded individuals are a result of their failure to share the common symbolic understandings that make up a culture, rather than their basic inability to reason and to make judgments. These questions (which we believe are worth pursuing) seem to demand, at least in the beginning, qualitative and quasi-experimental methods to find answers.

PERSONAL AND SOCIOEMOTIONAL ADJUSTMENT OF THE MENTALLY RETARDED IN COMMUNITY SETTINGS

For at least the past 50 years, there has been continuing interest in and speculation about the relationship between personality factors and mental retardation. Some of the major propositions explored and/or asserted in the literature include:

1. Mentally retarded persons have a significantly higher incidence of personality disorder than comparable normal populations (Beier, 1964; Garrison and Force, 1965; Hirsch, 1959; Hutt and Gibby, 1965; Johnson, 1963).
2. Certain personality characteristics (e.g., rigidity, anxiety, suggestibility, ego limitation) are concomitant with intellectual retardation (Feldman, 1946; Hirsch, 1959; Lewin, 1935).
3. Certain types of personality are characteristics of specific medical conditions. For example, individuals with Down's syndrome are friendly, amicable, easy-going, talented in music and mimicry, and rarely given to aggressive or destructive behavior (Blacketer-Simmonds, 1953; Ellis and Beechley, 1950; Rutter, 1971).
4. Certain personality traits are predictive of success and failure in post-institutional adjustment (Cobb, 1923; McPherson, 1935; Windle, 1962).

The evidential base for all of the above propositions is inconclusive, and although generalizations have often been accepted on the basis of apparent face validity, they can be neither accepted nor rejected on the basis of methodologically sound empirical evidence. Gardner (1968), for example, noted that "the sweeping generalizations which appear in the writings concerning the mentally retarded are mostly based on theoretic proclamation or on clinical observation of biased samples and not on data gathered in a scientifically suitable manner" (p. 54). Similarly, other reviewers have emphasized that most personality research on mentally retarded persons is methodologically weak in terms of the assessment procedures and control groups used (Heber, 1964; McCarver and Craig, 1974; Windle, 1962) and is generalized inappropriately from unrepresentative institutionalized samples. Thus, although older textbooks are replete with descriptive lore representing "the retarded personality," none of these purported attributes has been substantiated or refuted on the basis of available research data.

Methods For Predicting Adjustment Behavior

A major problem affecting both the quantity and quality of personality research with retarded persons is the questionable validity of traditionally favored self-report inventories, questionnaires, tests, and laboratory measures for individuals with restricted verbal skills (Gardner, 1968; Guthrie et al., 1964; Heber, 1964). Although a variety of measures including the Rorschach (Benton, 1956; Chambers and Hamlin, 1957; Molish, 1958; Sarason, 1959), the Thematic Apperception Test (Avila and Lawson, 1962; Bergman and Fisher, 1953), California Test of Personality (Gardner, 1967), Rosenzweig Picture-Frustration Study (Angelino and Shedd, 1956; Lipman, 1959), Manifest Anxiety Scale (Keller, 1957), and other assorted measures of self-concept (Guthrie, Butler, and Gorlow, 1962) have been employed with mentally retarded populations, the general pattern of results is inconclusive and interpretation is confounded by idiosyncratic variations in administration procedures. Furthermore, the research literature reveals very few studies in which any particular standardized test has been validated and successfully used to predict specific behavior patterns in mentally retarded persons (Clarke, 1974; Menolascino, 1970).

Perhaps the best conceptualized personality research with mentally retarded individuals has focused on motivational variables. For the most part, this research has relied on laboratory tasks rather than psychometric tests, and has involved application of the hypothetico-deductive method in studying personality characteristics of retarded persons as compared to normals. The two major theoretical formulations in this tradition are Rotter's (1954) social learning theory and Zigler's (1966, 1969) motivational-cognitive approach, which grows out of Lewinian personality theory (Lewin, 1936). Although these two lines of research have proceeded independently and have invoked differing explanatory constructs, both have been primarily concerned with the consequences of an experiential history of failure on the personality development of mentally retarded children. Reviews of the extensive experimental literature relevant to these theories are available for reference (Cromwell, 1963, 1967; Heber, 1964; Rosen, Clark, and Kivitz, 1977; Zigler, 1966, 1969). For present purposes, it is sufficient to note that this body of research has had little impact on programmatic intervention and habilitation, and its relevance to the everyday adjustment and coping problems of retarded adults has yet to be established.

The major point of this overview is to demonstrate that personality research with mentally retarded persons has had little success in relating personality and emotional variables to the successes and failures of day-to-day living of the noninstitutionalized mildly retarded adult.

There is, however, an emerging consensus regarding the type of research needed, and most reviewers of the personality literature emphasize the following points:

1. Attempts to discover personality characteristics that are universally descriptive of mentally retarded persons should be abandoned (Gardner, 1968; Heber, 1964; Rosen, Clark, and Kivitz, 1977).
2. The choice of which behavioral dimensions and personality variables to study should originate from the role of those variables in the everyday lives of the people being studied.
3. Research must seek to progress beyond the explanation that adjustment problems are caused by personality difficulties. It must further develop conceptual links between specified types of problematic behavior and criteria of adjustment that are less global (e.g., institutionalization, employment status, income, marital status). Instead, research should be more relevant to the day-to-day successes and failures of mentally retarded persons as they cope with situations and with significant persons.
4. There is a pressing need for the development of alternative approaches to the measure of personality variables in mentally retarded populations (Gardner, 1968; Heber, 1964; McCarver and Craig, 1974; Rosen, Clark, and Kivitz, 1977; Windle, 1962).
5. More research is needed that addresses itself directly to the implications of personality research for programmatic and clinical intervention (Beier, 1964; Gardner, 1968; Rosen, Clark, and Kivitz, 1977; Zigler and Balla, 1977).

On the basis of our own research efforts to document the everyday lives of mildly retarded adults, we have come to believe that generalized, situation-free, personality variables are of limited predictive and explanatory value in accounting for the level and quality of adjustment achieved in the community. Our observations, for example, do not support the idea that the mildly retarded individual possesses either adaptive or maladaptive personality traits that are generally manifest across a wide variety of settings and circumstances. Although some individuals appear to be more consistent in behavior and temperament than others, the large majority exhibit considerable transsituational variability in such qualities as aggressiveness, dependency, emotional control, self-esteem, and susceptibility to social influence (cf. Bem and Allen, 1974). Our data thus provide no evidence for some ideal set of personal characteristics that ensure or preclude successful, long-term community adjustment.

Similarly, in the course of following our mentally retarded informants' lives as they change jobs and residential arrangements and as they go in and out of various programs, we have been impressed by the variability in response of different individuals to the same or similar situations. We have consistently observed, for example, that what appears to be the ideal residential arrangement, employment, or training program for one individual can be a total disaster for someone else. In some cases, this variability of response occurs despite the apparent similarity of the individuals in such attributes as IQ, family background, history of adjustment problems, and personality tests. In such instances, we have found that, in addition to developing a more sophisticated model of complex person-setting interactions, it is important that we elicit, and include in our data, the subjective perspectives of the mentally retarded persons themselves. In our experience, mildly retarded adults have a great deal to say about their own behavior and about the relation of their behavior to the people, events, and circumstances of their lives. Furthermore, these self-descriptions and self-predictions are often crucial to describing, understanding, and predicting the problems of everyday life for the retarded person in the community.

Although we have found little indication that traditional trait theory notions of personality provide accurate descriptions or useful predictions of everyday behavior, it remains true that, for parents, social workers, and assorted service delivery system personnel, many adjustment problems of mentally retarded individuals are explained by invoking generalized personality traits. Our observations suggest that qualities like poor self-control, compulsive lying, and over-suggestibility are often attributed to individuals on the basis of only one, or at least relatively few incidents. However, the label persists despite the infrequency or nonrecurrence of the behavior, and such a label is often used as a justification for imposing a restricted lifestyle on the retarded individual. One man's parents, for instance, have refused to let him ride on the city bus system alone because he is "too suggestible." When asked for examples, the only evidence the parents could cite was an incident that had occurred 5 years earlier, in which a panhandler had talked their son out of 5 dollars at a bus stop.

The preceding considerations suggest some of the substantive issues that serve to guide our research on socioemotional adjustment of mildly retarded persons in community settings. Our major objectives are:

1. To develop extensive, detailed accounts of the emotional and behavioral adjustment strategies displayed by mentally retarded persons in the course of their everyday life in the community.
2. To analyze adjustment problems and coping behaviors from multiple perspectives, with particular emphasis on the interaction of personal variables, setting variables, and phenomenological factors.
3. To examine the role of personality trait attributions in facilitating or limiting access of retarded persons to normalizing experiences and less restricted lifestyles.

COMMUNICATIVE COMPETENCE OF MILDLY RETARDED PERSONS IN COMMUNITY SETTINGS

It is well known that the incidence of linguistic difficulties among mentally retarded populations is very high. Estimates of percentages of populations that exhibit some language problem vary with the type of population being studied and with the testing procedure or measurement instrument used. However, language problems are always found, and for some populations the incidence is as high as 100%. Even among mildly retarded populations, the incidence has been reported to be as high as 60% (Schlanger, 1967). Difficulty with language and speech is an important fact, if not a defining feature, of mental retardation (aside from the verbal component of most measures of intelligence that are used to classify individuals as mentally retarded in the first place).

The literature on the language and linguistic deficiencies of mentally retarded persons and on the programs designed to ameliorate those deficiencies is quite extensive (Blount, 1968; Cromer, 1974; Jordan, 1967; Yoder and Miller, 1972). However, with few exceptions, the linguistic research upon which this literature is based has been concerned with the analysis and description of linguistic competence of a rather narrow and traditional scope; that is, it has been concerned with phonological, grammatical, and syntactical abilities and with the physical realization of those abilities. The focus has been on the ability of mentally retarded persons to produce sentences that are grammatically and phonologically well formed and on their ability to understand such sentences when they hear them. There are a number of legitimate reasons for this restricted focus, two of which are probably most important.

Linguistic Competence

First, the ability to produce recognizable sounds, words, and sentences and to understand them is a fundamental ability. It is the necessary foundation upon which all other linguistic and speech skills are built. Without this underlying linguistic competence, language, of course, would not exist. Second, until quite recently, the discipline of linguistics itself has been concerned primarily with understanding this basic linguistic competency (Chomsky, 1965); research has concentrated on the structure of language and not on its use. As a result, there has been no analytical or theoretical model upon which research on broader aspects of language and its use can be conducted with mentally retarded populations.

Most of the research on language and mentally retarded persons has addressed itself to this first issue—that of underlying linguistic competence. Although much has been learned, much remains that is not known, and such research is necessarily continuing. However, recent developments in linguistics and the behavioral sciences have demonstrated that the linguistics abilities necessary for an individual to function as a fully competent member of his society go far beyond a competency to produce and to recognize phonologically and grammatically well-formed sentences. That is, the underlying skills and abilities that constitute an individual's communicative competency (Hymes, 1972) include the skills and abilities that constitute an individual's linguistic competence, but also go beyond those skills. A number of disciplines have developed a focus on various aspects of communicative competency, including the ethnography of communication, conversational analysis, linguistic pragmatics, discourse analysis, speech act theory, and sociolinguistics. Although these disciplines differ in their approach to and focus on different units or different dimensions of language use, they nevertheless share certain central themes: 1) the use of naturally occurring speech as the primary data source; 2) a concern with elements other than the sentence as basic units of analysis; 3) the recognition of the relevance of context to linguistic rules; 4) variability as a component of linguistic roles; and 5) an appreciation of the diversity of language functions (Ervin-Tripp and Mitchell-Kernan, 1977). Essentially, then, the focus is upon language use as it naturally occurs, as it changes according to the contexts in which it occurs, and as it serves the functions that the speaker intends. The concern is with all of the skills that underlie language use, not with phonological and grammatical skills alone. The expanded idea of the skills required to be a competent member of a speech community and the research that has been generated by this idea provide the basis for an examination of the communicative competence of mentally retarded individuals.

Language and Social Interaction

The current policy of community placement/deinstitutionalization of mentally retarded persons makes research about language and social interaction imperative. The use of language in the community involves participation in verbally mediated social interactions that are sensitive to such matters as politeness, social status, or appropriateness of topic. If there are deficiencies in language behavior that characterize a person as a mentally retarded individual, preparation for entrance into the community must include a type of language socialization program. Life in an institution or in sheltered family situations may make different communicative demands on the individual that do not prepare him to behave acceptably in the roles he might desire or need to assume in the community. There is a strong possibility, however, that such behavior is not beyond the ability of the mentally retarded individual, but that it simply has not been emphasized or learned during the acquisition of other language skills.

Although there is reason to believe that sociolinguistic and pragmatic aspects of language constitute a problem for retarded individuals, almost nothing is known about this area. We do not know, for example, what communicative demands are made of retarded individuals, especially those who reside in the community, or what abilities mentally retarded persons possess to meet those demands. We have not adequately studied the use of language by mentally retarded persons as it may relate to cognitive ability, especially the cognitive ability that is necessary to the everyday life of the community. We know little of the acquisition of sociolinguistic skills or of the use of speech in the socialization of retarded persons. Little is known about how the speech and language behavior of mentally retarded persons affects their self-image and self-presentation, or how it affects the way in which they are viewed, treated, and spoken to by others.

Our past research has suggested a number of problems encountered by mentally retarded persons in conversational interaction or in the organization and performance of various speech events. Many individuals fail to structure interaction through the use of situationally appropriate openings and closings, turn-taking, and topic selection. An individual may walk up to a visitor in the workshop and launch into a long story, without an appropriate greeting and without recognizing the inappropriateness of the topic, or another individual may start to talk while someone else is speaking.

The speech of many mildly retarded individuals is characterized by poor or inappropriate organization of information. Speakers may fail to introduce topics in such a way that the point they are trying to make is not clear. They may fail to describe or to identify persons, objects, and events introduced into the discourse in such a way that listeners can determine whom or what is being referred to. When talking about events sequentially ordered in time, speakers may introduce events in an incorrect temporal order. Poor design of this type might be related to an inability to determine the type or amount of information required by or already known to a listener, or to an inability to structure information relative to the needs of different listeners.

In responding to the questions of others, many mentally retarded individuals frequently give a great deal of irrelevant detail. This type of response may arise from the speaker's inability to determine his interlocutor's intention in asking the question, or from his inability to determine what type of information is relevant.

Conversations with retarded individuals are often characterized by the failure to locate and repair misunderstandings. Misunderstandings may continue until the nonretarded interlocutors notice discrepancies and attempt to repair them. Some mentally retarded speakers may simply fail to recognize that misunderstandings have occurred. However, because the work of Bedrosian and Prutting (1976) and Price-Williams and Sabsay (1979) indicates that even the severely retarded initiate can respond to certain types of misunderstanding repair work, there may be other factors involved, such as the retarded individual's reluctance to discredit himself by admitting that he does not understand something his interlocutor has said.

If the observational impression is correct that sociolinguistic and pragmatic aspects of language constitute a problem for the mentally retarded individual, the question then arises about the cause of the problem. We have already suggested some hypotheses; other causes might include an inability to adapt behavior to different situations (including different interlocutors), an insensitivity to the social cues that govern the use of particular speech forms or modes of behavior, an inability to learn the rules of speech that obtain in certain situations, or an inability to adapt to new situations after living in a language-learning environment in which individuals are not exposed to or required to learn those rules.

The ability to use language appropriately in various situations is central to one's ability to operate in, and to belong to, the social world. It is also part of one's identity as a member of a social group. The ability to learn and to make inferences about social facts and the ability to accomplish communicative and social goals are also related to one's use of language. Violations of sociolinguistic rules and conversational norms of conduct can be a source of communicative failure and can result in misinterpretations of speakers' intentions and attitudes (Mitchell-Kernan and Kernan, 1971; Sabsay and Bennett, 1977). More important, these violations can affect hearers' judgments about the personality and competence of the speaker. Those who cannot participate in conversation do not seem, to other speakers, to be competent members of society.

Poor communication skills affect the esteem that speakers are accorded by others and determine, to some extent, how they are treated. Speakers regularly make judgments about another individual's personality, background, and motivations on the basis of his or her use of language. They also make judgments about others' linguistic, social, and cognitive competencies and adjust their speech accordingly. Research in child language acquisition, communicative disorders, and other areas indicates that the linguistic and nonlinguistic behavior of an individual is systematically affected when he interacts with someone who displays some type of linguistic incompetence (Anderson, 1975; Ferguson, 1975; Sabsay and Bennett, 1977; Siegel, 1963; Spradlin and Rosenberg, 1964). It has been hypothesized, although not conclusively demonstrated, that the altered linguistic environment to which the mentally retarded child is exposed further impairs his learning of adequate communicative skills (Buium, Rynders, and Turnure, 1975).

The more severely retarded, isolated, or sheltered an individual is, the less likely he is to interact with nonretarded individuals in normal social interactions. Mentally retarded adults have already acquired a set of verbal behavior, much of which may be adaptive and appropriate to the situations in which they live and work. Hospitals, board-and-care facilities, and workshops are social systems, and a socialization process occurs in the course of an individual's acquiring and maintaining membership in those systems. However, a good adaptation to the particular demands of these social systems may be antithetical to adaptation to the broader community. The type of interaction in which an individual engages in the home or workshop, or in the company of his retarded peers, may not give him the skills he needs to get along in various other situations or to properly interpret the behavior of others.

Behavior that is acceptable in an institution or sheltered workshop may not be acceptable in public settings. The type of submissive behavior suggested by Bedrosian and Prutting (1976) and Bercovici (1977), for example, may not be conducive to effective self-presentation in everyday interactions but is actually reinforced by the attitudes of caregivers in various living and working situations—that is, there may be interactional norms particular to restricted settings that differ from the norms that obtain in the broader community. To be a member of the speech community of a residence or workshop, the individual must conform to those norms. At the same time, if he is to be able to enter and to operate in the broader community, he must learn about and adapt to that set of norms as well.

Adaptation to the norms of the more restricted settings does not necessarily mean that speakers do not still have the ability to switch styles of speech. Some mentally retarded individuals apparently recognize the necessity of altering their way of speaking in various situations and they have the ability to do so appropriately. Others, although they are perhaps capable of modifying their speech, do not do so, or do so inappropriately. There are no studies of the ways in which individuals interact with others outside of these restricted settings; yet outsiders, including research assistants, frequently react to something unusual in the behavior of these individuals that marks them as different. These reactions often seem to center around language or deviation from conversational norms.

Poor communication skills not only hinder the individual's entry into social life and affect how he is perceived and treated by others, they also affect his self-evaluation. Edgerton's previous work (1967), as well as our more recent observations, suggested that many mentally retarded persons are aware of differences in the way they speak and of the discrediting nature of these differences. Many comment disparagingly on their own speech and that of their peers. Some attempt to normalize their speech when they talk with nonretarded individuals in contexts other than institution, residence, or workshop. For example, they may attempt to avoid words that mark them as having once been institutionalized. One man in Edgerton's (1967) study reported, "I always got to watch myself that I don't slip and use some words which somebody would know I'm from the hospital. One day I called somebody a 'low-grade,' then I almost bit my tongue off because outsiders don't use that word. I'm usually real careful about that" (p. 163). A woman in the normalization study whose speech was loud and rapid in the workshop used well-modulated speech when she came to the research office to be videotaped. She explained that she did not want to appear "crazy."

Attempts to speak like "outsiders," however, are not always successful, and frequently constitute the most striking evidence of incompetence. Words and phrases are often used inappropriately. One man in Edgerton's (1967) study, for example, attributed his poor health to a "need for a lack of vitamins" (p. 163).

Poor communication skills can also depress learning ability (Schlanger, 1967). Lack of functional language ability has been associated with poor performance in school. At least among second language specialists, there is a growing consensus that tests of grammar and phonology do not accurately predict effective classroom participation, and that sociolinguistic and pragmatic competence is more important. According to Shuy (1977), "A child's ability to seek clarification or to get a turn seems much more crucial than his ability to use past tense markers correctly" (p. 79). Such difficulties in learning may be a problem for mentally retarded persons as well.

ETHNOGRAPHY OF COMMUNICATION

One of the goals of our future research is to provide an ethnography of the communication of mentally retarded individuals living in the community. We do not expect these individuals to constitute a speech community in and of themselves in the usual sense of a shared verbal repertoire and a set of sociocultural norms of use; differences in cause or type of retardation and differences in linguistic skills alone preclude that possibility. Sociolinguistic norms exist for mentally retarded individuals only insofar as they are imposed by the speech community in which the persons live or are expected to operate. Nonetheless, mentally retarded persons may constitute a subcommunity within the speech community, marked, perhaps, only by their deviation from its norms.

The ethnographic and sociolinguistic approach to communication is concerned with determining the linguistic resources available to speakers and the use to which those means are put. It is important to note, for example, that semantic functions can be expressed by speakers through means other than those used by normal adult members of the speech community. The fact that functions are expressed through different means must not be interpreted to signify that those functions do not exist in the repertoire of the speakers (Kernan, 1970). As Price-Williams and Sabsay (1979) point out, severely retarded individuals may make utterances that are linguistically ill-formed from the standpoint of the grammar of normal adult speakers, but, nevertheless, these utterances serve to express a wide range of functions. If only the normative means of expressing these functions is accepted as evidence of their presence in the repertoire of the speaker, an inaccurate picture of his competence is gained, as has been the case with children, mentally retarded persons, and dialect speakers. An ethnography of the communication of the mentally retarded, then, is concerned with describing the linguistic means available to, and the speech behaviors of, mentally retarded individuals. At the same time, it is concerned with determining the ways in which those means and behaviors differ from or conform to those of the speech community to which the speakers belong.

Observation of the speech of mentally retarded persons in a variety of settings, with different interlocutors and different communicative goals, should form the background for studies that seek to determine whether competence or incompetence is situationally specific or cross-situational, and whether it is linguistic, cognitive, social, or emotional in origin. It should be emphasized again that little is known about the communicative competence of mentally retarded persons as we have defined it here, and that a great deal of exploratory work is necessary. The questions we have raised can only be answered by research that observes the mentally retarded in naturally occurring verbal interactions.

SUMMARY

If our understanding of mental retardation and of the lives of mentally retarded individuals is to be increased and improved, the reasoning and judgment, the personal and socioemotional adjustment, and the communicative competence of mentally retarded persons are important—in our view, crucial—areas of study and research. The research that we are doing and that we hope to continue is perhaps not unique in terms of the subject areas with which it is concerned. Studies of personality, thought, and language of the mentally retarded are numerous and have a long history. Our research does, however, investigate these topics in terms of the whole lives of the individuals studied and in the context in which those lives are lived, which is a unique approach. We do not, however, pursue the research for its uniqueness; rather, we are convinced that the thought, personality, and language of mentally retarded people cannot be fully understood as isolated or separable entities but must be studied as aspects of whole individuals who live their lives in the real world. Recent conceptual and methodological advances in the behavioral sciences have made it possible for this research to begin. Although the work is difficult, time-consuming, and expensive, we are convinced that it is worthwhile and necessary, and it is our intention to pursue it as we have outlined here.

ACKNOWLEDGMENTS

We would like to thank Ronald Gallimore, Harold G. Levine, and Sharon Sabsay for their helpful advice, comments, and contributions to this paper.

REFERENCES

Adams, J. 1973. Adaptive behavior and measured intelligence in the classification of mental retardation. Am. J. Ment. Defic. 78:77–81.

Anderson, E. 1975. A selected bibliography on language input to children. Stanford Papers Rep. Child Lang. Dev. 9:75–86.

Angelino, H., and Shedd, C. L. 1956. A study of the reactions to "frustration" of a group of mentally retarded children as measured by the Rosenzweig Picture-Frustration Study. Psychol. Newsletter 8:49–54.

Avila, D. L., and Lawson, J. R. 1962. The Thematic Apperception Test as a diagnostic tool with retarded adults. Percept. Mot. Skills 15:323–325.

Bedrosian, J., and Prutting, C. 1976. The communicative performance of the mentally retarded adult. Unpublished paper, University of California, Department of Speech and Hearing, Santa Barbara.

Beier, D. C. 1964. Behavioral disturbances in the mentally retarded. In: H. A. Stevens and R. Heber (eds.), Mental Retardation: A Review of Research. The University of Chicago Press, Chicago.

Bem, D. J., and Allen, A. 1974. On predicting some of the people some of the time: The search for cross-situational consistencies in behavior. Psychol. Rev. 40:17–26.

Benton, A. L. 1956. The Rorschach test and the diagnosis of cerebral pathology in children. Am. J. Orthopsychiatry 26:783–791.

Bercovici, S. 1977. Applied research and program development for the retarded adult in the community. Paper presented at the Annual Meeting of the American Association on Mental Deficiency, New Orleans.

Bergman, M., and Fisher, L. A. 1953. The value of the Thematic Apperception Test in mental deficiency. Psychiatr. Q. Supplement 27:22–42.

Birenbaum, A., and Seiffer, S. 1976. Resettling Retarded Adults in a Managed Community. Praeger Publishers, New York.

Bjaanes, A. T., and Butler, E. W. 1974. Environmental variation in community care facilities for mentally retarded persons. Am. J. Ment. Defic. 78:429–439.

Blacketer-Simmonds, D. A. 1953. An investigation into the supposed differences existing between mongols and other mentally defective subjects with regard to certain psychological traits. Journal of Ment. Sci. 90:702–719.

Blount, W. R. 1968. Language and the more severely retarded: A review. Am. J. Ment. Defic. 73:21–29.

Bogdan, R., and Taylor, S. J. 1975. Introduction to Qualitative Research Methods. Riley, New York.

Braginsky, D. D., and Braginsky, B. M. 1971. Hansels and Gretels—Studies of Children in Institutions for the Mentally Retarded. Holt, Rinehart and Winston, Inc., New York.

Buium, M., Rynders, J., and Turnure, J. 1975. Early maternal linguistic environment of normal and Down's syndrome language-learning children. Am. J. Ment. Defic. 79:52–58.

Chambers, G. S., and Hamlin, R. M. 1957. Rorschach "inner life" capacity of imbeciles under varied conditions. Am. J. Ment. Defic. 62:88–95.

Cherkes, M. The understanding and use of formal logic in the mentally handicapped. Unpublished manuscript. University of Connecticut.

Chomsky, N. 1965. Aspects of the Theory of Syntax. MIT Press, Boston.

Clarke, D. F. 1974. Psychological assessment in mental subnormality: Social competence, vocational and rehabilitative prospects, personality measures. In: A. M. Clarke and A. D. B. Clarke (eds.), Mental Deficiency: The Changing Outlook. 3rd Ed. Free Press, New York.

Cobb, H. V. 1972. The Forecast of Fulfillment: A Review of Research on Predictive Assessment of the Adult Retarded for Social and Vocational Adjustment. Teachers College Press, Columbia University, New York.

Cobb, O. H. 1923. Parole of mental defectives. Proc. Am. Assoc. Study Feebleminded 28:145–148.

Cole, M., Gay, J., and Sharp, D. W. 1971. The Cultural Context of Learning and Thinking. Basic Books, Inc., New York.

Cole, M., and Scribner, S. 1974. Culture and Thought. John Wiley and Sons, Inc., New York.

Cromer, R. F. 1974. Receptive language in the mentally retarded: Processes and diagnostic distinctions. In: R. L. Schiefelbusch and L. L. Lloyd (eds.), Language Perspectives: Acquisition, Retardation, and Intervention, pp. 237–268. University Park Press, Baltimore.

Cromwell, R. L. 1963. A social learning approach to mental retardation. In: N. R. Ellis (ed.), Handbook of Mental Deficiency. McGraw-Hill Book Company, New York.

Cromwell, R. L. 1967. Success-failure reactions in mentally retarded children. In: J. Zubin and G. Jervis (eds.), Psychopathology in Mental Development. Grune and Stratton, New York.

Dingman, H. F., and Tarjan, G. 1960. Mental retardation and the normal distribution curve. Am. J. Ment. Defic. 64:991, 994.

Edgerton, R. B. 1967. The Cloak of Competence: Stigma in the Lives of the Mentally Retarded. University of California Press, Berkeley.

Edgerton, R. G. 1975. Issues Relating to the Quality of Life Among Mentally Retarded Persons. In: M. J. Begab and S. A. Richardson (eds.), The Mentally Retarded and Society: A Social Science Perspective, pp. 127–140. University Park Press, Baltimore.

Edgerton, R. B., and Bercovici, S. M. 1976. The cloak of competence: Years later. Am. J. Ment. Defic. 80:485–497.

Edgerton, R. B., and Langness, L. L. 1978. Observing mentally retarded persons in community settings: An anthropological approach. In: G. P. Sackett (ed.), Observing Behavior, Vol. 1. Theory and Applications in Mental Retardation, pp. 335–348. University Park Press, Baltimore.

Ellis, A., and Beechley, R. M. 1950. A comparison of matched groups of mongoloid and non-mongoloid feebleminded children. Am. J. Ment. Defic. 54:464–468.

Ervin-Tripp, S., and Mitchell-Kernan, C. 1977. Introduction. In: S. Ervin-Tripp and C. Mitchell-Kernan (eds.), Child Discourse, pp. 1–23. Academic Press, Inc., New York.

Falmagne, R. J. (ed.). 1975. Reasoning: Representation and Process in Children and Adults. Lawrence Erlbaum Associates, Publishers, Hillsdale, N.J.

Feldman, A. 1946. Psychoneurosis in the mentally retarded. Am. J. Ment. Defic. 51:247–254.

Ferguson, C. 1975. Baby talk as a simplified register. Stanford Papers Rep. Child Lang. Dev. 9:75–86.

Gardner, W. I. 1967. Use of the California Test of Personality with the mentally retarded. Ment. Retard. 5:12–16.

Gardner, W. I. 1968. Personality characteristics of the mentally retarded: Review and critique. In: H. J. Prehm, L. A. Hamerlynck, and J. E. Crosson (eds.), Behavioral Research in Mental Retardation. Rehabilitation Research and Training Center in Mental Retardation, Monograph no. 1, Eugene, Oregon.

Garrison, K. C., and Force, D. G., Jr. 1965. The Psychology of Exceptional Children. 4th Ed. Ronald Press, New York.

Guthrie, G. M., Butler, A., and Gorlow, L. 1962. Patterns of self attitudes of retardates. Am. J. Ment. Defic. 66:222–229.

Guthrie, G. M., Butler, A., Gorlow, L., and White, G. N. 1964. Non-verbal expression of self-attitudes of retardates. Am. J. Ment. Defic. 69:42–49.

Heber, R. 1964. Personality. In: H. A. Stevens and R. Heber (eds.), Mental Retardation: A Review of Research. The University of Chicago Press, Chicago.

Henle, M. 1962. On the relation between logic and thinking. Psychol. Rev. 69:366–378.

Henshel, A. M. 1972. The Forgotten Ones. University of Texas Press, Austin.

Hirsch, E. A. 1959. The adaptive significance of commonly described behavior of the mentally retarded. Am. J. Ment. Defic. 63:639–646.

Hutt, M. L., and Gibby, R. G. 1965. The Mentally Retarded Child. 2nd Ed. Allyn and Bacon, Boston.

Hymes, D. 1972. On communicative competence. In: J. B. Pride and J. Holmes (eds.), Sociolinguistics: Selected Readings, pp. 269–293. Penguin Books, New York.

Inhelder, B. 1968. The Diagnosis of Reasoning in the Mentally Retarded. Chandler Publishing Company, Novato, Calif.

Johnson, G. O. 1963. Psychological characteristics of the mentally retarded. In: W. M. Cruikshank (ed.), Psychology of Exceptional Children and Youth. 2nd Ed. Prentice-Hall, Inc., Englewood Cliffs, N.J.

Johnson-Laird, P. N. 1975. Models of deduction. In: R. J. Falmagne (ed.), Reasoning: Representation and Process, pp. 7–54. Lawrence Erlbaum Associates, Publishers, Hillsdale, N.J.

Jordan, T. E. 1967. Language and mental retardation: A review of the literature. In: R. L. Schiefelbusch, R. Copeland, and J. Smith (eds.), Language and Mental Retardation, pp. 20–38. Holt, Rinehart and Winston, Inc., New York.

Kamin, L. J. 1974. The Science and Politics of I.Q. John Wiley and Sons, Inc., New York.

Keller, J. E. 1957. The relationship of auditory memory span to learning ability in high grade mentally retarded boys. Am. J. Ment. Defic. 61:574–580.

Kernan, K. T. 1970. Semantic relationships and the child's acquisition of language. Anthropol. Linguist. May:171–187.

Landesman-Dwyer, S., Stein, J. G., and Sackett, G. P. 1978. A behavioral ecological study of group homes. In: G. P. Sackett (ed.), Observing Behavior, Vol. 1. Theory and Applications in Mental Retardation. University Park Press, Baltimore.

Langness, L. L. 1964. Socio-cultural aspects of mental retardation. In: H. A. Stevens and R. Heber (eds.), Mental Retardation: A Review of Research. The University of Chicago Press, Chicago.

Langness, L. L. 1965. The Life History in Anthropological Science. Holt, Rinehart and Winston, Inc., New York.

Lewin, K. 1935. A Dynamic Theory of Personality. McGraw-Hill Book Company, New York.

Linder, S. 1978. Language context and the evaluation of the verbal competence of the retardate. Working paper no. 1. Socio-Behavioral Research Group, Mental Retardation Center, University of California at Los Angeles.

Lipman, R. S. 1959. Some test correlates of behavioral aggression in institutionalized retardates with particular references to the Rosenzweig Picture-Frustration Study. Am. J. Ment. Defic. 63:1038–1045.

McCarver, R. B., and Craig, E. M. 1974. Placement of the retarded in the community: Prognosis and outcome. In: N. R. Ellis (ed.), International Review of Research in Mental Retardation, Vol. 7. Academic Press, New York.

McPherson, G. E. 1935. Parole of mental defectives. Proc. Am. Assoc. Ment. Defic. 40:162–176.

Madge, J. 1953. The Tools of Social Science. Longmans Green, London.

Menolascino, F. J. 1970. Psychiatric Approaches to Mental Retardation. Basic Books, Inc., New York.

Mercer, J. P. 1973. Labeling the Mentally Retarded: Clinical and Social System Perspectives on Mental Retardation. University of California Press, Berkeley.

Mitchell-Kernan, C., and Kernan, K. T. 1971. A sociolinguistic approach to the relations between language, society, and the individual. In: L. Nader and T. W. Maretzki (eds.) Cultural Illness and Health. Anthropological Studies, no. 9, pp. 104–114. American Anthropological Association, Washington, D.C.

Molish, H. B. 1958. Contributions of projective tests to problems of psychological diagnosis in mental deficiency. Am. J. Ment. Defic. 63:282–292.

Muehlberger, C. E. 1972. The socio-psychological experiences of adult former residents of a state school for the mentally retarded. Ed.D. dissertation, Syracuse University.

O'Connor, G. 1976. Home is a good place: A national perspective of community residential facilities for developmentally disabled persons. Monograph no. 2, Am. Assoc. Ment. Defic.

Price-Williams, D. R. 1975. Explorations in Cross-cultural Psychology. Chandler and Sharp Publishers, Inc., San Francisco.

Price-Williams, D. R., and Sabsay, S. 1979. Communicative competence among severely retarded persons. Semiotica 26:35–63.

Rosen, M., Clark, G. R., and Kivitz, M. S. 1977. Habilitation of the Handicapped: New Dimensions in Programs for the Developmentally Disabled. University Park Press, Baltimore.

Rotter, J. B. 1954. Social Learning and Clinical Psychology. Prentice-Hall, Inc., Englewood Cliffs, N.J.

Rutter, M. L. 1971. Psychiatry. In: J. Wortis (ed.), Mental Retardation: An Annual Review, Vol. 3. Grune and Stratton, New York.

Sabsay, S., and Bennett, T. L. 1977. Communicative distress. In: E. O. Keenan and T. L. Bennett (eds.), Discourse Across Time and Space. South. Californ. Occas. Papers Linguist. 5:181–212.

Sarason, S. B. 1959. Psychological Problems in Mental Deficiency. 3rd Ed. Harper Brothers, New York.

Schatzman, L., and Strauss, A. 1973. Field Research: Strategies for a Natural Sociology. Prentice-Hall, Inc., Englewood Cliffs, N.J.

Schlanger, B. 1967. Issues for speech and language training of the mentally retarded. In: R. L. Schiefelbusch, R. H. Copeland, and J. O. Smith (eds.), Language and Mental Retardation, pp. 137–145. Holt, Rinehart and Winston, Inc., New York.

Shuy, R. W. 1977. Quantitative language data: A case for and some warnings against. Anthropol. Educ. Q. 8(2):73–82.

Siegel, G. 1963. Adult verbal behavior in "play therapy" sessions with retarded children. J. Speech Hear. Disorders Monogr. 10:34–38.

Spiro, M. 1964. Religion and the irrational. Proceedings of the American Ethnological Society, pp. 102–115.

Spradlin, J., and Rosenberg, S. 1964. Complexity of adult verbal behavior in a dyadic situation with retarded children. J. Abnorm. Soc. Psychol. 68:694–698.

Tarjan, G. 1964. The next decade: Expectations from the biological sciences. In: Mental Retardation: A Handbook for the Primary Physician, pp. 123–133. 3rd Ed. Report of the American Medical Association Conference on Mental Retardation, April 9–11.

Wallace, A. F. C. 1962. Culture and cognition. Science 135:351–357.

Windle, C. 1962. Prognosis of mental subnormals. Am. J. Ment. Defic. 66, Monograph Supplement.

Yoder, D. E., and Miller, J. G. 1972. What we may know and what we can do: Input towards a system. In: J. E. McLean, D. E. Yoder, and R. L. Schiefelbusch (eds.), Language Intervention with the Retarded: Developing Strategies. University Park Press, Baltimore.

Zigler, E. 1966. Motivational determinants in the performance of retarded children. Am. J. Orthopsychiatry 36:848–856.

Zigler, E. 1969. Developmental versus difference theories of mental retardation and the problem of motivation. Am. J. Ment. Defic. 73:536–556.

Zigler, E., and Balla, D. 1977. Personality factors in the performance of the retarded: Implications for clinical assessment. J. Am. Acad. Child Psychiatry 16:19–37.

Living Environments for Developmentally Retarded Persons
Edited by H. Carl Haywood and J. R. Newbrough
Copyright 1981 University Park Press Baltimore

Utilization of Habilitation Services by Developmentally Disabled Persons in Community Residential Facilities

Daniel W. Close, Ph.D.
Rehabilitation Research and Training
  Center in Mental Retardation
College of Education, Clinical Services Building
University of Oregon
Eugene, Oregon 97403

Gail O'Connor, Ph.D.[1]
Office of Research
Planning and Research Division
Department of Social and Health Services
Olympia, Washington 98504

Susan L. Peterson
Rehabilitation Research and Training Center
  in Mental Retardation
College of Education, Clinical Services Buiding
University of Oregon
Eugene, Oregon 97403

INTRODUCTION

Foremost among the rights long denied mentally retarded individuals
in North America has been the opportunity for habilitation in the least

---

[1] Now at 916 64th Avenue, East, Tacoma, Washington 98424

restrictive residential environment. The large public institution, once regarded with promise as a setting where retarded persons could learn competence and independence, has fallen far short of these optimistic goals. The principle of normalization has now been introduced and specifically focused on providing services for mentally retarded and other developmentally disabled persons. The movement toward deinstitutionalization of mentally retarded persons to the least restrictive residential setting is the zeitgeist for services in the next decade (O'Connor, 1976).

Some immediate effects of deinstitutionalization have been a decrease in the number of placements in state institutions (Butterfield, 1976) and a development of programs for early detection and remediation of developmental disabilities. The outcome of these programs has been to reduce the severity and scope of these disabilities, making institutional placement unnecessary (Hanson, 1977; Meier, 1975). As the number of placements has decreased, the number of developmentally disabled persons being served in community residential facilities has correspondingly increased (Scheerenberger, 1976).

CURRENT STUDIES ON HABILITATION SERVICES

Although many states have aggressively implemented policies of deinstitutionalization, unfortunately, legislators, parents, and human service professionals have not been able to agree on the value or the goals of deinstitutionalization. Furthermore, there is little empirical evidence available to guide program planners in its implementation. Landesman-Dwyer, Stein, and Sackett (1978) stated: "In effect, the movement to small community-based facilities may be viewed as a large scale, poorly controlled human experiment, guided by the good intentions and economic considerations of politicians, planners, parents, and professionals" (p. 349).

According to the normalization principle, all human services should be provided in the home community, where each developmentally disabled child can be aided by early intervention and public school programs. However, some disabled children and most disabled adults cannot be kept at home, and some form of residential service is needed (Larsen, 1977). Unfortunately, the development of community programs for retarded and other developmentally disabled persons has not progressed as rapidly as is desirable (Scheerenberger, 1976). Present figures estimate that over 150,000 retarded individuals presently reside in state and private residential facilities (Bruinincks, personal communication, April 18, 1978). These figures indicate that a concerted effort is needed to effectively integrate institutionalized individuals back into their home communities, while continuing to develop quality programs for those who have not been institutionalized.

Integration is the foundation of true normalization. Wolfensberger (1972) posited that normalization cannot be accomplished unless the developmentally disabled are physically and socially integrated into their communities. Physical integration includes: housing in a typical residential neighborhood with landscaping and homelike furnishings, the availability of privacy, a personalized sleeping area, a supportive atmosphere, and competent management. Social integration refers to the quality and quantity of resident involvement in the resources of the community. Specific resources include the availability and adequacy of educational, social, recreational, vocational, and transportation services. Physical and social integration is achieved when persons interact with the general community in normal ways: residing in ordinary housing, shopping at the neighborhood store, traveling on public transportation, visiting with neighbors, working at a meaningful job, and participating in cultural and recreational activities. Integration, then, is accomplished when retarded persons are physically and socially members of their community.

The commitment to normalized living for the previously institutionalized retarded person requires a high level of economic support, program planning, and implementation. Ideally, this process would begin as a cooperative relationship between the institution and individual communities. The institution would provide habilitative training for the residents to ensure a smooth transition to the community. Personnel within the institution should gear their programs to the individual characteristics of the residents and their communities. In turn, communities should prepare to receive retarded persons and actively plan to ensure their long-term adjustment (Gollay, 1977). This coordinated effort would be implemented on a flexible timetable to account for any problems that may arise.

A perusal of the literature on community adjustment of retarded persons indicates that the deinstitutionalization movement is not as successful as the original theorists and planners had hoped. In the quest for an idealized living environment for retarded persons, legislators and agency personnel have mistaken physical movement from the institution to the community to be equivalent to normalized living. Rosen (1976) states: "The current controversy over institution versus community placements is pointless . . . if either institutions or community placement programs adhere to accepted standards of quality, the argument neutralizes itself" (p. 1).

Present research information on the success of the small,

community-based residential facility is sparse and rarely empirically sound. The majority of the programs described in the literature are simple case studies of the type of residents served, the range of services provided, and a subjective impression of the success of the program. McCarver and Craig (1974) summarized much of this literature up to 1972 and concluded: "With the present state of knowledge, community placement is typically on a trial and error basis and evaluation is mainly subjective" (p. 199).

One of the first systematic studies of retarded persons in community settings was conducted by Bjaanes and Butler (1974). Bjaanes and Butler used a direct observation method to study the components of the environment of community-care facilities for retarded persons. They reported substantial differences between board-and-care (larger facilities with between 30 and 50 residents) and home-care (small facilities with between 4 and 6 residents) on a number of critical dimensions. One major finding was that home-care facilities were geographically and socially isolated, whereas there was considerable contact with the community in the board-and-care facilities. The results of this study were limited because of the small sample size and the limited number of observations per facility. In a follow-up to the 1974 study, Butler and Bjaanes (1978) reported more striking results. Again using an observational method of data collection, they studied 171 care facilities in southern California. The results of this study indicated that larger care facilities "generally use agencies services and programs and have more internal normalizing activities . . . than smaller facilities" (p. 398). The researchers concluded that a care facility must have an active habilitation program within the facility and must encourage interaction and use of existing community facilities.

In another major study, conducted as a long-term follow-up of the landmark *Cloak of Competence* study, Edgerton and Bercovici (1976) reported that mildly retarded persons who successfully adjusted to the community were those who interacted in their communities in normal modes and who had some benefactor or affiliate to assist them in the difficult aspects of daily living. Edgerton and Bercovici emphasized that the assistance given these deinstitutionalized persons is not from the social service system, but from neighbors and other interested friends.

Landesman-Dwyer and colleagues (Landesman-Dwyer, Stein, and Sackett, 1978) utilized the direct observation method for describing the daily behaviors of mildly, moderately, and severely retarded adults living in group homes in Washington State. These researchers provided extensive documentation on neighborhood and group home characteristics and on the major activities of residents. Fully 98% of the residents who were studied regularly participated in school, work, and other training programs during weekdays. However, in investigating the relationship between daily activity and client ability, the researchers found that the activities of mildly retarded persons are significantly different from the activities of severely and profoundly retarded persons. Specifically, mildly retarded persons spend less time in inactive and undesirable behaviors and more time in household maintenance and in social and community activities than severely and profoundly retarded persons. The mildly retarded residents engaged in activities ranging from "visiting friends in neighboring group homes to participating in community activities, such as dances, bowling, swimming, talent shows, or shopping" (p. 359). This result is in striking contrast to the behavior of the severely and profoundly retarded residents, who were maintaining many of the so-called institutional behaviors, e.g., extended periods of inactivity, undesirable behavior, and little positive or productive behavior. The Landesman-Dwyer et al. study (1978) seems to indicate that a higher level of program development exists for those mildly retarded persons living in residential facilities, at least in the state of Washington.

A study that compared the differences between institutional and community living for severely and profoundly retarded adults was presented by Close (1977). Close employed an observational system to obtain information on the social interactions of two groups of severely retarded adults. The residents in the group home were exposed to a systematic self-care and socialization training program, an adult education program, and a community vocational training program (Bellamy, Petersen, and Close, 1975). The residents in the institution received the standard habilitation program of self-care training and social/recreational programming. The result of this study indicated that persons living in the group home produced more significant gains in self-care, socialization, and vocational skills than the group remaining in the institution (Bellamy, Close, and Crowley, 1975). Assessing the Landesman-Dwyer et al. (1978) and Close (1977) data together, it would appear that the level of program specificity and the availability of community resources are significant factors in developing residential programs for retarded persons.

One of the problems with these studies is that they represent a small sample of the total population of community residential facilities in North America. Only two studies from a national perspective have been conducted and presented in the literature. Elinor Gollay (1977) presented a description of data obtained under contract by ABT Associates Inc. The purpose of the study was to "assess the adjustment of deinstitutionalized mentally retarded persons to community life"

(p. 137). One of the primary focuses of the study was to obtain information on the characteristics of communities, specifically the amount
of services and training provided or available in the community. Of
interest are two general findings that indicate that the residents studied
were involved in an average of 1.2 day placement (either sheltered
workshop, school, or day activity program) per resident. Although this
is encouraging, further data indicate that 50 individuals or roughly 12%
of the individuals studied were not involved in any placement. In addition, 30% of the parents studied perceived that most of their child's
needs were not being met in the community.

Another study of national significance was published by O'Connor
(1976). O'Connor's *Home is a Good Place* was the first comprehensive description of the population of community residential facilities
with a national perspective. This project sought to "determine the
number, size, and general characteristics of existing community residential facilities, to identify patterns of use and needs for community
services; and to ascertain the characteristics of residents" (p. 10). In
the monograph, O'Connor attempted to differentiate those facilities
that met the physical criteria of normalization from those that did not.
The results indicated that 69% of the facilities studied met the physical
normalization criteria. These criteria included: 1) type of housing,
2) presence of special features in the home, 3) type of furnishings,
4) personalization of sleeping area, 5) opportunity for privacy, and 6) an
interviewer's subjective impressions of the general atmosphere of the
living situation and of the management and physical set-up of the home.
Given positive results on the degree of normalization of the physical
environment, it is also important to determine whether these physically
normalized facilities also differ in the social dimension.

In this chapter, information from O'Connor's (1976) report is used
to compare physically normalized and non-normalized facilities that
utilize community habilitation services. Specifically, it examines the
differences between the physically normalized and the non-normalized
facilities in terms of the availability and adequacy of community
services.

Method

The information for this chapter was obtained using data collected by
O'Connor (1976) for the monograph. The data were collected using an
extensive questionnaire that covered the following areas: 1) facility
description, including management, staffing, and costs; 2) resident information, including background and characteristics, and lifestyle; and
3) utilization of community services. In order to maximize response
validity, only professional interviewers were employed. All interviews

were conducted within the facility itself. The average length of time for the interview was 4 hours, allowing the interviewer the opportunity to observe and to validate many points under study.

O'Connor classified each facility as normalized or non-normalized based on a physical integration definition of normalization. For this chapter, physically normalized and non-normalized facilities were compared on the social integration component of normalization, e.g., the availability and adequacy of community services that are necessary to promote and support the normalization process.

Results

Results of the study included evaluation of the normalized and non-normalized group on the availability and adequacy of general community services and client-oriented community services. No statistical tests were used in analyzing the data because of the marked similarity between the groups. When sample facilities were analyzed using the social integration definition, 33% of the normalized facilities and 33% of the non-normalized facilities reported that five or more community services were needed but were unavailable or inadequate (see Figure 1). When the definition of community services is restricted to client-oriented (educational, vocational, social-recreational, and transportation) services, similar results are obtained. Twenty-two percent of the normalized group reported no need for services, 32% needed one service, 24% needed two services, 12% needed three services, and 10% needed all four services. This is similar to the non-normalized group, which reported 21% in need of no services, 30% in need of one service, 24% in need of two services, 12% in need of three services, and 9% in need of all four services (see Figure 2). The need for client-oriented facilities was similar across all categories (see Figure 3).

DISCUSSION

The purpose of the study was to investigate whether community residential facilities that had been classified as normalized according to a physical definition differed when compared according to a social definition of normalization. Six variables comprised the physical dimension: 1) type of housing; 2) presence of special features in the home; 3) type of furnishings; 4) personalization of the sleeping area; 5) opportunity for privacy; and 6) an interviewer's subjective comments about the facility environment. The four aspects of the social dimension of normalization were facility administrator's response to the availability and adequacy of 1) educational, 2) vocational, 3) social-recreational, and 4) transportation services in the community.

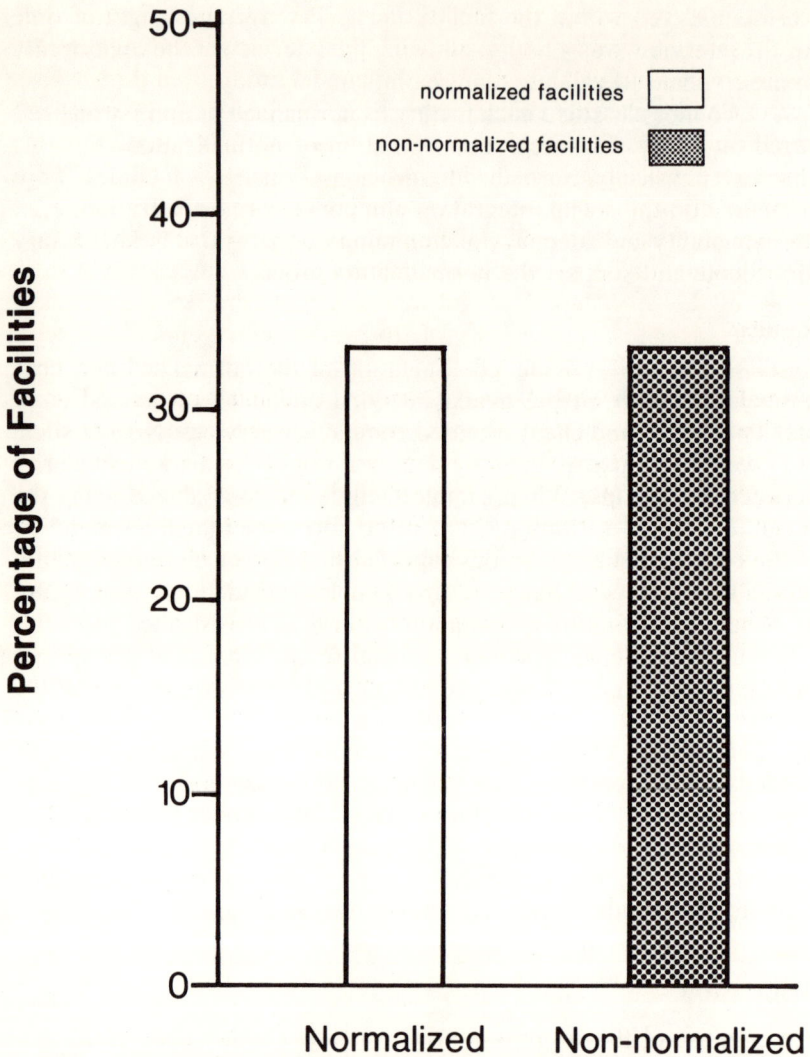

Figure 1.   Facilities reporting a need for five or more community services.

The results showed that physically normalized and non-normalized facilities do not differ when analyzed using a definition of normalization based on the interaction of physical and social integration. The results indicate that physical characteristics are not a sufficient basis for defining normalized community residential facilities. This point supports Zigler and Balla's (1977) assertion that the quality of human interaction is far more important than the physical characteristics of settings in determining programmatic effectiveness. Although these findings suggest that many community residential facilities are providing a quality living environment, the residents of these facilities often do not have access to the full array of habilitation services needed to promote and support normalized behavior.

These results are disturbing when placed against the idealistic rhetoric that preceded the current impetus for community living for the developmentally disabled. Theoretically, movement from the large custodial institution to smaller community-based facilities would solve many of the problems involved in residential care for the developmentally disabled. The results of this study offer support to recent findings that indicate that small community residential facilities have limited interaction with the community (Butler and Bjaanes, 1978) and that they are associated with less positive social behavior than larger facilities (Landesman-Dwyer, Stein, and Sackett, 1978). Given these tentative results indicating a limited effectiveness of community residential facilities, it is desirable to theorize about some of the potential factors contributing to these findings and to suggest some possible directions for future research and program development in community residential facilities for the developmentally disabled.

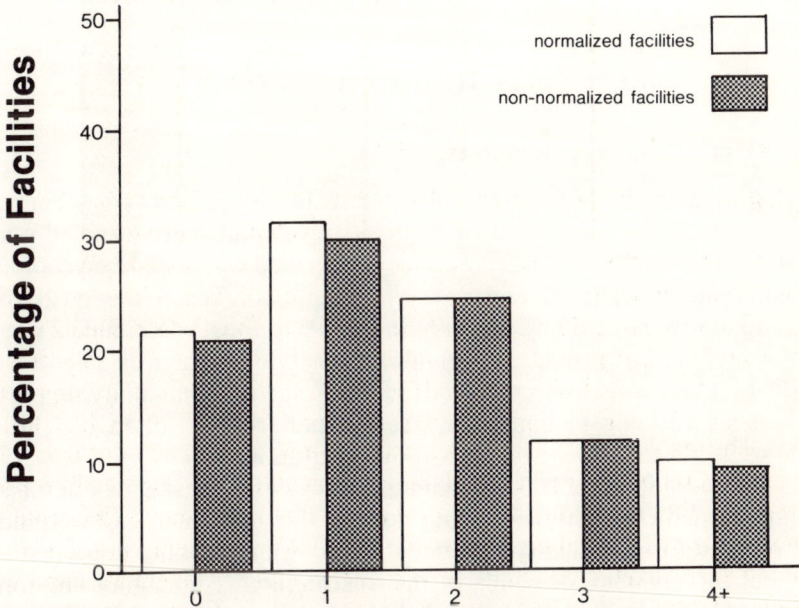

Figure 2.   Client-oriented services unavailable or inadequate.

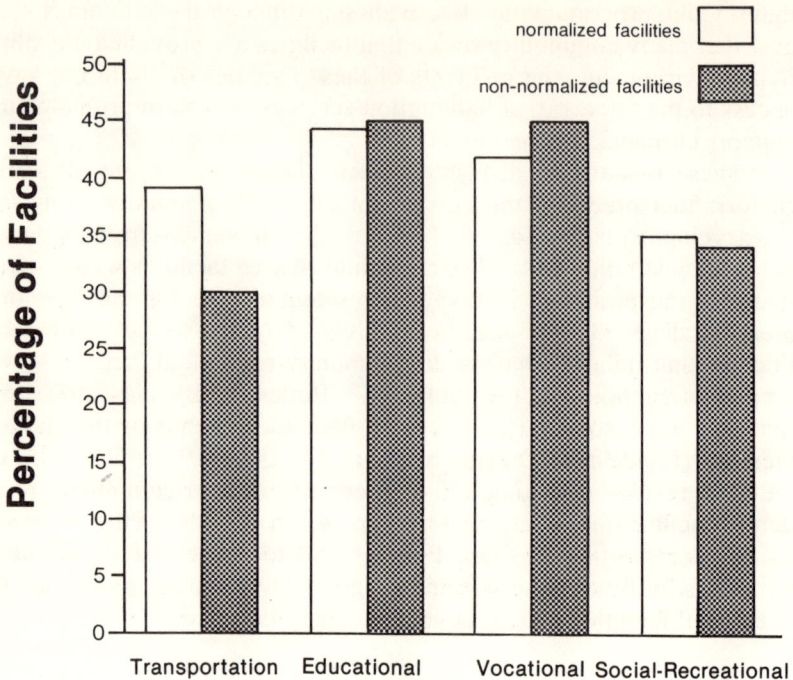

Figure 3.   Percentage of facilities reporting need for client-oriented services.

IMPLICATIONS FOR DEINSTITUTIONALIZATION

Lack of Community Resources

Historically, the large, state-operated institutional facility has been a major provider of residential care for developmentally disabled persons. The institution was a setting where medical, social, psychological, and educational expertise was centered. When the push for community-based living occurred in the 1960s, most communities were not prepared to provide a normalized lifestyle for their disabled residents. There were few residential facilities and little community support. Persons residing in community residential facilities often had little more to do than was available in the institution.

In addition to a lack of community resources, residents often had not learned effective daily living skills in the institution, and were not prepared for community placement. They were not only untrained to meet the complex demands of the unstructured community environment, but they had also acquired many personal behaviors that are incompatible with community standards (Gladden, 1973). Thus, communities were not equipped to provide a normalized lifestyle for their developmentally disabled residents, much less remediate many of the bizarre behaviors of those who had lived in institutional settings.

A number of problems occurred as communities began developing residential services. As was mentioned earlier, there were few persons of expertise available in many communities to initiate residential and supportive services. Programs were either started by parent or consumer groups (Wehbring and Ogren, 1975), or by private profit-making organizations (O'Connor, 1976). Facilities attempted to simulate normal family environments, attending to many of the physical aspects of the living, while ignoring the necessity for resident involvement in the community. Because of the rapid placement of individuals into community settings, staff without the skills necessary to work with developmentally disabled persons were hired. There were few standards for staff competence and little paraprofessional or professional training. This lack of programmatic expertise has resulted in dramatic differences in the quality of staff supervising these facilities and a marked variability in the effectiveness of the programs. The apparent inability of community residential facilities to promote normalized behavior in developmentally disabled persons has led to criticism of these programs (Payne, 1976).

Opposition to Deinstitutionalization

Advocates for community living originally assumed that the integration of the developmentally disabled would have positive effects on the majority of the community (Wolfensberger, 1972). Presumably, neighbors and other community members would become more accepting, develop positive attitudes, and desire social contact after interaction with handicapped persons. The movement of developmentally disabled individuals into regular schools, into neighborhood settings, and into competitive employment was predicated on this assumption. Unfortunately, the research literature indicates that these positive social attitudes have not developed. In fact, there is adequate documentation that the general public holds essentially negative attitudes toward integrating the developmentally disabled into the community (Berdiansky and Parker, 1977, Gottlieb, 1975).

This attitudinal barrier has caused many problems for the development of community programs. Armstrong (1976) asserted that some communities are enacting restrictive zoning ordinances to prevent developmentally disabled persons from living in particular neighborhoods. Payne (1976) indicated that many parents of institutionalized persons are fighting deinstitutionalization efforts because of the perceived fears of community living.

In part, some of the resistance was to be anticipated. Any major social change naturally has its detractors. The distressing part of the present criticism is that much of this criticism is based on the substantive fact that community-based programs are not as effective as they were originally envisioned to be. The lack of coordinated planning, the inadequacy of program models, and the absence of public education activities are products of a naive concept of social change.

CONCLUSIONS

The results of this study support the following conclusions:

1. Community residential facilities cannot be differentiated on the basis of a physical normalization criterion.
2. Social integration of the developmentally disabled into community settings must include both the physical aspects of the home environment and the opportunity for residents to utilize community agencies.
3. Further efforts should be undertaken to develop exemplary systems of program coordination.
4. Public education programs should be an integral aspect of any deinstitutionalization process.

A normalized community residential facility is defined by the quality of the physical environment and the habilitative programs both within and outside the facility. The proponents of deinstitutionalization must be aware that the simple movement of persons from one setting to the next does not constitute progress.

REFERENCES

Armstrong, B. 1976. Preparing the community for the patient's return. Hosp. Community Psychiatry 27(5):349–356.
Bellamy, T., Close, D., and Crowley, R. 1975. Multiple evaluation of a deinstitutionalization program. Paper presented at the Annual Convention of the American Association on Mental Deficiency, May, Portland.
Bellamy, T., Petersen, L., and Close, D. 1975. Habilitation of the severely and profoundly retarded: Illustrations of competence. Educ. Train. Ment. Retard. 10:174–186.
Berdiansky, H. A., and Parker, R. 1977. Establishing a group home for the adult mentally retarded in North Carolina. Ment. Retard. 15(5):8–11.
Bjaanes, A., and Butler, W. 1974. Environmental variation in community care facilities for the mentally retarded. Am. J. Ment. Defic. 78:429–439.
Butler, E., and Bjaanes, A. 1978. Activities and the use of time by retarded persons in community care facilities. In: G. P. Sackett (ed.), Observing Behavior, Vol. 1. Theory and Applications in Mental Retardation. University Park Press, Baltimore.

Butterfield, E. 1976. Some basic changes in residential facilities. In: R. Kugel and A. Shearer (eds.), Changing Patterns in Residential Services for the Mentally Retarded. U.S. Government Printing Office, Washington, D.C.

Close, D. 1977. Community living for severely and profoundly retarded adults: A group home study. Educ. Train. Ment. Retard. 12:256–262.

Edgerton, R., and Bercovici, S. 1976. The cloak of competence: Years later. Am. J. Ment. Defic. 80:485–497.

Gladden, J. 1973. Sheltered living programs at the Lubbock State School. In: C. K. Sigelman (ed.), Group Homes for the Mentally Retarded, Monograph no. 1. Research and Training Center in Mental Retardation, Texas Tech. University, August, Lubbock, Texas.

Gollay, E. 1977. Deinstitutionalized mentally retarded people: A closer look. Educ. Train. Ment. Retard. 12:137–144.

Gottlieb, J. 1975. Public, peer, and professional attitudes toward mentally retarded persons. In: M. J. Begab and S. A. Richardson (eds.), The Mentally Retarded and Society: A Social Science Perspective. University Park Press, Baltimore.

Hanson, M. 1977. Teaching Down's Syndrome Children: Manual for Parents. University of Oregon, Eugene.

Landesman-Dwyer, S., Stein, J., and Sackett, G. P. 1978. A behavioral and ecological study of group homes. In: G. P. Sackett (ed.), Observing Behavior, Vol. 1. Theory and Applications in Mental Retardation. University Park Press, Baltimore.

Larsen, L. 1977. Community services necessary to program effectively for the severely/profoundly handicapped. In: E. Sontag, J. Smith, and N. Certo (eds.), Educational Programming for the Severely and Profoundly Handicapped. The Council for Exceptional Children, Reston, Va.

McCarver, R. B., and Craig, E. M. 1974. Placement of the retarded in the community: Prognosis and outcome. In: N. R. Ellis (ed.), International Review of Research in Mental Retardation, Vol. 7. Academic Press, Inc., New York.

Meier, J. H. 1975. Dimensions of early detection of developmental disabilities. Themes Issues 3:3–12.

O'Connor, G. 1976. Home is a Good Place: A National Perspective of Community Residential Facilities for Developmentally Disabled Persons, Monograph no. 2. American Association on Mental Deficiency, Washington, D.C.

Payne, J. 1976. The deinstitutionalization backlash. Ment. Retard. 14:43–45.

Rosen, D. 1976. Deinstitutionalization. In: J. Stamm and J. Carta (eds.), Perspectives on Programming for the Severely Handicapped. University of Oregon, Eugene.

Scheerenberger, R. C. 1976. A study of public residential facilities. Ment. Retard. 14(1):32–35.

Wehbring, K., and Ogren, C. 1975. Community Residences of Mentally Retarded People. National Association for Retarded Citizens, Arlington, Texas.

Wolfensberger, W. 1972. The Principle of Normalization in Human Services. National Institute on Mental Retardation, Toronto, Canada.

Zigler, E. and Balla, D. A. 1977. Impact of institutional experience on the behavior and development of retarded persons. Am. J. Ment. Defic. 82:1–11.

Living Environments for Developmentally Retarded Persons
Edited by H. Carl Haywood and J. R. Newbrough
Copyright 1981 University Park Press Baltimore

Community Placement of Mentally Retarded Persons
Clinical and Environmental Considerations

Jeffrey L. Crawford, Ph.D.
Director, Clinical Systems Development
Information Sciences Division
Rockland Research Institute
Orangeburg, New York 10962

Donna E. Thompson, Ph.D.
Faculty of Arts and Science
Department of Psychology
Psychology Building
New York University
6 Washington Place, Room 550
New York, New York 10003

John R. Aiello, Ph.D.
Department of Psychology
Douglass College
Rutgers-The State University
New Brunswick, New Jersey 08903

Over the years, mentally retarded persons have passed through cycles from segregated institutionalization to community care. The current trend is to phase out large, publicly operated institutions by moving mentally retarded persons from state hospitals and training schools to

Supported by the New York State Health Research Council Grant 1410 and the New York State Office of Mental Retardation and Developmental Disabilities.

community-based residential alternatives (Barton, 1952, 1953, 1954, 1955, 1959, 1960, 1963; Barton and St. John, 1962; Bindman, 1969; Comptroller General, 1977; Crawford, Aiello, and Thompson, 1979; Crissey, 1975; Fairweather et al., 1969; Hutchison, 1970; Koch and Okada, 1972; Lee, 1963; Macht, 1974; Mamula and Newman, 1973; Miles, 1974; Shearer, 1972). Although some mentally retarded persons will always require extensive supervision in highly structured environments, a large majority of mentally retarded persons can function in smaller, less structured community environments (Nihira and Nihira, 1975).

Several factors must be taken into account prior to the placement of mentally retarded persons in community-based residences. This chapter examines the clinical and environmental factors. The review is based on the assumption that successful community placement is, in part, functionally related to the interaction of client demographic and behavioral characteristics with the sociophysical environmental structures of community-based residences.

NORMALIZATION, DEINSTITUTIONALIZATION, AND COMMUNITY PLACEMENT

Normalization

The process of community reintegration referred to as deinstitutionalization is based largely on the concept of normalization (deSilva and Faflak, 1976; Nirje, 1970; Wolfensberger et al., 1972). Normalization emphasizes the civil rights of mentally retarded persons and supports placement of institutionalized clients in the least restrictive environments available, within reason.

The Community Mental Health Centers Act and the Mental Retardation Facilities and Community Mental Health Centers Construction Act of 1963 signalled the beginning of a national policy of comprehensive community services for developmentally and psychiatrically disabled persons. The principles of the 1963 Act have had an international impact (Bindman, 1969; Hutchison, 1970; Koch and Okada, 1972; Miles, 1974). The Act emphasized the integration of the client and the community; consequently, the trend in mental retardation has become to care for and to educate developmentally disabled persons in their homes, foster homes, day-care centers, special classes, sheltered workshops and group homes rather than to commit them to large, depersonalizing institutions (Birnbrauer, 1976).

With the 1976 report of the President's Committee on Mental Retardation came a recommendation that every retarded person should have the "maximum opportunity to live in a local community setting of his or her choosing.'' The act further assured: 1) that the mentally retarded person has an increasing range of choices about where he/she shall live; 2) that services required to maintain the client in the community are available; 3) that restrictive fire, safety, and zoning codes are modified to recognize the degrees of independence and the responsibilities of retarded persons in the community; 4) that centralized, comprehensive residential institutions are changed from traditional warehouses to facilities for specific purposes, governed by those purposes; 5) that states and communities utilize the resources of environmental designers to enhance environments of existing and developing services; and 6) that comprehensive review and research continue to be carried out.

Deinstitutionalization

The deinstitutionalization process is predicated upon several interrelated events that include, but are not limited to: 1) placing those clients who have the skills to adapt outside the institution in community residences, 2) developing institutional programs for teaching clients those skills necessary for continued stay in the community, 3) developing community-based residential environments, 4) providing services in the community of residence, 5) educating the community in order to prevent or overcome resistance to residential placements, 6) specifying criteria for inpatient admission to avoid inappropriate admissions, and 7) generating mechanisms for placing clients in the particular community residence that matches the client's social, physical, and psychological needs.

Community response to the Mental Health Centers Act has lagged noticeably behind initial expectations (Comptroller General, 1977). Deinstitutionalization connotes the mass influx of patients from state institutions into communities that are not prepared to provide the residences and services required (Bachrach, 1976; Lamb, 1975; Lamb and Goertzel, 1971, 1972a, 1972b; Rutman, 1976). What the news media has dubbed the "revolving door" phenomenon has been the unfortunate result of poor preplacement screening, lack of community services, apathy on the part of local and state officials, and inadequate follow-up. Although many mentally retarded persons have been successfully placed in the community, many other mentally retarded persons enter, re-enter, or remain in public institutions when they could be treated in the community. Other persons have been placed in crowded, substandard facilities in unsafe neighborhoods. Many of these facilities are without provision for needed services and are even without the assurance that the client received the needed services (Comptroller General, 1977). Morrissey (1966, 1967) noted that somewhat less than half of the available hospitals had, at that time, developed the facilities necessary for community placement.

Community Placement

Community placement is the activity of a community agency that provides openings for X clients with certain, general characteristics (e.g., age between 25–44, male). The inpatient facility searches its records, finds X-plus clients fitting the criteria, and then selects the appropriate number of persons. The process of selecting a subset of all the clients in the facility that fit certain characteristics is highly subjective, often political, and generally does not reflect the actual needs and abilities requisite for survival in the community. The "process," such as it is, is antithetical to the principles of normalization, although it is a truer approximation of reality than are the principles themselves. Successful placement is left to the prowess of the individual placement agent and is the exception rather than the rule (Conroy, 1977; Dollins, 1967; Jansson, 1975; Nihira and Nihira, 1975).

Consequently, many persons with the behavioral skills required for placement remain in institutions, while others without the requisite skills are placed into communities. Community placements often result in a loss of the skills required to live in these less restrictive environments (Blatt, 1970; Blatt and Kaplan, 1966; Dentler and Mackler, 1961; Nirje, 1969; Wolfensberger et al., 1972). Those individuals must then return to the institution and, as a result, public statements about the presence of mentally retarded persons in communities are not often favorable.

CLINICAL FACTORS

Research that has been carried out in the last two decades to establish criteria predictive of successful placement has determined little. The only positive findings are: 1) that sex, age, IQ, and area of pre-admission residence are sometimes predictive of success in family care (Jackson and Butler, 1963); 2) that age (under 15, males only), long hospitalization (those under 15 years only), and being male (IQ less than or equal to 49) are favorable prognosticators of success in family care (Brown, Windle and Stewart, 1959); and 3) that age, sex, IQ, and diagnosis "do not greatly influence the probability of the release remaining in effect" (Tarjan et al., 1959).

In a case study of the community placement process, Calkins (1976) indicated that the majority of placement settings differed little from the institutions themselves. Institutional behavior patterns accompanied the client into the community, largely because there was neither a systematic procedure for placement nor a continuum of client characteristics correlated to community-based alternatives. Cohen et al. (1977) supported these findings with data indicating that higher functioning residents increased withdrawal following community placement, which resulted in setbacks in language development. Eyman and Call (1977), on the other hand, found a higher prevalence of maladaptive behavior in institutions than in community residences. Males were more likely to present behavior problems than females. Furthermore, there was an inverse relationship between intelligence test scores and the occurrence of maladaptive behavior. The data of Eyman, Demaine, and Lei (1979) and Birenbaum and Re (1979) further support the beneficial effects of community placement.

The research literature indicates that some clients benefit from community placement and others do not. Methods and procedures for predicting which mentally retarded persons will continue to develop are at present not available. There is, however, a considerable amount of data indicating that the occurrence of maladaptive behavior in community settings is the primary factor associated with reinstitutionalization rather than the lack of functional skills (Crawford, Aiello, and Thompson, 1979; Eyman and Call, 1977; Gollay, 1976; Gottesfeld, 1977; Nihira and Nihira, 1974, 1975; Schalock and Harper, 1978). Schalock and Harper (1978) found that the occurrence of inappropriate behavior (not explicitly defined in their paper) was the best predictor of unsuccessful placement in competitive employment. Gollay (1976), using the Adaptive Behavior Scale, found that all mentally retarded persons readmitted to inpatient status scored higher on all maladaptive areas than persons not readmitted. Because most mentally retarded persons residing in institutions are severely and profoundly retarded and/or are males, the prognosis for successful community placement and continued stay is not optimistic (Eyman and Call, 1977).

With the absence of specific behavioral criteria for placing a client, deinstitutionalization becomes the most challenging task facing those persons functioning in the mental retardation service delivery system (O'Connor, Justice, and Warren, 1970; Zerolis, 1971). The evidence indicates that few institutions systematically evaluate the behaviors required by a person to adapt successfully to specific types of noninstitutionalized settings. Therefore, they fail to place the client in the environment that indicates the highest likelihood of success (Bachrach, 1976; Baumanis, 1970; Place and Weiner, 1974). Instead, placement units are primarily concerned with the client's eligibility and are only marginally concerned with client characteristics for placement.

Under normalization, the salient goal of inpatient treatment becomes the return of the client to his or her community, to homelike environments such as halfway houses, or to other small group facilities where they presumably receive guidance and more individualized care (Blatt, 1970; Blatt and Kaplan, 1966; Dentler and Mackler, 1961; Nirje, 1969; Wolfensberger et al., 1972). Treatment programs must now teach mentally retarded persons the skills necessary for living in normalized environments while at the same time eliminating maladaptive behaviors. Until research systematically defines maladaptive behavior (or the absence of such behavior), we can expect a less than desirable outcome from placement efforts.

A promising approach aimed at successful community placement and continued stay has been implemented by the Association for the Developmentally Disabled (ADD), Franklin County Mental Health and Retardation Board in Ohio (Gardner, 1977). Their model consists of four levels of progress; advancement is contingent upon performance at each level. The behavioral criteria for entrance to and exit from each level are explicitly defined, as is the time required for acquisition. Clients may progress toward independent living arrangements (apartment or home) or toward more structured environments (foster home, group home). A client's maximum attainment level is reached when he or she fails to make continued behavioral progress within the time required for acquisition. Once the client is placed in the community residence best suited to his or her level of functioning, ADD resources focus on increasing the client's competency level, while community programs ensure that current levels are maintained. There are constant client and program evaluations adding to the overall quality control process. In addition, there are pre-placement homes in which the client's behavior can be.monitored, ensuring a better fit between person and environment. Gardner (1977) reports that the program results in substantial behavior gains by clients and that it is economically feasible.

CLIENT ASSESSMENT AND TREATMENT PLANNING

Our own work in the area of behavioral rehabilitation attempts to systematically increase the client's independence through a structured set of procedures for client assessment and treatment planning (Crawford, 1980; Crawford et al., 1978; Crawford, Orens, and diStefano, 1980). The assumption of the program is that the length of community stay increases as dependency on staff decreases.

The program begins with a detailed analysis of a client's repertoire using the Rockland Assessments of Functional Behavior (AFB). Each AFB consists of a temporally organized task analysis of the specific behaviors that comprise a skill. Staff assess clients on the type of assistance required for successful behavioral performance. Levels of assistance are defined in terms of the prompts that a staff member must produce for the client to emit the behavior. Prompting precedes the behavior and can be verbal and/or visual and/or tactile. Once the client is assessed, the treatment planning function begins. The delineated behavioral objectives involve decreasing the amount of prompting necessary for the behavior to occur. For example, if a client performs a response only with verbal and tactile prompting, the short-term objective could be to teach the client to emit the response with only verbal prompting. The long-term objective could be to teach the client to perform the behavior in the proper sequence without prompting.

The next step is to select the treatment programs designed to meet the behavioral objectives. A dictionary of interventions has been developed that documents approximately 1,000 programs across several disciplines. The dictionary provides a description of the program, a listing of required equipment, special restrictions, and references. A treatment plan is completed for each behavior targeted for change (Crawford, 1980).

The behavioral rehabilitation system uses computers to store all client assessments and treatment plans, which allows staff to obtain information about a client or group of clients not ordinarily available (without great cost) from manual systems. Client progress can be reviewed precisely and treatment efficacy can be evaluated systematically. Using specific behavioral assessments, treatment planning activities are focused on decreasing the amount of staff assistance required for skill performance. The assessments document each treatment plan and use computers to feed-back to clinicians precise information about the client's current repertoire and response to treatment. Through this method, we can begin to systematically evaluate which type of placement alternative will best serve each client.

A further obstacle to continued community stay is that the logical and empirical referents of the concept "successful placement" are at best ill-defined and vary from one study to the next (Crawford, Aiello, and Thompson, 1979). Criteria for success have been 1) length of stay out of the institution (Tarjan et al., 1959), 2) increases in functional and decreases in nonfunctional behaviors (Hollis, Gorton, and Chester, 1967; MacKay and Sidman, 1968), and 3) parental classification of the client as successful or not successful (Gray and Parr, 1957). The client characteristics, as well as environmental and treatment service characteristics required for successful community adaptation, will vary, depending upon the criteria used for defining success or failure.

Although Baumanis (1970) and Nihira and Nihira (1974, 1975) emphasize the importance of a comprehensive assessment of client adaptive and nonadaptive behaviors prior to release from inpatient service, existing assessments, such as they are, are grossly inadequate for screening the disabled for placement, especially the mentally retarded (Crawford, 1980; Crawford, Orens, and diStefano, 1980; Eagle, 1967; Masland, Sarason, and Gladwin, 1958; O'Connor et al., 1970; Tarjan et al., 1959; Windle, 1962; Zerolis, 1971). Most assessments do not provide the detail required to actually reconstruct the mentally retarded person's repertoire of behaviors. Instead, most standardized assessments result in a summary statement of a person's behavior with dependent variables, such as severity, that are inferences rather than descriptions. Using such subjective data to place clients into community settings benefits neither clients nor communities.

The need for objective, empirically determined criteria for predicting successful community adaptation among the array of placement alternatives is clearly indicated. Equally important is the development of criteria that inform placement units of the types of community residences to which a client will *not* successfully adapt. These criteria must be based, however, upon objective, reliable assessments of client behaviors and of the characteristics of the environments to which the client may be referred (Crawford, Aiello, and Thompson, 1979).

ENVIRONMENTAL CONSIDERATIONS

Considerable evidence supports the existence of a relationship between the environment and human behavioral development. The research literature indicates that cognitive functioning is enhanced if an institution provides environmental enrichment and nurturance, but intellectual functioning is debilitated in unstimulating institutional environments (Clarke and Clarke, 1954; Crissey, 1937; Kephart and Strauss, 1940; Skeels and Dye, 1939; Spitz, 1949). Skeels and Dye (1939) reported dramatic changes in IQ scores when preschool-aged mentally retarded children were moved from a regular orphanage ward with little stimulation to a high-stimulation ward environment with many adult contacts. Equally dramatic declines in IQ scores were reported for a control group that remained in an orphanage nursery setting where there were few adult contacts and little opportunity for development. Several other investigations have suggested that cognitive functioning is influenced by a change in general environmental configurations. McKay (1942) and Mundy (1957) noted positive changes in IQ scores when mentally retarded persons were moved to more normalized environments. These studies as well as those of Barrett (1971), Klaber and Butterfield (1968), Norris (1971), and Tizard (1960) all point out the significance of the relationship between environment and behavioral development.

Bloom (1964) suggests that the quality of the home environments of economically disadvantaged families may be a contributing factor in the etiology of mental retardation. In a recent study, Ramey et al. (1975) compared the home environments of infants from families in the general population and from families in what was identified as a "high-risk" population. Significant differences were found between these two groups on factors of maternal warmth, organization of the environment, appropriate toys, maternal involvement, opportunities for variety, and absence of restriction and punishment.

Influence of Physical Environment on Behavior

Objective and reliable assessment of the physical environment is critical because the architecture of a location can have important behavioral consequences for residents. Certain physical features may cause too much or too little privacy, which results in feelings of crowding or isolation that may then hinder or enhance a treatment program (Aiello and Baum, 1978; Baum, Aiello, and Calesnick, 1978). For example, many alternative residential facilities emphasize small, home-like living units. The suitability of these settings for the profoundly retarded or nonambulatory individual may be questionable for a number of reasons (Roos, 1970). First, small living units segmented into separate rooms may restrain a nonambulatory resident from receiving necessary, constant supervision. Second, in a small segmented living unit, effective programming may be impaired, because bathing, feeding, and crawling areas may be less accessible (Roos, 1970). Therefore, approximating the home environment for the nonambulatory, profoundly retarded individual may be less effective than designing the environment to facilitate conditioning (Watson, 1967). Third, privacy may be less desirable for the nonassertive, profoundly retarded resident who may benefit from maximum stimulation in the environment (Dorman, 1967). Thus, the physical environment may limit the range of possible behaviors occurring within the setting and may determine the patterns of behavior.

Until recently, however, research focusing on the relationship between the physical environment and behavior has been somewhat limited. Of particular interest are the effects of constructed features of the environment on people's behavior (Heimstra and McFarling, 1974). Three possible forms of this functional relationship between human behavior and the physical environment have been differentiated by Wohlwill (1970). In the first kind of relationship, the environmental context limits the particular behavior or behavior patterns that can occur within it. The second type of relationship is one in which some of the qualities that characterize specific environments affect the behavior and the personality of individuals residing within them. In the third type of relationship, the environment serves as a motivating force that may result in either strong feelings or attitudes, approach or avoidance behavior, or adaptation. According to Heimstra and McFarling (1974), research on the relationship between the built environment and resident behavior has considered two main categories of variables: 1) integral structural features (e.g., size and shape of rooms, placement of doors, space) and 2) components of particular settings (e.g., color of walls, furniture arrangement, decorating scheme). In general, a number of different types of behaviors have been found to occur within or as a result of the above features.

Levy and McLeod (1977) investigated the effects of the environmental design of an institutional dayroom on the behavior of severely and profoundly retarded adolescents. Observations of the behavioral interaction patterns of residents and staff were first made within the initial existing dayroom. Observations of the same dayroom after it was redesigned to provide an enriched environment that reinforced and supported learning activities indicated a reduction in stereotyped behaviors and an increase in productive activity. New patterns of space utilization emerged as a result of environmental restructuring. The authors suggest that further research needs to be directed toward determining the factors that instigate and maintain behavioral change in enriched environments.

Modifying the physical environment can lead to increasing functional and decreasing nonfunctional behaviors. One possible environmental manipulation involves the introduction to the setting of novel or specific materials or equipment. For example, Quilitch and Risley (1973) demonstrated that normal children's social play behavior within a free-play setting was significantly influenced by the types of toys given to them. Berkson and Mason (1964) found that stereotyped behaviors of institutionalized retarded individuals decreased when they were provided with toys and social stimulation.

Influence of Residence Size on Behavior

The size of the physical environment has received a considerable amount of attention in the mental retardation literature (Balla, Kossan, and Zigler, 1976; Cleland, 1965). Cleland (1965) reviewed the literature on the relationship between institution size and quality of care and concluded that even though the most popular opinion was that institutions should be limited in size, there were, in actuality, very few well-established criteria that had been used to evaluate the impact of this variable. Furthermore, he found that a number of organizational variables (e.g., staff turnover rate) needed to be further investigated to determine their relationship to the effectiveness of a treatment program. Similarly, Balla, Butterfield, and Zigler (1974) failed to find a relationship between several demographic characteristics (including size) of four residential institutions. In a more recent review of residence size, Balla (1976) discussed quality of care along the dimensions of caregiving practices, resident behavior, the rate of discharge, and the extent of parental and community involvement. The general finding was that care was more satisfactory in small, community-based facilities. However, Balla (1976) noted that the small community facilities differed considerably from one another. More importantly, there was little evidence that the behavior systematically varied as a function of the size of the residence. Balla (1976) concluded by emphasizing the fact that the relationship between institution size and other demographic variables needs further attention.

Knowledge of relevant organizational variables, such as client/ caregiver ratio, program cost, and background characteristics of participants in a particular setting may provide important additional information about the social and interpersonal characteristics of a setting. Harris et al. (1974) examined the relationship between aide/resident ratio, ward population density, and the social interactions of retarded children and their caregivers. In general, the results of this study suggested that the random addition of attendants to a moderately dense ward did not improve the quality of staff-resident interaction even though the average number of aide-initiated interactions did increase. In contrast, the quality of the aide-resident interactions did improve when there were fewer residents present on the ward. The authors interpreted these findings as indicating that ward attendants work most effectively when they are alone and are assigned a small group of residents.

Influence of Social Environment on Behavior

The social environment or climate of a particular setting can have a significant effect on behavior. Defined as the "personality" of a setting, the social climate may be represented by qualities like "supportive," "rigid," and "controlling," adjectives often used to describe the personalities of people (Moos, 1975). Social climate scales have been designed to assess the environments of hospitals, community-based facilities, and families.

Most studies using the social climate inventories focus on psychiatric settings with mentally ill patients. Recently, Zigler and Balla (1977) have indicated the need for characterizing the social-psycho-

logical climate of residential facilities for the mentally retarded. Pankratz (1975) used the Community Oriented Program Evaluation Scale
(COPES) developed by Moos (1972) to study the social climates of
halfway houses for mentally retarded persons. Staff and clients completed the COPES assessment, after which the perceptions of social
climate between the groups were compared. Clients had each question
individually presented. Questions were often reworded or paraphrased
at the examiner's discretion when the client seemed confused. Staff's
and clients' reported perceptions of social climate were in general
agreement. On the basis of these findings, Pankratz (1975) suggested
that mentally retarded individuals were adequately able to describe
their own treatment program. Furthermore, the norms used to evaluate
psychiatric environments were applicable to the settings in which mentally retarded persons were receiving treatment. Nevertheless, re-
wording the questions at the examiner's discretion may have influenced
the findings. Most of the subjects used in this study were functioning
at the mild and moderate ranges of retardation, with the exception of
one male and one female who were at the borderline range. The individuals tested ranged in age from 18 to 36 years. More research is
needed to determine if an instrument like the COPES can also be used
effectively and reliably as a measure of the psychosocial environment
of community treatment programs for those individuals younger than
18 years old and for those functioning at all ranges of retardation. We
expect that both of these groups would have difficulty with the scale;
preliminary data support this belief (Alexander, Crawford, and Conklin, 1979). Even though a self-report measure like the COPES may
provide a reliable assessment of the perceived social climate, it may
not necessarily provide a valid evaluation. More comprehensive assessments are needed to provide an objective description of the social
environment. However, Pankratz's results do lend some support to
the use of the COPES in assessing the social milieu of community
facilities for some mentally retarded persons.

Ramey et al. (1975) used the HOME inventory to compare the
home environments of high-risk infants with those of infants drawn
from the general population and found significant differences between
these two groups on all of the above factors or subscales. Recently,
Bradley and Caldwell (1977) conducted a validation experiment on the
efficiency of the HOME Inventory in the screening for mental retardation and affirmed its predictive utility. Of particular interest was the
finding that it was possible to predict what IQ range six-month-old
children would be in at age three by using the scores obtained from
the HOME Inventory. These results affect the planning of intervention
programs to meet the specific needs of individual children.

COMPARISONS OF RESIDENTIAL FACILITIES

Sociopsychological characteristics of institutions, reflecting the nature of the interactions between caregivers and mentally retarded residents, have been investigated in a series of cross-international studies (King and Raynes, 1968a, 1968b, 1968c; Raynes and King, 1968). The Child Management Scale, administered to staff members, conceptualized residential care practices as either institutionally oriented (no acknowledgment of the children's individuality is made) or child-oriented (variation in routine or individual variations among children are considered). The authors found that management practices were more resident-oriented in hostel or group homes (ranging in size from 12 to 41 residents). In contrast, care practices were found to be more institution-oriented in the hospital settings (ranging in size from 121 to 1,650 residents) and practices in voluntary homes (ranging in size from 50 to 93 residents) fell somewhere between practices in group homes and hospital settings. Demographic data, such as staff resident ratio, institution size, and number of children living in a unit were generally not predictive of care practices. Lower staff turnover rates were found in resident-oriented settings than in those that were institution-oriented, and during active periods there were higher ratios of residents to staff in the more resident-oriented facilities.

Bjaanes and Butler (1974) examined the behavior components of the environments of two board-and-care facilities and two home-care facilities for mentally retarded persons. Four environmental components were used to assess these community facilities: 1) the supportive component, which reflected the extent to which the caregiver and the staff provided social and personal life support; 2) the physical component, which referred to the location, size, condition, layout, organization, and utilization of the facility; 3) the behavioral component, which reflected the ongoing behavior patterns within a given facility; and 4) the attitudinal component, which referred to the attitudes of the caregiver and staff of a facility toward retardation and retarded persons.

Observations of all the activities engaged in by individuals placed in these facilities were made. The structure of the activity (who initiated it) was noted along with the duration of the act, the number of individuals included, and with whom the act took place. On the basis of these observations, a set of modal behaviors and characteristics was developed to describe the nature and patterns of behavior in the various facilities. A set of characteristics was generated and used to distinguish among facilities that encouraged behavior leading to competence and normalization. Observed activities were divided into five main categories, each with a set of associated specific behaviors: 1) active leisure that required the use of skills, abilities, and knowledge; 2) passive leisure that involved no active involvement on the part of the individual and in which there was no interaction with others; 3) work or chores defined as activity involving the performance of various household duties; 4) personal activity that was primarily self-oriented and in which there was little or no interaction with others; and 5) interaction that was oriented toward others. Behavior, time spent in specific types of behavior, and characteristics of behavior within a particular setting varied between the two board-and-care facilities and the two home-care facilities. Analysis of the frequency of specific types of behavior indicated that slightly over half of the behavioral acts of retarded persons in both of the board-and-care facilities were interactive. However, in one of the home-care facilities, interactive behavior accounted for 89.1% of the observed behavior, while in the other it accounted for only 38.5%. Variations were found in how the residents spent their leisure time. Residents in board-and-care facilities spent twice as much time in passive leisure than did residents in home care facilities.

RESULTS OF ENVIRONMENTAL STUDIES

These observations indicate that substantial differences in the behavioral component of community-care facilities exist. These differences seemed to be functions of variations in environmental climates of each facility. Board-and-care facilities were found to be closer to the objectives of normalization and the development of social competence than were home-care facilities. More independent behavior was found in board-and-care facilities than in home-care facilities and exposure to the community was an important factor in normalization. The geographic isolation of home-care facilities, rather than their size, appears to be related to the development of independent functioning and social competence. Specific types of community-care environments appear to be associated with different outcomes. However, the authors note that more systematic research comparing various environments and relating them to social competency over time must be accomplished before these hypotheses can be accepted. More recently, Butler and Bjaanes (1977) have concluded that "different types of environments result in different kinds of normalization and social competence outcomes" (p. 388).

In an ethnographic program of study, 500 mentally retarded persons in more than 50 community settings were observed using naturalistic procedures (Edgerton, 1975). The quality of life in the alternative community placement facilities studied varied considerably from one setting to another. Furthermore, in many cases, these living environments were no better than those found in larger, traditional institutional environments. Some seemed to be operating on a profit motive by failing to tell the mentally retarded individuals residing within their facility that they had the choice of living in that residential facility or in some other one. Of particular significance was the observation that these community settings were often structured to encourage dependency and incompetency on the part of the mentally retarded individuals residing within them. More recently, Edgerton and Bercovici (1976) suggested that the lack of reliable and supportive resources in the community for mentally retarded persons is an important factor in their failure to adapt to community living.

The potential risks as well as the benefits of the placement of mentally retarded persons in more normalized community settings need to be considered before these persons are relocated. Unfortunately there is to date no research on the effects of the transition from traditional residential institutions to community facilities. However, recent evidence has suggested that the inter-institutional relocation of mentally retarded individuals does result in short-term changes in adaptive behavior, mostly unfavorable (Cohen et al., 1977). Although lower-functioning residents demonstrated increases in their levels of adaptive and acting-out behavior, the higher-functioning individuals showed decreases in their level of adaptive behavior and evidenced withdrawal.

The sum of evidence indicates that environment can be related to human behavior. Varying degrees of emphasis have been placed on different environmental components, such as physical or structural, organizational or administrative, and social variables. In order to identify the specific environmental characteristics influencing the behavior of mentally retarded individuals, all of these components must be considered when evaluating a given setting. Research that has attempted to establish linkages between behavior of mentally retarded individuals and the sociophysical environment have not used standardized procedures. Furthermore, the scales that currently exist are not constructed to relate directly to specific behavior patterns with specific environmental characteristics. This characterization of variables depends on elaborate environmental descriptions that are currently not available.

Objective assessment of community residential environments is critical to the successful placement of the retarded. Just as there are wide differences among mentally retarded persons, there are wide differences among classes of placement alternatives. Residential placement units can vary on a number of sociophysical dimensions (e.g., staff qualifications, client/staff ratios, wheelchair ramps) that can affect the adequacy of support provided to clients. The placement objective is to provide the optimal balance between the client's behavior repertoire and sociophysical dimensions of the community residential alternative. The ability to match clients to community residences is critical to informed and successful placement of retarded individuals and is the first step in closing the so-called revolving door. However, at the present time few systematic data are available on the environmental determinations of adjustment by mentally retarded persons to community settings. Furthermore, even though lack of environmental support has been noted as an important factor in failure of community placement (Windle, Stewart, and Brown, 1961), little is known about the nature of the environments where mentally retarded persons are being sent.

CONCLUSIONS AND IMPLICATIONS

Delineation of Demographic and Behavioral Criteria

Several conclusions emerge from existing data. First, objective and empirically determined demographic and behavioral criteria for predicting successful adjustment to the various types of community-based residential alternatives are not available. Although we assume that individuals require different skills to adapt to the different types of community settings, the particular behaviors required for successful functioning in each of the residential alternatives have not been defined. Until these demographic and behavioral criteria are delineated, successful placement of mentally retarded persons from institutions into community residences will continue to be problematical.

Assessment of Sociophysical Environment

Second, research focusing on the environments of residential and community facilities for mentally retarded persons has placed varying degrees of emphasis on discrete components of the sociophysical environment. Assessment of the entire sociophysical environment leading to functional characterizations of residential alternatives (e.g., how group homes differ from foster homes), as well as specific descriptions of facilities within a class of residential alternatives (all foster home environments are not the same) are required. There is a need to develop ways of characterizing or profiling residential environments, and work has already begun in this area (Bjaanes and Butler, 1974; Butler and Bjaanes, 1977).

In order to identify specific environmental variables influencing the behavior patterns of residents, environmental assessment should be used systematically to assess the total environment of the various alternative facilities for the retarded. Environmental profiles reflecting the sociophysical variables that are characteristic of each type of setting can be created. The profiles of treatment settings may then be used to ensure that the environments in which mentally retarded individuals live enhance the specialized caregiving or formal training they may be receiving. Knowledge gained from these profiles will allow the construction of functional and appropriate community residential facilities that will coincide with the needs of the mentally retarded. Furthermore, with the current trend toward deinstitutionalization, information from these profiles can be used to place retarded persons in community environments that are best suited to their needs, thereby increasing the likelihood of successful community adjustment.

Environmental Manipulation

Third, behavior is often functionally related to both the physical and social structure of environments. Functional behavior can be enhanced through environmental manipulation. For example, stereotyped movements of severely retarded, institutionalized individuals do appear to be related to a number of environmental variables (Forehand and Baumeister, 1971). These factors include prior physical restraint, isolation, intense sound, and the presence of other individuals exhibiting rocking behavior (Baumeister and Forehand, 1970; Forehand and Baumeister, 1970a, 1970b, 1970c). Frequent occurrence of repetitious movements has been associated more with novel, restricting environments than with familiar, less restrictive settings (Berkson and Davenport, 1962). Berkson and Landesman-Dwyer (1977) have noted the significance of events in the natural environment in controlling the maladaptive behavior of severely and profoundly retarded individuals. The possibility that the residents might not be able to transfer some of the skills they have acquired in the institution to a new environment must be re-emphasized (Meredith, 1974). Community residential environments (family, foster home, and hostel group) need to be better understood to increase the probability that appropriate behaviors will generalize from the institution to these alternative settings. Perhaps institutions need transition facilities that will reflect these alternative residential environments. Clients might be placed in these specialized facilities within the institution preceding actual placement in order to ensure the generalizability of behaviors required for successful adaptation. Programs in the three alternative settings might also be developed to facilitate the clients' adaptation to the new residential environment. These programs would essentially be a continuation of the transitional programs in the institutions. Therefore, a step-by-step program designed to introduce the client gradually to the environmental variables characteristic of the new residence might prove to be useful in protecting the individual against potential risks that may be encountered in the transition from a large, traditional residential institution to a smaller, community facility. Research is needed that is designed to identify precisely the environmental variables that instigate and maintain functional as well as nonfunctional behavior.

Development of Statistical Models

Fourth, research in this area should have, as its long-range objective, the development of statistical models that relate client demographic and behavioral characteristics to the sociophysical environments of community residential alternatives. These models should, given a client profile, identify the specific community residences most likely to result in continued growth and development. Conversely, given a profile of a community residential environment, it should be possible to identify the mentally retarded persons who will successfully adapt to this particular setting. An important implication for clinical practice can be derived from these conclusions: Recognizing the potential influence of environmental factors in instigating and maintaining behavior, environmental assessments should be integrated into the treatment planning process.

Currently, treatment programs involve the manipulation of response-reinforcement parameters in order to bring about a change in the behavioral repertoire of a mentally retarded person. That is, given a behavior that is to be changed, the procedures usually involve a specific habilitative or rehabilitative program, such as time-out, differential reinforcement of other behaviors, crafts, sports or ultrasonic diathermy. Because environmental factors are not included in traditional clinical assessment, manipulation of environmental factors is rarely, if ever, considered as a method to effect behavior change. Although a specific behavior may be partly controlled by environmental variables, traditional clinical practice ignores these factors and places emphasis on changing response-reinforcement relationships. Consequently, a client may be placed in an expensive, time-consuming program that may ultimately prove ineffective.

Creating environments designed to increase the quality and frequency of behavior among groups can be effective. For example, Sommer (1962) found that the rearrangement of furniture within a hospital residential setting produced a significant increase in interactions among elderly residents. Quilitch and Risley (1973) demonstrated that normal children's social play behavior within a free-play setting was significantly influenced by the number and type of toys available. Determining the environmental factors that at least partially control the maintenance of behavior patterns should be an integral aspect of the clinical process.

Development of a Treatment Program

A comprehensive assessment of functional and nonfunctional behavior should be the first step in a treatment program (Crawford, 1980). The assessments of functional behavior should consist of detailed analyses of the specific behavioral components of each skill. The skill of toothbrushing can be divided into several components (e.g., gets toothbrush, gets toothpaste, gets towel, goes to sink). The client should be assessed on each of the behaviors in terms of the number and type of prompts (verbal, verbal and visual, visual and tactile, etc.) that a caregiver must generate for the mentally retarded individual to emit the response. Assessing behaviors on the prompts required for performance is based on the assumption that the larger the repertoire of behaviors performed with minimal staff assistance, the higher the likelihood of successful functioning in less restrictive, more normalized environments. Treatment planning focuses then on systematically reducing the dependency on staff, thereby facilitating independent behavior and community adjustment (Crawford, 1980; Crawford, Orens, and diStefano, 1980). This type of skill assessment differs from the traditional assessment in two ways. First, instead of toothbrushing capability being described in terms of "needs much assistance, needs some assistance, etc.," each of the behaviors comprising the skill area is assessed in terms of the specific type of assistance (prompts) required by the client. Second, behaviors are not assessed in the commonly used all-or-none framework where the rating is based on whether or not the behavior is performed. These scales ignore the possibility that a variety of stimulus conditions (e.g., prompts) might set the occasion for the response to occur. Assessment of nonfunctional behavior is easier because the staff do not have to produce specific prompts to discover whether the behavior is in the repertoire. Rather, nonfunctional behaviors (e.g., head banging) often appear as free operants, so the initial assessment of nonfunctional behavior can take the form of a frequency distribution over time or rate.

After the comprehensive behavioral assessment is completed, target behaviors and behavioral objectives are selected. Traditionally, after the behaviors and the objectives have been delineated, rehabilitation programs are ordered to modify the response-reinforcement relationship. However, it is at this point in the clinical process, prior to ordering treatment programs, that the staff should perform an assessment of the potential environmental determinants of the target behavior. The assessment would evaluate the concurrence of the target behavior and specific sociophysical environmental factors, using the onset and termination of behaviors that have been targeted for change as the conditions for the environmental assessment. For example, in order to learn what environmental factors are present when mentally retarded individuals engage in a maladaptive, self-injurious behavior, such as head banging, observations would be made at the beginning and at the end of the occurrence. For comparative purposes, similar assessments of environmental factors would be made at specific times when this behavior is not occurring.

The results of the behavior-environment assessment provide the clinical staff with several treatment planning options: 1) to manipulate environmental variables only, 2) to manipulate reinforcement contingencies only, or 3) to manipulate both environmental factors and reinforcement contingencies. Thus, if the environmental analysis clearly indicates that a self-injurious behavior occurs only under conditions of intense sound, then reducing noise levels may be more effective than implementing a differential reinforcement of other behavior programs. If environmental variables are not associated with the target behavior, then rehabilitation programs alone would be required. More likely than not, the target behavior will be controlled by both environmental and response-reinforcement relationships, in which case the manipulation of the environment in conjunction with the implementation of rehabilitation programs will be required.

The integration of clinical and environmental factors can facilitate the care of patients within institutions as well as in community residences. When it is developed, the use of environmental assessment as an aid in the development of successful rehabilitation strategies will be particularly significant in training mentally retarded persons in the skills necessary for community living.

REFERENCES

Aiello, J. R., and Baum, A. 1978. Residential Crowding and Design. Plenum Publishing Corp., New York.
Alexander, M. J., Crawford, J. L., and Conklin, G. 1979. Clinical and environmental criteria for community placement. Paper presented at the 87th Annual Convention of the American Psychological Association, September, New York, N.Y.

Bachrach, L. L. 1976. Deinstitutionalization: An Analytical Review and Sociological Perspective. DHEW Publication No. (ADM) 76-351, U.S. Government Printing Office, Washington, D.C.

Balla, D. A. 1976. Relationship of institution size to quality of care: A review of the literature. Am. J. Ment. Defic. 81(2):117–124.

Balla, D. A., Butterfield, E. C., and Zigler, E. 1974. Effects of institutionalization on retarded children: A longitudinal cross-institutional investigation. Am. J. Ment. Defic. 78:530–549.

Balla, D., Kossan, N., and Zigler, E. 1976. Effects of preinstitutional history and institutionalization on the behavior of the retarded. Unpublished manuscript, Yale University.

Barrett, B. H. 1971. Behavioral differences among an institution's backward residents. Ment. Retard. 9:4–9.

Barton, W. E. 1952. Outpatient psychiatry and family care: Review of psychiatric progress. Am. J. Psychiatry 108:542–544.

Barton, W. E. 1953. Outpatient psychiatry and family care: Review of psychiatric progress. Am. J. Psychiatry 109:531–534.

Barton, W. E. 1954. Outpatient psychiatry and family care: Review of psychiatric progress. Am. J. Psychiatry 110:533–534.

Barton, W. E. 1955. Outpatient psychiatry and family care: Review of psychiatric progress. Am. J. Psychiatry 111:539–542.

Barton, W. E. 1959. Family care and outpatient psychiatry: Review of psychiatric progress. Am. J. Psychiatry January, 115:642–645.

Barton, W. E. 1960. Family care and outpatient psychiatry: Review of psychiatric progress. Am. J. Psychiatry 116:644–647.

Barton, W. E. 1963. Family care and outpatient psychiatry: Review of psychiatric progress. Am. J. Psychiatry 119:665–669.

Barton, W. E., and St. John, W. T. 1962. Family care and outpatient psychiatry: Review of psychiatric progress. Am. J. Psychiatry 118(7):633–636.

Baum, A., Aiello, J. R., and Calesnick, L. E. 1978. Crowding and personal control: Social density and the development of learned helplessness. J. Pers. Soc. Psychol. 36(9):1000–1011.

Baumanis, D. 1970. Both sides of the coin: The retarded child and his family. Canada's Ment. Health (Ottawa), 18(3,4):23–28.

Baumeister, A. A., and Forehand, R. 1970. Social facilitation of body rocking in severely retarded patients. J. Clin. Psychol. 26:303–305.

Berkson, G., and Davenport, R. K. 1962. Stereotyped movements in mental defectives. Initial survey. Am. J. Ment. Defic. 66:849–852.

Berkson, G., and Landesman-Dwyer, S. 1977. Behavioral research on severe and profound mental retardation (1955–1974). Am. J. Ment. Defic. 81(5):428–454.

Berkson, G., and Mason, W. A. 1964. Stereotyped movements of mental defectives, 4. The effects of toys and the character of the acts. Am. J. Ment. Defic. 68:511–524.

Bindman, A. J. 1969. Perspectives in Community Mental Health. Aldine Publishing Company, Chicago.

Birenbaum, A., and Re, M. A. 1979. Resettling mentally retarded adults in the community—almost 4 years later. Am. J. Ment. Defic. 83(4):323–329.

Birnbrauer, J. S. 1976. Mental retardation. In: H. Leitenberg (ed.), Handbook of Behavior Modification and Behavior Therapy. Appleton-Century-Crofts, New York.

Bjaanes, A. and Butler, E. 1974. Environmental variations in community care facilities for mentally retarded persons. Am. J. Ment. Defic. 78:429–439.

Blatt, B. 1970. Exodus from Pandemonium. Allyn and Bacon, Inc., Boston.

Blatt, B., and Kaplan, F. 1966. Christmas in Purgatory. Allyn and Bacon, Inc., Boston.

Bloom, B. 1964. Stability and Change in Human Characteristics. John Wiley and Sons, Inc., New York.

Bradley, R. H., and Caldwell, B. M. 1977. Home observations for measurement of the environment: A validation study of screening efficiency. Am. J. Ment. Defic. 81(5):417–420.

Brown, S. J., Windle, C., and Stewart, E. 1959. Statistics on a family care program. Am. J. Ment. Defic. 64:535–542.

Butler, E. W., and Bjaanes, A. T. 1977. A typology of community care facilities and differential normalization outcomes. In: P. Mittler (ed.), Research to Practice in Mental Retardation, Vol. 1. Care and Intervention. University Park Press, Baltimore.

Calkins, C. F. 1976. The emergence of mentally retarded adults from a private culture to a public culture: A case study of the community placement process. Doctoral dissertation, George Peabody College for Teachers, Dissertat. Abstracts Int. University Microfilms No. 76-3714.

Clarke, A. D. B., and Clarke, A. M. 1954. Cognitive changes in the feeble-minded. Br. J. Psychol. 45:173–179.

Cleland, C. 1965. Evidence on the relationship between size and institutional effectiveness: A review and analysis. Am. J. Ment. Defic. 70:423–431.

Cohen, H., Conroy, J. W., Frazer, D. W., Snelbecker, G. E., and Spreat, S. 1977. Behavioral effects of interinstitutional relocation of mentally retarded residents. Am. J. Ment. Defic. 82(1):12–18.

Comptroller General of the United States. 1977. Report to the Congress: Returning the mentally disabled to the community: Government needs to do more. General Accounting Office, Washington, D.C.

Conroy, J. W. 1977. Trends in deinstitutionalization of the mentally retarded. Ment. Retard. 15(4):44–46.

Crawford, J. L. 1980. Computer support and the clinical process: An automated behavioral rehabilitation system for mentally retarded persons. Ment. Retard. June 18(3):119–124.

Crawford, J. L., Aiello, J. R., and Thompson, D. E. 1979. Deinstitutionalization and community placement: Clinical and environmental factors. Ment. Retard. April 17:59–65.

Crawford, J. L., Conklin, G. S., McMahon, D. J., Vitale, S. J., Robinson, J. A., Geller, J., and diStefano, O. R. 1978. An automated behavioral rehabilitation system for long-term patients. In: F. H. Orthner (ed.), Proceedings of the Second Annual Symposium on Computer Applications in Medical Care. The Institute of Educational and Electronics Engineers, Inc., New York.

Crawford, J. L., Orens, J., and diStefano, O. R. 1980. Clinical information and patient management. In: C. Siegel and S. Fischer (eds.), Psychiatric Records in Mental Health Cases. Brunner/Mazel, Inc., New York, In press.

Crissey, M. S. 1975. Mental retardation: Past, present, and future. Am. Psychol. 30(8):800–808.

Crissey, O. L. 1937. The mental development of children of the same IQ in differing institutional environments. Child Dev. 8:217–220.

Dentler, R. A., and Mackler, B. 1961. The socialization of institutional retarded children. J. Health Hum. Behav. 2:243–252.

deSilva, R. M., and Faflak, P. 1976. From institution to community—a new process. Ment. Retard. 14(6):25–28.

Dollins, C. N. 1967. The effect of group discussion as a learning procedure on the adaptive social behavior of educable adult mental retardates. Doctoral dissertation, Indiana University, Dissertat. Abstracts Int. University Microfilms No. 67-16398.

Dorman, G. 1967. A Summary of Concepts, Procedures and Organizations. Philadelphia Institute for the Achievement of Human Potential, Philadelphia.

Eagle, E., 1967. Prognosis and outcome of community placements of institutionalized retardates. Am. J. Ment. Defic. 72:232–243.

Edgerton, R. B. 1975. Issue relating to the quality of life among mentally retarded persons. In: M. J. Begab and S. A. Richardson (eds.), The Mentally Retarded and Society: A Social Science Perspective. University Park Press, Baltimore.

Edgerton, R. B., and Bercovici, S. M. 1976. The cloak of competence: Years later. Am. J. Ment. Defic. 80(5):485–497.

Eyman, R. K., and Call, T. 1977. Maladaptive behavior and community placement of mentally retarded persons. Am. J. Ment. Defic. 82(2):137–144.

Eyman, R. K., Demaine, G. C., and Lei, T. 1979. Relationship between community environments and resident changes in adaptive behavior: A path model. Am. J. Ment. Defic. 83(4):330–338.

Fairweather, G. W., Sanders, D. H., Maynard, H., and Cressler, D. L. 1969. Community Life for the Mentally Ill: An Alternative to Institutional Care. Aldine Publishing Company, Chicago.

Forehand, R., and Baumeister, A. A. 1970a. Body rocking and activity level as a function of prior movement restraint. Am. J. Ment. Defic. 74:608–610.

Forehand, R., and Baumeister, A. A. 1970b. Rate of Stereotyped Body Rocking of Severe Retardates as a Function of Frustration of Goal-directed Behavior. Unpublished manuscript, George Peabody College, Nashville, Tennessee.

Forehand, R., and Baumeister, A. A. 1970c. The effect of auditory and visual stimulation on stereotyped rocking behavior and general activity of severe retardates. J. Clin. Psychol. 26:426–429.

Forehand, R., and Baumeister, A. A. 1971. Stereotyped body rocking as a function of situation, IQ, and time. J. Clin. Psychol. 28:324–326.

Gardner, J. M. 1977. Community residential alternatives for the developmentally disabled. Ment. Retard. 15(6):3–8.

Gollay, E. A. 1976. A Study of the Community Adjustment of Deinstitutionalized Mentally Retarded Persons. Vol. 5. An Analysis of Factors Associated with Community Adjustment. Contract no. OEC-0-74-9183, U.S. Office of Education, Abt Associates, Cambridge, Mass.

Gottesfeld, H. 1977. Alternatives to Psychiatric Hospitalization. Gardner Press, Inc., New York.

Gray, P. A., and Parr, E. A. 1957. Children in care and the recruitment of foster parents. Soc. Survey, London, 249.

Harris, J. M., Veit, S. W., Allen, G. J., and Chinsky, J. M. 1974. Aide-resident ratio and ward population density as mediators of social interaction. Am. J. Ment. Defic. 79:320–326.

Heimstra, N. W., and McFarling, L. H. 1974. Environmental Psychology. Brooks/Cole Publishing Company, Monterey, Calif.

Hollis, J. H., Gorton, E., and Chester, E. 1967. Training severely and profoundly developmentally retarded children. Ment. Retard. 5(4):20–24.

Hutchison, A. 1970. Community care services for the mentally retarded in Britain. Am. J. Public Health Nation's Health 60(1):56–63.

Jackson, S. K., and Butler, A. J. 1963. Prediction of successful community placement of institutionalized retardates. Am. J. Ment. Defic. 68(2):211–217.

Jansson, D. P. 1975. Return to society: Problematic features of the reentering process. Perspect. Psychiatr. Care 13:136–142.

Kephart, N. C., and Strauss, A. A. 1940. A clinical factor influencing variations in IQ. Am. J. Orthopsychiatry 10:343–351.

King, R. D., and Raynes, N. V. 1968a. An operational measure of inmate management in residential institutions. Soc. Service Med. 2:41–53.

King, R. D., and Raynes, N. V. 1968b. Patterns of institutional care for the severely subnormal. Am. J. Ment. Defic. 72:700–709.

King, R. D., and Raynes, N. V. 1968c. Some determinants of patterns of residential care. In: B. W. Richards (ed.), Proceedings of the First Congress of the International Association for the Scientific Study of Mental Deficiency. Michael Jackson, Surrey, England.

Klaber, M. M., and Butterfield, E. C. 1968. Stereotyped rocking—A measure of institution and ward effectiveness. Am. J. Ment. Defic. 73:13–20.

Koch, R., and Okada, D. 1972. Educational services for the mentally retarded individual in California. Syracuse Law Rev. 23(4):1075–1083.

Lamb, H. R. 1975. Treating long-term schizophrenic patients in the community. In: L. Bellak and H. H. Barten (eds.), Progress in Community Mental Health, Vol. 3. Brunner/Mazel, Inc., New York.

Lamb, H. R., and Goertzel, V. 1971. Discharged mental patients: Are they really in the community? Arch. Gen. Psychiatry, 24:29–34.

Lamb, H. R., and Goertzel, V. 1972a. High expectations of long-term ex-state hospital patients. Am. J. Psychiatry 129:471–475.

Lamb, H. R., and Goertzel, V. 1972b. The demise of the state hospital—A premature obituary? Arch. Gen. Psychiatry 26:489–495.

Lee, D. T. 1963. Family care: Selection and prediction. Am. J. Psychiatry 120:561–566.

Levy, E., and McLeod, W. 1977. The effect of environmental design on adolescents in an institution. Ment. Retard. 15:28–32.

Macht, L. B. 1974. On community-based care. Psychiatr. Ann. 4(6):pp. 80–81; 85–86; 88–89; 92.

McKay, B. E. 1942. A study of IQ changes in a group of girls paroled from a state school for mental defectives. Am. J. Ment. Defic. 46:496–500.

MacKay, H. W., and Sidman, M. 1968. Instructing the mentally retarded in an institutional environment. In: G. Jervis (ed.), Expanding Concepts in Mental Retardation. Charles C Thomas, Publisher, Springfield, Ill.

Mamula, R. A., and Newman, N. 1973. Community Placement of the Mentally Retarded: A Handbook for Community Agencies and Social Work Practitioners. Charles C Thomas, Publisher, Springfield, Ill.

Masland, R. C., Sarason, S. G., and Gladwin, T. 1958. Mental Subnormality: Biological, Psychological, and Cultural Factors. Basic Books, Inc., New York.

Meredith, J. 1974. Program evaluation in a hospital for mentally retarded persons. Am. J. Ment. Defic. 78:471–481.

Miles, L. 1974. Recent developments in England and Wales. Aust. J. Ment. Retard. Victoria, 3(1):12–15.

Moos, R. 1972. The community-oriented program environment scales. J. Abnorm. Psychol. 79:9–18.

Moos, R. 1975. Evaluating Correctional and Community Settings. John Wiley and Sons, Inc., New York.

Morrissey, J. R. 1966. Status of family care programs. Ment. Retard. 4(5):8–11.

Morrissey, J. R. 1967. The Case for Family Care of the Mentally Ill. Behavioral Publications, New York.

Mundy, L. 1957. Environmental influence on intellectual function as measured by intelligence tests. Br. J. Med. Psychol. 30:194–201.

Nihira, L., and Nihira, K. 1974. From the shadows to success: A survey of successful adapting by community placed retardates. Exchange 2(3):5–9.

Nihira, L., and Nihira, K. 1975. Jeopardy in community placement. Am. J. Ment. Defic. 79(5):538–544.

Nirje, B. 1969. The normalization principle and its human management implications. In: R. B. Kugel and W. Wolfensberger (eds.), Changing Patterns in Residential Services for the Mentally Retarded. President's Committee on Mental Retardation, Washington, D.C.

Nirje, B. 1970. The normalization principle—implications and comments. J. Ment. Subnormal. December, 16:62–70.

Norris, D. 1971. Crying and laughing in imbeciles. Dev. Med. Child Neurol. 13:756–761.

O'Connor, G., Justice, R. S., and Warren, N. 1970. The aged mentally retarded: Institution or community care. Am. J. Ment. Defic. 75(3):354–360.

Pankratz, L. 1975. Assessing the psychosocial environment of halfway houses for the retarded. Community Ment. Health J. 11:341–345.

Place, D. M., and Weiner, S. 1974. Reentering the Community: A Pilot Study of Mentally Ill Patients Discharged from NAPA State Hospital. Stanford Research Institute, Menlo Park, Ca.

Quilitch, H. R., and Risley, T. R. 1973. The effects of play materials on social play. J. Appl. Behav. Anal. 6:573:578.

Ramey, C., Mills, P., Campbell, F., and O'Brien, C. 1975. Infants' home environments: A comparison of high-risk families from the general population. Am. J. Ment. Defic. 80:40–42.

Raynes, N. V., and King, R. D. 1968. The measurement of child management in residential institutions for the retarded. In: B. W. Richards (ed.), Proceedings of the First Congress of the International Association for the Scientific Study of Mental Deficiency. Michael Jackson, Surrey, England.

Roos, P. 1970. Evolutionary changes of the residential facility. In: A. Baumeister and E. Butterfield (eds.), Residential Facilities for the Mentally Retarded. Aldine Publishing Company, Chicago.

Rutman, E. D. 1976. Position Paper: Adequate Residential and Community-Based Programs for the Mentally Disabled. For Submission to the White House Conference on Handicapped Individuals. Horizon House Institute for Research and Development, Philadelphia.

Schalock, R. L., and Harper, R. S. 1978. Placement from community-based mental retardation programs: How well do clients do? Am. J. Ment. Defic. 83(3):240–247.

Shearer, A. 1972. Willowbrook revisited. World Med. London, 8(5):pp. 31–32; 35; 37–38; 40.

Skeels, H. M., and Dye, H. A. 1939. A study of the effects of differential stimulation on mentally retarded children. Proc. Am. Assoc. Ment. Defic. 44:114–136.

Sommer, R. 1962. The distances for comfortable conversation: A further study. Sociometry 25:111–116.

Spitz, R. A. 1949. The role of ecological factors in emotional development in infancy. Child Dev. 20:145–156.

Tarjan, G., Dingman, H. F., Eyman, R. K., and Brown, S. J. 1959. Effectiveness of hospital release programs. Am. J. Ment. Defic. 64:609–617.

Tizard, J. 1960. Residential care of mentally handicapped children. Br. Med. J. 1:1041–1046.

Watson, L. S., Jr. 1967. Application of operant conditioning techniques to institutionalized severely and profoundly retarded children. Ment. Retard. Abstr. 4:1–18.

Windle, C. 1962. Prognosis of mental subnormals. Am. J. Ment. Defic. Monograph, 66:1–180.

Windle, C. C., Stewart, E., and Brown, S. J. 1961. Reasons for community failure of released patients. Am. J. Ment. Defic. 66:213–217.

Wohlwill, J. F. 1970. The emerging discipline of environmental psychology. Am. Psychol. 25(4):303–312.

Wolfensberger, W., Nirje, B., Olshansky, S., Perske, R., and Roos, P. 1972. The Principles of Normalization in Human Services. National Institute on Mental Retardation, University of York, Toronto.

Zerolis, J. B. 1971. Preparing long-term retarded residents for community placement. Hosp. Community Psychiatry 22(6):148–150.

Zigler, E., and Balla, D. A. 1977. Impact of institutional experience on the behavior and development of retarded persons. Am. J. Ment. Defic. 82(1):1–11.

SOME ISSUES
IN RESIDENTIAL
PLACEMENT

Living Environments for Developmentally Retarded Persons
Edited by H. Carl Haywood and J. R. Newbrough
Copyright 1981 University Park Press Baltimore

Values and Limitations of Residential Care for Disadvantaged Youth

Michael J. Begab, Ph.D.
Vice President
University Park Press
300 North Charles Street
Baltimore, Maryland 21201

For more than a century, societies have struggled with how to care for, manage, and control their deviant, handicapped, or incompetent citizens. Many of these individuals, often children and youth, come to the attention of public authorities because of family and social pathology and community deficiencies rather than because of problems within the children themselves. Others manifest behavior problems, emotional disorders, mental handicaps, or socially unacceptable behavior that exceed parental management capabilities and community tolerance. In still others—perhaps the majority of those cases requiring care outside the parental home—deficiencies in the child, family, and community interact in ways necessitating societal intervention.

The undifferentiated almshouses of the nineteenth century, with their unspeakable horrors, still find occasional expression in the current network of more specialized hospitals, prisons, and institutions for the mentally ill, mentally retarded, and aged. In some quarters the furor over inhumane conditions of care, human rights, and normalization has led to litigation in the United States calling for the complete abandonment of traditional forms of residential care.

These criticisms, although undeniably valid in many instances, have been generalized to all age groups and to nearly every form of deviance. Such extreme generalizations defy conventional wisdom, but as in every movement of social reform, sociopolitical considerations rather than scientific observations tend to dominate public policy. It is imperative that scientists and practitioners systematically investigate

---

Presented at the 103rd annual meeting of the American Association on Mental Deficiency, Miami Beach, May 27–June 2, 1979.

the elements of residential care programs, not as they presently exist (for every program can be improved upon), but from a theoretical and conceptual perspective of child development needs.

CHILD-CARING INSTITUTIONS: SOME MYTH-CONCEPTIONS

Residential care programs serve children who are disadvantaged, retarded, dependent, disturbed, and delinquent. To a large extent, the programs are self-contained, providing through their own resources the total range of experiences affecting the performance of children and youth in major life functions. The potential impact on behavior and on development of this all-pervasive intervention approach is most profound. Properly structured and staffed, such programs can enhance the cognitive and educational achievements of youth, socialize them to the value system of the culture, and prepare them for productive roles in society. Conversely, programs that are ill-conceived can be devastating, at least in their short-term effects. Unfortunately, much of the research on institutional care has been focused on inadequate programs, which has resulted in a host of myth-conceptions.

Today there is much criticism of residential care regarding dehumanizing consequences and damaging effects on development. These charges are not fully substantiated. Much of the research on which these accusations are based suffers from methodological weaknesses. For instance, the change-producing potential of the institution, because it is, in a sense, the child's total world, makes the effects of intervention strategies difficult to measure. Institutions differ from each other on a host of variables: 1) the staff/child ratio, 2) deployment of staff time, 3) opportunities for peer group interaction, 4) education and treatment procedures, 5) administrative patterns, 6) institution-community relations, 7) the physical plant, and 8) resident living arrangements. Controlling for these variables to determine which are most relevant to outcome poses obstacles to sound research design. The outcome criteria—applied in comparison studies—are often too crude or too hard to specify. For example, the continued maintenance of mentally ill or retarded persons in community placement from institutions has been the major criterion in assessing the effectiveness of the program (Office of Child Development, 1976). Many of these individuals are, however, unsuccessful and become a part of other human services systems, such as corrections or welfare.

Comparison of institutional populations with control groups outside the institution also suffers from other limitations. The residential group is easily accessible and subject to microscopic examination. By contrast, far fewer data are likely to be available on control groups.

As a rule, this tends to overstate the negative characteristics of the treatment (residential) group. Attempts to match experimental and control groups are also hazardous, because the very act of placement in the institution often reflects the presence of pathological behavior or special problems not shared by those able to remain within their own families or communities. Thus, observed differences in outcome behavior may be caused by biases in placement and may bear little relationship to the presumed independent variable of the institutional experience.

Another problem in assessing the impact of institutional experience relates to the exact time for measuring outcomes. Tests administered immediately after treatment can be misleading and unpredictive of later behavior, such as the short-term IQ gains of children in preschool enrichment programs. Evaluation at a later time, however, seldom considers the impact of intervening events, which would be possible only in intensive longitudinal studies. The impact on adult behavior of early learning is clearly influenced by the length and potency of the learning experience, the repetition of learning sequences, and the reinforcement and extinction of learning. Early learning, in whatever environment it takes place, is only one important link in the developmental chain (Clarke and Clarke, 1976). Disturbed children often evoke hostile responses from their caregivers that further reinforce their negative behavior. Interruption of this cycle would greatly reduce the correlation between early institutional experience and later behavior and the causal inferences to be drawn therefrom.

These few illustrations of commonly observed deficiencies in research method and design may account in part for the pervasive view that institutions are inadequate as child-caring facilities.

LIMITATIONS OF RESIDENTIAL CARE

Much of the disenchantment with residential care stems from the early research reported by Bowlby (1951), Spitz (1946), and Goldfarb (1943). Bowlby concluded that deprivation of maternal care for prolonged periods early in life results in severe handicap to personality development. This influential report had the salutary effect of stimulating much research on maternal-child interaction patterns and their differential effects. However, the studies suffered from many of the weaknesses noted above—sampling bias of clinic populations, limited data on personality characteristics of subjects, inadequate information about pre-institutional experiences, and the nature of the institutional experience itself (Shyne, 1973). Spitz's research failed to distinguish the element of separation from other probable causes of retardation and his findings have not been replicated (Klackenburg, 1956). Gold-farb, in comparing the inferior intellectual and behavioral performance of children placed in institutions with those in foster home care, failed to consider problems of selective placement, testing biases, and incomplete information.

Despite the limitations of these particular studies, certain characteristics are consistently associated with early and prolonged institutionalization, such as retardation in language development and general intelligence, and deficits in interpersonal relationships (Yarrow, 1961). These deficiencies have been related to the amount of individual stimulation, the age of the child at placement, the duration of placement, and the lack of maternal-child attachment relationships. Unfortunately, institutional programs frequently do not have the numbers and quality of staff needed for individualized attention and mothering, nor is the environment usually consciously structured to provide affective, social, and intellectual stimulation. It is not surprising that children living under these conditions would demonstrate social apathy or "affect hunger," an insatiable demand for affection and attention.

These adverse conditions, although common, are neither inherent elements of residential care nor inevitable concomitants of large facilities. A study by Raynes and King (1968), for example, indicated that the role of the person in charge of the living unit was the critical factor. Staff members who had been trained in child care maintained high verbal contact with children and showed resident-oriented patterns of care. Nurses, on the other hand, were more institution-oriented and spoke less to the children. These differential patterns of interaction were not related to the size of the institution but did have developmental consequences in the expected direction.

Another limitation of residential care is its potential for fostering and prolonging dependency. Normal dependency needs may go unmet in infancy and may be unnecessarily prolonged later on.

Any living arrangement that involves large numbers of persons demands rules, regulations, structure, and possible regimentation. The degree of restriction on individual freedom and decision-making clearly depends on the population under care, but is probably greater for all congregate care groups than in family-type settings. To the extent that children and youth have little opportunity to exercise self-responsibility and to experience success or failure and the consequences thereof, their emotional and social maturity will be impaired. For these reasons, the graduates of residential care programs, whether they be delinquents, mentally retarded persons, or mentally ill persons, are often ill-prepared to function independently in society. Here, too, compensations are possible. Replacement training, day work activities in the community, and halfway houses are some of the techniques employed to facilitate the transition from dependency to independence.

The sense of stigma felt by individuals of some residential programs may be another disadvantage that damages self-esteem and social adjustment. There are many illustrations of this point, both anecdotal and scientific. Mildly retarded youth, often placed because of behavior disorders rather than low intelligence per se, may be seriously ego-threatened by being placed in a facility housing the more severely handicapped.

Delinquents of normal intellect may feel the same way about retarded delinquents. Stigma is reinforced by influential persons in the community who react to an individual's past record rather than to that person's current performance. Juvenile judges, for example, are far more likely to send children to correctional institutions than to place them on probation if they have previously been residents of some form of institution than if they have not (Office of Children's Services, 1973). This discriminatory practice probably accounts for some of the differentials in recidivism rates reported in experimental delinquency treatment programs. The mildly retarded also try to conceal their institutional backgrounds as much as possible, which is often counterproductive, because it may shield them from needed protection and force them into devious but often futile subterfuge. The stigmatizing effects of institutional care, unlike some of the other limitations identified, cannot be remediated until or unless societal perspectives of deviance are changed. This concept has less application for neglected, dependent, or disadvantaged children—those who are victims of social pathology but not formally labeled as deviant.

Not all residential care programs are stigmatizing. In Israel, the Youth Aliyah Program, with its heterogeneous mixture of disadvantaged immigrant Israeli children and youth from abroad, is not saddled with a negative image. This could conceivably change in the future if the composition of the resident population continues to shift even more in the direction of seriously disadvantaged youth, as it has in recent years. Such youth will have more emotional and behavior problems, lower levels of educational achievement, and, in the absence of good peer models to emulate, a potentially higher incidence of failure. Should these eventualities occur, the Israeli public image of Youth Aliyah and the self-image of its resident youth may undergo negative change. This program is cited here because it reveals some of the potential advantages of residential care. Perhaps the most often cited limitation of residential care, especially with regard to correctional facilities, but not confined to that setting, is the phenomenon of peer learning (Lerman, 1968). Recidivism among juvenile offenders, it is claimed, is attributable in large measure to learned behavior and to the negative influences of peer group interaction. Others have argued that mental institutions, because of ther preoccupation with pathology, are also inherently pathological environments and therefore incapable of fulfilling their restorative missions (Rosenhan, 1973).

The literature on imitative behavior, role models, and peer cultures may be more supportive of these observations than the data on recidivism of offenders or discharge of mental patients. Studies comparing the recidivism rates of offenders released from institutions with those of individuals placed on probation suffer from some of the design problems noted earlier. Persons on probation are more often first offenders or their offenses are less serious in nature. Juveniles living in community-based group homes, however, are theoretically subject to similar effects of learned behavior, and any existing differences cannot therefore be explained on this basis. The issue is a critical one in need of further study. If this concept were carried to its logical conclusion, it would argue effectively against homogeneous grouping of any type of deviants in the fear that disturbed, retarded, and mentally ill youth would be reinforced in their negative behavior patterns. This fear is not groundless; the adolescent peer culture is notorious for its imitative and modeling behavior. Such typical behavior could, through deliberate structuring of groups, be turned to advantage.

Individuals who serve as natural role models tend to be the more effective, more powerful, or higher status members of the group. Searching for such individuals and elevating them to leadership positions in the group could direct learning in positive directions.

In this discussion of the role of residential care in the behavior and development of children and youth, the intent is not to deny the growth-stunting effects on those persons, especially in early life, of many such facilities, past and present. To do so would be to hold a clearly untenable position by ignoring the critical force of the social environment in the developmental process. Instead, it is not congregate care as such, but the nature of the program provided that determines outcome. Bad institutions are no worse than bad homes. In fact, many children are the casualties of pathological home environments and their subsequent progress in institutions is often attendant upon this earlier experience. Numerous studies have shown that socioculturally retarded children from severely disadvantaged homes show increases in IQ after several years in institutional care, even in facilities judged mediocre by professional standards (Clarke and Clarke, 1954; Zigler and Williams, 1963). Conversely, the shift of an organically retarded child from a good home to an institution might result in declining performance.

Every child needs to develop a permanent attachment to adults (Rheingold, 1960), to receive affection and verbal stimulation, and to learn through the mediation of his experience by meaningful adults. Speech is particularly important because it may represent externalized thinking and is thus essential to problem solving (Luria, 1961). Retarded speech can weaken the earlier stages of cognitive development and inhibit later progress upon which the integrity of previous stages depends.

These needs are admittedly more difficult to satisfy in institutional settings that are characterized by high staff turnover, poor staff/child ratios, and low verbal interaction (as contrasted with the interaction of the average family). However, language deficiencies are also noted in disadvantaged children living at home. The Scottish survey, as far back as 1947, identified an inverse relationship between family size and verbal intelligence, without regard to social class. The dilution of parental care in larger families, duplicated by low staff-child interaction in institutions, seems a plausible explanation for this finding (Nisbet, 1953).

The damaging effects on children of early experience in bad institutions or homes raises the logical question about the efficacy of intervention in adolescence. The data on the relationship between early deprivation and long-range effects suggest that the human personality is highly resilient and capable of recovery from severe isolation and trauma. Davis (1947) and Koluchová (1972) both reported on the dramatic recovery from imbecility to intellectual normality of children reared under conditions of almost total isolation during the preschool years. More recent studies of young adults who had been evacuated to residential nurseries in World War II (Maas, 1963) or who had lived as infants in institutional care (Heston, Denny, and Pauly, 1966) showed no lingering effects in later life.

Numerous studies of this kind, including work in the animal field (Harlow and Suomi, 1970), challenge the "critical periods" concept of development and the idea that early deprivation causes irreversible damage. The Piagetian view that all conceptual schemata are the product of the child's active interaction with his environment from infancy to adolescence seems more consonant with empirical findings. Intervention in adolescence is clearly not too late to effect positive change, as has been so convincingly demonstrated in Israel (Feuerstein, 1977).

THE VALUES OF RESIDENTIAL CARE

Thus far, this chapter has addressed the limitations of residential care, some of which are remediable, others of which are less so. The advantages of residential care systems should also be considered, with particular emphasis on those serving older children and adolescents.

The most important characteristic of residential care is the control that can be imposed over every major function in the daily life of the resident. Theoretically, in fully self-contained units, goals can be established, programs defined, and staff members trained to carry out specific roles in predetermined ways. This demands not only well-intentioned but also well-informed personnel; the former are readily available but the latter are more difficult to find. Studies of staff behavior in facilities for delinquents frequently indicate that cottage parents accept the values of the delinquent subculture to keep peace, and that their doing so works at cross-purposes with professional workers (Polsky, 1962).

Institutions also have some ability to regulate intake and admissions policies and thus to approximate an optimal mix of clients. Private facilities in particular can exercise this option to maximize special therapeutic activities and to design educational programs specifically for children with common learning problems. Special education classes in the public school system, by contrast, have less flexibility with respect to the choice of whom they will serve. Such classes are likely to contain several types of children—some who are disadvantaged, some with learning disabilities, some with emotional disorders, and some with mild brain dysfunction. Although there may be benefits for socialization in heterogeneous grouping, educational needs may suffer.

The peer culture as a forum for social learning through imitation is one aspect of status. Status among peers is an important adolescent value. In the open environment of the community, deprived youth who lack other compensatory skills may seek status through delinquent or antisocial behavior. This activity probably accounts in part for the high admission rate of mildly retarded, disadvantaged youth to institutions during the 15– to 19– year age period. Residential settings, on the other hand, can guide modeling behavior in positive directions by applying the dynamics of social interaction to structured group activities, by offering opportunities for leadership in more capable youth, by rewarding achievement behavior, and by promoting a sense of belonging. The adolescent's need to be part of a peer group can be a powerful tool for social learning when control of unacceptable behavior is made a condition for continued group membership. In the absence of indigenous leaders or effective models in the disadvantaged youth group, staff members may need to fulfill this vital role. The Youth Aliyah program of Israel, cognizant of the problems of isolating disturbed adolescents within a disturbed subculture, properly places these individuals with normally functioning models in the youth villages. The Camphill Village Program for the retarded in New York applies similar concepts. Other options, such as the Big Brothers and Big Sisters programs in the United States, which provide models outside the peer culture, have also proven effective.

Another advantage of the residential setting is protection from the pressures of a nonsupportive, frequently hostile, and uncompromising environment. Mentally retarded and disadvantaged youth are, by definition, highly vulnerable to community rejection and to conflict with the dominant values of the larger society. If children's behavior is viewed as a threat to family or to community, their continuation of residence in unrestricted settings may well exacerbate their problems. Placement in a residential setting may be a more desirable alternative, at least until their behavior can be brought under control and until they can be provided with the educational and vocational tools needed to master the external environment.

Residential facilities, especially those under public auspices, are more stable over time than are foster family-care or group-care homes. Foster parents have great difficulty in handling emotionally disturbed or aggressive children and are subject to burn-out over time. Such children often undergo numerous placements, an experience that only strengthens their feeling of total rejection. Furthermore, foster families are particularly difficult to find for adolescents.

Group homes share some of the peer culture advantages described earlier but lack the protective qualities of the residential setting—qualities that have a pervasive influence over the adolescents' daily functions. To the extent that these facilities are privately owned and operated, they may be closed on short notice, requiring peremptory reassignment of residents. Furthermore, to turn a profit they must operate at full capacity, and to accomplish this business objective some facilities have retained residents unnecessarily and have thus prolonged their dependency behavior.

Reliance on the peer group as the medium for effecting behavior change and for instilling in children more acceptable social and moral values is consistent with the adolescent's drive for emancipation from parental controls and with the struggle for social acceptance. Despite the social pathology to which many of these youngsters are exposed (or perhaps because of it in some instances), there is considerable resistance to forming trusting relationships with adults in parental roles. Even in the face of adverse living conditions, some children retain strong family loyalties and are poor candidates for placement in homes where the foster parent-child relationship serves as the primary focal point for socialization and development. For adolescents, the peer group offers a temporary haven from further adult rejection and an opportunity for self-identity and social learning.

In this paper I have made no serious attempt to contrast residential care with alternative forms of placement for retarded or disadvantaged children and youth. The concentration on the values and limitations of residential settings per se has been deliberate, prompted in part by the strident efforts by some persons to abolish this form of care. It is my view—and one that I believe is shared by a large segment of the professional community and supported by research—that children with various problems need a wide range of living environments at different stages of development.

Residential programs are an essential component in the spectrum of services needed by children and youth whose families are unable or unwilling to care for them. Although it is true that in practice many of these facilities fail to achieve their child development goals, it is doubtful that these failures are inherent in residential care. Throughout the world, there are many examples of child-caring institutions whose graduates are socially competent, educated, and healthy, and who have well-rounded personalities.

REFERENCES

Bowlby, J. 1951. Maternal Care and Mental Health. World Health Organization, Geneva.

Clarke, A. D. B., and Clarke, A. M. 1954. Cognitive changes in the feeble-minded. Br. J. Psychol. 45:173–179.

Clarke, A. D. B., and Clarke, A. M., 1976. Early Experience: Myth and Evidence. Open Books, London.

Davis, K. 1947. Final note on a case of extreme isolation. Am. J. Sociol. 52:432–437.

Feuerstein, R. 1977. Instrumental Enrichment: Studies in Cognitive Modifiability. Final report: Grant #04634, NICHD, NIH, Washington, D.C.

Goldfarb, W. 1943. The effect of early institutional care on adolescent personality. J. Exp. Educ. 12:106–129.

Harlow, H. F., and Suomi, S. J. 1970. The nature of love—simplified. Am. Psychol. 25:161–168.

Heston, L. L., Denny, D. D., and Pauly, I. B. 1966. The adult adjustment of persons institutionalized as children. Br. J. Psychiatry 112:1103–1110.

Klackenburg, G. 1956. Studies in maternal deprivation in infants' homes. Acta Paediatr. 45:1–12.

Koluchová, J. 1972. Severe deprivation in twins: A case study. J. Child Psychol. Psychiatry 13:107–114.

Lerman, P. 1968. Evaluative studies of institutions for delinquents: Implications for research and social policy. Soc. Work 13(3):55–64.

Luria, A. R. 1961. The Role of Speech in the Regulation of Normal and Abnormal Behavior. Pergamon Press, Inc., London.

Maas, H. S. 1963. The young adult adjustment of twenty wartime residential nursery children. Child Welfare 42:57–72.

Nisbet, J. D. 1953. Family Environment: The Direct Effect of Family Size on Intelligence. Occasional papers on Eugenics, no. 8, Cassell, London.

Office of Child Development. 1976. Statement for priorities of research and demonstration activities in the area of children at risk and the child welfare system. DHEW, February, pp. 1–2.

Office of Children's Services. 1973. Juvenile Justice. Judicial Conference of the State of New York, p. 68.

Polsky, H. 1962. Cottage Six: The Social System of Delinquent Boys in Residential Treatment. Russell Sage Foundation, New York.

Raynes, N. V., and King, R. D. 1968. The measurement of child management in residential institutions for the retarded. In: B. W. Richards (ed.), Proceedings of the First Congress of the International Association for the Scientific Study of Mental Deficiency. Michael Jackson, Surrey, England.

Rheingold, H. L. 1960. The measurement of maternal care. Child Dev. 31:565–575.

Rosenhan, D. L. 1973. On being sane in insane places. Science 179(1):250–258.

Shyne, A. W. 1973. Research in child-caring institutions. In: D. M. Pappenfort, D. M. Kilpatrick, and R. W. Roberts (eds.), Child-Caring. Aldine Publishing Company, Chicago.

Spitz, R. A. 1946. A follow-up report. Psychoanal. Study Child. 2:113–117.

Yarrow, L. J. 1961. Maternal deprivation: Toward an empirical and conceptual reevaluation. Psychol. Bull. 58:459–490.

Zigler, E., and Williams, J. 1963. Institutionalization and the effectiveness of social reinforcement: A three year follow-up study. J. Abnorm. Soc. Psychol. 66:197–205.

Living Environments for Developmentally Retarded Persons
Edited by H. Carl Haywood and J. R. Newbrough
Copyright 1981 University Park Press Baltimore

Residential Provision for the Mentally Handicapped
Current Thinking, Provision, Research, and Emerging Research Issues in England and Wales

Chris Kiernan, Ph.D.
Deputy Director, Thomas Coram Research Unit
Institute of Education
University of London
41 Brunswick Square
London WC1N 1AZ
England

INTRODUCTION

In this chapter I outline some of the current thinking in England and Wales on residential environments for mentally retarded persons. It also sketches briefly the historical background of thinking about provision of services because the weight of our history bears heavily on present attitudes and philosophy. In addition, the current position on provision (within the context of isolated research issues that are being explored or could be explored in England and Wales) is outlined.

BASIC STATISTICS

There were 50,620 individuals in hospitals and units for the mentally handicapped in England on December 30, 1974 (Department of Health and Social Security, 1977). In addition, approximately 104,000 mentally handicapped persons were known to local authorities. These figures constitute the ascertained prevalence of mental handicap and are comprised of profoundly and severely mentally handicapped persons and a proportion of moderately mentally handicapped individuals who have

209

come to the attention of relevant agencies. With an estimated population of 46 million, these figures give England an ascertained prevalence of 3.4 per thousand mentally handicapped individuals who are considered in need of some form of service support.

HISTORICAL BACKGROUND

The current state of service provision in England should be understood against the background of the ideas and the physical provision that had been developed in the early years of this century. Tizard (1958) has argued that two ideas were crucial: 1) that intelligence could be measured, coupled with the development of means of measurement, and 2) that inherited mental handicap adversely affects society. The eugenics approach was represented by Tredgold (1909), who argued strongly for segregation of mentally handicapped persons from other persons. They would be placed in farm and industrial colonies where they could produce (at least minimally) toward their own upkeep, could be prevented from propagating, and meanwhile could be separated from the rest of society in order to protect it from the "definite criminal tendencies" that at least some of them possessed. The segregation approach was embodied in the Mental Deficiency Act of 1913, which (among other clauses) allowed an individual to be sent to an institution if "in addition to being a defective he was a person . . . guilty of any criminal offence . . . was an habitual drunkard . . . [was] found incapable of receiving education at school, or . . . might require supervision after leaving school." The Act provided for the institutionalization of children beginning at an early age.

The colonies conceived by Tredgold and required by the Act were normally constructed away from population centers. Many were old workhouses that had been designed and built in the nineteenth century with the stated intention that they should be as forbidding and as uncomfortable as possible in order to prevent the undeserving poor from entering them except as a final refuge from starvation. Some of these buildings are still in use today. The colony concept employed high-grade patients to produce goods and services that, if possible, would maintain the colony.

The terms of the Act (which was not replaced until 1959) meant that even persons of relatively high IQ could be incarcerated. Surveys by O'Connor and Tizard (1954), among others, found large numbers of individuals within the hospitals who had IQs of over 70. One provision of the 1913 Act that permitted this was the creation of the classification of moral defective, under which females who had illegitimate children could be certified. Brandon (1960) found that 50 of a group of 200 women discharged from a hospital had been committed because they had had illegitimate children. Even today, cases are still reported of women who had been certified under this clause gaining release from institutions.

Medical opinion was crucial in determining admission and discharge from the original colonies. In 1948, when the Ministry of Health took over the colonies from local councils, the colonies were brought under control of Regional Hospital Boards and became hospitals. To date they are administered by health authorities.

The decade of the 1950s was a period of considerable ferment. Influential studies were completed by O'Connor and Tizard (1954) and Ann and Alan Clarke (1958), inquiries were made about the conditions in institutions that showed serious deficiencies in care, international concern developed over mental handicap, and a Royal Commission on mental handicap led to the Mental Health Act of 1959. In addition to demonstrations that many institutionalized mentally handicapped persons were capable of living in the community, the main benefit of the 1959 Act was to eliminate compulsory detention except for restricted groups. There was very little impetus from the Act to promote the development of residential facilities outside the institutions, although the Act did encourage the development of community-based training and occupation centers. The recommendation of the Royal Commission was that hospitals should be responsible only for those individuals requiring specialist medical treatment, training, or continual nursing supervision. Local authorities were to provide small residential homes or hostels in centers of population where the residents were to be integrated into the life of the community (Her Majesty's Stationery Office, 1957).

Development of residential facilities in the 1960s was planned, but little was accomplished. Only 4,900 mentally handicapped people were housed in the community in 1969, as opposed to 58,850 individuals who resided in hospitals. During the 1960s, there was mounting pressure for small residential units (Tizard, 1964). The fact that these units had not emerged by the end of the 1960s may have been because Local Authority Health Departments essentially determined priorities by their control of education, further training or work, and residential accommodation for the mentally handicapped.

Apparently, mental handicap was not a priority to them, possibly because there was no cure. Only 43 of the 174 local authorities in England and Wales had homes of their own for children and adults (Her Majesty's Stationery Office, 1971). Nonetheless, there was grave concern over the state of mental subnormality hospitals. Surveying 35 hospitals, Morris (1969) found overcrowded, outdated wards in isolated hospitals where patients had few, if any, possessions and had nowhere to put possessions if they had them. The study also indicated a shortage of staff, a lack of treatment (partly a function of poor communication among specialists), and a general failure to adopt treatment objectives.

CURRENT LEGISLATION AND PHILOSOPHY

Medical control of provision for handicapped persons was broken by the creation of integrated social services departments in local authorities in 1970. These departments assumed responsibility for hostels, for day centers, and for adult training centers, as well as for the provision of support for families of mentally handicapped persons. In addition, the committee that recommended creation of the social services departments (the Seebohm Committee) also recommended that responsibility for the education of handicapped persons should pass to local authority education departments.

The Seebohm Committee created the opportunity for local development of residential facilities under the aegis of social work rather than of medicine. On the other hand, the Committee created complexities in services for mentally handicapped persons that central government is still trying to deal with (Court, 1976). Responsibility and authority were split between social workers and physicians; the social workers aligned with the community and the physicians aligned with the hospitals.

In 1971, what is now the Department of Health and Social Security published a major policy document entitled "Better Services for the Mentally Handicapped" (Her Majesty's Stationery Office, 1971). The document reviews all services for the mentally handicapped, acknowledging the need for advice and practical help for families and commenting on the need to develop day-care services. "Better Services for the Mentally Handicapped" argues for the principle of community placement in much the same terms as the Royal Commission had in 1957, except that it makes a plea for hospitals and community facilities to be used for different types of clients instead of a generalized plea for community residential placement. Hospitals should provide medical, nursing, and other specialist services on a day-to-day basis, plus inpatient treatment for those who "can no longer remain in the family home or in other residential care and require treatment or training under specialist medical treatment or constant nursing care. A high proportion will need this because their mental handicap is associated with severe physical disability or behaviour disorder" (Her Majesty's Stationery Office, 1971, p. 38). Hospitals should also provide treatment or training before discharge back to the community.

In the document, planning figures were produced based on esti-mates that were to be revised "in light of experience and further re-search" (Her Majesty's Stationery Office, 1971, p. 41). The investi-gators projected an increase from 4,900 residential places in the community in 1969 to 34,330 in 1991, and a reduction from the 59,500 beds allocated to mental handicap (some of which apparently were not being used) to a projected 33,400 by 1991.

The document omits many features that would have been desir-able. There is no clear reasoning behind the target figures; indeed, there is almost the admission that they were arrived at as a result of conflicting political pressures. There is no guidance on what type of provision is favored or how the transition from hospital to community should be effected. The document has been criticized from all sides (Campaign for the Mentally Handicapped, 1971; Elliott, 1972; Royal Medico Psychological Association, 1971) and has failed to give a strong lead on crucial questions (Jones et al., 1975), but it has provided con-crete figures and some direction for development.

The beginning of the 1970s was a watershed in the development of services for the mentally handicapped. Social service departments were created. Education departments assumed total responsibility for education and, as a result, all children were considered educable. A policy for development of services, although inadequate in several ways, did provide targets for the development of new residential facilities.

These changes brought with them substantial implications for training. Previously, there was a shortage of suitably trained staff at all levels. Subnormality hospitals were traditionally understaffed. The proportion of staff members holding professional qualification was low. More seriously, the training was and still is viewed by some profes-sionals and by the nurses themselves as substantially irrelevant. Jones et al. (1975) found that both trained and untrained nurses placed an emphasis on experience because nurse training did not represent an adequate knowledge basis for care. King, Raynes, and Tizard (1971) suggested that training was actually dysfunctional and was certainly inferior to child-care training. Although new training structures are evolving, it is estimated that only approximately 50% of hospital staff members have received any form of training, and it is the untrained staff members who are in direct contact with the patients (Department of Health and Social Security, 1976a).

Similar problems have emerged with local authority personnel, with the field social workers, and with staff members of residential homes. Here, the position has been complicated by the fact that, when social services were reorganized under the Seebohm Committee, specialization within social work training was abandoned. All social workers became generic, with common training and with caseloads consisting of a range of cases. This meant that social workers who had been employed specifically to work with mentally handicapped individuals in the 1960s were now required to become generic and, in addition, that contacts and administrative structures had to be abandoned or severely modified. Staff for residential homes simply did not exist in sufficient numbers and new training courses had to be developed in this area.

The pattern of training and service is still evolving within social services departments. Training under the Central Council for Education and Training in Social Work is becoming progressively more generic, with new generalized qualifications within which individual students can specialize (Central Council for Education and Training in Social Work, 1976). On the other hand, an increasing number of local authorities are moving toward the employment of specialized social workers to work with the handicapped. There is also a continued general practice of the segregation of mentally handicapped persons in residential homes for children or for adults.

Similar problems related to the shortage of adequately trained workers are evident in psychology and psychiatry. Part of the issue is specialization; the sectional lobby has little support from the professions or central government but still represents a vocal pressure group (Day, 1974; Elliott, 1972). Neither psychology nor psychiatry has given great attention to mental handicap in its training programs, and difficulties are still being experienced in making appointments to medical posts and (to a much lesser degree) to posts for psychologists in mental handicap hospitals. The position is further complicated by the fact that the local authorities do not normally employ clinical psychologists in social services departments. The local authority input from psychology is contributed by the educational psychologists, who, until 1970, had little or no contact with the mentally handicapped. They have very wide responsibilities, a situation that makes their direct involvement with mentally handicapped persons sporadic. They also have a very strong educational bias, are often not interested in the mentally handicapped, and, in any case, cease statutory contact completely when the children leave school at the age of 16 (Tizard, 1973).

The difficulties inherent in training are highlighted by problems in introducing behavioral techniques. Research and clinical psychologists have done the most work with introducing techniques, and a number of demonstration projects were established in the early 1970s in hospitals and clinics (Callias and Carr, 1976; Hattersley and Tennant, 1976; Kiernan, 1974). The demonstration projects attracted considerable attention, but nevertheless there was little clear change in practice.

In 1975, a group that met to discuss this situation agreed that those who conducted training courses lacked the necessary knowledge and practical experience and that experienced personnel could not fill these gaps solely by the type of short training workshops or day conferences that they were able to organize (Kiernan and Woodford, 1975). Furthermore, the group felt that the organizational climate and structure of hospitals and other residential establishments were not compatible with the introduction of behavioral techniques. The survey of nurse attitudes by Jones and associates (1975) revealed considerable skepticism over therapy, especially among untrained staff members—the primary emphasis was placed on care and kindness.

The process of change in areas as vast as those outlined above must necessarily be slow. Because of the status in 1970 and the economic stringencies of the early 1970s, however, the amount of progress made in developing new administrative structures and training courses has been substantial. The national government has continued to show interest in and concern for mental handicap with recurrent inquiries into abuse in subnormality hospitals. The most recent undertaking was the establishment of the National Development Group for the Mentally Handicapped in 1975, a multi-disciplinary group whose purpose is to act as a catalyst of development. The group has produced a number of brief pamphlets, the most recent on residential short-term care (National Development Group, 1977). These pamphlets contain outline ideas and brief guidance for local authorities and other concerned organizations. More detailed advice and guidance are available from a subgroup of the National Development Group—the National Development Team, which is a multi-disciplinary organization that can be called upon by hospitals, local authorities, or other interested bodies to provide detailed analyses of existing structures, provision and interpretation of policy, and guidance on how services may be developed. Experience of the Team has indicated that all levels of service provision require guidance in working out problems like what legislation is relevant, what can be used in obtaining central funds, and how available resources may be best deployed. However, the Team has no ruling powers and consulting authorities have no obligation to accept the advice given. Consequently, although the Team has been consulted extensively, there is as yet no indication of the effectiveness of the Team approach in changing practice (Simon, 1978). Thus, increasing research activity is evident in the field of mental handicap, with a considerable amount of research being funded by the Department of Health and Social Security.

Outside the government sphere, an independent organization—the Campaign for the Mentally Handicapped (CMH)—was established in the early 1970s and has exerted continued pressure for community provision (Campaign for the Mentally Handicapped, 1972). Initially, the CMH was constituted of people who lacked direct experience in working with mentally handicapped persons and who consequently lacked credibility with professionals and parents. In recent years, the basis of the organization has broadened; it now represents an active forum for questioning accepted wisdom and for presenting radical alternatives (Tyne, 1976b).

Finally, the parents' organization, the National Society for Mentally Handicapped Children, which tended in the early 1970s to adopt a rather bland posture, has become increasingly militant in suggesting that parents themselves should evaluate services and apply pressure where deficiencies emerge. Several checklists of minimum standards have been prepared under the title "Stamina," and other materials are in preparation (National Society for Mentally Handicapped Children, 1977). The level of detail involved is denoted by items relating to the education of multiply handicapped children. Parents are advised to ascertain that there is a staff/child ratio of one to three; that there is program stimulation, the effects of which are recorded; that the school has a specialist social worker and effective access to physiotherapy; that there are nursing and medical services; and that specialists are consulted when problems arise. If there is a failure to achieve minimum standards, parents are advised on the steps that can be taken to bring effective pressure for change.

Philosophically, the divisions of the 1960s are still present and, if anything, further entrenched. The conservative philosophy, more typical of medical and hospital thinking, still tends toward care and kindness as the sole solution to residential provision. Resistance to the dissolution of the subnormality hospitals has tended to be coupled with resistance to the release of control on the part of the medical profession (Primrose, 1974; Royal College of Psychiatry, 1976; Royal Medico Psychological Association, 1971). The argument of medical staff takes several forms. For instance, in response to pressure for more specific goals for treatment and for maintenance of records of progress in hospitals, they argue that these simply add to administrative loads. In any case, pressure to introduce new measures only shows lack of faith in the good will and expertise of the staff on the part of outsiders. Would it not be better to encourage parents and relatives to trust the system and to maintain a situation where one or two respected people whom relatives could meet—the doctors in charge—assume the role of looking after the overall well-being of the hospital?

The opposing philosophy is more characteristic of educators, psychologists, and social workers: mentally handicapped persons need recognition as individuals with rights and privileges, such as the freedom to take risks. In addition, the community needs to develop increased tolerance and acceptance and to realize that mentally handicapped individuals have something to contribute as persons. According to this philosophy, caring is caring about the individual by helping him to achieve the goals he wants to achieve; kindness is the acceptance of the individual on his own terms. The philosophy stresses the key issues of decentralization, suppport of the family and individual, education throughout life, and self-determination.

One almost certain index of an individual's philosophy is the terminology that he uses in referring to the mentally handicapped. Adherents of the first philosophy tend almost universally to refer to them as "patients." Adherents of the second philosophy have difficulty terminologically and use a variety of terms, such as "client," "resident," "the retarded," "the handicapped," "people with special needs," "handicapped individuals," or even just "people!"

PROVISION, RESEARCH, AND EMERGING RESEARCH ISSUES

This section outlines what is known of current provision ensuing from the philosophies described in the previous section. Research on mental handicap is a sociological phenomenon that is generated or should be generated by perceived needs but that is severely limited by practicalities. The function of research is to illuminate services and to guide them to the achievement of their goals by examining current practice and by pointing the way to future developments.

STATISTICAL REPORTS

Given the changes that have occurred, the first research issue to consider is whether the current position can be described in relation to hospital and community provision. Department of Health and Social Security statistics are available that give some overall indication of changes: the long-stay population of the hospitals is decreasing at a rate of just over 2% per annum, and the number of community residential places is rising (Department of Health and Social Security, 1977). There was a fall in the number of people in hospitals from nearly 59,000 in 1969 to 55,000 in 1974, and a rise from just under 6,000 community places in 1968 to 9,600 in 1974. When projected to 1991 (the target date set in 1971), these figures suggest a probable short-fall of nearly 14,000 community placements (around 40% by that date).

However, local authorities can be defended. Although capital grants were made available for hostel building in the early 1970s, only approximately 25% of loans requested by local authorities for the construction of hostels were granted by the Treasury. In recent years, economic difficulties have slowed progress of building and have forced some authorities to leave buildings standing empty (Mittler, 1976).

What is clear from several monitoring reports is that subnormality hospitals are achieving their function of housing more difficult or physically handicapped people. Spencer (1976) showed that over 50% of new long-stay admissions to one hospital were in the profoundly retarded category and needed nursing and specialized care. Two out of every three children were admitted because of behavior problems (Primrose, 1974). In addition, Department of Health statistics on admissions and discharges from subnormality hospitals show a substantial rise in the use of hospitals for short-term care (Department of Health and Social Security, 1977).

The most recent figures on physical provision (Department of Health and Social Security, 1976b) showed that by 1973 only four of the 71 hospitals covered achieved the minimum standards established by the Department for staffing, size of dormitories, and such basic necessities as provision of lockers for personal clothing. The number of physiotherapists, speech therapists, and occupational therapists was staggeringly low, despite the characteristics of the populations with whom they dealt.

This type of data is of obvious importance in monitoring the development of services and in indicating deficiencies. Spencer (1976) suggested that the trend for people with behavior problems and physical infirmities to become long-term patients was partly caused by inadequate provision for such persons in the community. On the basis of this type of data, the Royal College of Psychiatry (1976) argued that hospitals should be maintained at their present level or should even be increased in size.

SURVEY STUDIES

Hospital Provision

There is a clear need for research that examines the actual operation of the provision available. Since the publication of Morris's book (1969), a further major study of hospital provision has appeared. Jones et al. (1975) reported the results of a survey of provision in one Regional Health Authority and found problems similar to those revealed by Morris (1969). Little had been done to modify custodial attitudes, poor morale, institutionalization, lack of community contacts, and training of staff. To some extent, environments had been improved by the upgrading of some wards through remodeling and redecoration, but little can be done to disguise a work house effectively. Jones et al. (1975) reported that the introduction of some smaller units was welcomed. On the other hand, reorganization led to further problems, because of increased genericism in training, because of the feeling that training was irrelevant to needs, and because of worsening morale resulting from projected rundown of beds and discharge of the better patients.

The depressing picture presented by Jones et al. (1975) has been echoed by Grant (1974) and in a more recent study by Maureen Oswin (1978). Oswin found the same lack of direction, poor training, poor coordination of services within hospitals, and poor use and back-up by ancillary staffs that Morris (1969) had reported nearly a decade earlier.

To be fair, it must be pointed out that there is great variation among hospitals. The characterization given in the research reports tends to be outdated when reported. Several hospitals have introduced positive steps to offset the type of problem outlined above. They represent models of at least better practice within the institutional constraints of management and resources. Some Regional Health Authorities or hospitals have adopted a deliberate policy of integration with the community, or, as in the case of Sheffield, have never had monolithic hospitals to contend with (Gemmell, 1974). Notable among progressive authorities are the Wessex region in the South, Lea Hospital in the Midlands, and Northgate Hospital in the North. Developments have included new training programs founded on behavior principles, short-stay hostels in the community, and active interaction with community agencies.

Residential Community Provision

Information about style and operation of community provision is difficult to obtain. In general, authorities rely on 24-bed purpose-built hostels, although local authorities converted properties of several different types between 1971 and 1974. House parents or residential staff live in. The hostel size of 24 residents was determined through consideration of staffing arrangements (especially for night staff), absenteeism, and cost per head. Several pioneering demonstration projects, notably the Brooklands project (Tizard, 1964) and the Slough project (Baranyay, 1971), adopted this range of unit size. Kushlick (1974) noted that at the time such units were set up in Wessex, units of 24 were as small as the authorities would accept, but that units of 12 residents serving smaller catchment areas would have been preferable.

Surveying 20 hostels in 11 local authorities, Jones and her team (1975) found considerable variation. Purpose-built hostels were often found to be clinical in character—stark, gloomy, and isolated converted mansions. Normal residential housing, considered small and homely with as few as five residents, was most favored. The residents in the hostels were generally more capable than the hospital sample, evidence that reflects overt selection. Rules were few and attitudes toward activity varied from allowing people to do nothing because "it was their home" to "keep[ing] them occupied" (p. 175). Contacts with social services departments were good. Six of the 20 hostels surveyed said that they were receiving considerably more support than they had received from the health departments; however, contacts with social workers were apparently not encouraged (p. 177), and contacts with the community in general were almost nonexistent. Staff were poorly trained, and it was concluded that, if less capable people were to be moved from hospitals, then more intensive staffing would be required.

Sporadic but probably unreliable evidence of poor public attitudes toward mentally handicapped persons is given by occasional well-organized opposition to the placement of hostels or group homes in the community.

Group Homes, Lodgings, Fostering, and Short-term Care

Some homes have been established in which a group of mentally handicapped people has been placed in a community setting without residential supervision. Few of these group homes have been described. Race (1977) pointed out that there are probably two reasons for this omission: 1) the fear of unfavorable public reaction to publicity, and 2) the view that "the essential criterion of success for such homes is simply their existence and survival and thus evaluation is unnecessary" (p. 77).

The group homes described in the survey of Jones et al. (1975) vary from two purpose-built units of eight flatlets, each of which were felt to provide a "balance between necessary care and privacy for the residents," to a 30-bed converted house in which conditions were described as "rough" and where "some males frequently slept with their boots on" (p. 178).

The use of lodgings, where the mentally handicapped resident lives in a rooming house, is an additional alternative. Jones et al. (1975), who found this use infrequent and very inadequate in their survey, concluded their report with a slashing criticism of the attitudes of the authorities:

Social workers in the field, and their superiors, tended to see lodgings as a means of offloading the demand on hostels rather than as part of a range of choice. Lodgings were often used as dumping-ground for those for whom hostel places were not available, or who did not fit into the fairly middle class ethos of hostel life. It may be administratively convenient and currently fashionable to talk of "non-institutional forms of care" as though they were superior to hostel care. The reality suggests that a few genuinely are superior: the rest are much worse. (p. 178)

Although fostering and adoption of mentally handicapped children does occur, it is rare, and few reports have been published. Hibbert and Harman (1977) described a pilot scheme in Somerset that appears to have had substantial success for short-term care in foster homes.

Several centers are developing short-term care facilities for children who are closely linked with active treatment programs for the behavioral disabilities that may be preventing the child's adjustment to home. Notable among these are the programs at the Hilda Lewis Unit in London (Callias and Carr, 1976) and the Honeylands Center in Exeter (Brimblecombe, 1974; Raynor, 1977). The programs in these units are planned to include home and center, with intensive education of both family and child. The more typical pattern of short-term care is one in which the mentally handicapped individuals are admitted to the facility when the parents go on holiday, are ill, or simply need a break. There is apparently little preparation for the transition to these programs. One of the obvious and surprising omissions from survey research is the examination of the impact of this short-term care on the mentally handicapped person and his family. The separation experience must surely have effects in some ways paralleling those seen in normal infants, especially when the individual is profoundly retarded but there has been no previous study of the practices involved in short-term care or of the positive or adverse effects. A study of this type is currently being set up in the Thomas Coram Research Unit by Maureen Oswin.

Domiciliary Community Provision

Although this chapter is concerned with residential accommodation, the support and help provided to families with handicapped members also clearly affects demand for residential provision. Successive surveys since the early 1960s have paid considerable attention to families (Tizard and Grad, 1961). Bayley (1973) reported a developed structure for coping; other people who offered to help with the structure tended to be family, friends, or neighbors. Social work help at the time of the survey was not related to the everyday needs of the families and was generally ineffective. Bayley (1973) argued from his findings that there were strong reasons for keeping even the most profoundly retarded individuals at home or in local units very near to homes. The main basis for this argument was the benefit bestowed on the handicapped person from being "cared for and loved as a valued person" (p. 318). Bayley's research was completed before social services departments had begun to recover from the Seebohm reorganization. The current position within the community setting is complex.

The mentally handicapped individual or his family may have to deal with a variety of services: a family doctor (a general practitioner) who may know little or nothing about mental handicap; a pediatrician who acts independently of the general practitioner, but who similarly may know little of mental handicap; a Child Welfare Clinic independent of the family doctor; a Local Authority Social Services Department, which may not be in touch with medical aspects, and which may know little of mental handicap; a District Health Authority, which may be defined in geographic terms different from those of Local Authority Social Services, and which has its own assessment and (possibly) treatment functions; a Schools Psychological Service (Local Authority based, but not necessarily coordinated with other agencies), which may or may not have an interest in mental handicap as an educational problem; an education department with a statutory responsibility to educate; another branch of social services with responsibility for daycare or adult training; or a subnormality hospital, independent in management, policy, and responsibility from all the rest, which may eventually be the final residential accommodation for the mentally handicapped person. Parents and relatives need to know how, where, and when to apply for constant attendance allowance, disability allowance, national assistance, supplementary benefits and pensions—each of which may require separate visits and separate forms to be filled in, but which are worth applying for because they allow very substantial relief from the financial pressures of mental handicap.

It can be argued that, throughout all this, the social worker (who may be a specialist) should act as advocate and guide to the family, possibly within the structure of a community-based team with special responsibility for all mentally handicapped people (Court, 1976; Warnock, 1978).

Epidemiological Studies

Lewis's (1929) pioneer study of the epidemiology of mental handicap has been followed by a succession of elegant and important studies that have, of late, been crucial to service planning (Kushlick and Blunden, 1974). In general, it is now felt that the large-scale epidemiological studies of the 1960s need to be replaced by more intensive, limited focus studies in such areas as the epidemiology of communication disorders or mental handicap among immigrants (Wing, 1976). Locally based handicap observation registers should be routinely maintained, although it is doubtful that they now are.

Kushlick's (1974) epidemiological studies in Wessex examined various behavioral characteristics of a population, including mobility, continence, and behavior disorders. On the basis of this, he was able to show that a living unit of 20–25 places would be required to provide for all the residential care needs for all of the mentally handicapped children from a total population of 100,000. These figures have been tested in a number of projects in the Wessex region (Kushlick, 1974).

A small-scale survey in North London investigated the need for residential accommodation by interviewing parents about how they wished their mentally handicapped children to be placed (Wheeler, 1976). In rank order, their reasons for wanting residential care included death, illness or old age of parents, the happiness and development of the child, difficulty in coping with the child, and concern for the rest of the family. Estimates were also made of short-term needs. The report represents an excellent example of a small-scale epidemiological study directed toward a particular problem.

Analytic Studies

Survey research has produced crucial data bearing on the evolution and operation of services. The surveys tend to restrict themselves to descriptions and analyses that have possibly fostered a deepening of understanding, but that cannot lead to changes in practice when such changes are dependent on the acquisition of new skills or on the creation of new organizational structures.

One reason for the failure to change practice has been the argument that practices should not be changed until the relative benefits of different schemes are clear. This concept of evaluation as a sort of horse race has been generally unpopular with researchers, and one study by Race (1977) highlighted the reasons why. Race wanted to compare residents of hospitals, hostels, sheltered villages, and group homes in the gains they had made in social competence over a period of one year. He found that, in order to make a statistically and methodologically sound comparison, a new scale of social competence had to be developed that was relevant to the skills required in the contexts within which he was working. Then, because he could not representatively sample from certain groups because of group size, he was forced to discard several possible comparisons. Furthermore, because his scales were ordinal rather than ratio scales, he had to match subjects in different groups, thereby sampling only from the top end of the hospital group.

The study observed 81 subjects. No significant differences in social competence emerged in the study from one testing to the next or between groups. Race's thesis described the complex problems in designing studies in this area and the limitations of a single criterion (horse race) evaluation. He argued that adequate evaluation must take account not only of organizational climate and client satisfaction, but also of broader politico-social issues. As used here, the rubric "analytic studies" refers to attempts to study crucial aspects of process rather than to look merely to product measures as a focus of interest.

Possibly the most distinguished study of this type was completed by King, Raynes, and Tizard (1971), who have reported a series of studies on residential care of mentally handicapped persons. In their study, they developed scales from Goffman's concepts of rigidity of routine, block treatment, depersonalization, and social distance (Goffman, 1961). Using these scales, King, Raynes, and Tizard (1971) compared mental subnormality hospital wards, voluntary homes, and local authority hostels for mentally handicapped children. Within each scale, a child-oriented and an institution-oriented pole were identified. The hostels emerged as child-oriented, the hospitals as uniformly institution-oriented, and the three voluntary homes as mixed. Size of unit and ability of children were eliminated as crucial variables. A second main finding was that units run by directors trained in child care were significantly more child-oriented than those run by medically qualified staff. Heads of hostels tended not only to be much more involved in child care than heads of hospital units, but also to have significantly more responsibility for making decisions. Training was related to performance; judged from direct observation of behavior, child-care-trained directors were more likely to talk to children, less likely to reject them, and more likely to interact with children while engaged in domestic or administrative duties than were nurse-trained heads in equivalent situations (p. 187).

King, Raynes, and Tizard (1971) tracked the reported effects on the organizational structure encompassing the unit and on the climate created by the head of unit. Kushlick et al. (1976) raised the same points in discussing the nursing role in the care of mentally handicapped persons. They pointed out that direct-care staff have responsibility for care of the mentally handicapped but do not have the authority to make many of the decisions that affect how they can deal with problems of potential development (Richardson, this volume).

Research in social services departments by the Brunel University Institute of Organization and Social Studies (1974) has revealed structural constraints on the effective operation of residential care. Two patterns of organization have been isolated by the Institute: 1) functional organization in which workers are grouped in relation to their jobs (i.e., all fieldworkers, all residential care workers) and 2) functional groupings that have their own management hierarchy and geographical organization, and in which all workers within a certain geographical area are brought together into a single team. Functional organization tends toward a separation of various teams, so that communication is poor and working relationships are not adequately established. This separation is exacerbated by the fact that residential workers generally have received less training and therefore are on a lower salary scale than professional fieldworkers. The disagreements that arise, apparently (in particular) over transfer of residents from hostels to more independent living (Tyne, 1976a), can be seen as a function of differing perspectives: those derived from experience in fieldwork as opposed to those derived from experience in closed residential-care departments. Geographical organization overcomes the problems of communication but emphasizes the differences in salaries and training. Residential staff normally find themselves in a management structure headed by people with qualifications and experience irrelevant to their speciality.

DEMONSTRATION PROJECTS

The United Kingdom has a long and distinguished history of demonstration projects. Beginning in the 1950s with the Brooklands Project (Tizard, 1964) and the work of the Clarkes and of Tizard on training, the demonstration project approach has been used frequently in an attempt to model new services. The philosophy of the project is simple: a project is established within the reasonable constraints operating in mental handicap service contexts, progress is monitored (sometimes with control groups), and the resulting demonstration is publicized and made available for visits. The demonstration study is particularly appropriate in the context of service development in the United Kingdom in the 1970s. Survey studies reveal what is happening at a widespread level; analytic studies show some of the variables that might be in play, but, as we have seen, structure and training are being constantly and actively developed. Consequently, cross-sectional measurement studies are likely to be inconclusive. On the other hand, attractive and viable demonstration projects may be copied as part of new services.

Several studies on various types of residential development have been reported. Kushlick (1974) reported the results of a development project in which all mentally handicapped children from a predefined area of Southampton and Portsmouth were placed, regardless of level of disability, in residential homes within the cities concerned. The project, conducted in conjunction with service authorities, was epidemiologically based. Baranyay (1971) reported experiences in the Slough experiment, a demonstration project involving community residential provision and workshop experience for adolescents, and Johnson (1975) and Race and Race (1975, 1976) described developments of group homes. The Race and Race reports (1975, 1976) reveal gains in self-confidence and beneficial effects of group interaction. Cardiff Universities Social Services reported experiences in a home in which students and a number of mentally handicapped people lived together (Cardiff Universities Social Services, 1975).

Kiernan, Wright, and Hawks (1974) reported a demonstration project in a hospital ward that was reorganized in order to decrease institutionalization effects and to allow the introduction of a behavior modification program. Using a complex of measures, these researchers found that the scores of target children improved significantly in a 2-year program as compared to their initial scores and to the scores of a matched control group. The target ward improved on the Tizard scales, with other wards remaining at a high level of institutional orientation.

A large group of demonstration projects has been developed to investigate aspects of parent involvement with handicapped children. These include Sandow (1977), University of Manchester (Cunningham, 1975), the Hilda Lewis Unit at the Maudesley Hospital (Callias and Carr, 1976), and the Honeylands Center in Exeter (Brimblecombe, 1974).

ILLUMINATIVE EVALUATION

Almost by definition, the demonstration project is of limited duration when it is set up within an existing organizational framework and when it requires that some aspects of the organization be modified to accommodate it. When the project is completed, the organizational variables are allowed to operate again and the special schedules, extra stability of staff, increased autonomy of decision, or simply enhanced motivation disappear and the project dies. This experience makes it clear to change-oriented researchers that many potent variables that are substantially concerned with training and organization are not being controlled in these studies.

Therefore, researchers should become involved in the development of researched inservice training programs. One example is a training course in behavioral techniques developed for senior nurses by the Joint Board of Clinical Nursing Studies with research support from the Kings Fund. Another program of this type is being developed for social work personnel by Kiernan and colleagues (Kiernan, 1976). This type of research is considered by many to be the only effective means for dissemination of new developments, especially to those places where acquisition of new skills and ways of working is required.

There is general agreement that training on its own is ineffective as a means of changing practices within organizations. A second method for improving service is for the researchers to adopt a modified illuminative evaluation approach and to become involved in the development as well as the measurement of the effects of a service.

This model, without benefit of a name, was pioneered in the United Kingdom in the 1950s by the Clarkes, Tizard, and their colleagues. Its most effective proponent in the 1970s was Kushlick. Working in the Wessex region since the mid-1960s, Kushlick has played a dual role in the development of research by evolving or by introducing new concepts of community care and by devising means whereby the effects of these changes can be measured (Whatmore, Durward, and Kushlick, 1975). Within this framework of the Wessex research, the crucial element of systematic replication, which is impossible in the demonstration project, has been implemented. The original two hostels have been followed by others. Seven hostels—five for children and two for adults—have been built by the Regional Health Authority. Each hostel takes all the hospital population from the relevant catchment area (a 100% hostel scheme including the most profoundly retarded).

Kushlick and his collaborators have tried to compare the effects of local placement in hostel accommodation with placement of matched control clients in hospital units. Their results are being published in a series of working papers (Kushlick et al., 1977). Initial comparison of the two groups showed that the psychiatrists operating the scheme agreed to the procedure of transferring clients into hostels according to the geographical location of their homes. As a consequence, levels of handicap and behavior disorders were initially equivalent in both groups. Subsequent comparisons showed that hostel residents attained similar or better levels of progress over time on a developmental checklist (Smith et al., 1977a). There was similarly no evidence that more handicapped people were being moved back into hospitals as time went on (Palmer, Kushlick, and Dawes, 1977). Hostels were found to achieve higher levels of active engagement of clients throughout the day than hospital settings achieved (Felce et al., 1977a), and parents and other people from outside the settings visited hostel clients more frequently (Felce et al., 1977b). Death and injury rates were not different in the two settings (Glossop et al., 1977; Palmer, Kushlick, and Dawes, 1977).

One prediction made by opponents of hostels was that professionals would provide poorer services for the hostel clients than for the hospital clients. The results of comparisons here were interesting in several respects. Overall frequency of contact in both settings was low—often significantly so. For example, consultant psychiatrists made an average of only 0.3 contacts per patient per year! There was no difference between settings. Overall contacts with medical and other therapists and members of the helping professions were more frequent in the hostel than in the hospital settings—for example, 34% of hostel clients came in contact with a physiotherapist, 13% with a speech therapist, and 29% with an occupational therapist, while the corresponding figures for hospital settings were 7%, 19%, and 0% of clients (Glossop et al., 1977). Studies of parents' and relatives' reactions to hostel and hospital settings showed, in the hostel setting, a higher rate of visiting or taking clients out, greater contact with relevant external professionals, and a higher rate of favorable comments on the hostel settings (Smith et al., 1977b).

The results of the Wessex study are impressive in their extent and in their evaluation of a stabilized service delivery system. To that degree, they gain a credibility that is lacking in some demonstration projects that may rely on exceptional individuals and circumstances. The Wessex study showed the overall desirability of locally based hostels and provided substantial evidence on which to reject arguments in favor of hospitals. How influential the study will be in affecting practice remains to be seen.

Similar programs of collaborative research, in which the researcher has a broadly based brief and the assurance of actively involved service personnel, have been set up elsewhere. In Glamorgan, Blunden (a former coworker of Kushlick) has established an applied research unit for the development and evaluation of services for mentally handicapped persons (Blunden, 1976). The research is proceeding in six phases: setting up, pilot, demonstration, replication, dissemination, and end. Heron began a similar project in association with ongoing service developments in Sheffield (Gemmell, 1974). (Unfortunately, this evaluation was begun only after the Sheffield project was already underway.) Kiernan (1976) is involved in a similar project in North London, in which the particular reference of the project is the development of the role of social services departments with the handicapped. All projects in this group are epidemiologically based; the research worker functions to feed information and ideas into the development of services as well as to test objectively the practical consequences of these ideas.

This type of project seems particularly relevant at a time of rapid evolution of services. The model for residential services has clear ramifications. Taking as a baseline the epidemiological data used by

Kushlick (1974) in his estimates of need for residential care, it is apparent that development of services to the family may reduce pressures on the family by eliminating feeding, toileting, or behavior problems. Improved teaching may reduce problems caused by communication deficits (Bayley, 1973). Active development of fostering and short-term care facilities may reduce the demand for long-term residential care. Greater support to the families may lead them to feel more able to maintain the handicapped person at home. On the other hand, improved residential services may render parents more willing to see the handicapped person leave home. One school of thought in the United Kingdom suggests that the parents should have the right to expect the mentally handicapped child to leave home at around 19 years of age. The handicapped person himself may well want to leave home if he likes the alternatives offered. If any or all of these factors operate, they would disclaim single epidemiological studies of static types of problems experienced or felt needs.

The most effective way to chart the evolution and interplay of these trends is to monitor (in as controlled a way as possible) the effects of different variables. Specific projects on the effects of different types of living environments (Blunden, 1976; Durward and Whatmore, 1975) on the functioning of specialists as opposed to generic social workers (Fassam and Hart, 1978) and on the training and skills of residential care staff are planned or are in progress.

CONCLUSION

The preceding section argues that several types of research are needed to serve different functions in the development and evaluation of residential alternatives for mentally handicapped persons. One further function must be emphasized: research workers do not have enough adventurous ideas. Recently, the author visited a residential unit that had adopted a policy of maximum freedom and self-determination for the residents. A problem had arisen: one of the girls in the hostel was refusing to wash frequently enough. It would have been against policy to threaten her with return to a more restrictive unit if she didn't wash. How was her behavior to be changed within the framework of the organizational philosophy? As researchers, we have the obligation to encourage new developments by feeding in new techniques to solve such problems. More than that, we must try to develop new ways of helping society achieve the goals that it sets for itself to integrate and to free mentally handicapped individuals from the constraints that nature and man have placed on them.

REFERENCES

Baranyay, E. P. 1971. The Mentally Handicapped Adolescent. Pergamon Press, Inc., Oxford.

Bayley, M. 1973. Mental Handicap and Community Care. Routledge and Kegan Paul, London.

Blunden, R. 1976. The Development and Evaluation of Services for the Mentally Handicapped—An Outline Research Plan. Applied Research Unit, Welsh National School of Medicine, Health Park, Cardiff.

Brandon, M. W. G. 1960. A survey of 200 women discharged from a mental deficiency hospital. J. Ment. Sci. 106:355–370.

Brimblecombe, F. S. W. 1974. An Exeter project for handicapped children. Br. Med. J. 4:706–709.

Brunel University Institute of Social Studies. 1974. Social Services Departments: Developing Patterns of Work and Organisation. Heinemann, London.

Callias, M., and Carr, J. 1976. Behaviour modification programmes in a community setting. In: C. C. Kiernan and F. P. Woodford (eds.), Behaviour Modification with the Severely Retarded. Associated Scientific Press, London.

Campaign for the Mentally Handicapped. 1971. The White Paper and Future Services for the Mentally Handicapped. Campaign for the Mentally Handicapped, London.

Campaign for the Mentally Handicapped. 1972. Even Better Services for the Mentally Handicapped. Campaign for the Mentally Handicapped, London.

Cardiff Universities Social Services. 1975. Cardiff Universities Group Home Project. Cardiff Universities Social Services, Cardiff.

Central Council for Education and Training in Social Work. 1976. Professional Training in Social Work. The Certificate of Qualification in Social Work (CQSW). Central Council for Education and Training in Social Work, London.

Clarke, A. M., and Clarke, A. D. B. 1958. Mental Deficiency: The Changing Outlook. Methuen, London.

Court, S. D. M. 1976. Fit For the Future: Report on the Committee on Child Health Services. Her Majesty's Stationery Office, London.

Cunningham, C. 1976. Parents as therapists and educators. In: C. C. Kiernan and F. P. Woodford (eds.), Behaviour Modification with the Severely Retarded. Associated Scientific Press, London.

Day, K. 1974. Follow the northern lights. New Psychiatry 1:19–28.

Department of Health and Social Security. 1976a. Priorities in the Health and Social Services in England—A Consultative Document. Her Majesty's Stationery Office, London.

Department of Health and Social Security. 1976b. The facilities and services of mental illness and mental handicap hospitals in England and Wales. Stat. Res. Rep. Ser. No. 11. Her Majesty's Stationery Office, London.

Department of Health and Social Security. 1977. In-patient statistics from the mental health enquiries for England 1974. Stat. Res. Rep. Ser. No. 17. Her Majesty's Stationery Office, London.

Durward, L., and Whatmore, R. 1975. A Pilot Study on a Method of Measuring the Quality of Care in Two Residential Units for Severely Mentally Handicapped Children. Preliminary Report. Health Care Evaluation Research Team, Mimeo, Winchester.

Elliott, J. 1972. Eight propositions for mental handicap. Br. J. Ment. Subnorm. 18(1):41–46.

Fassam, M., and Hart, D. 1978. The Role of the Handicap Specialist in Haringey Social Services. Thomas Coram Research Unit, London.

Felce, D. J., Lunt, B., Powell, E., and Kushlick, A. 1977a. Evaluation of Activity Levels of Clients Attained Throughout the Day in 5 Wessex Locally Based Hospital Units and Traditional Units. Health Care Evaluation Research Team, Dawn House, Sleepers Hill, Winchester, Hampshire.

Felce, D. J., Lunt, B., Powell, E., and Kushlick, A. 1977b. Evaluation of External Activities of Clients, e.g., Interaction with Visitors and Members of the Local Community, Trips Out, in 5 Wessex Locally Based Hospital Units and Selected Traditional Units. Health Care Evaluation Research Team, Dawn House, Sleepers Hill, Winchester, Hampshire.

Gemmell, E. 1974. Progress in the rehabilitation of the mentally handicapped in Sheffield. In: H. C. Gunzburg (ed.), Experiments in the Rehabilitation of the Mentally Handicapped. Butterworths, London.

Glossop, C., Felce, D., Smith, J., and Kushlick, A. 1977. Comparative Evaluation of Locally-Based and 'Traditional' Hospital Units for the Mentally Handicapped in Wessex: 1) Contacts made by 'external professionals' with clients resident in the units; 2) morbidity experienced by the clients. Health Care Evaluation Research Team Research Report No. 127. Dawn House, Sleepers Hill, Winchester, Hampshire.

Goffman, E. 1961. Asylums: Essays on the Social Situation of Mental Patients and Other Inmates. Doubleday, New York.

Grant, G. W. B. 1974. The relationship between attitudes of nurses and their patterns of interacting with mentally handicapped individuals. In: J. Elliott, and E. Whelan (eds.), Employability of Mentally Handicapped People. Kings Fund Centre, London.

Hattersley, J., and Tennant, L. 1976. The Parent Participation Model. Paper presented to the British Psychological Society, Division of Child Psychology Conference on Parent Participation, May, Birmingham.

Her Majesty's Stationery Office, 1957. Report of the Royal Commission on the Law Relating to Mental Illness and Mental Deficiency, 1954–1957. Her Majesty's Stationery Office Command No. 109, London.

Her Majesty's Stationery Office. 1971. Better Services for the Mentally Handicapped. Her Majesty's Stationery Office Command No. 4683, London.

Hibbert, R., and Harman, J. 1977. Somerset Social Services Department: Pilot Project: Short-term Care in Foster Homes for Mentally Handicapped Children. Somerset Social Services Department, Somerset.

Johnson, M. 1975. Sheltered Housing Scheme—a Report for Northgate Hospital. Northgate Hospital, Morpeth.

Jones, K., Brown, J., Cunningham, W. J., Roberts, J., and Williams, P. 1975. Opening the Door: A Study of New Policies for the Mentally Handicapped. Routledge and Kegan Paul, London.

Kiernan, C. C. 1974. Application of behaviour modification in the ward situation. In: H. C. Gunzburg (ed.), Experiments in the Rehabilitation of the Mentally Handicapped. Butterworths, London.

Kiernan, C. C. 1976. A research, demonstration, and dissemination project on social services involvement with the handicapped. A research application to the Department of Health and Social Security. Thomas Coram Research Unit, London.

Kiernan, C. C., and Woodford, F. P. 1975. Training and organization for behaviour modification in hospital and community settings. Br. Assoc. Behav. Psychother. 3:31–34.

Kiernan, C. C., Wright, E. C., and Hawks, G. 1974. The ward wide application of operant training techniques. In: D. Primrose (ed.), Proceedings of the Third Congress of the International Association for the Scientific Study of Mental Deficiency. Polish Medical Publishers, Poland.

King, R. D., Raynes, N., and Tizard, J. 1971. Patterns of Residential Care: Sociological Studies in Institutions for Handicapped Children. Routledge and Kegan Paul, London.

Kushlick, A. 1974. The need for residential care: The Wessex experiment. In: H. C. Gunzburg (ed.), Experiments in the Rehabilitation of the Mentally Handicapped. Butterworths, London.

Kushlick, A., and Blunden, R. 1974. The epidemiology of mental subnormality. In: A. M. Clarke and A. D. B. Clarke (eds.), Mental Deficiency: The Changing Outlook. 3rd Ed. Methuen, London.

Kushlick, A., Felce, D., Palmer, J., and Smith, J. 1976. Evidence to the Committee of Enquiry into Mental Handicap and Nursing Care from the Health Care Evaluation Research Team. Health Care Evaluation Research Team, Winchester, Hampshire.

Kushlick, A., Palmer, J., Felce, D., and Smith, J. 1977. Summary of Current Research in Mental Handicap Work, 1977. Health Care Evaluation Research Team Research Report No. 126. Dawn House, Sleepers Hill, Winchester, Hampshire.

Lewis, E. O. 1929. The Report of the Mental Deficiency Committee Being a Joint Committee on the Board of Education and Board of Control: Part IV: Report on an Investigation into the Incidence of Mental Deficiency in Six Areas. 1925–1927. Her Majesty's Stationery Office, London.

Mittler, P. 1976. Priority for handicap. New Soc. 1:21–24.

Morris, P. 1969. Put Away: A Sociological Study of Institutions for the Mentally Retarded. Routledge and Kegan Paul, London.

National Development Group. 1977. Residential Short Term Care. National Development Group Pamphlet No. 4. National Development Group, London.

National Society for Mentally Handicapped Children. 1977. Stamina: Local Action for Services. Papers 1 and 2. National Society for Mentally Handicapped Children, London.

O'Connor, N., and Tizard, J. 1954. A survey of patients in 12 mental deficiency institutions. Br. Med. J. 1:16–20.

Oswin, M. 1978. Children Living in Long Stay Hospitals. Spasties International Medical Press, London.

Palmer, J. W., Kushlick, A., and Dawes, B. J. 1977. Evaluation of Locally Based Hospital Units for the Mentally Handicapped in Wessex: Report on Professionals' Following of Rules, Some Consequences for Clients and Changes in Demand for Residential Care. Research Report No. 123. Health Care Evaluation Research Team, Dawn House, Sleepers Hill, Winchester, Hampshire.

Primrose, D. 1974. The changing pattern of admissions to a mental deficiency hospital. Health Bull. 32, no. 5.

Race, D. G. 1977. Investigation into the Effects of Different Caring Environments on the Social Competence of Mentally Handicapped Adults. Unpublished Ph.D. thesis. University of Reading, England.

Race, D. G., and Race, D. M. 1975. Investigation into the Effects of Different Caring Environments on the Social Competence of Mentally Handicapped Adults. Operational Research Unit, Progress Report 1, Reading.

Race, D. G., and Race, D. M. 1976. The price of living in harmony. Commun. Care 1:624–628.

Raynor, H. 1977. The Exeter Home Visiting Project: The Psychologist as One of Several Therapists. Paper presented to the Annual Conference of the British Psychological Society, April, Exeter.

Royal College of Psychiatry. 1976. Mental deficiency section: Memorandum on the present and future development and organization of mental handicap services. Br. J. Psychiatry, News and Notes, 129:11.

Royal Medico Psychological Association. 1971. Royal Medico Psychological Association Memorandum on future patterns of care for the mentally subnormal. Br. J. Psychiatry 119:95–96.

Sandow, S. 1977. Comparison of Fortnightly and Bimonthly Parents' Groups with No-intervention Group in Terms of Very Young Children's Developmental Scores. Paper presented to the Exeter Annual Conference of the British Psychological Society, April, Exeter.

Simon, G. 1978. Development Team for the Mentally Handicapped. First report 1977-78. Her Majesty's Stationery Office, London.

Smith, J., Glossop, G., Hall, J., Kushlick, A., and Dawes, B. 1977a. Evaluation of Locally Based Hospital Units for the Mentally Handicapped in Wessex: A Comparison of the Changes in Behaviour of Clients in 5 Wessex Locally Based Hospital Units and Equivalent 'Control' Clients in Traditional Units. Health Care Evaluation Research Team, Dawn House, Sleepers Hill, Winchester, Hampshire.

Smith, J., Glossop, G., Hall, J., Kushlick, A., and Dawes, B. 1977b. Evaluation of Locally Based Hospital Units for the Mentally Handicapped in Wessex: A Comparison of the Performances of Professionals with Respect to Clients Before, During and After They Were Admitted to 5 Locally Based Hospital Units and to Equivalent 'Control' Clients Before, During and After They Were Admitted to Traditional Units. Health Care Evaluation Research Team, Dawn House, Sleepers Hill, Winchester, Hampshire.

Spencer, D. A. 1976. New long stay patients in a hospital for mental handicap. Br. J. Psychiatry 128:467–470.

Tizard, J. 1958. Introduction. In: A. M. Clarke and A. D. B. Clarke (eds.), Mental Deficiency: The Changing Outlook. 1st Ed. Methuen, London.

Tizard, J. 1964. Community Services for the Mentally Handicapped. Oxford University Press, London.

Tizard, J. 1973. Maladjusted children and the child guidance service. London Educ. Rev. 2:222–236.

Tizard, J., and Grad, J. 1961. The Mentally Handicapped and Their Families. Oxford University Press, London.

Tredgold, A. F. 1909. The feebleminded—A social danger. Eugenics Rev. 1:97–104.

Tyne, A. 1976a. Residential provision for mentally handicapped adults. Soc. Work Today 7(6):763–764.

Tyne, A. 1976b. Residential home for mentally handicapped adults: Is the guidance any good. Design Spec. Needs 11:2.

Warnock, H. M. 1978. Special Educational Needs Report of the Committee of Enquiry into the Education of Handicapped Children and Young People. Her Majesty's Stationery Office, Command No. 7212, London.

Whatmore, R., Durward, L., and Kushlick, A. 1975. Measuring the quality of residential care. Behav. Res. Ther. 13:227–236.

Wheeler, R. 1976. Planning for the Future. National Society for Mentally Handicapped Children, London.

Wing, L. 1976. Research on the Epidemiology of Mental Handicap. Paper presented to a Medical Research Council Conference on Priorities in Research with the Mentally Handicapped, autumn.

Living Environments for Developmentally Retarded Persons
Edited by H. Carl Haywood and J. R. Newbrough
Copyright 1981 University Park Press Baltimore

Handicap Prejudice and Social Science Research

Robert Bogdan, Ed.D.
Assistant Dean for Research and Development
School of Education
Syracuse University
150 Marshall Street
Syracuse, New York 13210

Douglas Biklen, Ph.D.
Director, Center on Human Policy
Syracuse University
Syracuse, New York 13210

Burton Blatt, Ed.D.
Dean, School of Education
Syracuse University, Huntington Hall
150 Marshall Street
Syracuse, New York 13210

Steven J. Taylor, Ph.D.
Senior Staff Associate
Center on Human Policy
Syracuse University
Syracuse, New York 13210

Although there were no organized groups who referred to themselves as psychologists, sociologists, and special educators four years after the close of the Civil War, we can imagine what such professionals might have said if they had been called together to discuss the demise of slavery. Undoubtedly, some would have suggested that freeing the slaves was not in the slaves' best interests, and that "Negroes" were better off under the rule of masters than they were in their new-found freedom. Others might have said that it should have occurred gradually, that the society was not ready for so many blacks to operate freely. The more progressive persons might have added that there was a need for an elaborate system of rehabilitation and services prior to release, and that until such a system was in place masters ought to be required to keep their slaves. They probably would have held the position that not all slaves can function in society and that the end of slavery should not be categorical.

Today these imagined remarks sound foolish. After the Emancipation Proclamation, we passed the time of questioning whether or not people should be held in the bonds of slavery (except penal slavery) even if they chose to live under those conditions. The law of the land was absolute despite the indefinite hardships that the newly freed and the never enslaved had to endure. Persons who did not understand or appreciate the significance of the events that had just occurred discussed what might have been and how much better it had been before. Certainly the decision to free the slaves was related to political and economic considerations. The decision was not made because it was certain to make life easier for everyone; it was made knowing that life might be more difficult. Moral and legal imperatives demanded it; the way the public thought about human beings had changed and there was no turning back.

Similarly, any group that meets to talk about least restrictive alternatives, normalization[1] of developmentally disabled persons, and related research has to deal with how these concepts will be considered one hundred years from now. Are the issues they raise similar to those of slavery; has the way of thinking about developmentally disabled people changed, with no turning back; or will these issues pass as a fad? We believe that there is change and that people have a significantly different conception of the rights of people labeled as developmentally disabled than they had in the past. Recent court rulings and litigation testify to the fact that normalization and least restrictive alternatives are not merely esoteric professional cliches that will pass by. They are the law and the foundation for service delivery to the developmentally disabled in the present and the future, a fact that should guide our research agendas.

Therefore, research that studies whether small institutions provide better care than large ones or whether community-based programs are

---

[1] For discussion of the legal interpretation of least restrictive alternatives in the education, residential care, police investigation, or guardianship of mentally retarded persons, see Kindred, Cohen, Penrod, and Shaffer (eds.), The Mentally Retarded Citizen and the Law (1976). Relevant sections are written by D. Chambers, L. Glenn, A. Abeson, L. Lippman, and D. Norely. Other sources are: Abeson (1974), Abeson et al. (1975), and Gilhool (1973). The concept of normalization is discussed comprehensively by Wolfensberger (1972).

as humane as institutional settings addresses irrelevant issues. Those are outdated research questions, constructed out of another paradigm. "Least restrictive alternative" and "normalization" are concepts that require a totally different way of thinking about the approach to research related to developmentally disabled persons.

Too often, the vocabulary used to frame research reflects previous ways of thinking that are part of the old paradigm but that do not reflect radically different changes that are demanded of us and our society. 'Deinstitutionalization' is such a word. The study of deinstitutionalization has come to mean the study of releasing people from state facilities. People leaving institutions have been put in large nursing homes, group homes, foster homes, or boarding homes—or simply left to live alone in such places as large motels or flop houses, with often less than adequate room and board. Deinstitutionalization has come to be thought of as a goal and a process that simply designates getting people out of institutions. Such usage of the term is a distortion of the new paradigm signified by the terms "least restrictive alternatives" and "normalization." The goal of deinstitutionalization is not simply to move people out of one setting and into another but to transform a dehumanizing system of service delivery. The existing principles of exclusion, segregation, and labeling should be changed to a zero-reject, integrated, noncategorical, community-based system. The problems surrounding that change and the barriers to it should be the central thrust of any research endeavor (Blatt et al., 1977).

A systematic way of thinking about and studying our society and our institutions that will help transform the present service delivery system into a model that is more in line with the new paradigm is needed. We call this system the "conversion plan":

> By conversion, we mean an orderly transition from an institutional to a community-based system of services with concomitant plans to transform existing physical facilities, resources, institutional ideologies, community attitudes, and agency policies to alternative, more humanizing uses and postures. (Blatt et al., 1977, p. 41)

Research concerning the movement toward community programs should be conceptualized in the context of the conversion of a system. Thus, the transformation of a society rather than the deinstitutionalization of individuals should be studied.

BARRIERS TO CONVERSION

The development of any research agenda directed at least restrictive alternatives and normalization should begin with an extensive study of the body of literature in the social sciences on the process of social change[2] and of its application to the specific change that is now required of us. In addition to the many barriers to change that are inherent in any society, those specific aspects of our society that resist change of the service delivery system for developmentally disabled people should be studied and delineated. This chapter discusses some of those barriers and suggests research strategies to study them.

Handicapism

Handicapism is a concept that allows us to study our own prejudices[3] and to understand the social experiences of those who are known as developmentally disabled, mentally retarded, deformed, deviant, abnormal, and handicapped. The phrase has many parallels to racism and sexism (Bogdan and Biklen, 1977) because it points to the assumptions and practices that encourage the differential and unequal treatment of people because of their apparent or assumed physical, mental, and behavioral differences.[4] Three terms are crucial to developing a research strategy for understanding how handicapism acts as a barrier to conversion: prejudice, stereotype, and discrimination.[5] Prejudice is any oversimplified and overgeneralized belief about the characteristics of a group or of a category of people. People are typ-

---

[2] See works by Alinsky (1971), Etzioni and Halevy (1964), Friere (1970, 1973), Kahn (1970), Lauer (1973), Needleman and Needleman (1974), and Sharp (1973).

[3] A few years ago we teamed up with two architecture professors to teach a course entitled "Designing Environments of the Developmentally Disabled." The students were in a master's degree program and represented an even mix from the architecture and special education departments. They were teamed to develop designs for a community-based residence for developmentally disabled people, with special education students serving as consultants to the architecture students. Students were required to do extensive bibliographical research, to spend time on wards in the local state schools, and to attend lectures by authorities on design and mental retardation. For one of the lecture sessions, a former state school resident who was employed and living in the community was asked to come to the class to share his thoughts on what a community-based home for developmentally disabled people might be like. The person was known to be articulate and forceful in his views concerning people labeled mentally retarded. Students in the course were asked to design a living center for the retarded and he told them what he thought was appropriate. His words revealed the obvious—that "they," the retarded, want the same things that other people want in a living situation, and to think that "they" needed a specially designed residential facility was the concretization of our own preconceived notions of what the retarded are like. By listening to him, we became keenly self-conscious of the prejudicial and stereotypical way we had approached the design problem (Bogdan and Taylor, 1976).

[4] Authors who have discussed handicapped categories as minority groups include Dexter (1964), Gellman (1959), Wright (1960), and Yinker (1965).

[5] Yuker (1965) and Allport (1954) give a social-psychological perspective on these terms.

ically not aware of how prejudiced they are (Berelson and Steiner, 1964, p. 501). Prejudice toward the so-called developmentally disabled is often indicated by such assumptions as: they are innately incapable; they are naturally inferior (the mind set is "Thank God, I'm not you"); they have unique personalities, different senses, and different needs than the typical citizen; and they have more in common with each other than with nondisabled persons and therefore like to be with "their own kind" (Goffman, 1963; Wright, 1960). These beliefs, which are at the heart of handicapism, provide the background assumptions for our action toward people labeled disabled.

Whereas prejudice is the general disposition, stereotype refers to the specific content of the prejudice directed toward specific groups. The mentally retarded, for example, are believed to be childlike, dangerous, and erratic in their behavior, and to enjoy boring and routine work (Wolfensberger, 1975). Although sets of stereotypes are often contradictory, they are nevertheless regarded seriously by a number of people and are used to justify particular modes of treatment. Thus, the mentally retarded can be treated like children, given boring work, and locked up.

Although it may be inaccurate, a stereotype is often steadfastly maintained. First, peer groups and the culture support the transmission of stereotypes and therefore constantly reinforce them. Second, the stereotyped groups, such as mentally retarded people, are isolated, have few opportunities for intimate relations to develop between themselves and the so-called normal people, and consequently have little chance of disproving the stereotypes. Last, and perhaps most importantly, they are treated in ways that correspond to their stereotypes and are rewarded for living up to the image that others have of them (Lemert, 1951). Thus, they learn the role of the handicapped and fall victim to self-fulfilling prophecies (Merton, 1968).

The occurrence of prejudices and stereotypes suggest that there are cognitive and ideological aspects of handicapism. The concept of discrimination provides the structural and behavioral aspect. Unfair and unequal treatment of individuals or groups on the basis of prejudice and stereotypes translates into discrimination. Standards of fairness and unfairness vary from society to society and from time to time as the social criteria for equality or discrimination change in accordance with social values. At one time it was considered the natural state of slaves to labor in the fields for the economic benefit of others and for married women to serve their husbands; the treatment they received was not thought to be unfair. Similarly, handicapped people are generally thought to experience relative equality in this society, especially since the advent of various categorical social service programs. They are believed to occupy their rightful place and to receive deserved treatment. For example, until recently, few people questioned the practices of fingerprinting and taking mug shots of people admitted to state institutions, despite the fact that there is no evidence that former patients are involved in any more crimes than typical citizens (Scheff, 1966). It is equally common for public school districts to segregate handicapped children into special classes and even into separate special schools, although there is no empirical evidence that supports any benefit, either educational or social, resulting from segregated services. Segregation policies and practices discriminate against people with disabilities and are a part of handicapism.

Handicapism can be observed at various levels and in various institutions of our society. The discomfort people feel around individuals who are developmentally disabled and the stylized, self-conscious communication between handicapped and nonhandicapped people are topics for socio-psychological and psychological research. Who exhibits the greatest discomfort? Under what conditions can this discomfort be reduced? What are the various ways in which people deal with their discomfort (such as withdrawing, being overly gracious or overly sympathetic, treating people as if they aren't there)? These questions are only a few of the important issues to be addressed at this level of analysis. Fifty years of research in the area of race relations indicate the direction this study might take. Any research directed at the psychological and social-psychological dimensions of handicapism should begin with a thorough review of the race relations literature, in order to sort out what aspects of that work are applicable to the relations between developmentally disabled and typical persons.

We also need to study the mass media carefully, using techniques and questions similar to those used by civil rights and women's rights scholars. To what extent do the mass media present prejudicial and stereotypic images of developmentally disabled persons? What is the specific content of that imagery? What effect does it have on those who view it? Our own survey of the media suggested that negative images of handicapped people were being portrayed (Biklen and Bogdan, 1976, 1977). Horror movies, for example, often establish a clear link between physical and mental disabilities and acts of physical violence and destruction, thus promoting distrust and fear among nonhandicapped individuals. Cartoons often promote stereotypic images of handicapped individuals. "Stupid idiot," "moron," and related epithets can be heard on prime time television, revealing not only the handicapist nature of television dialogue but also its use of everyday words, which at one time referred to specific diagnostic categories, as general words indicating contempt. Newspaper articles often link crimes with various disabilities as if the disability were the cause of the crime. When formally institutionalized individuals are involved in incidents of physical assault, their past is given prominence in the report (Scheff, 1966). A study of how the media promote certain images of handicapped people by the way they report charity drives and telethons is also needed. Human interest features often proclaim that the handicapped can be helped by charity, thus reinforcing an image of dependence. The effect on the public of images presented by the media has not been studied, but this might be a fruitful way of exploring how people relate to developmentally disabled individuals.

Another necessary area of research deals with physical literacy, legal, and policy barriers to the participation of developmentally disabled persons in the mainstream of society. What are some of the basic assumptions that people in our society make, and how do these manifest themselves in building designs, required procedures, and rules and regulations? Because it is generally assumed that everyone can and should read, it is terribly embarrassing and difficult for people who cannot read to live independently. In much the same debilitating fashion that architectural barriers deny access to physically disabled individuals, written directions (for tests, applications, forms, and signs) provide untold obstacles for the person who cannot read and write. People leaving state schools for the mentally retarded report that their inability to read and write creates barriers to their mobility in a society that relies so heavily on written communication. People who cannot learn these skills or who simply were never taught to read and write have an extremely difficult time with forms like income tax, employment application, credit application, and registration for school (Dexter, 1964). Literacy barriers have been mentioned to illustrate only one of many areas in which the discriminatory and exclusionary assumptions and structures of our society need to be explored. These assumptions are so widespread that they are difficult to recognize, and because nondisabled people do not experience their consequences directly, their impact on the lives of developmentally disabled people is seldom understood. This area is difficult to study and to understand, as most important issues are, because they do not easily lend themselves to standard research procedures.

One way to conduct research related to this area is to spend long periods of time with developmentally disabled individuals in order to understand the world from their point of view (Bogdan and Taylor, 1975). Studying the subjective states of developmentally disabled individuals can be done in a systematic and objective way and can be invaluable in helping nonhandicapped people to better see themselves and the world they have created.

Economics

Providing service to developmentally disabled people is a big business. The economics of that service delivery system is intimately tied to the economy of the larger society as well as to the political system. Very little research is directed toward understanding the economics and politics of developmentally disabled people (Fein, 1958). The efforts of Rockefeller, Carnegie, Mellon, Peabody, and other large-scale philanthropists led to significant changes in the extent and method of federal government aid to those in need. Big business leaders have demonstrated how to organize our philanthropies to serve the people, as well as how to organize the people (the state) to serve both business and philanthropy.

A cornerstone in the system of service delivery to developmentally disabled people is the assumption that services are a gift or a privilege rather than a right. The American public gives billions of dollars each year to charity, much of which is solicited in the name of helping the handicapped. This system of collecting funds supports the idea that handicapped individuals are inferior people. Professionals who require charitable contributions to support their programs tend to distort the image of handicapped people in order to play on public pity.

The other major funding sources for special services are the federal and state governments. Here, too, the money system promotes a categorical system of service delivery. To be eligible for state and federal funds, school workers and other human service personnel must label children according to certain clinical disability categories that provide reimbursement. They must list the name and the diagnosis of the handicap, and thereby people are labeled early in their careers as mentally retarded, autistic, or cerebral palsied, or are designated by some other diagnostic characteristic (Bogdan, 1976; Schrag and Divoky, 1975). In the reimbursement system, disabled individuals become commodities and agencies become headhunters. In every instance when funds become available for a particular disability group, the number of people so labeled soars geometrically.

There are many economic questions and issues; we know little about how the system works and what the implications for change are. Important questions to ask are: 1) How do we convert segregated facilities for handicapped people to useful purposes? 2) How can these thousands of people return to normal community life without the state bankrupting itself in attempts to meet bond obligations and other commitments to the business community? 3) How do the concepts of surplus labor and human capital fit into the conversion model? 4) What are the various economic interest groups that are threatened by changes in the system (Brown, 1978; Nassi, 1978)? 5) What is the relationship between various funding formulas and labeling?

Professionalism

Individuals responsible for providing services to developmentally disabled people often erect additional barriers that prevent changing the present categorical service-segregated system to an integrated noncategorical one. Many professionals working with handicapped individuals think in terms of categories and segregated services because this is the way they have been taught to diagnose and to prescribe. Thus, they may not have the philosophy or the skills needed to meet the requirements of conversion. Furthermore, the formal organizations that professions have created can stand as defenses against change. Our buildings, which represent great financial, career, and life investments, have been constructed to foster segregation and isolation. Civil Service organizations are heading up campaigns to stop deinstitutionalization. Expensive media campaigns are being launched with membership dues to tell the public to stop what is called "dumping." Although the aim of this effort is clearly directed at saving the disabled client, the interests of the members are also at stake. Such civil servant protest did not occur against the documented human abuse that occurred for years inside the walls of the institutions in which they are presently employed. Professional societies and professional schools have similarly been organized in ways that may be detrimental to conversion. Another barrier to conversion is the claim by professionals that special children need specially trained professional people to take care of them. Although this is true to some extent, it is not wholly or perpetually the case. A major challenge for professionals is to demystify themselves and to share freely some of their understanding with others so that they too can join in helping developmentally disabled people.[6]

Little is known about the professionals who work in the field and the structure of their organizations and conceptual framework because, in studying developmentally disabled people, we have forgotten their

---

[6] A related issue is that of self-help by handicapped persons. Professionals have frequently been unaware (or perhaps avoided awareness) of the ability of people with disabilities to lead autonomous, active lives. Systematic study is needed on the role handicapped individuals can play in their own clinical treatment within traditional human services (Gartner and Riessman, 1977; Levin, Katz, and Holst, 1976) or within self-help organizations (Hampden-Turner, 1976).

"keepers." We need to know about the nature of these professions and how members define their work and success. Histories of work in the field have been self-aggrandizing accounts that limit themselves to insiders rather than critical and analytical works that attempt to trace particular movements within the field and in the nation. (For the exceptions, see Wolfensberger, 1975.) At present, social historians are doing important work in placing professional ideologies in the proper perspective by studying them as outgrowths of the ascendance of science and the use of the professional class (Lasch, 1978). Such historians should be encouraged to work in the disability field so that we might be liberated from incomplete images of our past. The holistic care study is another research approach needed in the study of developmental disability professionals. Thomas Szasz (1961), Erving Goffman (1963), Thomas Scheff (1966), Robert Scott (1969), and Dorothea and Benjamin Braginsky (1971) taught us to understand handicap categories, as well as the term "handicap" itself, as metaphors. They laid the groundwork for thinking about so-called handicaps as societally created conditions rather than as natural or objective conditions. These same authors and their associates in the interactionist or labeling school pointed out the importance that the quality of interactions between labelers and those labeled plays in understanding handicap (Davis, 1963; Goffman, 1961; Lemert, 1967; Wiseman, 1970). The interface of human service agencies and clients became an area where social researchers could develop theoretical perspectives on how labels and definitions were applied (Bogdan, 1976; Gubrium, 1975).

This anthropological-sociological research approach needs to be applied to the study of professionals working in the area of developmental disabilities to a much greater extent than it has been in the past.

CONCLUSION

Societies have always created categories such as "handicapped" and "race" and have fostered prejudices, stereotypes, and discrimination. Some theorists have suggested that these categories fulfill real purposes, such as serving as targets for our hostility, as excuses for what goes wrong, as indicators of fear, and as a means of self-approval through the knowledge that we do not belong to the disapproved groups (Barzun, 1965; Erikson, 1966). Barzun suggested that the urge to classify and to categorize people is reinforced in modern societies by the belief that scientific theories and systems of facts can account for and explain distinctions between people, differences in temperament and ability, and variations in bodily features and mental habits. Because social science has conducted research and formulated theory on common sense notions of differences between preconceived categories, and has emphasized statistically significant differences rather than emphasizing the range within populations and the overlapping of characteristics between categories, it has done much to reify categories and therefore to entrench prejudice, stereotypes, and discrimination (Bogdan and Taylor, 1976). Professionals in fields related to disability have followed a research tradition that has hindered the questioning of basic concepts in disability research. A disturbing number of handicapist assumptions have been accepted as givens, as starting points for research.

The handicapism paradigm is presented so that researchers and practitioners can begin reassessing their assumptions concerning segregated service, differential treatment, the real source of the disability problem, labeling and language patterns, and the funding mechanisms tied to labeling. Furthermore, the concept of handicapism can facilitate research that will result in data related to policy. Although we have not yet explored the full ramifications of handicapism, we have attempted to provide the foundation for conceptualizing the experience of handicaps in a way that will not perpetuate prejudicial notions, but instead will reveal and eradicate injustice.

ACKNOWLEDGMENTS

We thank Andrejs Ozolins and Debra Doniger for their comments and suggestions.

REFERENCES

Abeson, A. 1974. Movement and momentum: Government and the education of handicapped children—II. Except Child. 41:109–115.

Abeson, A., Bolick, N., and Hass, J. 1975. A Primer on Due Process. The Council for Exceptional Children, Reston, Va.

Alinsky, S. 1971. Rules for Radicals: A Practical Primer for Realistic Radicals. Random House, New York.

Allport, G. W. 1954. The Nature of Prejudice. Beacon Press, Boston.

Barzun, J. 1965. Race: A Study in Superstition. Harper and Row Pubs., Inc., New York.

Berelson, B., and Steiner, G. 1964. Human Behavior. Harcourt, Brace, and World, New York.

Biklen, D., and Bogdan, R. 1976. Handicapism. Slide show with script, Human Policy Press, Syracuse, New York.

Biklen, D., and Bogdan, R. 1977. Media portrayals of disabled people: A study in stereotypes. Interracial Books Child. Bull. 8:6–7.

Blatt, B., Bogdan, R., Biklen, D., and Taylor, S. 1977. From institution to community: A conversion model. In: E. Sontag (ed.), Educational Programming for the Severely and Profoundly Handicapped, pp. 40–52. The Council for Exceptional Children, Reston, Va.

Bogdan, R. 1976. National policy and situated meaning: Head Start and the handicapped. Am. J. Orthopsychiatry 46:229–235.

Bogdan, R., and Biklen, D. 1977. Handicapism. Soc. Policy 17:14–19.

Bogdan, R., and Taylor, S. 1975. Introduction to Qualitative Research Methods. John Wiley and Sons, Inc., New York.

Bogdan, R., and Taylor, S. 1976. The judged not the judges: An insider's view of retardation. Am. Psychol. 31:47–52.

Braginsky, D., and Braginsky, B. 1971. Hansels and Gretels. Holt, Rinehart, and Winston, Inc., New York.

Brown, P. 1978. Political-economic and professionalistic barriers to community control of mental health services: A commentary on Nassi. J. Commun. Psychol. 6:384–392.

Davis, F. 1963. Passage Through Crisis. Bobbs-Merrill Company, Inc., Indianapolis.

Dexter, L. 1964. The Tyranny of Schooling. Basic Books, Inc., New York.

Erikson, K. 1966. The Wayward Puritans. John Wiley and Sons, Inc., New York.

Etzioni, A., and Etzioni-Halevy, E. (eds.). 1964. Social Change. Basic Books, Inc., New York.

Fein, R. 1958. Economics of Mental Illness. Basic Books, Inc., New York.

Friere, P. 1970. Pedagogy of the Oppressed. Herder and Herder, New York.

Friere, P. 1973. Education for Critical Consciousness. Seabury, New York.

Gartner, A., and Riessman, F. 1977. Self-help in the Human Services. Jossey-Bass, Inc., Pubs., San Francisco.

Gellman, W. 1959. Roots of prejudice against the handicapped. J. Rehab. 25:4–6.

Gilhool, T. 1973. An inalienable right. Except. Child. 39:597–609.

Goffman, E. 1961. Asylums: Essays on the Social Situation of Mental Patients and Other Inmates. Anchor, Garden City.

Goffman, E. 1963. Stigma. Prentice-Hall, Inc., Englewood Cliffs, N.J.

Gubrium, J. F. 1975. Late Life: Communities and Environmental Policy. Charles C Thomas, Springfield.

Hampden-Turner, C. 1976. Sane Asylum. San Francisco Book Company, San Francisco.

Kahn, S. 1970. How People Get Power. McGraw-Hill Book Company, New York.

Kindred, M., Cohen, J., Penrod, D., and Shaffer, T. (eds.). 1976. The Mentally Retarded Citizen and the Law. Free Press, New York.

Lasch, C. 1978. Haven in a Heartless World. Basic Books, Inc., New York.

Lauer, R. 1973. Perspectives on Social Change. Allyn and Bacon, Boston.

Lemert, E. 1951. Social Pathology: A Systematic Approach to the Theory of Sociopathic Behavior. McGraw-Hill Book Company, New York.

Lemert, E. 1967. Human Deviance, Social Problems, and Social Control. Prentice-Hall, Inc., Englewood Cliffs, N.J.

Levin, L., Katz, A., and Holst, E. (eds.), 1976. Self-Care: Lay Initiatives in Health. Prodist, New York.

Merton, R. 1968. Social Theory and Social Structure. Free Press, New York.

Nassi, A. 1978. Community control or control of the community? The case of the community mental health center. J. Commun. Psychol. 6:3–15.

Needleman, M., and Needleman, C. 1974. Guerillas in the Bureaucracy. John Wiley and Sons, Inc., New York.

Scheff, T. J. 1966. Being Mentally Ill: A Sociological Theory. Aldine Publishing Company, Chicago.

Schrag, P., and Divoky, D. 1975. The Myth of the Hyperactive Child. Pantheon Books, New York.

Scott, R. 1969. The Making of Blind Men. Russell Sage Foundation, New York.

Sharp, G. 1973. The Politics of Non-Violent Action, Vol. 1: Power and Struggle. Porter Sargent, Boston.

Szasz, T. S. 1961. The Myth of Mental Illness. Hoeber-Harper, New York.

Wiseman, J. 1970. Stations of the Lost. Prentice-Hall, Inc., Englewood Cliffs, N.J.

Wolfensberger, W. 1972. Normalization: The Principle of Normalization in Human Services. National Institute on Mental Retardation, Toronto.

Wolfensberger, W. 1975. The Origin and Nature of Our Institutional Models. Human Policy Press, Syracuse, N.Y.

Wright, B. 1960. Physical Disability: A Psychological Approach. Harper, New York.

Yinker, M. 1965. A Minority Group in American Society. McGraw-Hill Book Company, New York.

Yuker, H. 1965. Attitudes as determinants of behavior. J. Rehab. 31:15–16.

PRACTICAL PROBLEMS IN EVALUATION AND IMPLEMENTATION

Living Environments for Developmentally Retarded Persons
Edited by H. Carl Haywood and J. R. Newbrough
Copyright 1981 University Park Press Baltimore

Evaluating Sheltered Living Environments for Mentally Retarded People

Abraham Wandersman, Ph.D.
Department of Psychology
University of South Carolina
Columbia, South Carolina 20208

Rudolf H. Moos, Ph.D.
Department of Psychiatry and Behavioral Sciences
Director, Social Ecology Laboratory
Stanford University and Veterans Administration
  Medical Center
Palo Alto, California 94305

The enduring environments in which mentally retarded people live can have a powerful impact on them. Children's values may change differentially as a function of the expectations of long-term group care settings. The more intensive, committed, cohesive, and socially integrated the setting, the greater its impact (Shouval et al., 1975; Wolins, 1974). The hypothesis that environments may have particularly strong influences on individuals whose functional abilities are impaired (Lawton and Nahemow, 1973) indicates the importance of assessing the environments of mentally retarded people. This need is underscored by the fact that there is considerable variation in sheltered care facilities of the same type, such as community care facilities (Butler and Bjaanes, 1977) and institutions (Balla, Butterfield, and Zigler, 1974; Tizard, Sinclair, and Clarke, 1975). Although some investigators have shown a relationship between the type of milieu and personal and intellectual functioning (Bjaanes and Butler, 1974; Scarr and Weinberg, 1976), very

Preparation of this paper was supported in part by Veterans Administration Health Services Research and Development Service Funds and NIMH Grant MH28177 and in part by NICHD Grant HD04510 to the J. F. Kennedy Center, Peabody College.

few have included detailed assessments of the environment (exceptions: Eyman et al., 1977; King, Raynes, and Tizard, 1971). Therefore, there is little reliable information about the specific qualities of settings that are related to varied outcome criteria (Crawford et al., this volume).

In this chapter, we suggest methods for providing this type of information. We focus on three questions: 1) How can the characteristics of sheltered living environments for mentally retarded persons be assessed? 2) How can the impacts of these environments on mentally retarded persons be evaluated? 3) What practical uses can be made of the resulting information? We are concerned primarily with three major types of sheltered living environments: family settings, such as adoptive and foster homes; community settings, such as group homes and residential care facilities; and institutional settings, such as large hospitals for mentally retarded persons and those skilled nursing facilities in which an increasing number of mentally retarded people live.

We approach the issues in this chapter as social ecologists suggesting an outline for a program of research to study the influence of living environments on mentally retarded people. Two views guide our conceptualization of environments and our evaluation of the effects of environments: a social-ecological view (Moos, 1976, 1979a); and a social-developmental view (Ricks, Wandersman, and Poppen, 1976; Wandersman, 1976). Both approaches share the perspective that people affect their environments and are affected by them. This type of perspective is being integrated into clinical and community psychology (Holahan, 1978), developmental psychology (Bronfenbrenner, 1977), gerontology (Lawton and Nahemow, 1973), and health psychology (Moos, 1979b). The social-developmental view provides an approach for conceptualizing the qualities of environments best suited for people and suggests certain principles by which these qualities operate. Some of the principles can be stated as follows: 1) the characteristics of a rewarding environment depend on a person's behavioral repertoire, information-processing abilities, needs, and values; 2) qualities of environments need to be related to capacities of individuals to make use of them as real alternatives; and 3) settings need to reflect stability and change in relation to the input and feedback of people as they select and create environments.

ASSESSING THE ENVIRONMENTS
OF MENTALLY RETARDED PERSONS

There is considerable variation both among and within family, community, and institutional settings. For example, foster homes differ in the amount of freedom allowed, in the warmth and quality of emotional care, in the spontaneity and openness of the interaction between parents and children, and in the strictness and consistency of rules. Residential care settings also vary in these characteristics, as do hospitals and skilled nursing facilities. The movement toward deinstitutionalization and normalization and the intricate interrelationships among environments make comparable assessments of different types of settings a desirable goal. A common set of dimensions is needed to describe the range of variation within each type of setting, to compare different types of settings, and to assist in developing useful typologies of settings. Such dimensions could help to clarify how different environments function, to match mentally retarded persons with those settings most appropriate for them, and to make possible more informed decisions about the types of facilities that should be constructed with the limited resources society is able to provide.

Moos has been engaged in a program of research directed toward assessing and understanding the salient features of environments. The approaches used show promise in characterizing diverse environments on similar dimensions. This work recently has involved sheltered care settings for the elderly; many of these settings are similar to those for mentally retarded persons. This work has focused primarily on social climate (Moos, 1974a, 1975), but ongoing research has included the development of a Multiphasic Environmental Assessment Procedure (MEAP), which represents a more comprehensive approach to assessing environments (Moos and Lemke, 1979). The basic thrust of this work is social-ecological, that is, it emphasizes the inclusion of social-environmental (such as social climate) and physical-environmental (ecological) variables to create a multidimensional perspective of a setting.

The Social Climate Approach

The social climate approach has involved the development of a set of scales to measure the social environments of settings like families, classrooms, residence halls, and hospital-based and community-based treatment programs (Moos, 1974b; 1979a). An appropriate scale is available for each of the three types of environments we focus on here: family (Family Environment Scale), group homes (Community-Oriented Programs Environment Scale; COPES), and treatment institutions (Ward Atmosphere Scale). In the course of this work, we discovered that quite different social environments could be described in terms of common or similar sets of dimensions that are conceptualized in three major domains.

Relationship dimensions assess the extent to which people are involved in the environment, the extent to which they support and help one another, and the extent to which they express themselves freely and openly.

Personal Growth or Goal Orientation dimensions assess the basic directions along which personal development and self-enhancement tend to occur in a particular setting. For example, in psychiatric programs, there is autonomy (the extent to which residents are encouraged to be self-sufficient and independent) and practical orientation (the emphasis on jobs, getting released from the program, and preparing for the future), whereas in families there is independence (the extent to which family members are encouraged to be assertive and self-sufficient and to make their own decisions) and moral-religious emphasis (the degree of focus on ethical and religious issues and values).

System Maintenance and Change dimensions deal with the extent to which an environment maintains control and is orderly, clear in its expectations, and responsive to change.

Because the dimensions in the Relationship and System Maintenance and Change domains are common or similar in the three settings that are relevant here, it is possible to assess the social climate of these settings on some commensurate dimensions. On the other hand, most of the Personal Growth or Goal Orientation dimensions are relevant only to certain types of settings. For example, moral-religious emphasis discriminates among families but not (usually) among institutional treatment facilities.

Although it is useful to have people describe their own environments, mentally retarded people, like many cognitively impaired elderly people, may find it difficult or impossible to do so. This raises some problems in using instruments like the social climate scales with mentally retarded persons (Balla and Klein, this volume). Rephrasing items into a question-based interview format and/or tape recording them can help to overcome this problem (McGee and Woods, 1978; Pankratz, 1975). Information on the social environments of settings for mentally retarded people can also be obtained from families, nursing and administrative staff in institutions, visiting friends and relatives, volunteer workers, and other outside observers. The information can reflect how people in different roles view the environment. Therefore, although the social climate scales assess an individual's perceptions of an environment, their applicability and usefulness are not limited to the resident's perceptions.

One reason for assessing environments is the possibility of identifying certain types of mentally retarded people who might derive more benefit from one environment than from another. The assessment of family environments, group homes, and institutions on the three domains of social climate dimensions could help to move us in this direction. Because there is great heterogeneity in each of these types of settings, the next important step is to develop taxonomies of these environments. Using social climate scale data obtained in hospital-based and community-based treatment programs and in correctional facilities, it has been possible to identify six basic types of each: 1) therapeutic community, 2) relationship-oriented, 3) action-oriented, 4) insight-oriented, 5) control-oriented, and 6) disturbed behavior programs. Although the specific types of environments identified vary somewhat in relation to the sample and to the statistical method and criteria employed, such typologies can help to deepen our understanding of the essential characteristics of social environments (see Moos, 1975, for methodological details).

A Multidimensional Approach to Assessing Environments

The Multiphasic Environmental Assessment Procedure (MEAP) is used to assess the environmental resources of sheltered care settings for the elderly in terms of dimensions drawn from four major domains: physical and architectural resources, policy and program resources, resident and staff resources, and social-environmental resources (Lemke et al., 1979; Moos and Lemke, 1979). The MEAP represents an attempt to create a comprehensive, conceptually based environmental assessment procedure. There is enough commonality between sheltered care settings for the elderly and those for mentally retarded persons (in fact, many of the settings are identical) that the items and procedures used in the MEAP should apply to many of the community care and institutional settings in which mentally retarded persons live. The same four domains of variables also apply to family settings, although new items and observational procedures need to be developed to characterize such settings. A brief description of the four major parts of the MEAP follows.[1]

Physical and Architectural Resources

The Physical and Architectural Features checklist (PAF) assesses nine dimensions of the physical and architectural resources of a sheltered care facility. The PAF covers questions about the facility's location, its external and internal physical features, and its space allowances.

---

[1] Copies of the MEAP, a Handbook for Users, a Hand-Scoring Booklet, and a Preliminary Manual can be obtained from Rudolf Moos, Social Ecology Laboratory, Psychiatry Service, Veterans Administration Medical Center, Palo Alto, Calif. 94304.

Examples of some of these dimensions are:

1. *Physical Amenities*—a set of 31 items that measure the presence of physical features that add convenience and special comfort. (Is the main entrance sheltered from sun or rain? Are the halls decorated? Is there a writing surface by the phone? Is there wall space available where residents can hang pictures?)
2. *Social-Recreational Aids*—a set of 26 items that assess the presence of features that foster social and recreational behavior. (Is the lounge space by the entry furnished for resting and casual conversation? Is reading material available on tables or shelves? Is there a pool or billiard table? Is there a piano or organ?)
3. *Prosthetic Aids*—a set of 31 items that assess the extent to which the facility provides a barrier-free environment, as well as aids to physical independence and mobility. (Can one enter the building without walking up steps? Is the front door wide enough for a wheelchair? Are telephones accessible to wheelchair residents? Are there lift-bars next to the toilet?)
4. *Orientational Aids*—a set of 15 items that measure the extent to which the setting provides visual cues to orient the residents. (Is there at least one large-faced clock in the lobby or entrance area? Is there a reception area or reception desk? Are the residents' names on or next to their doors? Is there a posted list of staff?)

The other PAF dimensions are safety features, architectural choice (the extent to which certain architectural features provide choices for the residents), space availability, staff facilities, and community accessibility (the extent to which the community and its services are accessible both in terms of the existence of services and of their convenience to the facility).

Policy and Program Resources

The Policy and Program Information Form (POLIF) assesses ten dimensions of the policy and programmatic resources of a facility. The items cover the financial and entrance arrangements, the types of rooms or apartments available, the way in which the facility is organized, and the services provided for residents. Examples of some of these dimensions are:

1. *Expectations for Functioning*—a set of 10 items that assess the minimum level of ability acceptable in the facility to perform such daily living functions as making one's bed, cleaning one's room, and feeding and dressing oneself.

2. *Tolerance for Deviance*—a set of 18 items to measure the extent to which such aggressive or potentially destructive behavior as smoking in bed, wandering around the building or grounds at night, creating a disturbance, and verbally threatening another resident is tolerated in the facility.

3. *Policy Choice*—a set of 20 items that reflect the extent to which the facility provides options from which each resident can select individual patterns of daily living. The items tap such areas as whether the residents can drink liquor in their rooms, keep a fish or bird, and have their own furniture. Also included are scheduling issues, such as the hours during which breakfast, lunch, and dinner are served, and whether there is a curfew or a fairly set time at which residents are expected to go to bed (lights out) at night.

4. *Resident Control*—a set of 29 items that assess the amount of influence residents have in setting policies and in helping to govern or to run the facility. The items tap the extent to which residents perform chores or duties in the facility, whether there is a residents' council, and, if so, the number of residents who are on it and the frequency with which it meets, whether there are regular house meetings for residents, and the extent to which residents have input in areas like planning entertainment, organizing welcoming and/or orientation activities, setting visitors' hours, selecting new residents, and making rules about the use of alcohol.

The other dimensions assessed by the POLIF are selectivity (the criteria used to select new residents); policy clarity (the explicitness of the policies and procedures); provisions for privacy; the availability of health services, such as physical and occupational therapy and regularly scheduled nurses' hours; daily living assistance services, such as help in preparing meals, assistance with personal care or grooming, barber or beauty service, and laundry or linen service; and social-recreational activities, such as exercises or other physical fitness activities, reality orientation groups, films or movies, and classes or lectures (Lemke and Moos, 1979).

Resident and Staff Resources

The Resident and Staff Information Form (RESIF) assesses six dimensions that tap the basic characteristics of the residents and staff in the facility. The dimensions measure areas like the residents' social resources (educational and occupational background), the heterogeneity of the residents (in terms of sociodemographic characteristics, such as age, ethnic background, and religion), and residents' functional abilities (how many residents can eat their meals without help, can dress and undress themselves, can handle their own money, or can go shopping for groceries and clothes). The RESIF also evaluates the activity level of the residents (what proportion participate in certain activities, such as listening to music, reading a newspaper or book, playing pool or bingo, drawing or painting), and the degree of resident integration in the community (what proportion of residents participate in activities outside the facility, such as going on a picnic, attending religious services, eating in a restaurant, and engaging in volunteer or paid work). In terms of staff resources, the RESIF obtains information on staffing levels and includes a 14-item Staff Richness scale that focuses on the heterogeneity of staff, on the length of time staff have worked in the facility, and on the number of volunteers and the degree to which they participate in facility activities.

Social Climate Resources

A new social climate scale, the Sheltered Care Environment Scale (SCES), assesses the social-environmental resources of sheltered care settings (Moos et al., 1979). It includes two Relationship dimensions (cohesion and conflict), two Personal Growth or Goal Orientation dimensions (independence and self-exploration), and three System Maintenance and Change dimensions (organization, resident influence, and physical comfort). A self-administered yes/no questionnaire format is used to obtain information from staff and other caregivers. Information is obtained from residents using either the self-administered format or an interview format, depending on their capabilities. The SCES may be more appropriate than the other social climate scales for assessing mentally retarded people's perceptions of their environments. The items are simpler, using a question rather than a statement format, and they apply to a broad range of settings, varying from skilled nursing facilities to board-and-care homes and sheltered apartment facilities.

A comprehensive approach to assessing environments has broad potential utility. For example, it is possible to evaluate the assumption that architectural resources, such as social-recreational aids and space availability, or policy resources, such as policy choice and resident control, favorably influence the social environment. The assumption can be tested that group homes provide more normal environments than institutions because they have more privacy and allow more input from residents. A sobering fact is that 19 of 78 (approximately 25%) community-oriented psychiatric treatment programs evaluated with the COPES had control-oriented social environments that primarily emphasized order and structure and that lacked emphasis on relationship and personal growth factors (Moos, 1975). It is also possible to compare programs with and without professionally trained staff, to evaluate the effects of policy changes on other dimensions of the environment, to investigate the social climate and programmatic correlates of architectural and physical design features, and to determine how the types of residents in a facility and their level of functional ability interact with other factors to affect the overall functioning of a setting.

Procedures like the MEAP also make it possible to develop typologies of settings based on variables chosen from one domain (like a typology based only on architectural or only on policy and program variables), as well as to construct a typology based on variables chosen from all four domains. Different methods of describing settings may be useful for different purposes. For example, a typology based on social climate may be most relevant for staff training and for facilitating short-term social-environmental change. A typology based on the aggregate characteristics of the people in a facility may be most useful for giving prospective residents and staff an idea of the kinds of people and behaviors they are likely to encounter in a setting. A typology based on policy and program indices may be most valuable for making relatively quick comparisons among institutions and for planning long-term changes, whereas a comprehensive general typology might be most useful for placement decisions.

SYSTEM PERFORMANCE

We have focused on several sets of indices by which the environments of mentally retarded people can be assessed. Although these indices help to describe a setting, direct measures of system performance are also useful. In fact, the quality of care in institutional settings is often defined by indicators of system performance, such as the number of errors in medication use and the consistency and accuracy of medical records. These and other comparable indices provide another perspective on a facility and can be related to the other sets of indices discussed above.

Staff perception of the work environment, staff turnover, absenteeism, and accident rates can serve to measure system performance. The high rate of direct-care staff turnover and absenteeism in facilities for the retarded (as well as for the elderly) are economically costly, and can result in reduced quality of service delivery (indexed by lower proficiency), disruptions in staff communication, increased formalization of rules, lower job satisfaction, and less progress toward meeting rehabilitation objectives. Zaharia and Baumeister (1978) cite several studies to suggest that continuity of care is related to quality of care and organizational effectiveness. They describe three categories of variables associated with turnover: extra-institutional factors, intra-institutional management, and the characteristics of the employees.

One important measure of system performance involves employee's perceptions of the work setting. Residential care and institutional settings provide a treatment or living environment for residents and a work environment for staff. These two environments serve different functions but are closely related. For example, it may be difficult for staff to provide a supportive, clear environment for residents when they feel little support from peers or supervisors and are unclear about their job and role performance expectations. The Work Environment Scale (WES), which is one of the set of social climate scales previously described (Moos and Insel, 1974), can be used to assess the work settings of the staff (Waters, 1978) and to relate these descriptions to other sets of environmental indices.

The combined use of multi-dimensional assessments of environments and of criteria by which to evaluate the effects of these environments on mentally retarded people may eventually contribute to placement and policy decisions. The diversity of relevant environments suggests that such a goal might be facilitated by national cooperative studies similar to those that have been successfully carried out in Veterans Administration Hospitals (Linn et al., 1977).

EVALUATING THE IMPACTS OF ENVIRONMENTS ON MENTALLY RETARDED PEOPLE

Although the description of environments is useful in comparing and contrasting settings, we also need to evaluate the effects of environments on relevant outcome criteria. For example, it has been found that institutions with lower limits of tolerance for deviance have lower reinstitutionalization rates (Freeman and Simmons, 1963). Many issues need to be investigated, such as the extent to which an environment that encourages achievement leads to independence or distress, or both independence and distress, in mentally retarded persons; and whether an environment composed of individuals who are similar to each other leads to satisfaction or boredom.

Environments influence the behavior and mood of their inhabitants, even though people can select and change their settings to some degree. Therefore, the characteristics of an individual must be considered when the effects of an environment are evaluated. We need to specify the differential effects of environments on different types of people. A group home that encourages achievement may have different effects on an educable mentally retarded person than on a severely retarded one. Appropriate methods of assessing the abilities, moods, and behavioral repertoires of mentally retarded persons are needed to evaluate the effects of alternative environments (Nihira et al., 1974).

The importance of studying the interaction of environmental dimensions in relation to different types of people is illustrated in the contrasting results of two studies on the effects of the treatment environment of psychiatric wards on patients' self-esteem and morale (Moos, 1974a, pp. 149–175). In one study of eight programs, patients felt more anxious in active, directed, clear treatment programs that fostered the expression of personal problems and angry feelings, that emphasized greater responsibility and independence, and that exerted pressure to perform and get moving. In a second study of 23 programs, the results were exactly the opposite. Patient anxiety was lower in programs that emphasized clarity of expectations and the open expression of angry feelings. These differences probably occurred because the more psychiatrically disturbed patients involved in the first study found that the strong performance pressure was beyond their capabilities and was thus anxiety-provoking, whereas the healthier patients involved in the second study welcomed a more active, psychotherapeutically oriented program. Furthermore, the relative influence on independence (in relation to support and the mutual sharing of feelings) was higher in the first than in the second set of treatment programs.

This section discusses research approaches that can be used to evaluate the effects of environments and outcome criteria that can be used in evaluating such effects.

NEEDED RESEARCH ON ENVIRONMENTAL IMPACT

Several types of studies are needed to investigate the effects of environments on mentally retarded people. The first type might focus on naturalistic or ethnographic case-studies of contrasting settings, which would primarily develop hypotheses and deepen our understanding of how mentally retarded individuals interact with their settings. Edgerton (1967) illustrates this approach in his use of naturalistic observation and interview techniques to study people who were released from a hospital for the mentally retarded and who were living in the community. The book provides rich descriptions of the effects of hospitalization and of stigma as well as of the strategies of passing and denial that were used to establish what Edgerton calls a "cloak of competence."

A second type of study might focus on institutions or community-care facilities to ascertain the relationship between environmental features and individual behavior and psychological characteristics. For example, Bjaanes and Butler (1974) found more independent behavior in board-and-care facilities than in home-care settings.

A third type of research might consist of quasi-experimental studies (Campbell and Stanley, 1963) of different types of settings. Settings could be selected to differ on salient characteristics (certain types of members, a large setting reputed to be functioning unusually well). Residents would be assessed either prior to or immediately upon entry into the setting and would be followed longitudinally. With appropriate methodological and statistical control, changes in characteristics of the residents could be linked to environmental factors. Eyman et al. (1977) focused on two institutions and on several community care facilities and examined the relationship among characteristics of the residential environment (autonomy, activity), special intensive programs (behavior shaping) and changes in three factors of adaptive behavior (personal self-sufficiency, community self-sufficiency, and personal-social responsibility) of mentally retarded individuals over a period of two to three years. The data were organized by types of residents (under 20 and over 20, profoundly retarded and less retarded) as well as by types of facilities. Several interesting relationships were found, for example, "the younger, higher functioning children in the foster care and board and care homes underwent changes in all three factors that were moderately related to environmental measures or programs. In contrast, similar children in the institutions evidenced lower relationships between change on the factors and environmental measures or programs, with the exception of Factor II (community self-sufficiency)" (p. 311).

In order to clarify the inevitable questions raised by quasi-experimental studies (such as the effects of selection biases), a fourth type of research would be desirable when practically feasible. This type includes experimental studies in which new environments are developed, prospective residents are evaluated and randomly assigned or are selected on specific criteria, and changes are measured longitudinally and related to particular environmental factors. Budoff and Gottlieb (1976) studied 31 special class EMR children who were assigned randomly either to regular classes or who were retained in special education classes. Academic, personal, and social growth were assessed at three intervals: prior to assignment, two months after assignment, and at the conclusion of the school year. The authors showed that, at the end of the school year, children in the regular classes were more internally controlled, more reflective in their behavior, and more positive in their attitudes toward school.

SELECTING CRITERIA FOR
EVALUATING ENVIRONMENTAL IMPACTS

In performing studies focusing on environmental impact, it is often difficult to select the outcomes to be evaluated. Most evaluation research on mentally retarded people has tended to focus on only one type of outcome, such as behavior competence or self-concept. Because there is considerable diversity in the conceptual approaches and goals used in facilities for mentally retarded people, we need to develop a broad set of applicable criteria. Ricks, Wandersman, and Poppen (1976) were faced with a similar problem when they attempted to design a set of criteria to guide evaluations of all schools of psychotherapy and systems interventions and to provide an unbiased comparison of different approaches. They proposed a general set of criteria, based on a social-developmental approach, ranging from indices of basic minimum personal functioning to those concerned with maximum development and actualization. Ricks et al. (1976) and Thomas and Wandersman (1977) described how these criteria could evaluate the effects of outcomes of therapy and system interventions in the mental health area; Wandersman (1976) also used them to suggest guidelines for evaluating planned environments. The criteria are discussed below to help guide the selection of an inclusive set of measures for evaluating the effects of varied settings on mentally retarded persons.

Mortality, Morbidity, and Physical Health

This first class of criteria is concerned with mortality (death rate), morbidity (incidence of disease), and physical health. Mortality is an important issue in institutionalization and transition from one care setting to another. Tarjan et al. (1973) reported that mortality is high for mentally retarded people during the initial period of adjustment to an institution. In a suggestive study, Pense et al. (1961) studied 415 severely and profoundly retarded children who were less than five years old and who were admitted to a state institution. They found that 131, or 32%, died during the first four years after admission; 53 of them died within two months after admission. Most of the children who were on the waiting list of the institution lived at home. Their mortality rate was 10%–20%, although they may not have been as severely retarded as those in the institution. Further indications of the possible effects of institutionalization are suggested by the fact that every one of the 415 children had either a relatively major or minor intercurrent disease, such as asthma, bronchopneumonia, shigellosis, infectious hepatitis, or measles. Every child in the sample required medical attention for a physical condition during his stay in the institution. Measures of mortality and gross indices of morbidity and physical health are relatively easy to obtain and are an important component of an overall program evaluation.

Vulnerability to Stress

This criterion is concerned with vulnerability to stress as indicated by avoidance, "paralysis," or other maladaptive responses to situations that generally are considered routine or only mildly stressful. Descriptions of the lives of mentally retarded people (Edgerton, 1967; Spencer, 1972) indicate that they often avoid common situations, such as going to a party, because they are afraid of failure. Vulnerability to stress in a particular situation may be measured in terms of psychological indicators, such as anxiety and tension; physiological measures, such as skin conductance (GSR); and behavioral measures, such as avoidance and withdrawal. Such vulnerability can arise from environmental factors like overprotection in homes or institutions, which leads to limited practice and interaction with everyday environments, thereby making otherwise routine situations stressful (Perske, 1972).

An innovative research and demonstration project called Project Change[2] uses a variety of techniques (including behavior modification) to teach severely and profoundly retarded children the behaviors required for adjustment to less restrictive environments. As part of the project, children were taught how to behave appropriately in public environments. They were taken successfully to environments that they had never entered before, such as restaurants and churches. These types of experiences decrease the likelihood of avoiding future opportunities to interact in public settings.

Competence

Sundberg, Snowden, and Reynolds (1978) define competence as "personal characteristics (knowledge, skills, and attitudes), which lead to achievements having adaptive payoffs in significant environments" (p. 196). We view this criterion in terms of people's abilities to deal with their current environments. Increased competence is an explicit goal of deinstitutionalization and of many programs. A major focus of recent research in mental retardation has been on measuring the adaptive behavior of people who may be mentally retarded. The Adaptive Behavior Scales (ABS) has been developed to assess competencies in several areas, such as physical development, economic activity, language development, numbers, and time (Nihira et al., 1974). Eyman et al. (1977) used the ABS to measure longitudinal changes in the functioning of mentally retarded individuals living in different types of settings.

Morale, Well-Being, and Satisfaction

This class of criteria is concerned with variables like enjoyment, satisfaction, well-being, depression, and morale. There are relatively few

---

[2] Project Change. 1976. Contract 300-75-0305 to George Peabody College, Nashville, Tennessee.

studies in the mental retardation literature that use these criteria; perhaps there is an assumption that mentally retarded persons cannot tell us how they feel. In a study by Scheerenberger and Felsenthal (1977), mentally retarded persons who were former residents of a public residential facility and who had moved into the community were interviewed to determine their attitudes toward living in the community and their impressions of the community-care facility. The IQ scores of the people interviewed ranged between 42 and 84. In general, they reported liking their residence and their job. Relatively simple measures that assess morale and subjective well-being might be adapted for use with mentally retarded people. Dupuy (1973) developed the General Well-Being Schedule to assess subjective well-being in the general population. Several of the subscales are pertinent to this set of criteria and are relatively easy to administer, e.g., satisfying life (fullness of daily life) and mood (downhearted and blue, depressed/cheerful). Information derived from such measures could contribute to our understanding of the moods and of the affective experiences in the everyday lives of mentally retarded people in relation to environmental factors.

Personality Structure

This class of criteria focuses on individual personality structure and orientation toward the world. It involves the concepts of expectancy of success or failure, locus of control, inner- and outer-directedness, and self-esteem. These types of variables have been related to mentally retarded children's perceptions and behavior. Moss (1958) suggested that the expectancy of success or failure in determining an individual's behavior may be especially important in explaining the performance of mentally retarded children, who often experience a history of failure. Self-concept measures have been used to evaluate the effects of placing mentally retarded children in special versus regular classes. Budoff and Gottlieb (1976) found that highly able students placed in an integrated setting regarded themselves more favorably as students than did their highly able counterparts in a segregated setting. However, less able students in the segregated placement felt more positive about themselves than did the less able students in the integrated class.

Capacities and Skills to Adapt and Cope with New Situations

The focus in this set of criteria is the ability of an individual to adapt and to adjust to future life changes and new settings (thus distinguishing it from the earlier criteria of competence that are concerned with current environments). "Adaptation" primarily involves changes in the person to fit the environment, whereas "coping" primarily involves modification of the environment to suit the person's needs and values. This class of criteria includes the development of capacities for planning, communication, and problem-solving skills needed to cope with new situations. D'Zurilla and Goldfried (1973) suggested that learning effective problem-solving skills contributes significantly toward the long-range goals of independence, self-determination, and flexibility of action. Interpersonal skills, for example, are required to adjust to new people in novel situations. They are, therefore, very important for mentally retarded persons who are being integrated into the community. Weiss and Weinstein (1968) explored the interpersonal abilities of institutionalized and noninstitutionalized mentally retarded children in simulated interpersonal problem situations. Surprisingly, the institutionalized children used more advanced styles of interpersonal communication and were more cognizant of the motivations of others. The differences were thought to result from differing interpersonal environments in which noninstitutionalized retarded children were somewhat pampered and over-protected by their parents.

Intimate Relationships and Competent Parenting

A criterion of effective reproduction and competent parenting was included in descriptions of this set of criteria used to evaluate mental health interventions and planned environments. In relation to mental retardation, this is a difficult criterion from an ethical and social standpoint; it requires a long-term perspective beyond the scope of most evaluations. To the extent that it is relevant, this set of criteria might be separated into intimate relationship development and effective family planning and competent parenting. In terms of intimate relationships, the focus is on the extent to which an environment (e.g., family, group home) educates and encourages the development of skills necessary in relationships like marriage (Meyers, 1978). The focus on effective family planning and competent parenting concerns the mature choice of whether or not to conceive and nourish a child, the ability to bear healthy children, and the quality of parenting. Robinson and Robinson (1976) suggested that relatively few mentally retarded parents can provide an optimal environment for childrearing, and they cited a study by Scally that concluded: "nearly two-thirds of the retarded mothers, many of them single, needed help with child care or even removal of the child from the home" (p. 464). Although some mentally retarded women, given appropriate training and assistance, can nurture young children (Skeels, 1966), the skills and resource limitations of many mentally retarded persons may preclude effective parenting. Primarily, this criterion relates to the extent to which an environment has prepared a mentally retarded person for responsible decision-making regarding parenting, not whether mentally retarded individuals should or should not have children.

UTILIZING KNOWLEDGE ABOUT ENVIRONMENTS

New information is needed to better our understanding of environments and their effects on the behavior and lives of mentally retarded people. Such information has a broad array of uses (Moos, 1974b, 1976, 1979a), some of which are illustrated here.

Facilitating Environmental Change

Feedback and utilization of information on social and physical environments can facilitate environmental change. Feedback can be provided about a particular program, about how different groups within a program compare with each other (such as residents and caregivers), and about how the current setting compares to what is considered ideal. Ways in which specific changes can be made can then be outlined. These procedures allow caregivers (and residents, where possible) to define the type of environment they have, and to formulate and implement changes that might improve their program.

There are four steps involved in this process of facilitating and monitoring environmental change: 1) systematic assessment of the environment, 2) feedback to participating groups with particular stress on real/ideal setting differences, 3) planning and instituting specific changes, and 4) reassessment. Curtiss (1976) used these methods to facilitate and assess changes desired by patients and staff in a token economy program in a large state mental hospital. The Ward Atmosphere Scale (WAS) revealed that patients and staff shared dissatisfactions with particular aspects of the program. Consultants used workshops and other techniques to facilitate change, and the WAS was readministered to assess changes in environment.

Because many aspects of mentally retarded people's environments are under local control (the emphasis on expressiveness, autonomy, and organization is alterable), caregivers can plan and implement beneficial changes. This often leads to increased staff satisfaction and morale, and thereby improves the quality of care. These techniques can also serve an important function in staff training and inservice activities.

Formulating Clinical Case Descriptions

Information about mentally retarded people's environments can be used in case descriptions and in the creation of treatment and placement plans. Data about each individual's community settings can be sought in terms of the four major domains of variables assessed by the MEAP. For example, the architectural resources of a mentally retarded person's living environment might include the number of social-recreational and orientational aids, the amount of available space, and the degree to which the space is public or private. This type of information can be helpful in describing the ecological niche in which a person functions. Predictions about people's behavior and mood following release from large institutions might be more accurate if more information about their community living environments were available.

Maximizing Environmental Information

Environmental assessment procedures may be useful in compiling more accurate and complete descriptions of the living environments of mentally retarded people. Giving residents and caregivers information about a program can enhance the accuracy of residents' perceptions and/or expectations and make it easier for them to adapt to a new environment. The information can also be used to select an appropriate placement for a particular person, and thereby may help to increase the individual's satisfaction and morale. The selection of suitable environments is becoming more important as the number of possible placements increases, and as new types of group homes develop.

Comparing and Contrasting Programs

Environmental assessment procedures can provide more differentiated information upon which to compare programs than do current data, which are usually limited to staff/resident ratios, cost-per-resident, and the like. The data can be used by administrative personnel as a management tool to provide an up-to-date picture of ongoing resident care, to identify potential trouble spots, and to institute preventive action. If living environments are to be held accountable, we need to have common standards against which these settings can be evaluated. Procedures by which sheltered care environments can be described and compared may help to develop a broader and more relevant set of standards than those currently used for licensing.

Enhancing Environmental Competencies

Knowledge concerning the ways in which the environment relates to human functioning can be used to teach people how to create, select, and transcend environments; that is, it can teach them to enhance environmental competence. People can be sensitized to the characteristics of varied behavior settings and can be taught what to expect and how to act in these settings. In addition, those responsible for selecting the environments of others, such as social workers who make decisions concerning community placement for mentally retarded people, can do so with a greater awareness of the traits or behaviors that alternative environments encourage. There is a need for trained educators who can teach people about their environment—how to conceptualize its component parts and their interrelationships, and how to understand and control its potential impact in their everyday lives.

The use of knowledge about settings and the implementation of placement and policy decisions are affected by such complex pragmatic judgments as: 1) how many people can potentially benefit from a particular type of setting, 2) how efficiently the setting can be operated, 3) how much professional training is needed to implement and sustain the setting, 4) how easy it is to disseminate or recreate the setting, 5) how acceptable the setting is to prospective residents and staff, and 6) how much the setting costs to operate on a day-to-day basis. [These considerations are based on the ideas presented by Kazdin and Wilson (1978) on outcome research in psychotherapeutic procedures.]

Although such pragmatic considerations are important, we must not forget that they are based on value judgments about the relative desirability of different social objectives. Given that a society with sufficient resources can decide to explore outer space and to engage in other costly technological endeavors, the development of optimal environments for those less fortunate than we are is certainly a worthwhile and achievable objective.

CONCLUSION

Mentally retarded people are generally viewed as dependent and powerless. They are often cared for and planned for, but they have little or no opportunity to play an active role in their environment. There have been attempts to assess and to increase the behavioral competencies of mentally retarded people, but relatively little work has focused on evaluating their capacity to participate actively in their environment and to have more control over their lives. Recent evidence suggests that participation increases feelings of control over the environment and thus may enhance physical and psychological well-being (Langer and Rodin, 1976; Rodin and Langer, 1977; Schulz, 1976; Wandersman, 1979). We need to know more about environments and their effects so that existing settings can be used more effectively and so that mentally retarded people can be taught how to function and participate more actively in them.

In the approaches advanced here, we have emphasized that planning should be specific to the environment and to its social-ecological interrelations. Planning needs also to be specific to people and to their values and adaptive skills. In the social learning framework, "freedom is defined in terms of the number of options available to people and the right to exercise them. The more behavioral alternatives and social prerogatives people have, the greater is their freedom of action" (Bandura, 1976, p. 372). One implication of the social learning view is that freedom can be increased by enlarging the number of options available by increasing people's abilities to obtain options, and by using social and legal contracts to insure their rights. However, providing potential behavioral alternatives is not enough; such alternatives need to be translated into meaningful choices by relating them to the needs and abilities of the individual involved.

We hope that the procedures described here can help to monitor the quality of care, to provide caregivers with guidelines to improve morale and program effectiveness, to plan new environments that can be used effectively by mentally retarded people, and to increase the involvement of mentally retarded individuals in evaluating and changing the environments in which they live.

ACKNOWLEDGMENTS

The comments and suggestions of Al Baumeister, Steven Greenspan, Charles Holahan, Sonne Lemke, Susy Schleuning, Monte Smith, and Lona Davis Spencer have helped us in clarifying this chapter and in providing examples. We would like to acknowledge the special contribution Lois Pall Wandersman has made through her editorial comments and through her help in conceptualizing a number of key points.

REFERENCES

Balla, D., Butterfield, E., and Zigler, E. 1974. Effects of institutionalization on retarded children: A longitudinal, cross-institutional investigation. Am. J. Ment. Defic. 78:530–549.
Bandura, A. 1976. Behavior theory and the models of man. American Psychological Association Presidential Address (1974). Reprinted in: A. Wandersman, P. Poppen, and D. Ricks (eds.), Humanism and Behaviorism: Dialogue and Growth. Pergamon Press, Inc., New York.
Bjaanes, A. T., and Butler, E. W. 1974. Environmental variation in community care facilities for mentally retarded persons. Am. J. Ment. Defic. 78:429–439.
Bronfenbrenner, U. 1977. Toward an experimental ecology of human development. Am. Psychol. 32:513–531.
Budoff, M., and Gottlieb, J. 1976. Special-class EMR children mainstreamed: A study of an aptitude (learning potential) x treatment interaction. Am. J. Ment. Defic. 81:1–11.
Butler, E. W., and Bjaanes, A. T. 1977. A typology of community care facilities and differential normalization outcomes. In: P. Mittler (ed.), Research to Practice in Mental Retardation, Vol. 1. Care and intervention. University Park Press, Baltimore.

Campbell, D. T., and Stanley, J. C. 1963. Experimental and Quasi-Experimental Designs for Research. Rand McNally, Chicago.

Curtiss, S. 1976. The compatability of humanistic and behavioristic approaches in a state mental hospital. In: A. Wandersman, P. Poppen, and D. Ricks (eds.), Humanism and Behaviorism: Dialogue and Growth. Pergamon Press Inc., New York.

Dupuy, H. L. 1973. The General Well-Being Schedule. Vital and Health Statistics, PHS Ser. 1., no. 106, Public Health Service, Government Printing Office, February, Washington, D.C.

D'Zurilla, T. J., and Goldfried, M. R. 1973. Cognitive processes, problem-solving, and effective behavior. In: M. R. Goldfried and M. Merbaum (eds.), Behavior Change Through Self-Control. Holt, Rinehart and Winston, Inc., New York.

Edgerton, R. B. 1967. The Cloak of Competence: Stigma in the Lives of the Mentally Retarded. University of California Press, Berkeley.

Eyman, R., Silverstein, A., McLain, R., and Miller, C. 1977. Effects of residential settings on development. In: P. Mittler (ed.), Research to Practice in Mental Retardation, Vol. 1. Care and Intervention. University Park Press, Baltimore.

Freeman, H. E., and Simmons, O. G. 1963. The Mental Patient Comes Home. John Wiley and Sons, Inc., New York.

Holahan, C. 1978. Environment and Behavior. Plenum Publishing Corp., New York.

Kazdin, A., and Wilson, G. T. 1978. Evaluation of Behavior Therapy: Issues, Evidence, and Research Strategies. Ballinger, Cambridge, Mass.

King, R., Raynes, N., and Tizard, J. 1971. Patterns of Residential Care: Sociological Studies in Institutions for Handicapped Children. Routledge and Kegan Paul, London, England.

Langer, E., and Rodin, J. 1976. The effects of choice and enhanced personal responsibility for the aged: A field experiment in an institutional setting. J. Pers. Soc. Psychol. 34:191–198.

Lawton, P., and Nahemow, L. 1973. Ecology and the aging process. In: C. Eisdorder and P. Lawton (eds.), The Psychology of Adult Development and Aging. American Psychological Association, Washington, D.C.

Lemke, S., and Moos, R. 1979. Assessing the institutional policies of sheltered care settings. J. Gerontol. 19:74–82.

Lemke, S., Moos, R., Mehren, B., and Gauvain, M. 1979. The Multiphasic Environmental Assessment Procedure (MEAP): Handbook for Users. Social Ecology Laboratory, VA Medical Center and Stanford University, Palo Alto, Calif.

Linn, M., Caffey, E., Klett, J., and Hogarty, G. 1977. Hospital vs. community (foster) care for psychiatric patients. Arch. Gen. Psychiatry 34:78–83.

McGee, M., and Woods, D. 1978. Use of Moos' Ward Atmosphere Scale in residential setting for mentally retarded adolescents. Psychol. Rep. 43:580–582.

Meyers, R. 1978. Like Normal People. McGraw-Hill Book Company, New York.

Moos, R. 1974a. Evaluating Treatment Environments: A Social-Ecological Approach. John Wiley and Sons, Inc., New York.

Moos, R. 1974b. The Social Climate Scales: An Overview. Consulting Psychologists Press, Palo Alto, Calif.

Moos, R. 1975. Evaluating Correctional and Community Settings. John Wiley & Sons, Inc., New York.

Moos, R. 1976. The Human Context: Environmental Determinants of Behavior. John Wiley and Sons, Inc., New York.

Moos, R. 1979a. Evaluating Educational Environments: Procedures, Measures, Findings, and Policy Implications. Jossey-Bass, Inc., Pubs., San Francisco, Calif.

Moos, R. 1979b. Social-ecological perspectives on health. In: G. Stone, F. Cohen, and N. Adler (eds.), Health Psychology. Jossey-Bass, Inc., Pubs., San Francisco, Calif.

Moos, R., Gauvain, M., Lemke, S., Max, W., and Mehren, B. 1979. Assessing the social environments of sheltered care settings. Gerontologist 19:74–82.

Moos, R., and Insel, P. 1974. The Work Environment Scale Preliminary Manual. Consulting Psychologists Press, Palo Alto, Calif.

Moos, R., and Lemke, S. 1979. The Multiphasic Environmental Assessment Procedure (MEAP): Preliminary Manual. Social Ecology Laboratory, VA Medical Center and Stanford University.

Moss, J. W. 1958. Failure-avoiding and success-striving behavior in mentally retarded children and normal children. Unpublished doctoral dissertation, George Peabody College.

Nihira, K., Foster, R., Shellhaas, M., and Lealand, H. 1974. Adaptive Behavior Scale: Manual. American Association of Mental Deficiency, Washington, D.C.

Pankratz, L. 1975. Assessing the psychosocial environment of halfway houses for the retarded. Community Ment. Health J. 11:341–345.

Pense, A. W., Patton, R. E., Camp, J. L., and Kebalo, C. 1961. A cohort study of institutionalized young mentally retarded children. Am. J. Ment. Defic. 66:18–22.

Perske, R. 1972. The dignity of risk. In: W. Wolfensberger (ed.), The Principle of Normalization in Human Services. National Institute of Mental Retardation, Toronto.

Ricks, D. F., Wandersman, A., and Poppen, P. 1976. Humanism and behaviorism: Towards new syntheses. In: A. Wandersman, P. Poppen, and D. Ricks (eds.), Humanism and Behaviorism: Dialogue and Growth. Pergamon Press, Inc., New York.

Robinson, N. M., and Robinson, H. B. 1976. The Mentally Retarded Child. 2nd Ed. McGraw-Hill Book Company, New York.

Rodin, E., and Langer, E. 1977. Long-term effects of a control-relevant intervention with institutionalized aged. J. Pers. Soc. Psychol. 35:897–902.

Scarr, S., and Weinberg, R. 1976. IQ test performance of black children adopted by white families. Am. Psychol. 31:726–739.

Scheerenberger, R. C., and Felsenthal, D. 1977. Community settings for mentally retarded persons: Satisfaction and activities. Ment. Retard. 15:3–7.

Schulz, R. 1976. Effects of control and predictability on the physical and psychological well-being of the institutionalized aged. J. Pers. Soc. Psychol. 33:563–573.

Shouval, R., Kav-Venaki, S., Bronfenbrenner, U., Devereux, E., and Kiely, E. 1975. Anomalous reactions to social pressure of Israeli and Soviet children raised in family versus collective settings. J. Pers. Soc. Behav. 32:477–489.

Skeels, H. 1966. Adult status of children with contrasting early life experiences: A follow-up study. Monograph, Vol. 31, Society for Research in Child Development.

Spencer, L. D. 1972. A "retarded" graduate student looking at the institutional world through the eyes of a resident. Western Carolina Center Papers and Reports in Mental Retardation, Vol. 2, no. 1, February.

Sundberg, N. D., Snowden, L. R., and Reynolds, W. M. 1978. Toward assessment of personal competence and incompetence in life situations. Annu. Rev. Psychol. 29:179–221.

Tarjan, G., Wright, S. W., Eyman, R. K., and Keeran, C. V. 1973. Natural history of mental retardation: Some aspects of epidemiology. Am. J. Ment. Defic. 77:369–379.

Thomas, J. and Wandersman, A. 1977. A general system of criteria as a basis for the assessment of mental health interventions. Working paper, Department of Psychology, University of South Carolina.

Tizard, J., Sinclair, I., and Clarke, R. V. G.(eds.). 1975. Varieties of Residential Experience. Routledge and Kegan Paul, London, England.

Wandersman, A. 1976. Applying humanism, behaviorism, and a broader social developmental view to understanding and researching the design process. In: P. Suedfeld and J. Russel (eds.), The Behavioral Basis of Design, Vol. 1. Dowden, Hutchison, Ross, Stroudsberg, Pa.

Wandersman, A. 1979. User participation: A study of types of participation, effects, mediators, and individual differences. Environ. Behav. 11(2):185–208.

Waters, J. 1978. Assessing the work environment of long-term health care facilities. Long-Term Care Health Serv. Adm. Q. 2:300–307.

Weiss, D., and Weinstein, E. 1968. Interpersonal tactics among mental retardates. Am. J. Ment. Defic. 72:653–661.

Wolins, M. 1974. Successful Group Care: Explorations in the Powerful Environment. Aldine Publishing Company, Chicago.

Zaharia, E. S., and Baumeister, A. A. 1978. Technician turnover and absenteeism in public residential facilities. Am. J. Ment. Defic. 82:580–593.

Living Environments for Developmentally Retarded Persons
Edited by H. Carl Haywood and J. R. Newbrough
Copyright 1981   University Park Press   Baltimore

Mentally Retarded Persons in Some Atypical Settings

H. Carl Haywood, Ph.D.[1]

*Director, John F. Kennedy Center for Research
   on Education and Human Development
Box 40, Peabody College
Vanderbilt University
Nashville, Tennessee 37203*

Mentally retarded persons are found in many different settings and situations, and often it is as much the nature of their environments as the nature of the persons themselves that determines how well they function and develop. In fact, some social scientists argue that, from a social-ecological standpoint, the very definition of mental retardation inheres in the environment and its demands rather than in the individual (Mercer, 1975). Recognizing the close relationship between the behavioral development of an individual and the structure and functioning of the nervous system, it is apparent that a given pattern of behavior can be adaptive in one situation and maladaptive in another. Furthermore, the adjustment of mentally retarded persons and of nonretarded persons depends to a considerable extent on the demands placed upon them by their environments, as well as on the assets for individual development afforded them by those environments (Schoggen, 1963).

Only about 150,000 of the six million retarded individuals in the United States (about 2.5%) live in residential institutions for retarded persons. The remaining 97.5% are distributed across a variety of settings, not all of which have been designed to enhance the development of retarded persons. The majority of profoundly retarded individuals are in residential institutions, and a very large proportion of severely

---

[1] This chapter is based largely on an invited paper entitled "Mentally Retarded Persons in Atypical Settings," given by the author as part of the First International Congress on Developmental Disabilities, Lisbon, March 1980. A second version was presented at the Third International Workshop on Special Education, Taipei, March–April, 1980. Observations reported herein were gathered from two studies by Human Development Associates, Inc. (those on adult prisons and psychiatric hospitals) and from an earlier research and demonstration project on mentally retarded juvenile offenders, of which Floyd Dennis was principal investigator.

retarded persons reside in institutional or quasi-institutional settings, such as nursing homes, large group homes, and, occasionally, convalescent hospitals. Moderately and mildly retarded persons are distributed across the greatest variety of settings, a fact that helps to define the nature of the problems associated with the development and functioning of those persons, and that presents particular problems for identification, diagnosis, and treatment.

I shall consider here three settings not designed for retarded persons, but in which large numbers of retarded persons are to be found (at least in the United States). I shall also consider associated problems in identification, diagnosis, and treatment. The settings are adult prisons, juvenile correctional facilities, and psychiatric hospitals. In such a consideration, it is useful to examine the following dimensions for each setting: 1) demography and epidemiology of mild and moderate mental retardation; 2) identification; 3) assessment and program planning; 4) programming (activities of daily living, social skills, vocational skills, academic education, cognitive processes); 5) social services; 6) medical services; 7) special problems of re-entry; and 8) separation or integration of services. Unfortunately, research with retarded persons in these settings has not been sufficiently comprehensive to permit such a review, so each dimension is examined whenever there is sufficient knowledge to do so; the significant knowledge gaps are apparent.

ADULT PRISONS

Depending upon the definition of mental retardation and the diagnostic methods used, the number of mentally retarded persons who are in adult prisons in the United States at any given time ranges from 5% to 30% of the prison population (Brown and Courtless, 1968; Cull, 1975; Santamour and West, 1977; Zeleny, 1933). The percentage, which varies considerably by state, is directly related to the sophistication of diagnosis and social services. Many prisoners who are identified as mentally retarded yield assessment patterns that appear to be in the mentally retarded range but are instead the results of cultural, social, and economic disadvantage, poor education, and other environmental factors that mask greater potential for learning and for satisfactory adjustment. Motivational factors often further depress test scores.

However, some mentally retarded adults in prison are never identified as retarded because they make adequate adjustments to a system that is not highly demanding. When such individuals are identified, it is often because they have been systematically victimized by other prisoners. Retarded prisoners are sometimes willing or unwilling servants and scapegoats of more adequately functioning prisoners and are often objects of verbal, physical, and sexual abuse (Morgan, 1973; Santamour and West, 1977). Observation of prison social patterns is a good way to begin to identify retarded prisoners.

Examination of educational achievement and IQ is not a completely adequate method of identification, because these variables are not greatly different from average levels of attainment among prisoners. In some state prisons, mildly retarded persons may have IQs that are no more than 10 to 15 points less than the mean IQ of the prison population. In educational achievement the difference may be even less. Standard measures of adaptive behavior, such as the Vineland Social Maturity Scale and the American Association on Mental Deficiency's Adaptive Behavior Scale, are not fully satisfactory, because by definition the adaptive behavior of all prisoners is significantly impaired (especially on the maladaptive behavior dimension). One must, then, rely heavily on the social history, which is the single most important source of diagnostic information, and which includes school records, records of institutionalization, early diagnoses, and levels of functioning of parents and siblings. Developmental histories, if available, are also important, as are observational reports by prison personnel, clinical interaction with the prisoners, and, to some extent, standardized testing (although test results cannot be used in complete conformity with usual standards).

Adults who enter prison most often are from lower socioeconomic levels, are relatively poorly educated, and, at least in the United States, are a disproportionate representation of ethnic minorities, especially blacks (McCollum, 1973; Santamour and West, 1977; Velde, 1977). Most inmates are not so-called white collar criminals, in prison for sophisticated crimes such as embezzlement or conspiracy to commit fraud, but are instead from marginal segments of society and are in prison for crimes of passion or theft, malicious destruction of property, or other relatively unsophisticated offenses. These same subgroups of American society produce 80% of mildly and moderately mentally retarded persons (Haywood and Stedman, 1969). Thus, the proportion of mentally retarded persons in a prison population may be no more than the representation of retarded persons in those segments of society from which most prisoners have come. Procedures for assessment, program planning, and program implementation must take these social variables into account.

My colleagues, Robert Orlando and Katherine Smits, and I were given the task of identifying mentally retarded adults in the Tennessee state prison system, doing diagnostic assessments on those who were thought to be retarded, and developing broad recommendations to habilitate these persons. The observations that follow are the results of that experience.

Although record keeping in prisons is not good (Bell, Conrad, and Laffey, 1979), the examination of records is an essential first step in identifying retarded persons. The same information is not present for everyone, but it is possible to establish broad categories and to find in most records some information in each category, including fairly standard information on social history, circumstances of imprisonment, education, previous psychological tests, health problems, and reports of disruptive or strange behavior. Presence of this information was useful, but absence of information was not taken as negative evidence of mental retardation.

Our first level of screening identified maladapted individuals whose educational achievement was below fifth-grade level. We then determined which members of that group had either low IQs or no record of intelligence tests. Next we examined developmental history, including placement in special education classes, retarded parents or siblings, previous institutionalization, or even verbal reports by parents, teachers, or others that the individual had been thought to be "slow."

Each prisoner identified by this process was given an intelligence test and the AAMD Adaptive Behavior Scale (Public School Version—Lambert et al., 1975), modified so that some items could be given directly to the prisoners because of the unreliability of reports by prison employees. The Adaptive Behavior Scale was not useful for differentiating mentally retarded prisoners, because everyone made low scores. As a result, we developed an informal interview schedule for examining the domains of Residence/Living Skills, Academic/Vocational Attainment, Recreation/Socialization Behavior, Transportation, Health, Money Management, Sociolegal Understanding, and Communication. The Adaptive Behavior Survey Interview schedule is shown at the end of this chapter (Appendix A). We selected functional items from standard adaptive behavior scales indicating whether the individual could prepare meals, take care of fundamental needs of daily living, handle money, understand the rules of popular games, such as football and basketball, take public transportation, and use the telephone to summon emergency help. Mental retardation was usually diagnosed when the IQ on an individually administered intelligence test was significantly below 70 (but always questioned when IQ was at least 65), when educational attainment was below the fifth grade, when adaptive skills appeared to be significantly impaired, and when there was some history of developmental abnormality (such as placement in special classes). If any one of these elements was missing, we questioned the diagnosis and examined further. For example, we used one simple experimental procedure that I had used frequently in research on cognitive processes—administering the Similarities Test under both regular and enriched conditions. In the regular condition, one might ask, "In what way are an orange and a banana alike?"; while in the enriched condition one would ask "In what way are an orange, a banana, a peach, a plum, and a pear alike?" On 20 such items, if the subject's score in the enriched condition showed at least a 50% improvement over his score in the regular condition, we inferred that he had greater learning potential than would be expected of a mentally retarded person and that the apparent retardation was the result of cultural disadvantage (Gordon and Haywood, 1969; Haywood and Switzky, 1974; Haywood et al., 1975). For such individuals, even an IQ of 60 might not warrant a diagnosis of mental retardation. There are more extensive and formal clinical procedures for the assessment of learning potential (Feuerstein, Rand, and Hoffman, 1979), and these should be used when one has both sufficient time and well-trained examiners.

Medical examinations revealed a general pattern of poor health. Many new prisoners, especially those bordering on mental retardation, were malnourished, were suffering extensive dental problems, and were host to various parasites. These conditions were readily treated.

Programs to teach daily living skills did not have to be extensive, because even the most clearly retarded prisoners that we examined had more highly developed self-help skills than do most persons of comparable IQ and educational achievement who reside in institutions for retarded persons (Haywood, 1976). On the other hand, social-interpersonal skills were particularly lacking. The prisoners did not know how to relate to other people, how to indicate their needs and wishes to others, how to deal with aggression, or how to participate in group activities.

Vocational skills, although often deficient, were not as severely deficient as were academic skills. Many prisoners were functionally illiterate, and retarded prisoners were frequently performing at about first- or second-grade level in basic areas, such as reading, arithmetic, and spelling. This finding was consistent with the major literature on educational levels of prisoners (Bell et al., 1979; Kilty, 1979; Law Enforcement Assistance Agency, 1979; Reagan et al., 1976). Even so, upon release from prison these adults do not return to school. Therefore, unless it is possible to bring these skills up to functional levels of fifth or sixth grade, other needs should be emphasized.

Another major deficit in retarded prisoners was in cognitive processes, the fundamental processes of thought. These processes include functions like inducing a principle from various examples, deducing an application of that principle to new situations, analyzing problems into their component parts and attacking those parts separately, relating parts to wholes, thinking through a possible action to its eventual consequences, weighing alternative courses of action, comparing two sets of events with respect to a variety of dimensions, seeing oneself from the perspective of others, and seeing contemporary events within the contexts of their history and their probable future. These basic processes, in which everyone engages daily, constitute some of the important building blocks of more complex thought (Feuerstein, Rand, and Hoffman, 1979; Feuerstein et al., 1980), but we found them to be sadly deficient in this population. It is possible that much of the maladaptive and illegal behavior of prisoners is more directly related to such cognitive (thought process) deficits than to low intelligence per se. Such a thesis has been suggested both by Feuerstein and by Haywood in a videotape presentation on thought processes of criminals (Griffin, 1979).

As was true in Edgerton's (1967) and Edgerton's and Bercovici's (1976) study of deinstitutionalized mentally retarded persons, individuals in our prison sample who had failed on the outside had apparently failed not for lack of vocational skills but for lack of social and planning skills. For re-entry into nonprison life, mentally retarded prisoners were especially in need of medical services for chronic poor health and of social services directed toward fundamental daily living skills, including maintaining a residence, finding and keeping employment, making purchases, saving money, and getting along with other people.

The question that we were repeatedly asked by state officials was whether retarded persons should be housed and treated in prison with nonretarded prisoners or segregated in a separate facility. We answered at two levels:

1. Prisons are not equipped to deal with the multitude of problems raised by individuals who are at least moderately mentally retarded. Because it is highly unlikely that they are dangerous to society, we recommended that adults who are at least moderately retarded be extruded from the correctional system and transferred to settings that are more appropriate for mentally retarded persons.

2. With respect to mildly retarded persons, we consistently observed that they are more competent than are comparable persons in mental retardation settings. This led us to conclude that mildly retarded persons should not be segregated, but should continue to interact with nonretarded individuals who may function as models for behavior. We saw that such modeling often results in learning

inappropriate behavior, but the variety of appropriate social and personal skills that they learned was sufficiently strong compensation to justify the recommendation. Another consideration was that even though a determinate prison sentence might be completed in a reasonable amount of time, after which the individual is returned to society, a transfer to a mental retardation setting often constitutes a life sentence (Haywood, 1976).

JUVENILE CORRECTIONAL FACILITIES

On two occasions, almost ten years apart, my colleagues and I have conducted studies of the juvenile correctional system in Tennessee. On the first occasion (Dennis and Mankinen, 1973; Lucker and Wright, 1971), our major focus was the study of adolescents who were both mentally retarded and in trouble with the law. On the second occasion (Human Development Associates, Inc., 1979), we were commissioned to evaluate the adequacy of the juvenile correctional system in Tennessee for any adolescent in trouble with the law. The observations reported here are based upon these studies and upon a review of related research literature in the United States.

Even more than adult prisoners, adolescents adjudicated as juvenile delinquents and committed to correctional institutions come overwhelmingly from lower socioeconomic levels. In Tennessee they tend to be poor, black, from urban rather than rural homes, from single-parent homes, and from poor educational backgrounds, characterized by frequent absences from school and low levels of achievement. By the time the typical adolescent offender in Tennessee first reaches a juvenile correctional facility, he has been in trouble with the law on several occasions, has been expelled from school at least once for misbehavior ranging from truancy to aggression against students or teachers, and his family has been in contact with at least three or four social agencies. Boys outnumber girls by a factor of approximately nine to one.

From examination of 1,054 adolescents in institutions for delinquents, we found that 34% had IQs between 70 and 84, while 18% had IQs below 70 (as opposed to 2.5% in the population at large). In one institution for adolescent males between 12 and 14 years of age, only 28% of the population had IQs of 85 or above, while 72% were at least one standard deviation below the national mean (as compared with 16% in the general population). Because school achievement levels were characteristically very low in this population, we decided to administer individual intelligence tests to all those who scored below 85 on group tests, and the picture changed markedly with respect to IQ. The percentage who achieved IQs in the mentally retarded range fell from over 30% on the basis of group administered tests to about 9% on the basis of individually administered tests. That finding simply indicated that large numbers of these youths cannot read. This inference was validated by achievement tests that showed that the average 16-year-old in this population was performing at about the fifth-grade level or below. Of course, mentally retarded adolescents in this group were achieving at even lower levels.

As was the case with adult prisoners, correct identification of retarded juvenile offenders was a complex process. Some had not been identified because they were similar in many ways to their nonretarded peers. Others had been categorized as retarded through their inadequate social behavior, through poor school performance, and through the comments of other youths. Formal testing and examination followed these informal leads.

As in the case of adult prisoners, juveniles who had been identified as mentally retarded were for the most part mildly retarded, although a few were in the moderate range. Most were without obvious signs of genetic, metabolic, toxic, or traumatic etiology, and their mild retardation seemed to be a product of environments unconducive to optimal development in combination with hereditary factors that would have placed them, in any case, at the lower end of the normal range of variation.

Assessment included intelligence testing, classification of adaptive behavior, personality assessment, and ecological assessment (identification of important social systems in their lives, ranging from families to schools to larger community systems). Results of our assessment procedures revealed surprising strength in self-help skills compared with persons of similar IQ in other settings. Social skills were usually impaired, revealing ineptitude at getting along with peers; consequently, retarded offenders were often involved in fights and were led into trouble by more sophisticated age-peers. Many of these youths had promising vocational skills, sometimes functioning as carpenters' helpers, plumbers' helpers, and general laborers in construction, forestry, dairy farming, and related tasks. Most were severely deficient in basic cognitive processes, indicating that some of their learning failures in school did not result so much from the incapacity to learn as from the lack of instruction in how to learn.

Program plans for these juveniles concentrated sharply upon cognitive education, social services, and medical services. An experimental program of cognitive education has been instituted to teach adolescents basic thought processes so that they can learn on their own once they leave the correctional system, but that program is severely limited by the average short duration of their stay in the correctional system. Social services were focused on rearranging the home environments to which they would return so that the circumstances that put them in trouble with the law would not recur. Medical services were aimed at nutrition, freedom from parasites, dental treatment, correction of vitamin deficiencies, and identification and treatment of chronic illness.

As was the case with adult prisoners, we recommended that mildly retarded juveniles remain integrated with their nonretarded age-peers. This decision was based on the observation that in many areas their skills were comparable to those of nonretarded age-peers and were usually superior to those of persons with similar IQ who were in mental retardation settings. As with adult prisoners, the situation was different for levels of mental retardation below the mild category. The correctional system had no facilities or trained personnel for meeting the needs of moderately or severely retarded persons. We concluded that the correctional system should not attempt to acquire that capability but instead should extrude moderately and severely retarded persons from the system. If an individual within the juvenile correctional system was moderately or severely retarded, the probability increased dramatically that he would be the subject of verbal, physical, and sexual abuse by age-peers, and sometimes even by staff members. Because such retarded persons rarely constitute any threat to society, it was fairly easy to reach an agreement with correctional officials that all moderately and severely retarded persons should be extruded from the juvenile correctional system, after which services could be sought from appropriate mental health and human service agencies.

Mildly retarded adolescents who remained within the juvenile correctional system, usually for periods varying from 3 to 9 months, were examined for various personality characteristics. On self-concept scales, juvenile delinquents typically describe themselves as persons who dislike themselves; they reveal considerable conflict, confusion, variability, and uncertainty in self-perceptions and they believe that they have little to say about their destinies. We found not only that juvenile delinquents have less positive estimates of themselves than do nondelinquent adolescents, but also that mentally retarded delinquents have even more negative self-concepts than do their intellectually advantaged, but also delinquent age-peers. Mentally retarded juvenile delinquents are more concerned about what they are than are nonretarded delinquents or nondelinquent adolescents. They also are more concerned about their worth in relation to others and about their social interactions. Even after controlling statistically for differences in intelligence, self-concept turned out to be an extremely important variable in accounting for differences in both institutional behavior and academic achievement. The more positive the self-concept, the less likely the individual is to become a discipline problem in the institution and the more likely he is to score higher on academic achievement tests.

In addition to the self-concept difference, retarded delinquents were more often characterized by a task-extrinsic motivational orientation than were nonretarded delinquents, and both groups were more task-extrinsic than were nondelinquent adolescents of comparable age and social class. For this dimension, we were measuring the extent to which individuals seek their principal satisfactions in life through task-intrinsic variables, such as achievement, responsibility, learning, creativity, and aesthetic considerations, as opposed to the extent to which they simply seek to avoid dissatisfaction by concentrating on nontask aspects of the environment, including ease, comfort, safety, security, and material gain (Haywood, 1971). Retarded delinquents did not often seek satisfaction in positive terms; instead, their lives were oriented toward an incessant effort to avoid failure and to avert discomfort and dissatisfaction. They did not try many new things, because trying usually meant failing, and if one does not try, one is not confronted with the possibility of failing. Because it is impossible to learn without risking exposure to new situations, the original low learning abilities of these students were compounded by their own motivational systems that made them unwilling to attempt new learning tasks (Haywood and Burke, 1977). Whatever programs of remediation are undertaken, these motivational variables must be considered, because without improvement in task-intrinsic motivation, even restructuring of cognitive functions will not have maximum beneficial effect.

One additional personality characteristic we examined was the variable known in personality theory as "locus of control." Derived from Rotter's (1954) social learning theory, the construct refers to individual differences in the extent to which persons see themselves as responsible for their own destinies. Internal locus of control refers to the belief that one's behavior can help to determine one's fate; external locus of control refers to the belief that one's fate is determined by chance or by the actions of others. In our samples, nondelinquent adolescents were most often characterized by internal locus of control, nonretarded delinquents were next, with scores much more toward the external end of the locus of control continuum, and mentally retarded delinquents were strongly characterized by an external locus of control. Although this orientation might have been somewhat realistic, given their histories of being unable to control events in their lives, it also constituted a very pessimistic view of the future. Treatment that would have any success must include efforts to improve the extent to which retarded delinquents believe that they can have some control over the direction of their lives.

With respect to their institutional behavior, we divided our samples into three groups: mentally retarded, borderline (IQs between 70 and 85), and intellectually average. The mentally retarded and borderline groups were cited more often for rule infractions and involvement in fights than were intellectually average adolescents. Escapes were the only category in which the average group exceeded the below-average group. We also found that borderline and mentally retarded delinquents were more frequently placed in maximum security, were more frequently given physical punishment, and more frequently received all other types of punishment combined.

Examination of school records for the three groups indicated that the retarded delinquents had consistently received more unsatisfactory conduct ratings than had students in the other groups, beginning with the first year in school and continuing throughout their school careers. As early as first grade, they had engaged in behavior that was judged to be disruptive. Furthermore, we discovered a strong correlation between school absences and increasing chronological age, but the correlation was exactly the opposite for retarded and intellectually average delinquents. Our retarded group started school with very few absences in the first year, but by the ninth year in school these students were absent significantly more often than were borderline and intellectually average students. As absences increased from year to year, the retarded group's inherent learning difficulty was compounded. The problem is one of progressive failure and alienation that culminates in expulsion despite numerous indications, some evident in the first year in school and others appearing certainly by the fourth year, that intervention and special training are needed.

As a result of these studies and others conducted on this same population, our group of investigators devised an education-based system for the treatment of retarded juvenile offenders, concentrating on training in the basic processes of thought and decision making; functional competence in basic subjects such as reading, arithmetic, and spelling; social skills; and prevocational training. An essential component of the system was to allow the retarded offenders as much interaction with nonretarded age-peers as possible. A token reinforcement system allowed us to emphasize that behavior has consequences and that one can control those consequences by controlling behavior. Definitive results cannot be cited because follow-up studies have not been completed. From the standpoint of the teachers and correctional officers who worked with the program, it was successful in producing more competent individuals than would have been produced otherwise. In addition, it probably contributed to reducing the rate of recidivism in the correctional system. The fundamental and most powerful conclusion was that, even though by living at home and circulating freely in the community, they had much more opportunity to get into trouble, the mildly retarded adolescents who participated in this community-based education-oriented program got into no more trouble than did their peers who were sent to residential juvenile correctional facilities (Dennis and Mankinen, 1973).

These studies suggested some intriguing possibilities for further study, including the following: 1) the level of social competence of mentally retarded adolescents may be strongly a function of the settings, including the social environments, in which they live, learn, work, and develop; 2) correctional settings may have some characteristics that predispose to negative developmental outcomes, e.g., negative self-concept, external locus of control, task-extrinsic motivation, although it is difficult to separate the contribution of correctional settings from the selective contribution of the home-community environments from which most juvenile offenders come; 3) residential juvenile correctional settings are no more successful at preventing maladaptive behavior in mildly retarded adolescents than are carefully programmed community settings.

PSYCHIATRIC HOSPITALS

To our great surprise, we have found a substantial number of obviously mentally retarded persons among the patient populations of psychiatric hospitals. The President's Committee on Mental Retardation (PCMR, 1975) reported that in 1971 there were 29,272 persons in state mental hospitals diagnosed as mentally retarded. Of that number, 81% were at least 24 years old.

Such persons often are different from retarded persons in the prisons and the juvenile correctional system described earlier. One difficulty is that, for many years, developmental and mental health professionals were accustomed to seeking a differential diagnosis, i.e., whether an individual was mentally ill or mentally retarded. Often that was a pseudo-question, having no reasonable answer, because the two conditions are not mutually exclusive. In fact, some investigators maintain that the frequency of mental illness is significantly greater among mildly and moderately retarded persons than among nonretarded persons, and that much of the difficult behavior that we attribute to the mental retardation may be at least a result of the interaction of the mental retardation with the mental illness. Another confounding variable is that institutionalization itself tends to produce strange and often socially unacceptable behavior. Thus, when examining older patients, one must consider that mental retardation and mental illness may occur together in an individual, and that the length of institutionalization may affect behavior.

Unlike retarded persons in correctional systems, those found in psychiatric hospitals are not so predominantly from lower socioeconomic levels. Although there are significant numbers from such environments, the number is not disproportionate to that within the basic population distribution. There is a great preponderance of older patients, many being above age 65. It is unusual to find children and adolescents among retarded psychiatric patients, although it does occur.

Identification at the first level usually occurs when a staff member offers the opinion that a patient might be retarded, and, as a consequence, assessment is sought. Diagnostic assessment is particularly difficult with this group, especially if there is active psychotic process. In about 400 patients that my colleagues and I examined over the last year, almost 30% were either totally nonverbal or had such poor communication skills that formal psychological and educational testing were useless. Without such quantitative criteria, nonquantitative standards assume even greater importance. The social history, always the most important source of diagnostic information, is, in these cases, sometimes the only reliable source of information other than direct and immediate observation. Sophisticated and subtle techniques of diagnosing psychiatric disorder are useless, including projective techniques and the usual mental status examination.

In order to get some rough estimate of functional ability in the most rudimentary requirements of social living, we developed and used the brief Checklist for Awareness of Self and Surroundings, which is presented at the end of this chapter (Appendix B).

The critical question is: Is this individual behaving at a retarded level because he or she is constitutionally unable to behave otherwise, or is the low level of behavior the result of a psychiatric disorder that, if relieved, would reveal a greater capacity for intelligent behavior? One also needs to ask what difference the answer would make in treatment, in social planning, and in the placement and disposition of a case. We examined several patients who were past 70 years of age, who were nonverbal or uncommunicative, and who had only the most rudimentary daily living skills. Devising complicated training programs for such individuals, with goals of independent living outside institutions (except some perhaps being placed with their own families), seemed unrealistic and even unkind. Instead, we asked questions like: Is it possible that increasing this patient's understanding might enhance the quality of life, might make the patient happier, more comfortable, more dignified, or more capable of doing things that he or she would find personally rewarding? Program plans were then built around the answers to these questions.

For younger patients, the difficulties were often compounded. Acute psychiatric distress was much more likely to be found in younger patients, who sometimes were mute, hostile, delusional, or actively hallucinating. When formal psychological testing failed, as it usually did with this group, we relied strongly upon the social history and the personal observations of staff members, supplemented by nonstandard techniques. Rather than trying to assess the products of past learning opportunities, we found that it was more productive to introduce new learning tasks that the patient could not have encountered in the past, and then to help the patient to learn the tasks in every possible way, recording the amount of help and the kinds of help required to solve the problems. Indications of ability to solve new problems argued against a hypothesis of mental retardation in addition to the mental illness. All of these interpretations had to be made despite traditional knowledge that, especially with schizophrenic disorders, there is a transient intellectual deficit of 10 to 20 IQ points that seems to vary with the severity of psychiatric symptoms (Haywood and Moelis, 1963; Hunt and Cofer, 1944).

In spite of the diagnostic difficulties encountered, about 40% of the patients that we examined, referred by staff members who thought that they might be retarded as well as mentally ill, were diagnosed as mentally retarded. A diagnosis of mental retardation meant that the diagnostic team considered their developmental needs to exceed their psychiatric needs; in other words, the greatest need of individuals diagnosed as mentally retarded was to acquire elementary skills of self-help and communication, with the prospect that their behavior and social adjustment might improve on these developmental bases alone without further psychiatric intervention.

SUMMARY

Mentally retarded persons are to be found in adult prisons, in juvenile correctional facilities, and in psychiatric hospitals. From examination of clinical studies conducted in these three settings, several conclusions are suggested. First, it is likely that when mentally retarded persons disappear at early adulthood from the rolls of retarded individuals, they reappear in other and frequently even less desirable places (Charles, 1953; Edgerton, 1967; Edgerton and Bercovici, 1976), such as prisons, juvenile correctional facilities, and psychiatric hospitals. Still others may be found on the margins of urban society, living on welfare, causing constant trouble with the police, and managing only minimally to maintain daily existence. Such persons are not to be ignored simply because they reside outside institutions for mentally retarded persons, or because they are classified primarily in other categories. They require specialized services. Because most such individuals are mildly or moderately retarded, their prospects for improvement in social adjustment, given adequate treatment and social services, are very good. Thus, they represent a potentially good investment of money, time, and professional services.

Examination of mentally retarded persons in these three atypical settings, as well as in other more traditional settings, reinforces the idea that physical and social environments are significant determinants of the behavior, the development, and the adjustment of retarded persons. In addition to this generalization, one must take into account the broad array of individual differences that one finds within the mental retardation category. Study of both environmental variables and individual differences variables can be expected to yield important inferences with respect to differential effects, demands, assets, and apparent characteristics of a variety of settings, depending upon the individual strengths, histories, weaknesses, needs, abilities, preferences, and personality configurations of mentally retarded persons. Given the complexity of such interactions of settings and persons, it is clear that it would be a mistake to attempt to devise the "best" setting for all retarded persons, or even for all mildly or moderately retarded persons, for all retarded juvenile offenders, or for all psychiatrically ill retarded persons. The array of settings that society makes available must be very large in order to accommodate the diversity of needs and strengths that individual retarded persons bring to the settings. Therein lie the major challenges: first, to devise reliable procedures for determining optimal person-setting matches, based upon developmental criteria; and second, to discover the sociopolitical processes that will be adequate to bring about the matching.

ACKNOWLEDGMENTS

The author is grateful to Katherine Smits, Robert Orlando, and Joel Rothaizer for their participation in the studies of retarded persons in prisons and in psychiatric hospitals, and to Floyd Dennis, William G. Lucker, and Richard Mankinen for observations on mentally retarded juvenile offenders.

REFERENCES

Bell, R., Conrad, E., and Laffey, T. 1979. National evaluation program—phase 1 report: Correctional education programs for inmates. Law Enforcement Assistance Administration, National Institute of Law Enforcement and Criminal Justice, U.S. Department of Justice, Washington, D.C.

Brown, B. S., and Courtless, T. F. 1968. The mentally retarded in penal and correctional institutions. Am. J. Psychiatry 124:1164–1166.

Charles, D. C. 1953. Ability and accomplishments of persons earlier judged as mentally retarded. Genet. Psychol. Monogr. 47:3–71.

Cull, W. H. 1975. Adult offenders. In: Mentally Retarded Offenders in Adult and Juvenile Correctional Institutes, Research Report no. 125, Kentucky Legislative Research Commission.

Dennis, H. F., and Mankinen, R. 1973. Our house: A report to Tennessee about the mentally retarded juvenile offender project. Progress report for the J. F. Kennedy Center, George Peabody College, Nashville.

Edgerton, R. B. 1967. The Cloak of Competence: Stigma in the Lives of the Mentally Retarded. University of California Press, Berkeley.

Edgerton, R. B., and Bercovici, S. M. 1976. The cloak of competence: Years later. Am. J. Ment. Defic. 80(5):485–497.

Feuerstein, R., Rand, Y., and Hoffman, M. 1979. The Dynamic Assessment of Retarded Performers: The Learning Potential Assessment Device, Theory, Instruments, and Techniques. University Park Press, Baltimore.

Feuerstein, R., Rand, Y., Hoffman, M., and Miller, R. 1980. Instrumental Enrichment: Intervention Program for Cognitive Modifiability. University Park Press, Baltimore.

Gordon, J. E., and Haywood, H. C. 1969. Input deficits in cultural-familial retardates: Effect of stimulus enrichment. Am. J. Ment. Defic. 73:604–610.

Griffin, D. K. (producer). 1979. Crime and Reason. Videotape, Education and Training Division, Correctional Service of Canada, Toronto.

Haywood, H. C. 1971. Individual differences in motivational orientation: A trait approach. In: H. I. Day, D. E. Berlyne, and D. E. Hunt (eds.), Intrinsic Motivation: A New Direction in Education. Holt, Rinehart, and Winston, Inc., Toronto.

Haywood, H. C. 1976. How "special" are retarded offenders? In: M. Kindred, J. Cohen, D. Penrod, and T. Shaffer (eds.), The Mentally Retarded Citizen and the Law. Free Press, New York.

Haywood, H. C., and Burke, W. P. 1977. Development of individual differences in intrinsic motivation. In: I. C. Uzgiris and F. Weizmann (eds.), The Structuring of Experience. Plenum Publishing Corp., New York.

Haywood, H. C., and Moelis, I. 1963. Effect of symptom changes on intellectual function in schizophrenia. J. Abnorm. Soc. Psychol. 67:76–78.

Haywood, H. C., and Stedman, D. J. 1969. Poverty and mental retardation. Staff position paper prepared for the President's Committee on Mental Retardation. J. F. Kennedy Center, George Peabody College, Nashville, Tennessee.

Haywood, H. C., and Switzky, H. N. 1974. Children's verbal abstracting: Effects of enriched input, age, and IQ. Am. J. Ment. Defic. 78:556–565.

Haywood, H. C., Filler, J. W., Jr., Shifman, M. A., and Chatelanat, G. 1975. Behavioral assessment in mental retardation. In: P. McReynolds (ed.), Advances in Psychological Assessment, Vol. 3. Jossey-Bass, Inc., Pubs., San Francisco.

Human Development Associates, Inc. 1979. Final report of an evaluation of the six institutions for juvenile offenders in the Tennessee Department of Correction. Prepared for the Attorney General of Tennessee, Nashville.

Hunt, J. Mcv., and Cofer, C. N. 1944. Psychological deficit. In: J. McV. Hunt (ed.), Personality and the Behavior Disorders, Vol. 1. Ronald Press, New York.

Kilty, T. K. 1979. A study of the characteristics of reading programs in federal, state, and city-county penal institutions. Kalamazoo School of Education, Western Michigan University.

Lambert, N., Windmiller, M., Cole, L., and Figueroa, R. 1975. AAMD Adaptive Behavior Scale—Public School Version. American Association on Mental Deficiency, Washington, D.C.

Law Enforcement Assistance Agency. 1979. Profile of state prison inmates: Sociodemographic findings from the 1974 survey of inmates of state correctional facilities. Special report SD-NDS-SR-4, National Institute of Law Enforcement and Criminal Justice, U.S. Department of Justice, Washington, D.C.

Lucker, W. G., and Wright, W. E. 1971. Retarded juvenile offenders research and demonstration project. Progress report for the J. F. Kennedy Center, George Peabody College, Nashville.

McCollum, S. G. 1973. New designs for correctional education and training programs. Fed. Probation 37:6–11.

Mercer, J. R. 1975. Sociocultural factors in educational labeling. In: M. J. Begab and S. A. Richardson (eds.), The Mentally Retarded and Society. University Park Press, Baltimore.

Morgan, F. 1973. The mentally retarded adult offender. A study of mental retardation in the South Carolina Department of Education, Division of Research, Planning and Development of South Carolina, Department of Corrections.

President's Committee on Mental Retardation. 1975. Mental retardation: The known and the unknown, DHEW Publication no. OHD 76-21008, U.S. Government Printing Office, Washington D.C.

Reagan, M. V., Stoughton, D. M., Smith, T. E., and Davis, J. C. 1976. School Behind Bars: A Descriptive Overview of Correctional Education in the American Prison System. Scarecrow Press, Metuchen, N.J.

Rotter, J. B. 1954. Social Learning and Clinical Psychology. Prentice-Hall, Inc., Englewood Cliffs, N.J.

Santamour, M., and West, B. 1977. The mentally retarded offender and corrections. Law Enforcement Assistance Administration, National Institute of Law Enforcement and Criminal Justice, U.S. Department of Justice, Washington, D.C.

Schoggen, P. 1963. Environmental forces in the everyday lives of children. In: R. G. Barker (ed.), The Stream of Behavior. Appleton-Century-Crofts, New York.

Velde, R. W. 1977. Blacks and criminals in justice today. In: C. E. Owens and J. Belle (eds.), Blacks and Criminal Justice. Lexington Books, Lexington, Mass.

Zeleny, L. D. 1933. Feeblemindedness in criminal conduct. Am. J. Sociol. 39:564–576.

ADAPTIVE BEHAVIOR SURVEY INTERVIEW©

Name: _____ ID#: _____

Facility: _____ Date: _____

Examiner: _____

I. INTRODUCTION
— This is part of a classification project.

— Asking questions about you before you got here.

— Some will be personal.

— Do the best you can; if can't remember, say so.

II. RESIDENCE/LIVING SKILLS
Type of Dwelling _____

Own, Lease, Rent, Other _____

Household Composition _____

Domestic Responsibilities _____

Personal Belongings _____

Source and Amount of Income _____

Self-Care Skills _____

Use of Telephone _____

Sends/Receives Mail _____

Pets _____

Writes and/or Draws _____

Other_____

_____

_____

III. ACADEMIC/VOCATIONAL

School History ⎯⎯⎯⎯⎯⎯⎯⎯⎯⎯⎯⎯⎯⎯⎯⎯

Vocational Training ⎯⎯⎯⎯⎯⎯⎯⎯⎯⎯⎯⎯⎯⎯

Type and Duration of Employment ⎯⎯⎯⎯⎯⎯⎯

Rate of Pay ⎯⎯⎯⎯⎯⎯⎯⎯⎯⎯⎯⎯⎯⎯⎯⎯⎯⎯

Vocational Interests ⎯⎯⎯⎯⎯⎯⎯⎯⎯⎯⎯⎯⎯⎯

Attitude Toward Work ⎯⎯⎯⎯⎯⎯⎯⎯⎯⎯⎯⎯⎯

Other ⎯⎯⎯⎯⎯⎯⎯⎯⎯⎯⎯⎯⎯⎯⎯⎯⎯⎯⎯⎯

⎯⎯⎯⎯⎯⎯⎯⎯⎯⎯⎯⎯⎯⎯⎯⎯⎯⎯⎯⎯⎯⎯⎯⎯⎯

IV. RECREATION/SOCIALIZATION BEHAVIOR

Hobbies ⎯⎯⎯⎯⎯⎯⎯⎯⎯⎯⎯⎯⎯⎯⎯⎯⎯⎯⎯

Reading Preferences ⎯⎯⎯⎯⎯⎯⎯⎯⎯⎯⎯⎯⎯⎯

Sports Interests ⎯⎯⎯⎯⎯⎯⎯⎯⎯⎯⎯⎯⎯⎯⎯

Use of Recreation Facilities ⎯⎯⎯⎯⎯⎯⎯⎯⎯⎯

Circle of Friends ⎯⎯⎯⎯⎯⎯⎯⎯⎯⎯⎯⎯⎯⎯⎯

Family Relationships ⎯⎯⎯⎯⎯⎯⎯⎯⎯⎯⎯⎯⎯

Sexual Experience and Affiliations ⎯⎯⎯⎯⎯⎯⎯

Street Savvy ⎯⎯⎯⎯⎯⎯⎯⎯⎯⎯⎯⎯⎯⎯⎯⎯⎯

Other ⎯⎯⎯⎯⎯⎯⎯⎯⎯⎯⎯⎯⎯⎯⎯⎯⎯⎯⎯⎯

⎯⎯⎯⎯⎯⎯⎯⎯⎯⎯⎯⎯⎯⎯⎯⎯⎯⎯⎯⎯⎯⎯⎯⎯⎯

⎯⎯⎯⎯⎯⎯⎯⎯⎯⎯⎯⎯⎯⎯⎯⎯⎯⎯⎯⎯⎯⎯⎯⎯⎯

V. TRANSPORTATION

Driving Skills ⎯⎯⎯⎯⎯⎯⎯⎯⎯⎯⎯⎯⎯⎯⎯⎯⎯

License(s) ⎯⎯⎯⎯⎯⎯⎯⎯⎯⎯⎯⎯⎯⎯⎯⎯⎯⎯⎯

Public Transportation ⎯⎯⎯⎯⎯⎯⎯⎯⎯⎯⎯⎯⎯

Map Reading ⎯⎯⎯⎯⎯⎯⎯⎯⎯⎯⎯⎯⎯⎯⎯⎯⎯

Knows and Follows Directions ⎯⎯⎯⎯⎯⎯⎯⎯⎯

Plans Trips to Distant Places ⎯⎯⎯⎯⎯⎯⎯⎯⎯⎯

Other ⎯⎯⎯⎯⎯⎯⎯⎯⎯⎯⎯⎯⎯⎯⎯⎯⎯⎯⎯⎯

⎯⎯⎯⎯⎯⎯⎯⎯⎯⎯⎯⎯⎯⎯⎯⎯⎯⎯⎯⎯⎯⎯⎯⎯⎯

VI. HEALTH/MEDICAL
Major Illness or Health Problems _____

_____

Medications _____

Hospitalizations and Surgeries _____

Other Institutionalization _____

Dental Work _____

Drug or Alcohol Use _____

Diet _____

Weight Control _____

Exercise _____

Hearing or Vision Problems _____

Other _____

_____

VII. MONEY MANAGEMENT
Making Change _____

Budget Skills _____

Bank Accounts _____

Loans or Savings _____

Charge Accounts _____

Pays Bills _____

Other _____

_____

VIII. SOCIOLEGAL
(Current offense and history of priors, attitude toward
authority, respect for rights of others, concepts of
probation and parole, understands rehabilitation, etc).

_____

_____

_____

_____

IX. COMUNICATION

(After interview, describe verbal behavior, including scope
of vocabulary, articulation, voice quality, etc).

_____

_____

_____

_____

Appendix B
CHECKLIST FOR AWARENESS OF SELF AND SURROUNDINGS©

Name: _____ Case: _____

Facility: _____ Date: _____

1 . Does client know his/her name?
    __ a. Receptive
    __ b. Expressive
    __ c. Uses other name (specify _____)

2. Does client know his/her age?
    __ a. Expressive
    __ b. Receptive

3. Does client know why he/she was brought to the testing situation? __ Yes __ No (Explain to client: "here for test")

4. Can client tell what he/she had to eat at his/her last meal? __ Yes __ No

5. Regarding clothing:
    __ a. Can client describe degree of satisfaction with what he/she is wearing? (Conversation)
    __ b. If not, can he/she describe what he/she is wearing?
    __ c. If not, can client point to basic clothing items?
    __ d. None of the above

6. Awareness of surroundings:
    __ a. Knows name of residential unit
    __ b. Knows name of facility
    __ c. Knows name of nearest city
    __ d. Knows name of state

7. Awareness of time:
    __ a.   Knows the day of the week
    __ b.   Knows the year
    __ c.   Knows the date
    __ d.   Knows the time of the day
    __ e.   Can tell what the usual times are for getting up
            and bed
    __ f.   Can tell the time of favorite TV program
    __ g.   Can tell what he/she did right after breakfast

8. Awareness of other people
    __ a.   Knows name of facility director
    __ b.   Knows name of his/her physician
    __ c.   Can name favorite staff member
    __ d.   Can name a friend or acquaintance (resident)

9. Awareness of family:
    __ a.   Knows where family lives (Specify _____)
    __ b.   Can tell who lives there
    __ c.   Can tell members of family who visit at facility

10. Awareness of program
    __ a.   Can describe or at least name one therapeutic or
            instructional activity he/she participates in
    __ b.   Can describe or at least name a favorite program

11. Other observations which would contribute to conclusions
    regarding awareness of self and surroundings:

    Completed by: _____
                            (Examiner)

Living Environments for Developmentally Retarded Persons
Edited by H. Carl Haywood and J. R. Newbrough
Copyright 1981   University Park Press   Baltimore

On Becoming a "Retarded" Person
The Institutional Experience Nine Years Later

Lona Davis Spencer, Ph.D.[1]
Director, Diagnostic and Evaluation Services
Piedmont Regional Center
South Carolina Department of Mental Retardation
Clinton, South Carolina 29325

I have experienced being a retarded person by spending six nights and seven days in a cottage at an institution.

There were many goods things about the place. The fact that every one of us had her own key to her own locker taught property values. Having morning coffee in the cafeteria did a lot for our concept of being a real person here. The residents were not on peonage, and I saw no evidence of squads of so-called working boys and girls on substandard wages. The token economy seemed to be teaching a realistic approach to work and privileges that reflected normal life contingencies.

I found the cottage parents to be generally fair and, at times, ingenious in working with residents.

There was a pervasive attitude of working your way out of the institution that was very good. Residents I knew had adopted this as a realistic goal.

Movies and recreation I attended were paced correctly for my age group (early and late teens). Regimentation to maintain order among 36 girls and two cottage parents was kept to a minimum. Every cottage I saw had a good television set. The provision of gym, pool, movies, television, and outdoor playground equipment and areas was important. The cottage parents gave each of us a place to go to avoid the crush of living in a group all the time.

---

[1] Now at Owen School of Management, Vanderbilt University.

Another way to get away was to spend a few tokens to see the Director of Cottage Life. He was available for plain talks as well as emergencies. The residents were encouraged to talk to staff who were pertinent to their problems. I was happily stunned when a cottage parent introduced one of my friends to the cafeteria dietician when she asked about sugar in the coffee. We had access to service staff on request and to management personnel for a small (token) price.

There were some bad things about this institution as well as good. I noticed immediately when I was admitted (being designated "retarded") that no one looked me in the eye. I was a nonperson. I could not get anyone to look at me directly for the length of my stay.

Private lockers had no drawers or shelves, so there was no neat way to store personal items. Classes could have been better coordinated than they were; I wondered why my math teacher wasn't teaching fractions at the same time that my cooking teacher was teaching cups and measures. Many of us were bored with primary school books that matched abilities but fell short of age-appropriate interests.

There was a chronic shortage of staff in residents' personal lives. An overall staff/resident ratio of 2:1 resulted in one or two cottage parents for 36 persons per shift. Teachers stayed in the school building. Social workers visited all of us from time to time. Recreation staff sat on the stage playing the record player while we bungled attempts to find dance partners out of ineptitude. I estimate that I had a total of six minutes per day of an adult's individual attention.

The lack of adult attention showed up in table manners, grooming, and interpersonal behavior. With a staff dining room, there were no role models left for table manners, and the chance to eat with a "real person" was lost. Television characters demonstrated make-up well, but essential bathing and clothing care were slighted. Residents needed someone with them who could take advantage of daily opportunities for adequate parenting.

There was absolutely no privacy. There was a constant bedlam caused by the dayroom television set, the ward radio, and the echo of terrazzo floors throughout. On a day when we were all sick and had all that noise, I was as irritable as any of my friends in the cottage. The large numbers of residents, the shortage of staff, and the ward architecture combined to eliminate any true personal choice or the exercise of that choice.

It is not surprising that cottage parents' morale seemed lousy. They identified with us and our needs most closely. They shared our living space with us in their job. They were almost as helpless as we were to have an apparent affect on our shared lives.

Those bad things could be remedied, but there was one thing happening here that could undo all of the good things and exacerbate all of the bad: None of us did anything without the ward streetgang's permission. I lay awake nights full of fear for my physical safety. I dreaded foggy days because retaliations outside the buildings were so much easier then. I could not function under such fear, and I wondered how my retarded friends could either. Some of us learned tyranny and the rest of us learned hatred. As I said in 1972: "I don't know why the advocates don't do anything. I don't know why the cottage parents can't seem to get anything done. I don't know why the parents are not told. The only thing I do know is why the little kids don't say anything. Because they are as afraid as I was made to feel while I was here."

REFLECTIONS

Looking back, I find it was amazingly simple to pass for someone ten years my junior and approximately sixty points lower on an intelligence test. The physical transformation was merely a lack of adult make-up (techniques and materials) and a supply of new clothing from the institution clothing shop to augment my own jeans and cotton shirt. The major transformation was psychological. It had two parts—attitude and academic skills. My attitude was a quiet resignation to failure based on a case history of graduation from lifelong special education, of dead parents, and of life with a married sister. Any plans to do or to learn elicited my own murmurs of "I'm not too good at things" or "I can't do that stuff." I avoided reading magazines, newspapers, or books; this was easily accomplished because the only reading material was elementary school textbooks available only in the classrooms. It seemed to be a vicious cycle of no supply, no demand, no supply, and so on. The only arithmetic skills required were at school, and I went along with the skill level demonstrated by my institutional peers.

The touchstone of the psychological transformation was a limited vocabulary. Whenever a simple word sufficed for a more complex one, I used it. Many things were "good" rather than "excellent," "permissible," or any gradations of meaning in between. An intriguing incident occurred as a result of my restricted vocabulary. One cottage parent was off duty the day I was admitted, and no one told her about me. Because I thought she knew who I really was, I used the word "flexible" in a private conversation that none of the residents could hear. She immediately turned toward me and exclaimed, "Where did you learn that word?" I quickly mumbled some failure response, reverted to the truncated vocabulary of one and two syllable words, and kept my cover up the rest of the week. The moment passed.

Although I believe I would have passed with other staff members as well, I had decided that all levels of staff should be informed of my true identity. The administration's original plan had been that only the superintendent, psychology department, and admitting staff would know who I was. I vetoed that because anything I would have to feed back to staff on my final consultation day would be undermined if my role was construed as "spy." At the time, I did not stop to realize the human need of the residents not to be betrayed about my identity. As I stayed in the institution, I gained valuable insights about mentally retarded people's feelings because I was one of them. Before my stay, abhorrence about deceiving staff readily came to mind; I held no opinion about deceiving residents until later in the week. The most stinging memory of my insensitivity concerns a crippled resident from an impoverished home who encouraged me again and again that I could learn to write my name and that she would show me how if I would let her. She did so with great patience and was sincerely delighted at my "progress." I found I could not betray her accomplishment by revealing my identity.

The violence I reported was not the only indignity we encountered. One day when all of us became ill with a gastro-intestinal flu, orders went out to restrict us to the ward and to serve bouillon broth. The staff made the bouillon with cubes sent over from the dining room building and with hot water from the ward shower room. Because the hot water tank had a governor on it for the residents' protection, the result was an unpalatable combination of tepid water and partially dissolved cube. I politely objected and asked the staff if there was any other source of hot water. In full view of the large coffeepot full of boiling water in the nurses' station, I was solemnly told that the bouillon was good for me as it was given. None of us ate anything that day.

I am left with great wonderment about the entire institutional experience. Did I make too much of the fear I felt? I remember a Down's syndrome girl shrinking back from going out to the swing on the grounds because a gang member came by. Was I too outraged by the laxity in the staffing pattern that allowed extortion on the ward? I remember my resident friend sobbing herself to sleep because her bag of apples and cookies from home was gone before she had gotten any. Did I expect too much of an environment set up for previously deprived 15-year-old girls? I remember our watching TV hour after hour for our role models because no one else could spend enough time to relax with us; people spent time with us because that was their job. Should I have stayed two weeks rather than only one? I left earlier than originally planned because, had I stayed, I would have felt compelled to form a counter-gang for protection that would have severely embarrassed my professional colleagues there and, more importantly, would have left my resident friends more vulnerable to abuse after my departure from the leadership position. Was mine an isolated experience? I stayed in a modern institution run by an administration that regularly invited professional students to stay and to report back to the staff the effects of staff actions on residents. The superintendent was a fully qualified, politically powerful, enlightened professional. The research and service staff were exemplary in their backgrounds and professional activities. With one exception, the cottage parents were warm and caring people with residents. The community seemed proud of the institution in their town.

The central question then is: What was indeed happening while I was "retarded"? Apparently the role constraints of resident and staff are as strong as sociological evidence suggests (Berkowitz and Mc-Cauley, 1961; Mercer, 1965; Merton, 1945; Scheff, 1966; Steadman, 1972). The failure of staff to identify with residents as persons was continually exemplified in everything from lack of eye contact, to tepid boullion, to ignored injury. No one among us could transcend his role.

A related incident has more than confirmed for me the power of role constraints. Some years after these events, I was seeking (as a bureaucrat) an alternative to prison or maximum security hospitalization for a mentally retarded defendant who had previously been convicted of a felony and who had been judged incompetent to stand trial for current felony charges. I found myself arguing for his admission to an institution for mentally retarded people knowing that release to his home would not be tolerated. The superintendent of that institution patiently explained to me that he could not provide a setting secure enough to satisfy the sheriff or bondsmen. Not once did my memory stop my argument, even though the superintendent alluded to the gentle innocence of his organically retarded residents. My professional role as container of deviance in society (Rhodes, 1972) had overridden some intense personal memories.

Coupled with the role constraints of my institutional experience was the centralized hierarchy of the institution. Tizard (1970) alluded to the difference in daily life for residents of hospital-type and of home-like facilities. Balla (1976) concluded that size is not the determinant of the degree of institutionalization in residents' behavior. Both findings can be explained in terms of the distance between a person's daily life and the place where decisions about that daily life are made; this is the measure of institutionalization. Decisions affecting the daily life of residents where I stayed were made two or more steps up the hierarchy from active participation in that daily life. Furthermore, the central hierarchical organization of the pyramid did not accurately reflect the streams and pools of power therein. I concluded from my institutional experience that those persons in middle management were the holders of determining power.

On our consultation day, the psychology and teaching professional staff objected strongly to my verbal report of the violence that existed, even though they were strangely silent to my query whether they wanted any one of the gang members to come live with their families for a week. Immediately after my departure from the institution, I related in an open letter to the superintendent the violence and fear I had found in the facility, sending copies of the letter to all the staff members whom I named or to those who worked with the individual residents who were named. I received no official response to my letter. Later I did hear a rumor that the situation was changed some months afterwards. At the time of my stay, however, the middle management objectives were more important than the clear and present physical danger threatening any resident who objected to unfairness. These decision-makers would not decrease the distance from their own position to that of the residents in daily life, which is necessary to establish the contingencies that maintain normal relations (Skinner, 1969). In the original report (Spencer, 1972), I estimated that I spent approximately six minutes a day in direct contact with an adult. Newbrough (personal communication, January 5, 1979) suggested that, in the absence of supervision of this population of unsocialized persons, the basis of the ethical system had become one of power. According to the Kohlberg framework of moral development (Kohlberg and Turiel, 1971), the level I felt operating was Stage 1 (Preconventional), wherein unquestioning deference to power and avoidance of punishment are valued in their own right. The circumstances I encountered were unlike Kohlberg's Stage 4, in which an underlying moral order is supported by authority and punishment. This is not to say that staff and administration of the institution were lacking in morality or that when questioned they would have professed no moral basis to their actions. However, the reasoning by which we conducted daily life as residents quickly sank to this Stage 1 because of the lack of a social order that could promote and enforce elements of fairness among residents and reciprocity between mentally retarded people and others.

In my memory, the most lasting effect of institutional life on residents' behavior was the truncated language and vocabulary. I have since wondered whether mentally retarded people cannot remember three syllables in succession or whether no one ever uses three-syllable words with known mentally retarded individuals. I suspect strongly that the lack of three-syllable words is part of the hallmark of an English-speaking mentally retarded person and serves to alert the community that this person is different. It is a subtle aspect of community functioning that might be profitable to study. I muse at the surprise that would be engendered in an examiner testing a labeled mentally retarded person who could define the more difficult words in the Wechsler Adult Intelligence Scale Vocabulary subsection. The humor of the situation is lost in the realization that humanity is often loosely defined in terms of language capabilities—to the detriment of the natural rights of porpoises, cerebral palsied people, and Down's syndrome infants. It is in the common values of humanity that I found the institutional experience most lacking.

The most recent, widely available work that reverberates my own experience is the review by Zigler and Balla (1977) of twenty years of research. Their focus is the effect of institutionalization on specific kinds of behavior and development, but their analyses of institutions clarify some of the inconsistencies in my impressions of my own experience. Salient among these results is the finding that, in sorting out institutional effects, one must "go beyond the simple question of size" (Zigler and Balla, 1977, p. 2).

Somewhere a better balance must be struck between hard-pressed families with too few supporting services and penurious legislators doling out funds for restricted institutional budgets in lagging economic conditions. If size is not the problem and money is not the answer, then we must ask other questions. At the least, records of institutional experiences might help to discern a just balance. For myself, the impact of the one-week institutional experience is still powerful, nine years later.

REFERENCES

Balla, D. A. 1976. Relationship of institution size to quality of care: A review of the literature. Am. J. Ment. Defic. 81:117–124.
Berkowitz, L., and McCauley, J. R. 1961. Some effects of differences in status levels and status stability. Hum. Relations 14:135–148.
Kohlberg, L., and Turiel, E. 1971. Moral development and moral education. In: G. Lesser (ed.), Psychology and Educational Practice. Scott, Foresman and Company, Chicago.
Mercer, J. R. 1965. Social system perspective and clinical perspective: Frames of reference for understanding career patterns of persons labeled as mentally retarded. Soc. Probl. Summer, 13:18–34.
Merton, R. 1945. Sociological theory. Am. J. Sociol. 50:462–473.
Rhodes, W. C. 1972. Behavioral Threat and Community Response. Behavioral Publications, New York.
Skinner, B. F. 1969. Contingencies of Reinforcement: A Theoretical Analysis. Appleton-Century-Crofts, New York.
Scheff, T. J. 1966. Being Mentally Ill: A Sociological Theory. Aldine Publishing Company, Chicago.
Spencer, L. D. 1972. A "retarded" graduate student: Looking at the institutional world through the eyes of a resident. Western Carolina Center Papers and Reports in Mental Retardation. 2(1):1–12. (Available from De-

partment of Psychology and Education, Western Carolina Center, Morgan-
ton, N.C. 28655).

Steadman, H. J. 1972. The psychiatrist as a conservative agent of social control. Soc. Probl. 20:263–271.

Tizard, J. 1970. The role of social institutions in the causation, prevention,
and alleviation of mental retardation. In: H. C. Haywood (ed.), Social-Cultural Aspects of Mental Retardation. Appleton-Century-Crofts, New York.

Zigler, E., and Balla, D. A. 1977. Impact of institutional experience on the
behavior and development of retarded persons. Am. J. Ment. Defic. 82:1–11.

Living Environments for Developmentally Retarded Persons
Edited by H. Carl Haywood and J. R. Newbrough
Copyright 1981   University Park Press   Baltimore

A Letter to a Service Provider

Gershon Berkson, Ph.D.
Illinois Institute for the Study of
 Developmental Disabilities
Behavioral Sciences Building, Box 4348
University of Illinois at Chicago Circle
Chicago, Illinois 60680

Daniel Romer, Ph.D.
Illinois Institute for the Study of
 Developmental Disabilities
University of Illinois at Chicago Circle
Chicago, Illinois 60680

To: Mr. Jack Dinero Semolians
        President
        Diamond Catering Service
        18 Easy Street
        Silver City, Kentucky

Dear Mr. Semolians:

Thanks for your letter of early June asking for advice about establishing a community living facility for moderately and severely retarded adults. Our understanding is that your firm plans to develop a sheltered-care home on the south side of Chicago and that you have heard that doing so sometimes is complicated. We also understand that you want the venture to be profitable and that, at the same time, you want to provide a decent quality of life for the people you will serve.

We confess that we were somewhat surprised to receive your letter. It has become somewhat unfashionable lately for service providers to consult researchers like us about how to proceed. We are not sure that the way we go about things can be helpful to you. However, we will do what we can. What we have to tell you is based on our experience, working with sheltered workshops and sheltered living

307

facilities in the Chicago area and also on some research we have done there during the last couple of years.

Our letter has three parts. In the first part, we discuss the current status of the so-called community-reintegration normalization, or dein-stitutionalization, movement. (These terms have slightly different meanings for the knowledgeable, but they are poorly defined and people interpret them differently, so we don't think we need to be too concerned with the subtleties.) In the second part, we discuss some practical issues that will affect the management of your facility. In the third part of the letter, we describe some of the research we have been doing. We are not sure yet that the details of the research give an accurate picture of what could happen in facilities like yours, but perhaps our general approach will give you some ideas.

CURRENT STATUS OF DEINSTITUTIONALIZATION

The deinstitutionalization movement has ideological, fiscal, and demographic underpinnings. Ordinarily, people argue about the ideological issues, but the fiscal and demographic influences are also important. Beginning approximately 40 years ago, an empiricist orientation in the social sciences gained power, particularly regarding influences on child development. One familiar result of this orientation was the position that large state-operated residential institutions, isolated in rural areas, were not adequate environments for rearing handicapped children. Despite the growing scientific evidence supporting this philosophy, pressure for any kind of services for the mentally retarded in the 1950s produced, not a decrease, but a net increase in the number of people in institutions between the early 1950s and the middle 1960s. This increase was made up mainly of children (Butterfield, 1976).

A clue to the apparent contradiction between the current deinstitutionalization ideology and the simultaneous increase of young populations in institutions is that those institutionalized children were most often severely handicapped. What was really happening was a general shift of severely handicapped children out of their homes into the only alternative residential facilities available at that time. In the same period, there was a movement of more mildly retarded adults from institutions into the general geographic region where their homes had once been.

In the early and middle 1960s, there were few community agencies ready for these people. Edgerton's (1967) description dramatized the problems encountered by mildly retarded persons living with minimal societal support. However, soon afterward, the community movement began growing rapidly. Privately run agencies like yours began to take over at least some of the responsibilities for the retarded. Increasingly, schools and sheltered workshops provided daytime services, and various types of living arrangements were experimented with informally. A normal, family-like environment with at least a semblance of normal work available was the principle that many people espoused vigorously as a basic human need and a basic human right.

To understand what was going on back then, however, it is essential to look at some of the more direct influences. It was becoming clear that the demands for high-quality state-operated programs were costing a lot of money. The price tag for providing services in institutions was approaching $15,000 per year per person. This high cost not only came from improved services in institutions but also from higher labor costs associated with unionization of state employees. Officials of Departments of Mental Health and their counterparts in increasingly influential Bureaus of the Budget were embarrassed by rapidly expanding budgets. It seemed to them that deinstitutionalization might be a partial solution. Fiscal conservatives argued that private operators would do a more efficient job than expanded bureaucracies could. It was thought that it would be less expensive if existing services in the community were tapped or new ones were developed. Of course, there was as yet no union movement in community facilities. Furthermore, federal social security, welfare, public health, housing, and vocational rehabilitation systems could be drawn on for partial support of the community programs. This meant that, as the fiscal burden shifted to other agencies, the Department of Mental Health's budget looked better to taxpayers and to their representatives.

Aside from the ideological and fiscal factors promoting deinstitutionalization, geographic and demographic factors were also important. When the first institutions were built in this country 100 years ago, the population of America was largely rural. Early in this century, the population began moving to urban areas. More recently, there has been a tendency to move from the central city to suburbs and perhaps to a certain extent back to formerly rural areas that are now being industrialized. These population trends meant that deinstitutionalization was part of deruralization. Later the holes left in deteriorating centers of cities left demographic gaps, especially in lower-class neighborhoods. There was a clear need for federal and state government support to offset the losses of the declining economies of the cities. Mental health programs in these areas provided jobs for the populations there.

By the middle of the 1970s, there had been massive changes in services for the retarded. Many more retarded people and their families were receiving some kind of service. It is interesting that, despite the deinstitutionalization rhetoric, the state-operated institutions were serving almost as many persons as they had 10 years before (U.S. General Accounting Office, 1977). However, their populations were more severely handicapped than they had been, and services for them were more decent. More mildly and moderately retarded persons were now living in suburban, urban, and even rural areas near their homes, and many of them participated somewhat more fully in their communities. A large private service network was emerging, funded by numerous government agencies. Studies of overall costs made it appear that, in general, it cost no less for private agencies to provide services comparable to those in state-operated facilities than it cost the state to provide those services. Multiple funding produced more types of service options than had been previously available, and no single agency's budget looked too big.

A 10-year study of the community adjustment of adult retarded males in Los Angeles showed them to be better adjusted in the middle 1970s than they had been 10 years before (Edgerton and Bercovici, 1976), but the difficulties in the private community system began to be visible to almost everyone who cared to look. You are going to encounter some of these things when you get started on your own facility.

PRACTICAL CONSIDERATIONS FOR MANAGEMENT

In the city, a service provider who is reasonably efficient and honest can expect to earn about 15% on his investment, which seems like a good return. However, you are going to have to work for it. To begin with, the area in which you are proposing to develop your facility has no other residential programming at this time. That seems like good news because you are almost sure to be funded and should not have the difficulty that other agencies are experiencing in finding enough clients of the type they feel comfortable working with. The bad news is that there are reasons that there are no other facilities there. As you know, the area has the lowest per capita income in the city and the highest crime rate. You may also have trouble finding a building that the Department of Public Health will approve. HUD money may be available for renovation, but it may be difficult to get.

After you have found and fixed up a building, you will look for staff. In order for you to qualify for Developmental Disability funding, you need to hire the required ratio of professional staff. First-class professionals are not ordinarily willing to work full time for the salaries that government agencies allow, so you must depend on consultants and less-qualified personnel. In this state, add-on money is not available to for-profit providers. You will therefore need to make contact with nonprofit agencies that can provide vocational rehabilitation, recreation, and other services for your clients. Because there are none in the neighborhood in which you wish to work, you will have to arrange to bus your more severely disabled clients and to teach the others to use public transportation.

Once your operation is under way, your staff will want to monitor the rapid changes in funding regulations and standards for each of the government bureaucracies (state and federal) that you deal with. Because many of them are on annual funding cycles that sometimes are inconsistent with each other, your people will need to keep close contact with the personnel representing the agencies so that your applications for funding are timely and in proper form. This may be difficult to do since staff turnover in those government agencies is sometimes as great as it will be in your own.

Funding of services by many agencies makes life complicated for the service provider. Each agency monitoring you (and in fact each representative of each agency) has its own philosophy of what clients need. Your professional staff can easily become involved in administrative tasks rather than in providing the services they were trained to provide, which makes for a service system in flux.

The instability is further evident in staff turnover rates. Rates of 100% per year are not rare. The causes of high staff turnover are not clearly understood, but there is some evidence that availability of other jobs is part of the story. In our system, the easiest way to move up is to move out, so the whole business is like musical chairs.

All of this sounds unpleasant, and many people think it is. Professionals are not happy with their bureaucratic roles. Direct-service personnel do their jobs with little leadership. Program reorganizations are frequent, and much decision-making is done in an atmosphere of change and crisis.

Nevertheless, there are signs now that the systems are beginning to stabilize somewhat. Restricted budgets are slowing the growth of the system. There are incipient movements to integrate the activities of various government agencies. Standards and monitoring procedures are becoming more explicit. Some private agencies are becoming larger and forcing smaller ones out of business. However, in our opinion, the most effective force for stability is the growing unionization of employees in community facilities. This not only is going to improve salary levels but also is going to require private and government agencies to be more explicit about their management practices.

Of course, these forces that increase stability are not necessarily going to be beneficial to clients. After all, the total institutions described by Goffman were very stable. The real question is whether they will also be oriented to the human needs of the clients. We are not sanguine about this.

The preceding information is background. What you specifically wanted from us was a description of how to serve clients decently and economically. The reason that we have emphasized these broader considerations is that we think it is impossible to understand how to organize services without a consideration of the political and economic context in which they occur. Now let us move on to other issues. To do so, we will need to become somewhat more formal.

THREE CONCEPTS OF SERVICE

Two major concepts have dominated services for the mentally retarded. The first has emphasized the assurance of security and good health through decent residential programming, nutrition, and medical care. This assurance will be the main expectation that society will have of your agency. However, this caregiving concept is not adequate without a second principle that has dominated progressive services during the last generation. This second principle has emphasized the development of cognitive and social skills through education and training. Because you are establishing a residential facility, you will not be expected to engage in a lot of training, but progressive service providers think of their task as increasing the level of functioning of their residents. Even though government agencies do not always provide enough of the right kinds of funds to do this well, a well-run organization that is committed to training can usually accomplish a good deal. The first two principles, caregiving and training, are now traditional. However, they are not, by themselves, enough to meet the goals of high-quality programming. A third approach emphasizes social ecology. There has been some research in this area, but very little relative to the amount of effort given to the development of training technologies. The social-ecological approach recognizes that a person is part of a community and that his development and welfare are determined in crucial ways by the social context he is in. (Although an ecological orientation can include analysis of the physical environment, we are going to concentrate on social factors because we believe that social organization is more important than architecture in determining quality of life.)

Following this general approach, the first thing to emphasize is that consideration of residential programming alone denies the fact that people in the community do more than eat, sleep, and stay healthy. A heavy emphasis on residential programming in funding patterns, and for that matter, in research, neglects the person's participation in everyday work and recreation activities.

A second thing to consider is that most services for retarded adults living away from their families involve supervised communal living. Whether we are talking about small group homes, mini-institutions, sheltered workshops, or large total institutions, retarded adults generally live and work mainly with other people of their same age and intellectual level, and they are supervised by staff members who have little permanent relationship to them.

There are very few studies about what staff members actually do with mentally retarded people on a day-to-day basis, and those studies that exist are more encouraging to people who emphasize a caregiving ideology than to those who favor a training orientation. In our own research we look at another aspect of supervised communal living—the social relationships among the clients. There are three general issues that we have looked at: the relationship of social behavior to general intellectual level, the nature of social interactions among retarded adults, and the relationship between residential placement and social behavior.

We have dealt with three major assumptions. The first states that there ought to be a fairly clear relationship between cognitive level and social behavior among retarded persons. The second suggests that people are most likely to socialize with people of their own cognitive level. The third states that social choice is related to both historical and situational opportunity to interact. That is, people will tend to socialize with others to the degree that they have had an oppportunity to do so.

I am sure that you are smiling to yourself now because these are such simplistic notions and because the results must be obvious. However, watch for some surprises.

RESULTS OF SOCIAL BEHAVIOR RESEARCH

The data we are going to summarize are from four studies. They include observations by James Becker in a state-operated institution; peer relationship data provided for analysis by Sharon Landesman-Dwyer from her group home study (Landesman-Dwyer, Stein, and Sackett, 1978); and two studies of sheltered workshops, one by Adalton Caram (1974) and one by our current group.

Because many of our subjects have limited verbal skills, the major method we use is to observe the behavior of people when they are free to do what they wish. Typical situations we look at are coffee breaks, meals, outings, dances, and other recreational activities. The people we observe are comfortable with our presence. We do not intrude on their activities and do not interfere with their privacy.

We do an adequate number of momentary observations of many individuals, and we employ behavior checklists that reveal who does what with whom. The sociometric data that emerge from these observations correlate only moderately well with staff and client estimates of client friendships. We think that this is important. Because our interobserver reliabilities are generally satisfactory, we attribute the lack of agreement between behavioral measures and the more traditional social choice data to the fact the the the different sources of data are, at least to some extent, measuring different things.

Our first major finding is that, with the exception of nonverbal profoundly retarded persons, there is a negligible correlation between intellectual level and the amount of social behavior among retarded individuals living in groups. This finding was characteristic of the data in Dr. Landesman-Dwyer's study of group homes and was also true of our studies in sheltered workshops. Correlation coefficients between general intellectual level and total social behavior were -0.03 and -0.07, respectively, for the two studies.

It is the case that, among profoundly retarded persons in institutions, nonverbal individuals show less social behavior (Table 1) than do verbal people. This is consistent with the findings of Wills (1973) and others. On the other hand, if one looks carefully, one can see social behavior among even nonverbal profoundly retarded people, although the activities are infrequent, fleeting, and occur primarily in response to initiation by others (Table 2).

Although there is negligible correlation of IQ with general social behavior, one might suspect that the correlation would be larger if one considered verbal interactions. However, in Dr. Landesman-Dwyer's group home study there was, again, little correlation of intellectual

Table 1. Activities of nonverbal (NVR), partially verbal (PVR), and verbal (VR) profoundly retarded persons at a dance

Activity	Distribution by percentage		
	NVR	PVR	VR
Dance*	0	7	20
Conversation*	0	1	10
Gesture*	6	7	1
Music	2	18	23
Rock*	47	12	2
Hand before eye	3	1	0
Pace	3	1	0
Other stereotypy*	7	1	3
Walk*	5	12	7
Other	6	8	3
Nothing	21	34	31

* $p < 0.05$.

Table 2.   Distribution of social behavior of nonverbal profoundly retarded persons in their cottage[a]

Behavior initiated		Response to others	
Behavior	Rate	Behavior	Rate
Approach	0.6	Nothing	0.9
Sit down	0.2	Start stereotypy	0.2
Lead	0.1	Stop stereotypy	0.1
Follow	0.2	Approach	0.1
Contact play	0.1	Follow	0.01
Touch	0.1	Contact play	0.1
Affection	0.01	Directed play	0.1
Answer door	0.1	Touch	0.1
Grab	0.03	Affection	0.03
Avoid	0.1	Look away	0.1
Eye contact	0.8	Resist	0.1
Observe	0.1	Avoid	0.1
Look at	0.8	Let go	0.1
Smile	0.1	Not respond	0.7
Gesture	0.2	Follow instructions	0.6
Laugh	0.01	Disobey	0.1
Vocalize	0.04	Eye contact	0.1
Give object	0.02	Orient	0.1
Take object	0.04	Look at	0.2
		Smile	0.2
		Gesture	0.2
		Laugh	0.1
		Take object	0.1
		Pace	0.04

[a] Rate = Behavior/hour/subject.

level with amount of either verbal or nonverbal social interactions. Thus, there is information from several sources that the general frequency of verbal or nonverbal social interactions is not clearly related to intellectual level except in the case of nonverbal profoundly retarded persons.

A common concept in social psychology is that people are attracted to those whom they perceive to be similar to themselves. Applied to intellectual level, there are studies suggesting that school children choose to affiliate with others of similar intelligence, and this is also generally true of mate choice in adults. We were therefore interested in knowing whether the principle also predicted affiliation among retarded adults in group settings. In the group home data, a similarity choice principle seemed evident. That is, there was a correlation of IQ of clients and the people they were seen with ($r = 0.30$). However, this correlation was reduced to zero when the average IQ of the clients in their group home was partialled out. That is, the similarity choice for IQ was associated with the fact that people had been assigned to different homes according to intellectual level and therefore had limited choice of associates other than those of their own intellectual level. This assignment artifact was not characteristic of the sheltered workshop in which we tested the idea further. There we found no evidence for a similarity choice effect, but there was a tendency of individuals to have as their closest associates others who were more intelligent than they. Thus it seems that, although intellectual level may not be related to the general level of social behavior or similarity choice as we had believed when we began our studies, there may be a tendency for more able people to be more popular.

One way of looking at the nature of informal social interactions in these groups is to explore the frequency of association in groups of various sizes. Figure 1 shows the distribution of observations in which retarded individuals were seen alone and in dyads, trios, and larger

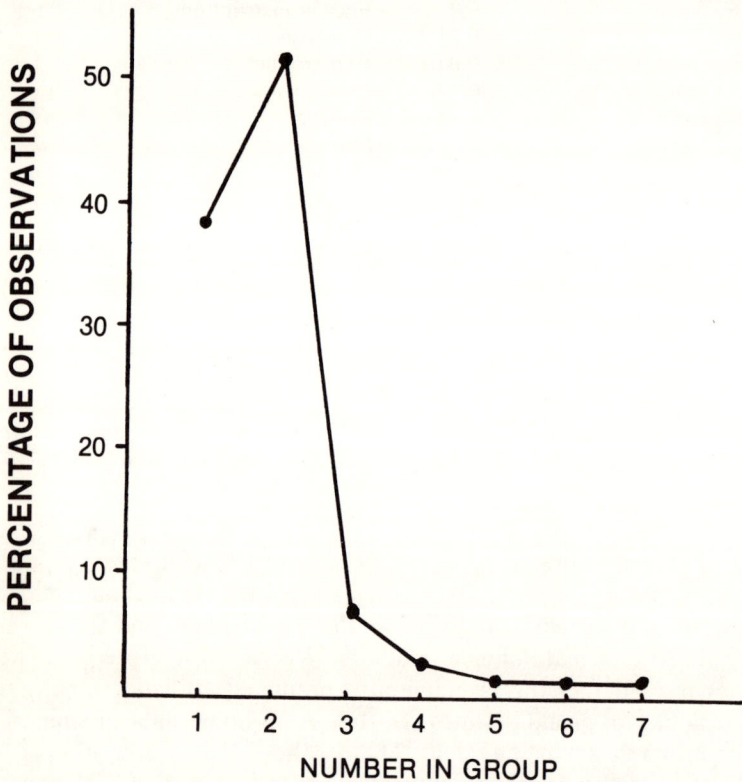

Figure 1.   Frequency of subjects' association with groups of different sizes.

Table 3. Ten most frequently observed types of behavior

Behavior	Definition	Frequency	Percentage of total
Verbal dyadic interaction	Interacts verbally with one other person within four feet	937	33
Eat and drink	Consumes food or beverages	257	9
Look around	Observes environment without attention to others	211	7
Isolated observation	Attends to activity of others without participation	164	6
Verbal projected interactions	Interacts verbally with one or more persons at a distance of more than four feet	152	5
Eat and drink and look around	Same as above	132	5
Locomote	Moves more than two feet	98	3
Verbal group interaction	Participates in group discussion with at least two other persons within four feet	86	3
Affectionate touch and verbal dyadic interaction	Touches another person in friendly or sexual manner and interacts verbally	80	3
Vocalize to self	Talks to self or no one in particular	48	2

sized groups in a sheltered workshop. Note that dyadic interactions are somewhat more frequent than monadic ones and are certainly more frequent than supradyadic groupings.

Table 3 shows the distribution of various types of social behavior during coffee breaks and lunch periods in the same sheltered workshop. These data and others we have obtained suggest that conversation is the most frequent type of social interaction, constituting a significant proportion of subjects' social behavior. Other social behavior occurs but is infrequent. Disruptive behavior is very rare.

We also looked further into the social organization of the group we studied by measuring the number of groups each person interacted with, and the frequency of interaction with each group. The data on frequency of interaction allowed us to ask whether people who interact with more people also interact more frequently with them. In two different correlational analyses we found that the average amount of affiliation (intensity) is independent of the number of groups one affiliates with (extensity). That is, for these data, there is no evidence that people who interact with a greater number of individuals are either more or less likely to interact frequently with them. The significance of the independence of social intensity and extensity will become evident later.

To give you an idea of the strength of social relationships, Figure 2 contains the frequency distribution of the most intense groups observed in group homes. About 80% of the residents did not have a group that they were observed in more than 10% of the time. Also shown in Figure 2 is the distribution of time college students at a large urban university reported spending in their most intense groups. Notice that, although the form of their distribution is similar, the students, on the average, spend more time with their friends or relatives than do the retarded persons in a group home setting. Over 60% of the students have a relationship in which they claim to spend at least 10% of their waking day (1.6 hours). Admittedly, these data are not comparable (one is based on observations and the other on self-reports), but they suggest that deinstitutionalized mentally retarded persons have less intense friendships than do young, nonretarded adults.

In summary, the social behavior of people in the groups we have looked at is primarily dyadic. In many cases, relationships are not

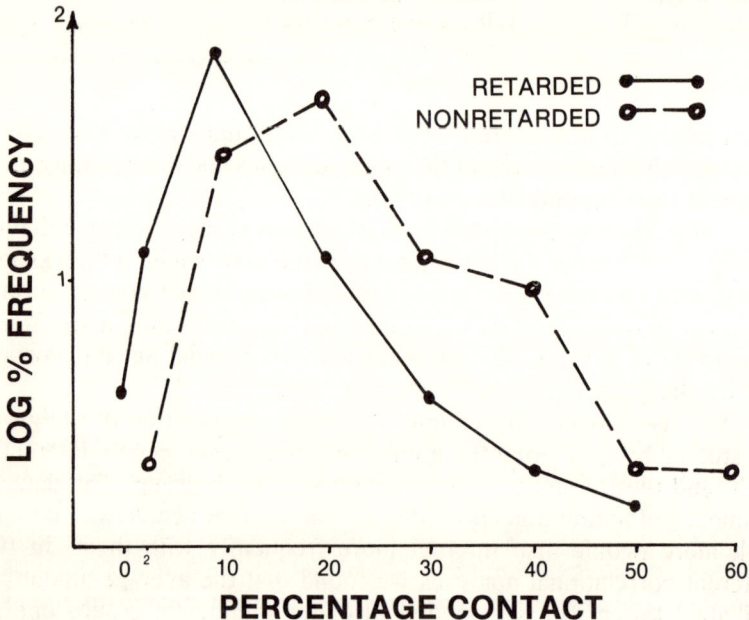

Figure 2.   Proportion of time spent in most frequent group for retarded and nonretarded adults.

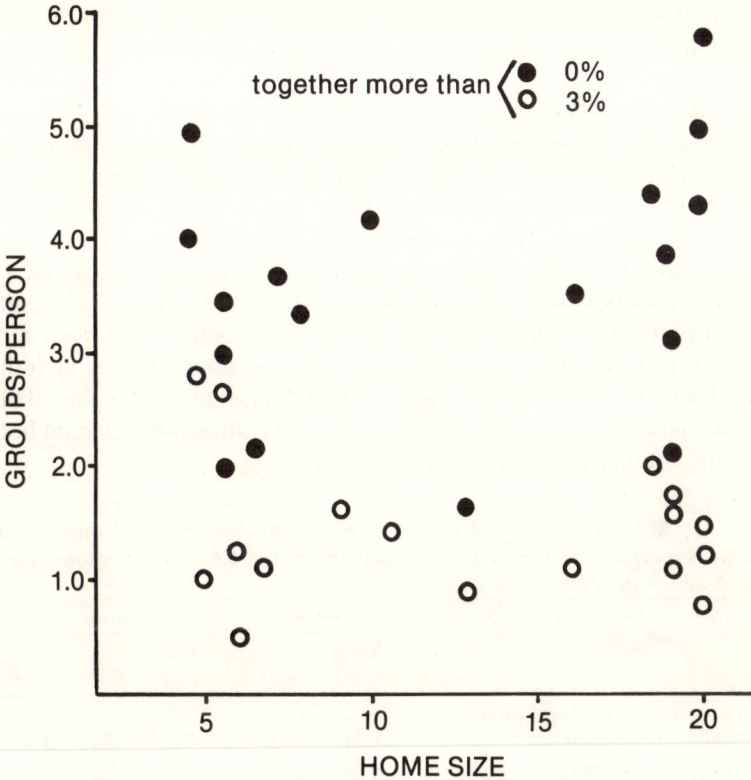

Figure 3.   Average number of groups per person in homes of various sizes.

intense. In fact, the relationships might be regarded as social, but superficial.

The third issue is the relationship between residential placements and social behavior. The central concept that has guided our thinking about this issue is that people will interact with those people with whom they have an opportunity to interact. This rather obvious and simplistic idea was necessary at the beginning of our studies; however, the data we have collected so far present a more complex picture than we had expected.

The first question is the extent to which social behavior is related to size of a residential facility. This represents an instance of situational opportunity. In large homes one might expect greater extensity because there are more people available with whom to affiliate. Perhaps there would be greater intensity in small homes because of a greater probability of association. Dr. Landesman-Dwyer's group home study allowed us to compare the social behavior of people in group homes ranging in size from 6 to 20 residents. As Figure 3 indicates, the number of groups a person interacted with increased with home size. However, this result merely means that large homes provide more opportunity for superficial interactions. When one considers only those groups who affiliate more than 3% of the time, the effect of home size disappears.

Although there was a relationship between home size and extensity, there was no such relationship with intensity. That is, frequency of association with peers was neither lower nor higher in small as compared with larger homes. If the relationships had been more intimate in small homes (as was expected by some people, including ourselves), Dr. Landesman-Dwyer's data did not reveal the fact. Thus, for our data there seems to be no important relationship between home size and intensity of social relationships.

Table 4. Mean frequency of occurrence of behavior observed during lunch and work periods expressed as a percentage of the total observations: home-reared and institutionalized subjects[a]

Type of behavior	Home		Institution		
	Mean (%)	S.D.	Mean (%)	S.D.	p^b
Social behavior during lunch					
Dyadic interaction	11	9	11	10	n.s.
Group interaction	33	22	31	23	n.s.
Combined interaction (dyadic, group, and projected)	49	24	48	26	n.s.
Noninteractive/Proximity	27	18	39	20	< 0.05
Noninteractive/Isolation	21	22	12	21	n.s.
Social behavior during work					
Dyadic interaction	6	5	4	5	n.s.
Group interaction	12	12	6	7	< 0.05
Projected interaction	6	5	6	5	n.s.
Combined interaction (dyadic, group, and projected)	26	18	17	13	< 0.05
Noninteractive/Proximity	45	25	36	23	n.s.
Noninteractive/Isolation	26	22	43	27	< 0.01
Interaction with staff	6	7	5	4	n.s.
Work-related behavior					
On-task	58	20	66	18	n.s.
Work activity/Waste	6	10	4	12	n.s.
Idle	7	9	9	12	n.s.
Appropriately idle	20	17	14	15	n.s.

[a] Only types of behavior occurring with a frequency of at least 5% are listed. For this reason, the category Projected interaction does not appear among the lunch period behavior. However, it was included in the computation of Combined interaction.

[b] Two-tailed t test, 63 df; n.s. = not significant.

One way to approach the question of whether previous or historical association with others will affect a person's affiliation is to compare people who live together in a group home with people who still live with their families. Adalton Caram did this in his study of adaptation to a sheltered workshop (Caram, 1974). He found that the group-living people were somewhat more sociable and more productive than were people who lived in their own home (Table 4).

More direct support of the historical opportunity-to-interact principle comes from the demonstration that people in a sheltered workshop generally associate with people from their own residence in preference to people from other group residential facilities.

The results about the influence of residential arrangements can be summarized as follows: group home size is not obviously related to intensity of social relationship, although large homes do provide more opportunity for new association with other retarded people; people who live with each other seem more sociable with each other than those who do not.

Well, you got more than you asked for. Let us summarize and suggest a few possibilities.

SUMMARY

Mentally retarded people are sociable. Their social relationships with peers in community facilities appear superficial. We don't know whether or not the superficiality of their relationships is a consequence of intrinsic cognitive deficits. We doubt that this is a complete explanation, but it may play a part. We are worried that the current turmoil in the service system may interfere with friendship formation and maintenance, but we can't yet prove that. However, the data we have do suggest that stability and increased opportunity to interact with peers might enhance social integration. Perhaps that is obvious without our data, but then why do service personnel generally ignore it during the referral process and in program assignment?

Here are some suggestions of things you might try in order to enhance peer relationships. You might want to evaluate your efforts with naturalistic observation methods.

1. Make your staff sensitive to the importance of friendship among retarded persons.
2. Encourage informal organizations, because they are the important ones.
3. Have staff members avoid dependency relationships with clients that might interfere with client friendships.

4. Don't split up people who like each other. Arrange their lives so that they can be together.
5. Avoid faddish program reorganizations that move people around unnecessarily.
6. Manage your home decently so that the facility won't be closed, resulting in the distribution of clients all over the city.
7. Protect your professional staff from the demands of government bureaucracies. So-called standards do not make good programs. Trained and motivated personnel do.
8. Remember that caregiving and training are necessary but not sufficient conditions for better peer relations.
9. Above all, remember that your clients are potential members of a community. If you analyze that unique community, and look for opportunities for each client to interact with it, you surely will enhance their participation in it.
    With best wishes.

Sincerely,

Gershon Berkson
Research Scientist IV

Daniel Romer
Research Fellow B

References

Butterfield, E. 1976. Basic changes in residential facilities for the mentally retarded. In: R. B. Kugel (ed.), Changing Patterns in Residential Services for the Mentally Retarded. U.S. Government Printing Office, Washington, D.C.
Caram, A. C. 1974. Sheltered workshop adjustment of institutionalized and noninstitutionalized mentally retarded adults. Unpublished master's thesis, University of Illinois-Chicago Circle.
Edgerton, R. B. 1967. The Cloak of Competence: Stigma in the Lives of the Mentally Retarded. University of California Press, Berkeley.
Edgerton, R. B., and Bercovici, S. M. 1976. The cloak of competence: Years later. Am. J. Ment. Defic. 80:485–497.
Landesman-Dwyer, S., Stein, J. G., and Sackett, G. P. 1978. A behavioral and ecological study of group homes. In: G. P. Sackett (ed.), Observing Behavior, Vol. 1. Theory and Application in Mental Retardation. University Park Press, Baltimore.
United States General Accounting Office. 1977. Returning the Mentally Disabled to the Community: Government Needs to Do More. U.S. General Accounting Office, Washington, D.C.
Wills, R. H. 1973. The Institutionalized Severely Retarded: A Study of Activity and Interaction. Charles C Thomas, Publisher, Springfield, Ill.

Index

Social integration
  community residences, 77
  language and, 142–146
  research on, 78
Social learning theory, 137, 204, 270
Social policy, research needs, 96
Social reinforcement, responsiveness
    to, 25
Social relationships
  choices related to opportunity to
    interact, 313, 319
  cognitive level and, 313–321
  ecological approach, 32, 38–40
  results of social behavior research,
    313–321
  strength of, 317–320
Social workers, 221–222
Socialization process, 24
  form and manner of, 29
  need for, 27
Socioemotional factors
  community adjustments, 139–140
  personality traits and, 136–137
Special classes, 240
Special education, 204
  barrier to conversion, 243
Speech, see Language and speech
Stability over time, living environ-
    ments, 205
Staff and administration
  attitudes toward clients, 107–108
  avoidance of dependency relation-
    ships with clients, 321
  community residences, 71–73
  failure to identify with residents,
    303–304
  hierarchy of institution, 303–304
  hiring, 310–311
  institutional experiences with,
    302–306
  job design, 111–112
  job satisfaction, 41, 109–110
  motivation, 108
  number per resident, 22
  operation guidelines, 117
  organization and administrative
    characteristics, 22–23, 310–312
  impact on helpers, 106–110
  oriented to human needs, 314
  participation in decision-making,
    119

  perception of work environment,
    259–260
  quality of care, 41–42
  Resident and Staff Information
    Form, 257–258
  role strain, 112–113
  role structure, 110–112
  staff/nurse relationships, 22
  staff/resident ratio, 22, 181
  staff/resident relationships, 23–25,
    200, 303–304, 321
  supervision by, 313
  turnover and absenteeism, 22, 41,
    110, 181, 311
  unionization of employees, 114,
    309, 311
  welfare, 117, 120
  work setting, 110–112
  working conditions, 117, 259–260
"State schools," 18
Statistical models, development of,
    186–187
Stigma attached to mental retarda-
    tion, 201
Stress, vulnerability to, 263–264
Success achieved by retarded persons,
    45
Support systems, 27–28
  family networks, 37, 49
  for improving quality of life, 49
  liaison teacher-counselors, 37–38
  self-help and advocacy groups, 37
  service professionals, 37
Surgery, corrective, 28

Task performance, 32, 35–38
  coping and, 35
  skills acquired, 35
Taxonomies, 7–11, 257
  caregiving environments, 3–14
  excess meaning of labels, 4, 7–8, 10
  labels and, 139, 237, 242, 245
Teacher-counselors, 37–38
  See also Staff and administration
Television, prejudicial and stereo-
    typic images, 240–241
Terminology and classification, 3–5
Tests and testing
  biases, 202
  methods for predicting adjustment

behavior, 137–140
procedures for testing, 131–132
validated, 137–138
Thematic Apperception Tests, 137
Therapeutic techniques, 34
Thought, reasoning and judgment,
130–132
Time-usage patterns, 182
Token economy concept, 119, 285
Training programs
ecological approach, 45–46
inservice training, 226–229
on-the-job, 46
United Kingdom, 215
Transitions to different living environments, 28–29, 188
conversion plans, 237
from parent's home, 18, 26–27, 29
See also Deinstitutionalization
Treatment programs
administrative policies, 79–80
behavioral assessment, 187–188
behavioral rehabilitation, 174–176
client assessment and, 174–176
community residences, 74, 174
manipulation of environmental factors, 186–187
skill assessment, 187–188

Unionization of employees, 114, 309,
311
United Kingdom, *see* England and
Wales

Vineland Social Maturity Scale, 277
Violence and fear, 302, 304
Visits and visitors to residential facil-
ities, 27
Vocabulary of mentally retarded, 301,
304–305
Vocational rehabilitation, 313
Volunteer programs, 22, 42

Ward Atmosphere Scale, 253
Well-being, sense of
assessing, 264–265
ecological approach, 32, 40–42
environments for, 40–42
Wessex research project, 219, 227–228
Work setting, organizational design,
110–112
Workshops, *see* Sheltered workshops
World Health Organization, 4

Young adults, mentally retarded,
27–28
See also Adolescence
Youth Aliyah program, Israel,
201, 204

Zero-reject, 237
Zoning restrictions, 165